AF224156

Sketchy People – Year Eight

Sketchy People: Year Eight
by Jack Kent

Sketchy intro:

This comic is about celebrating, documenting, and drawing the
people I see. Sketchy People has me as part cartoonist and part
journalist. I guess you could call me a "cartoonalist".
My favorite thing about Sketchy People is what you think just
happened, or what's about to happen in each drawing. I just
provide a snapshot in a time and place. You can fill in the rest.

If you can't get out there to go people watching, just flip
through this book. I bring the people watching to you.

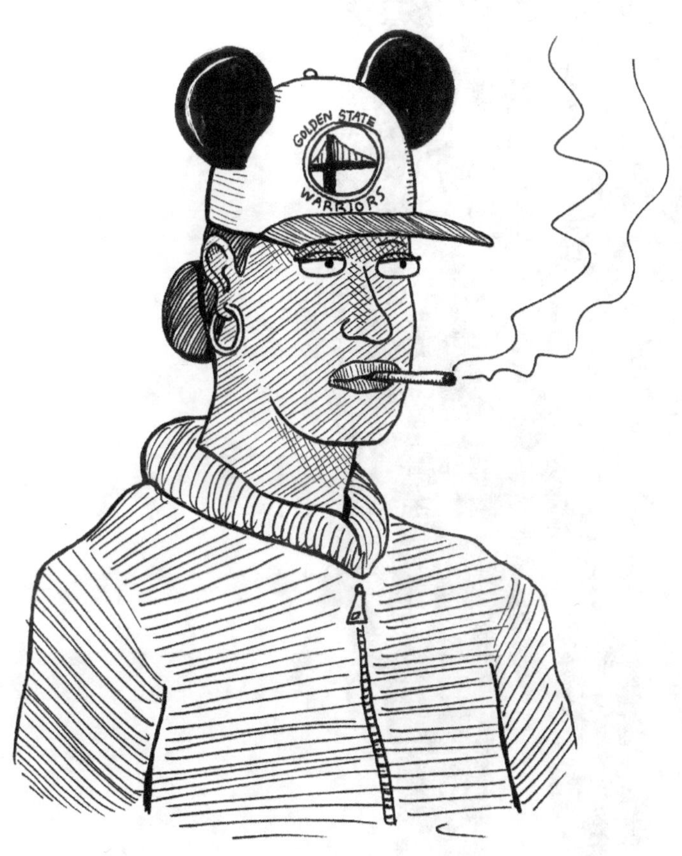

All originals are for sale!
A portion of the proceeds go to Meals on Wheels!
DM or email me to buy.
@sketchypeoplepdx or sketchypeoplepdx@gmail.com

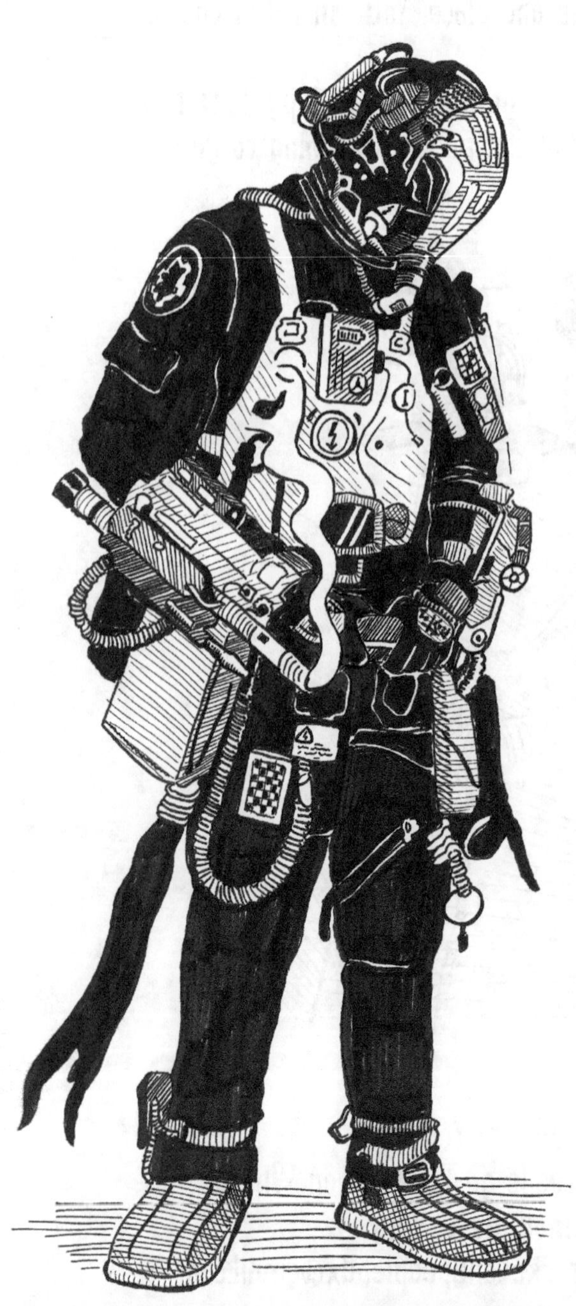

Sketchy Process:

Here's an insight on how I create my sketches.

Qualifications of sketchy:

One: What they are doing?
Two: What they are wearing?
Three: What they are saying?
(Or a combination of any of these)

How I remember Sketchy People:

If it's what someone is doing. I can remember the action.
I'll draw a rough sketch to capture the scene. then put pen to paper.

If it's what someone is wearing. that's a little harder to get the details.
I like to get a picture to capture their wardrobe.
This is where I really like to connect with the people I draw.

If it's what they're saying. I'll jot down the quote. I love sitting and
listening. People can be hilarious without even trying.

How I draw Sketchy People:

I don't use pencils. Sketchy People are drawn with no rough sketches. It's
just a blank page and a pen. Once the pen starts. there's no going back.
The reason why I do this is I like the style I get with using only pens. It's
kinda wonky. Hands might be too small. heads might be too big — it has a
sketchy look I like. I'm not after perfection. I'm after the moment.

Welcome to Year Eight
You Could Be Next!

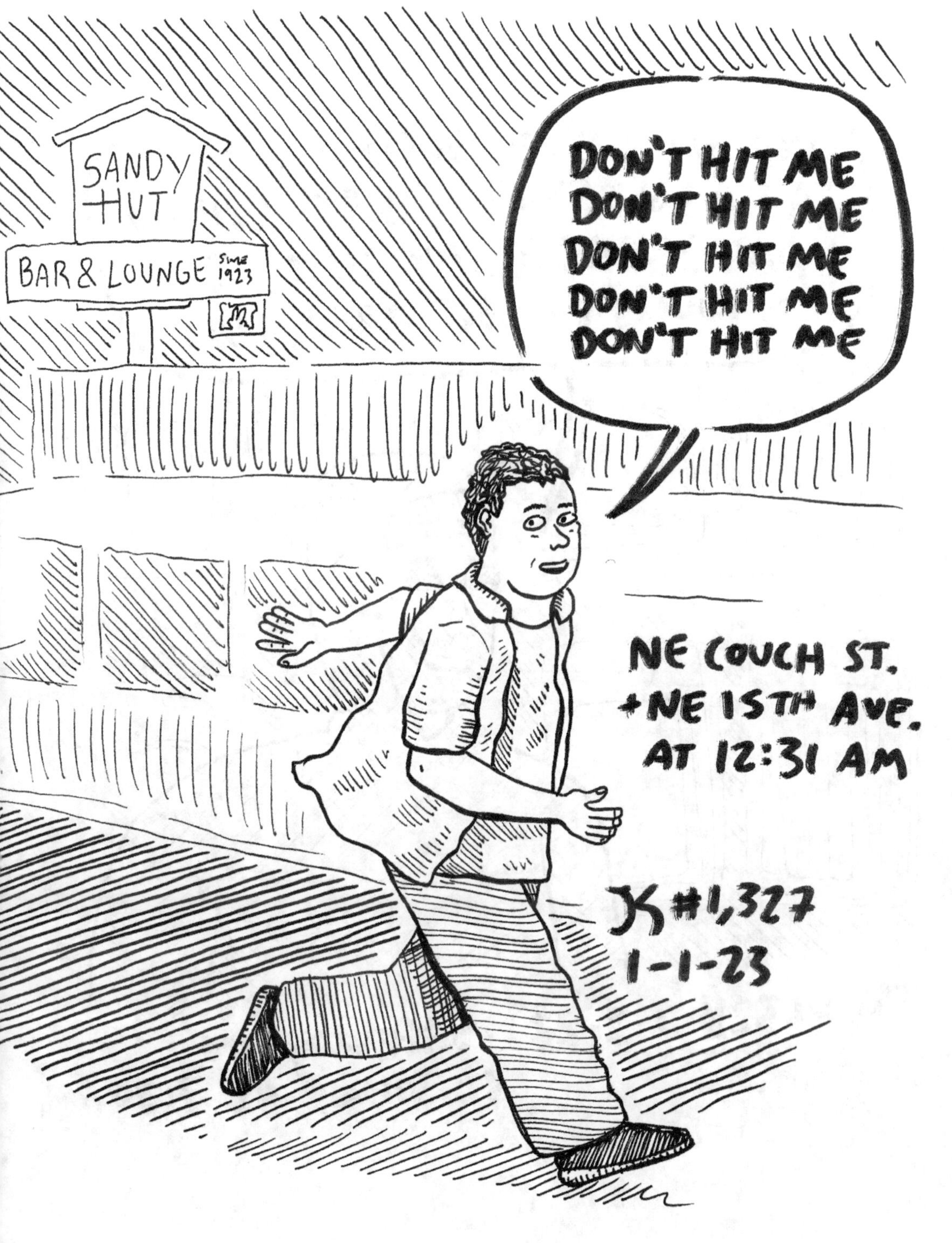

SANDY HUT
BAR & LOUNGE SINCE 1923
DON'T HIT ME
DON'T HIT ME
DON'T HIT ME
DON'T HIT ME
DON'T HIT ME
NE COUCH ST.
+ NE 15TH AVE.
AT 12:31 AM
JS #1,327
1-1-23

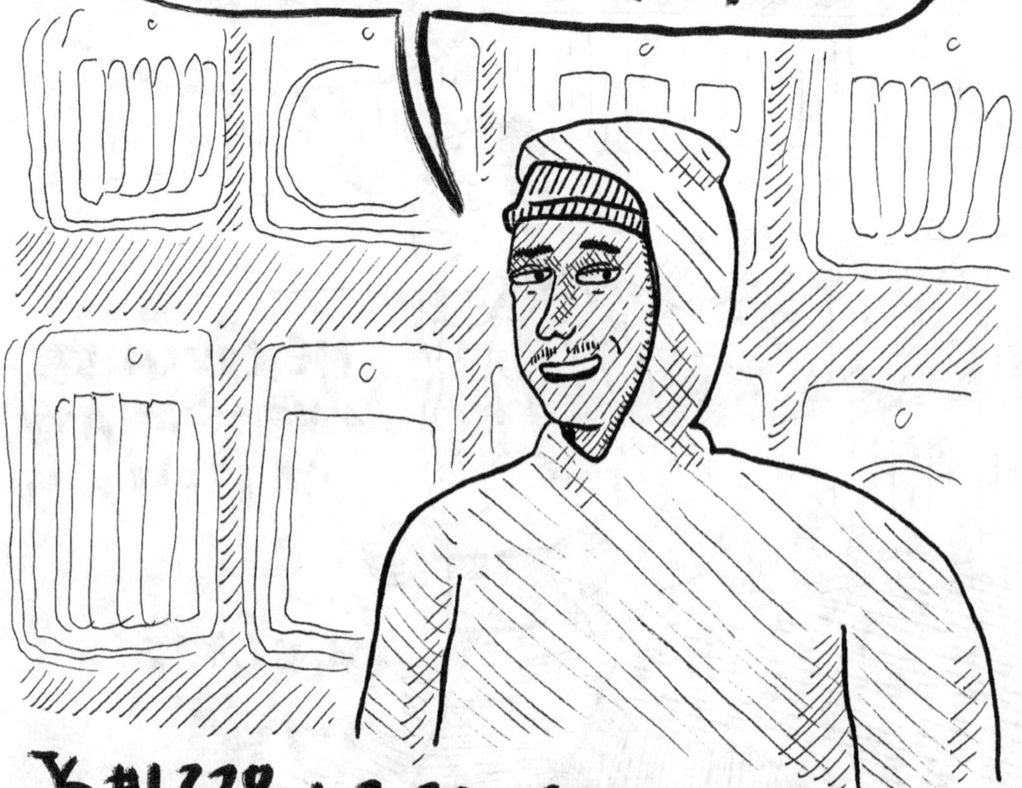
WE SHOULD'VE GOTTEN INTO AN ARGUMENT FIRST. WHEN YOU GRABBED MY HAT, I SHOULD'VE HIT YOU, HA!
#1,328 1-2-23 SAFEWAY IN ST. JOHNS AT 7:20 AM

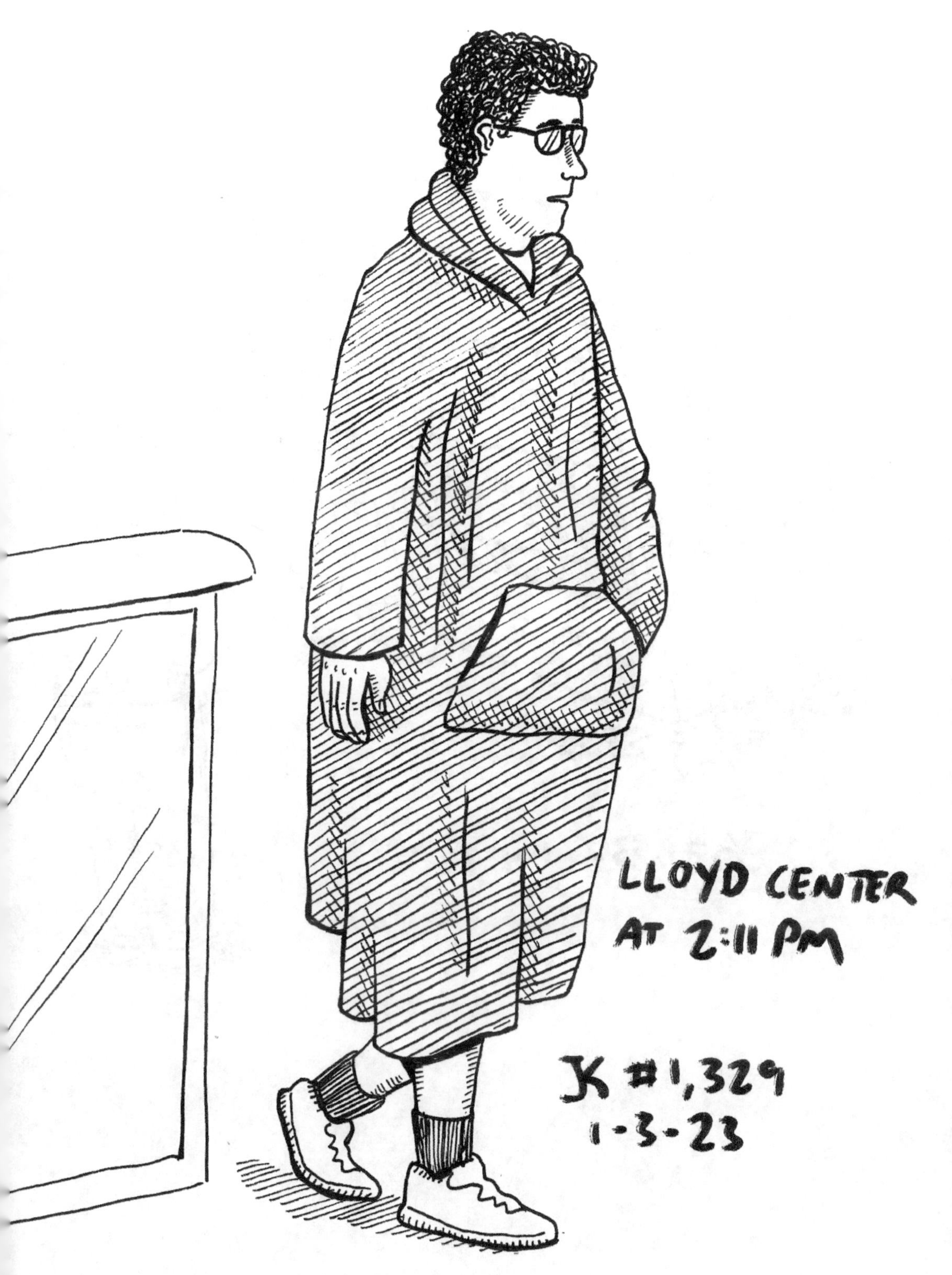

LLOYD CENTER
AT 2:11 PM

K #1,329
1-3-23

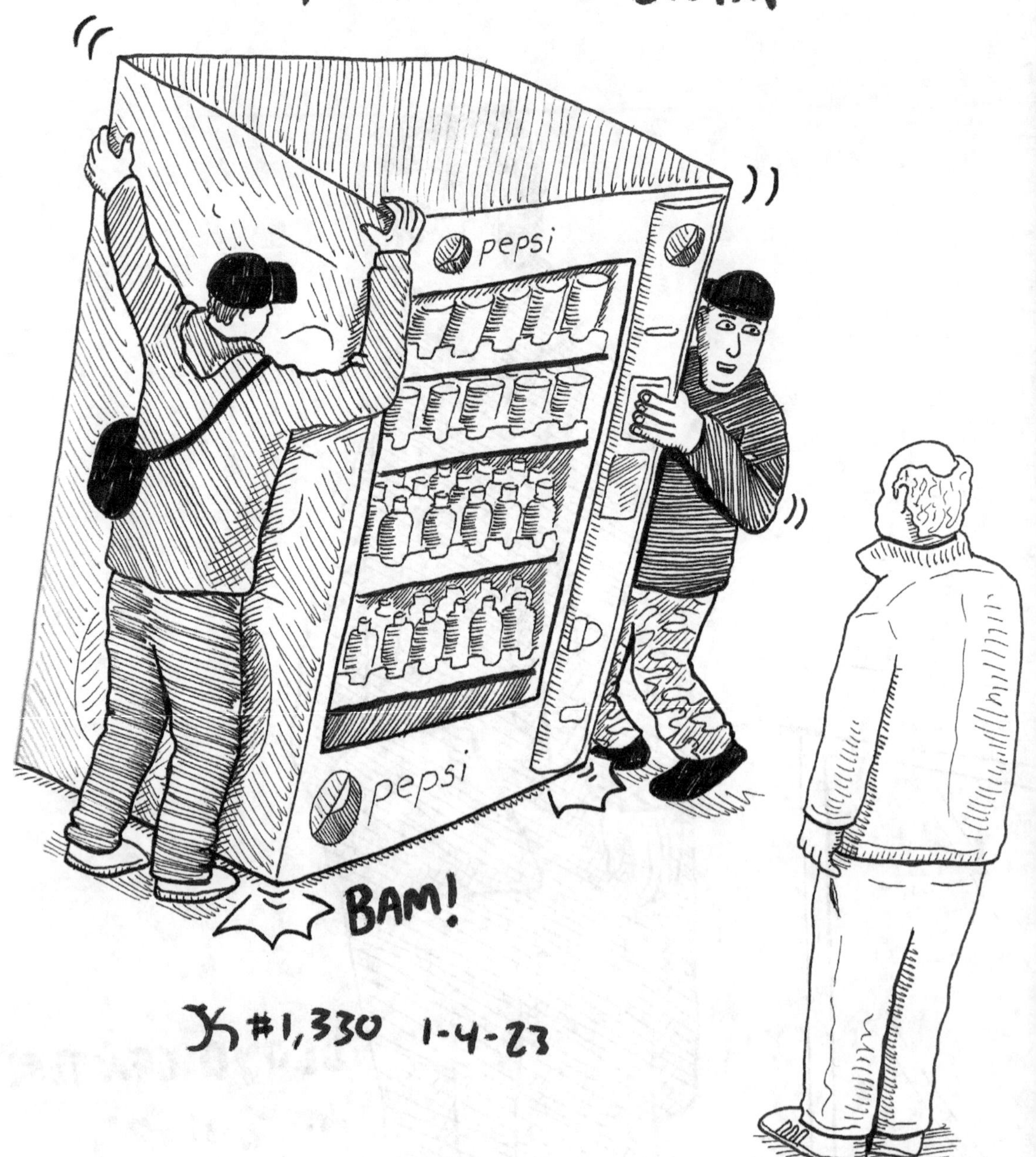

#1,330 1-4-23

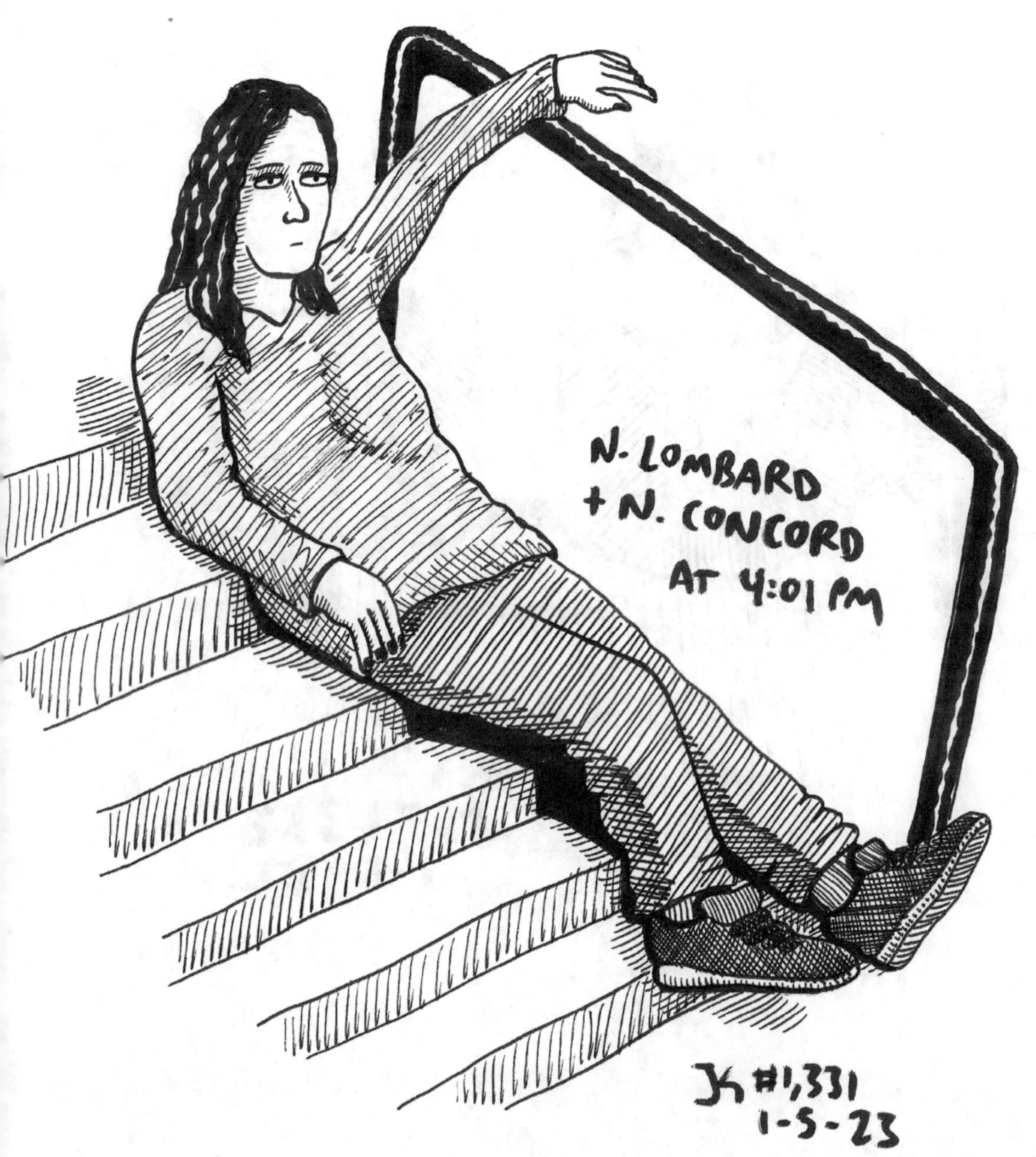

N. LOMBARD
+ N. CONCORD
AT 4:01 PM
JH #1,331
1-5-23

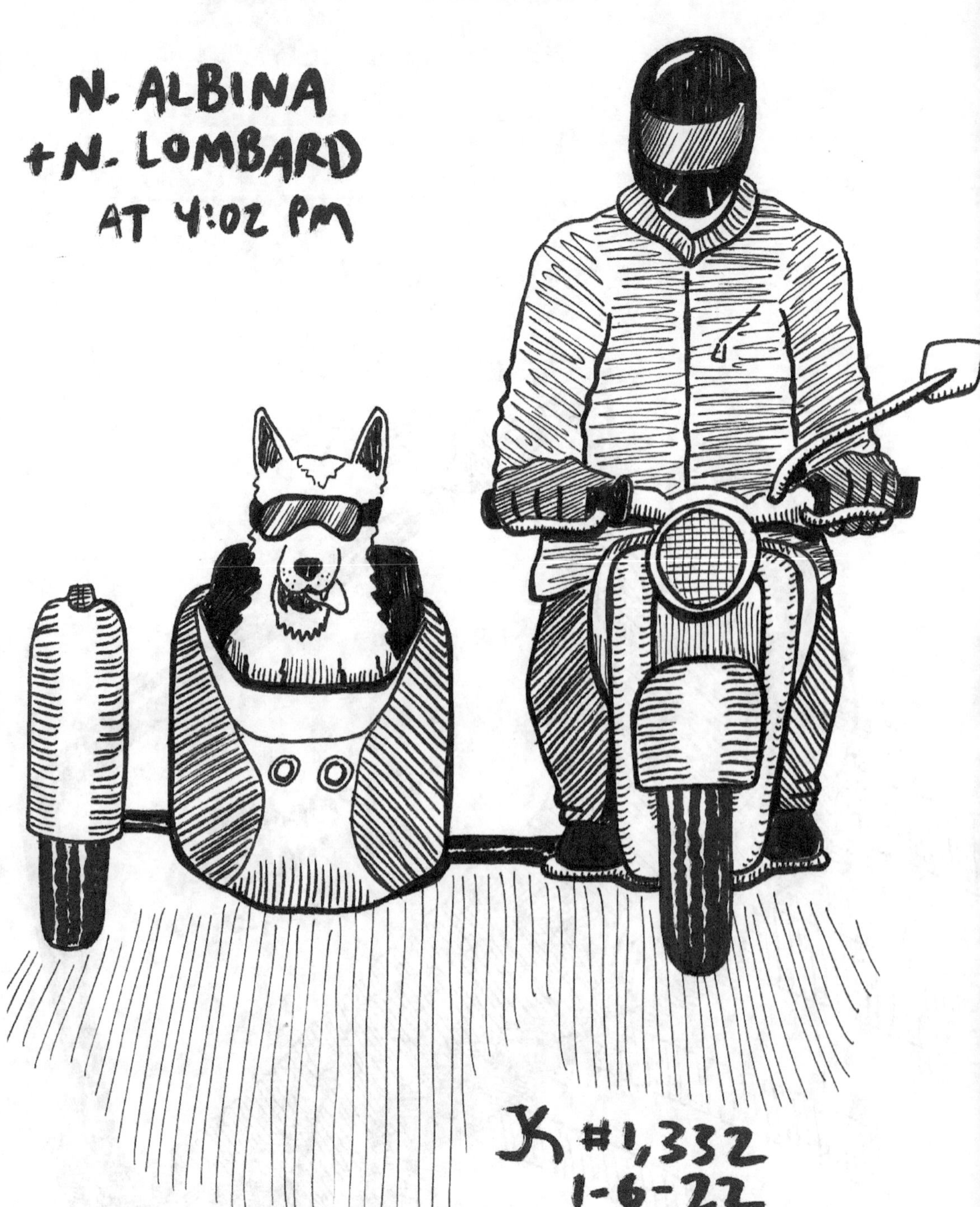

N. ALBINA
+ N. LOMBARD
AT 4:02 PM
#1,332
1-6-22

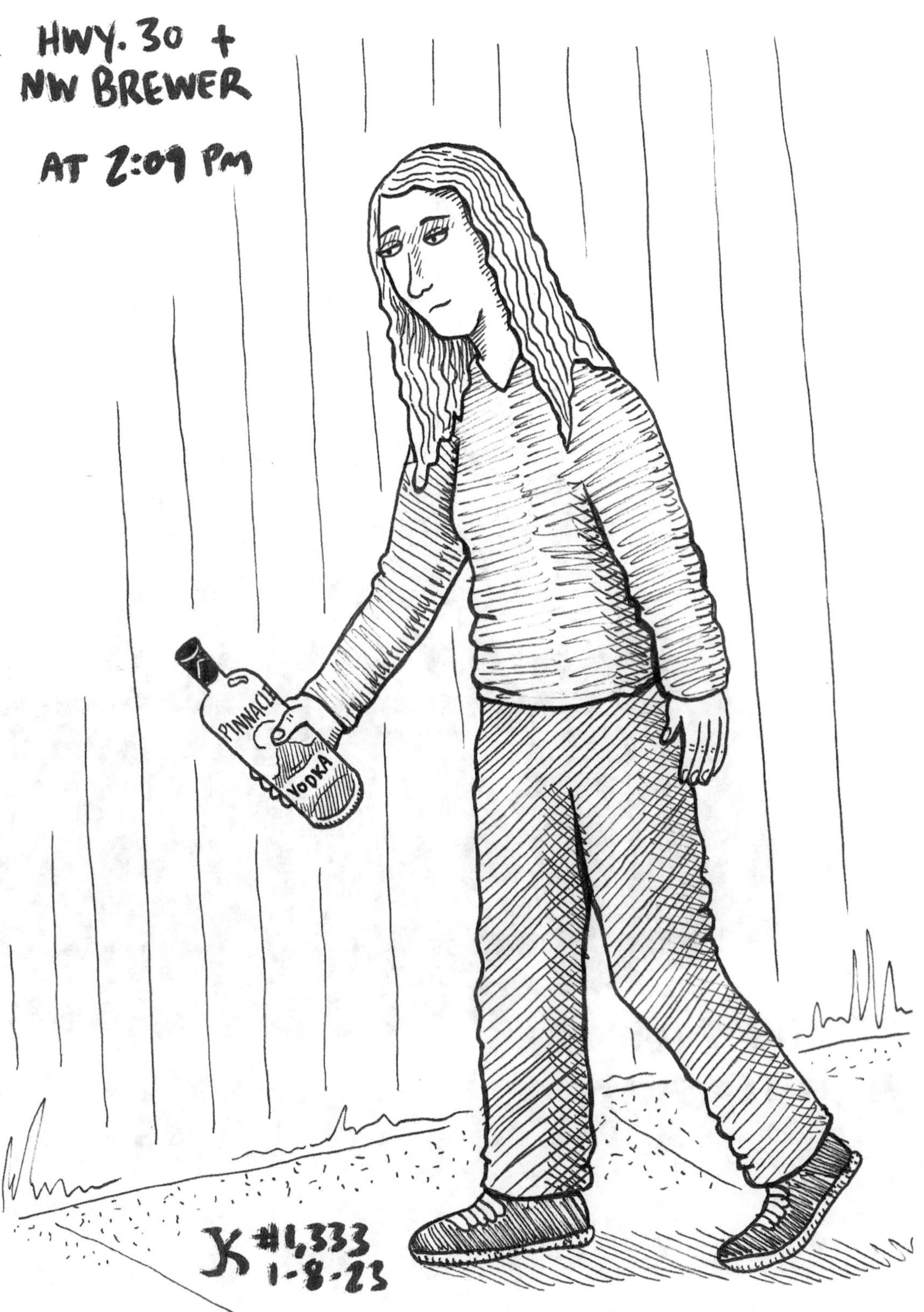

HWY. 30 +
NW BREWER

AT 2:09 PM
PINNACLE
VODKA
JK #1,333
1-8-23

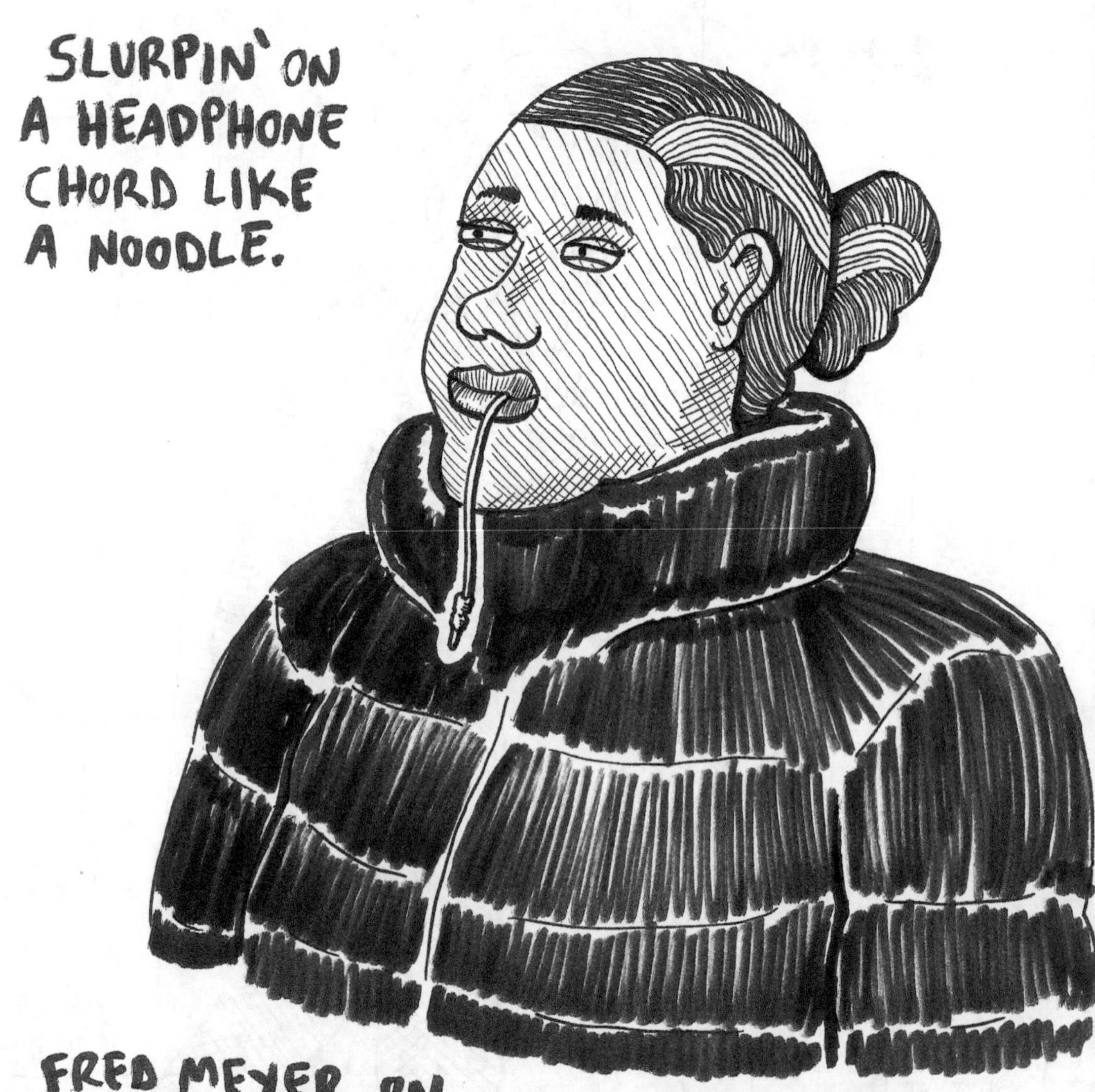

SLURPIN' ON
A HEADPHONE
CHORD LIKE
A NOODLE.

FRED MEYER ON
N. INTERSTATE
AT 5:30 PM

1,334
1-9-23

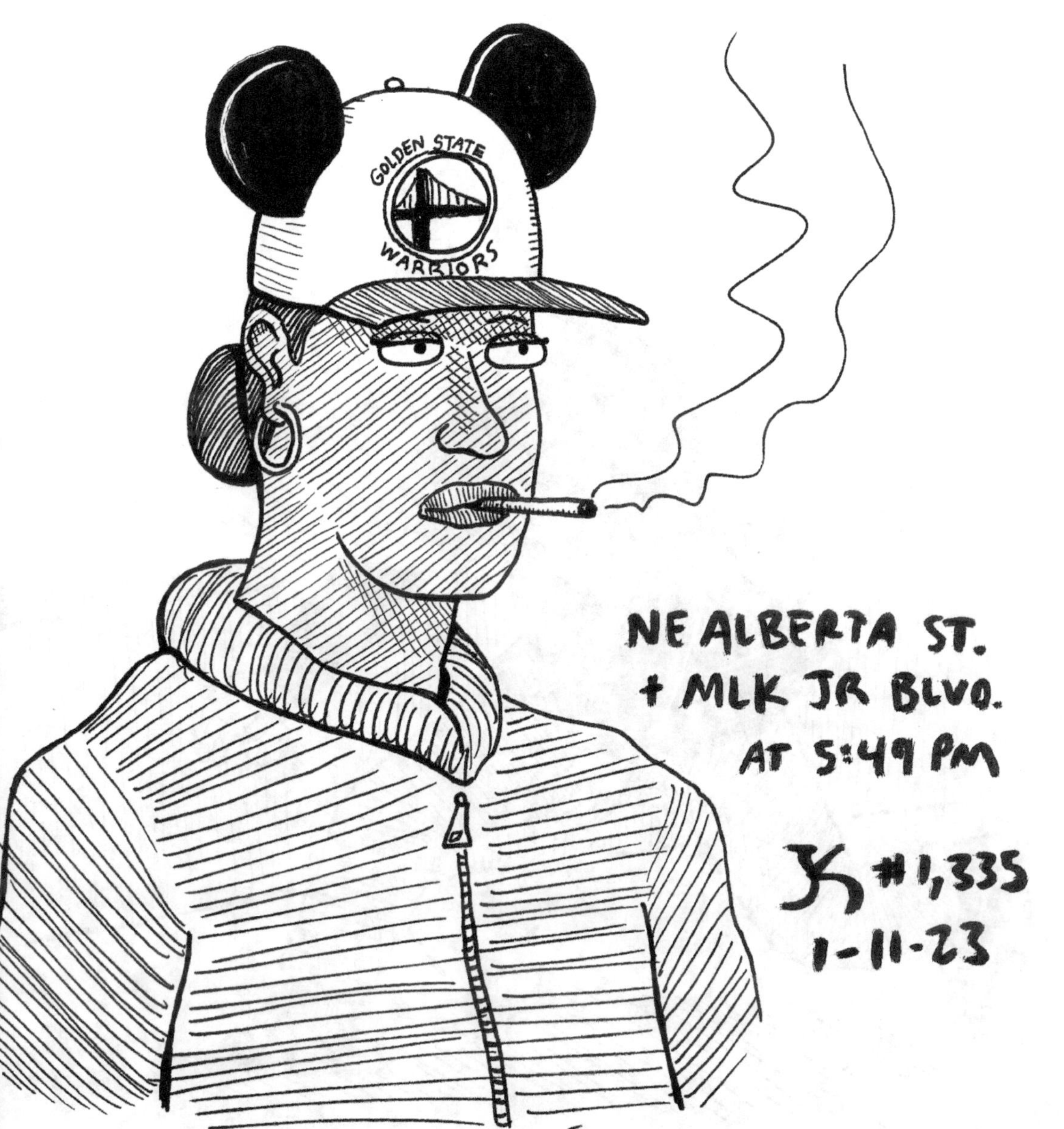

GOLDEN STATE
WARRIORS
NE ALBERTA ST.
+ MLK JR BLVD.
AT 5:49 PM
#1,335
1-11-23

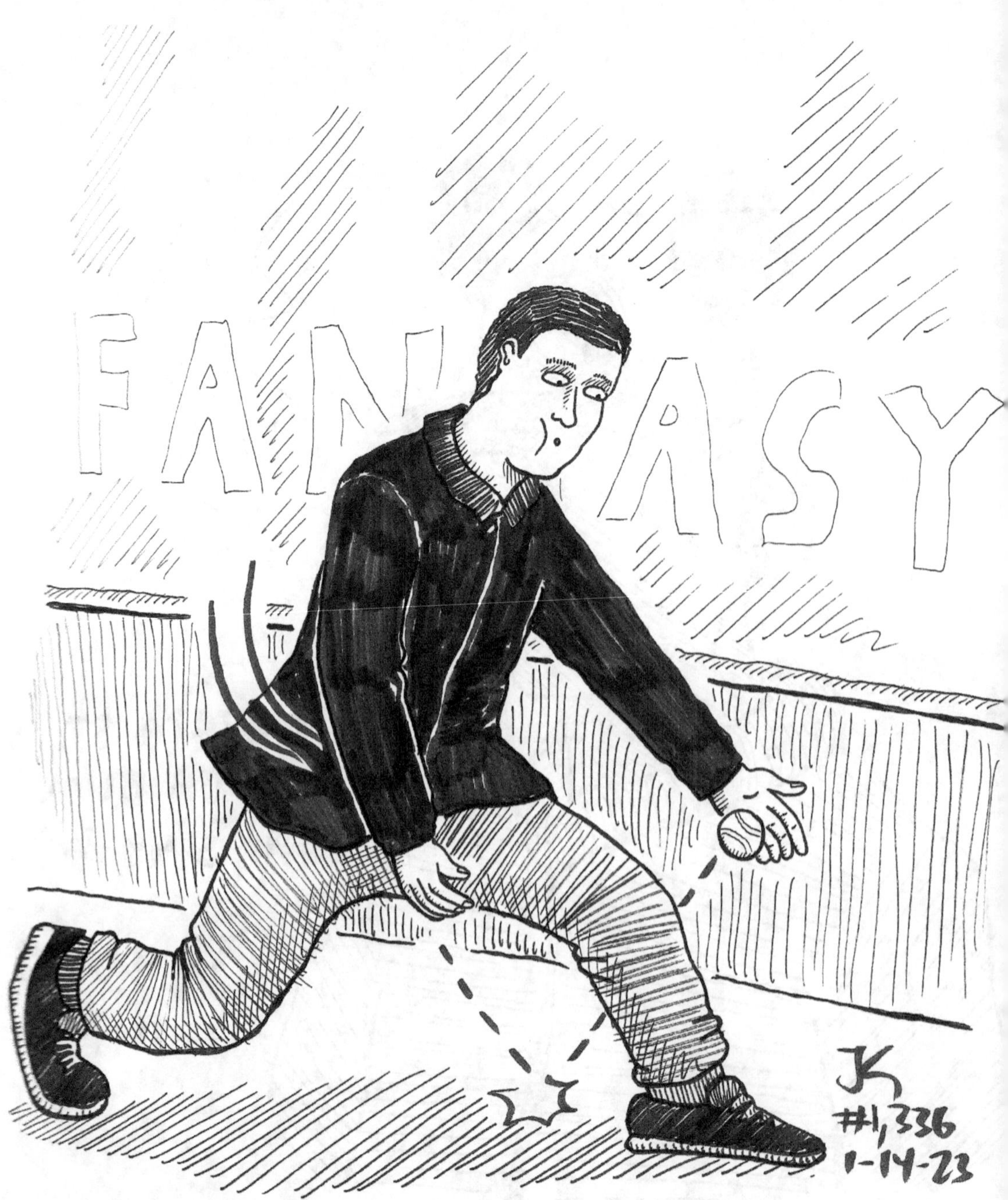

NW 17TH AVE. + W. BURNSIDE ST. AT 6:10 PM

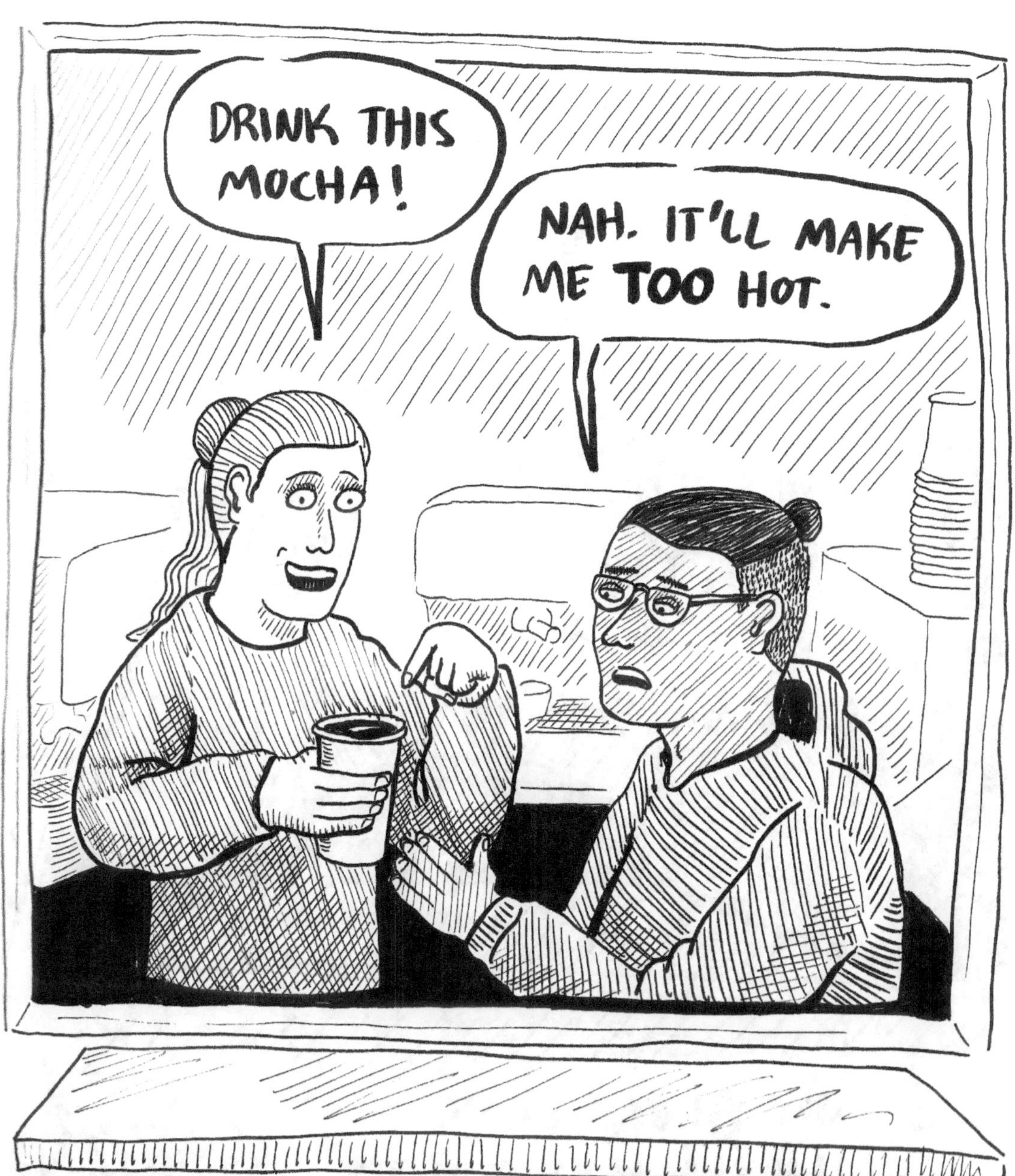

AT 5:55 PM

JK #1,337 1-15-23

DUTCH BROS. DRIVE-THRU
ON NE GRAND AVE. + NE LLOYD

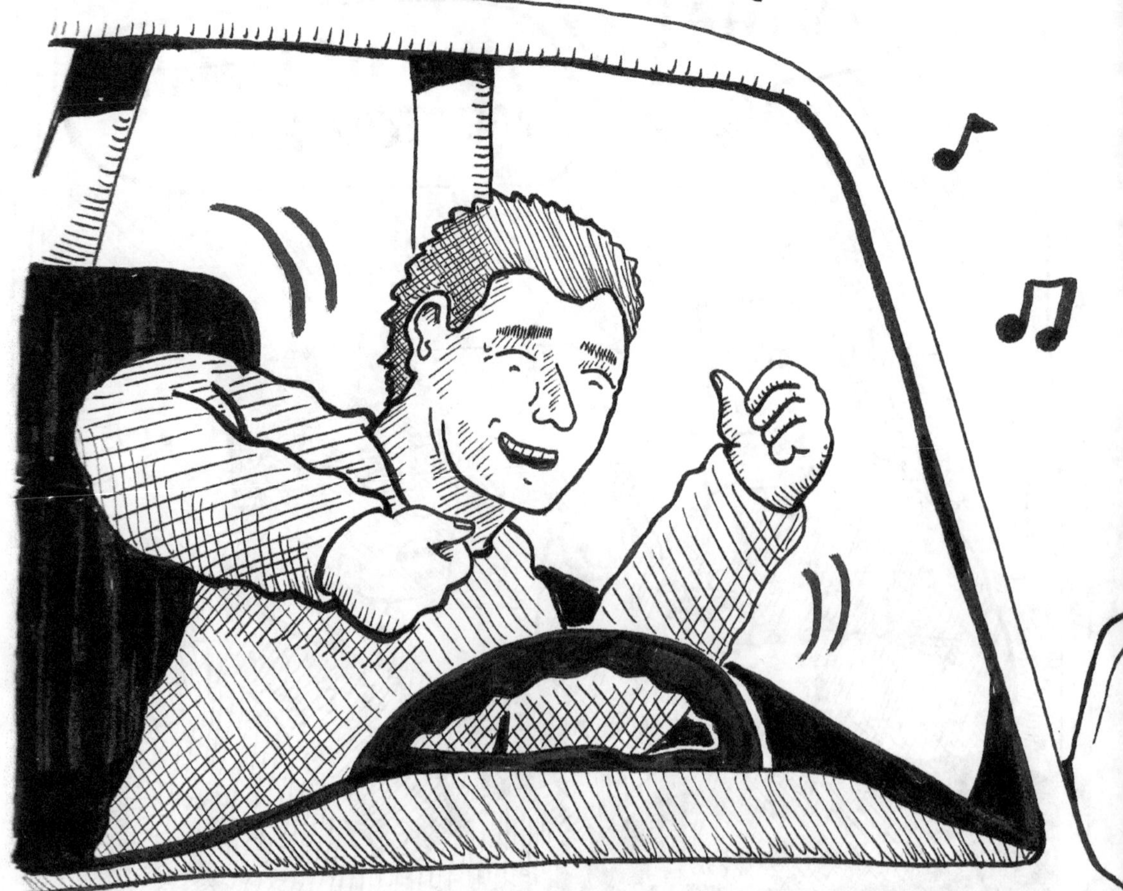

GRAND BLVD. +
COLUMBIA HOUSE BLVD.
IN VANCOUVER, WA AT 11:25 AM

#1,338
1-16-22

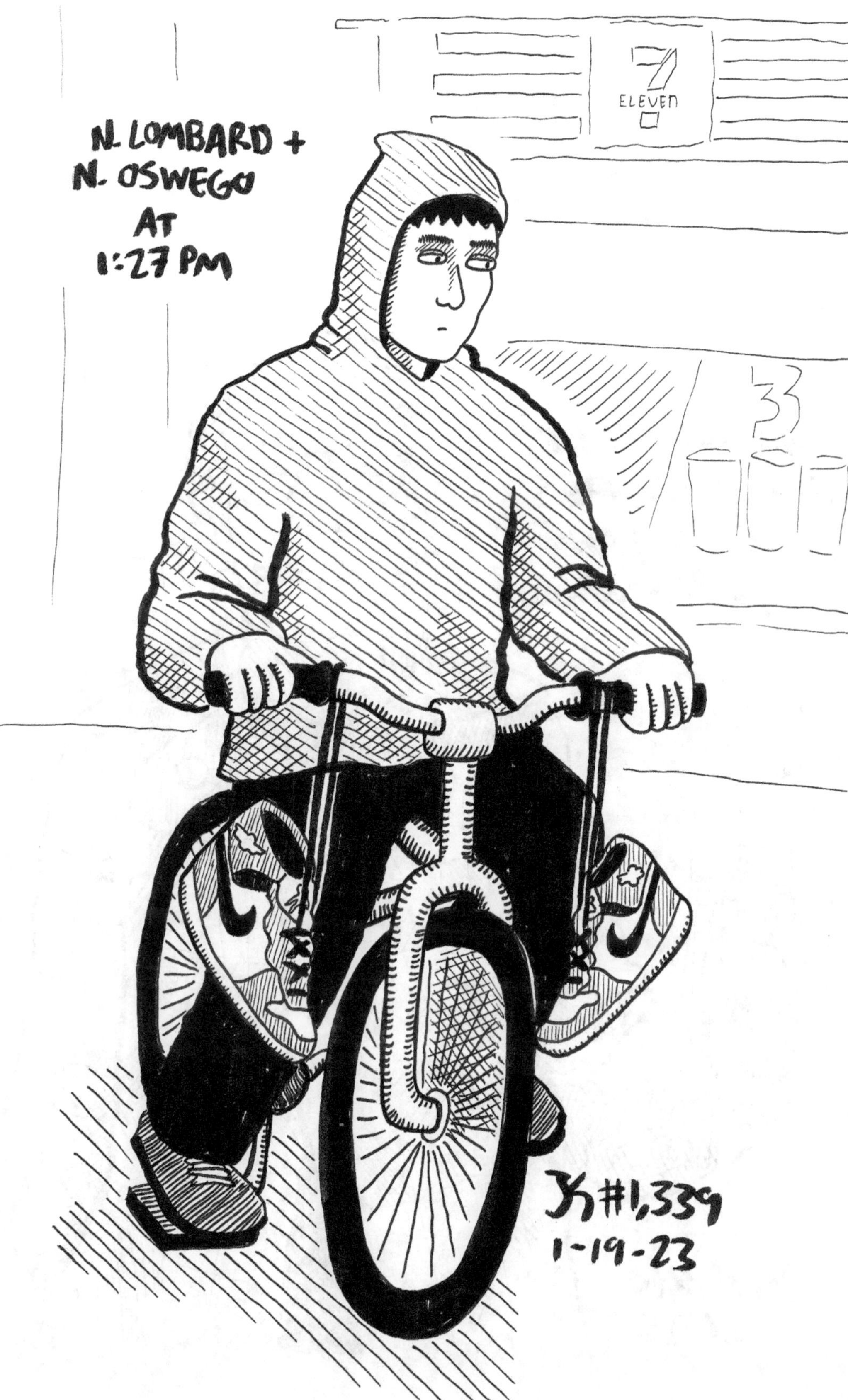

N. LOMBARD +
N. OSWEGO
AT
1:27 PM
ELEVEN
JS #1,339
1-19-23

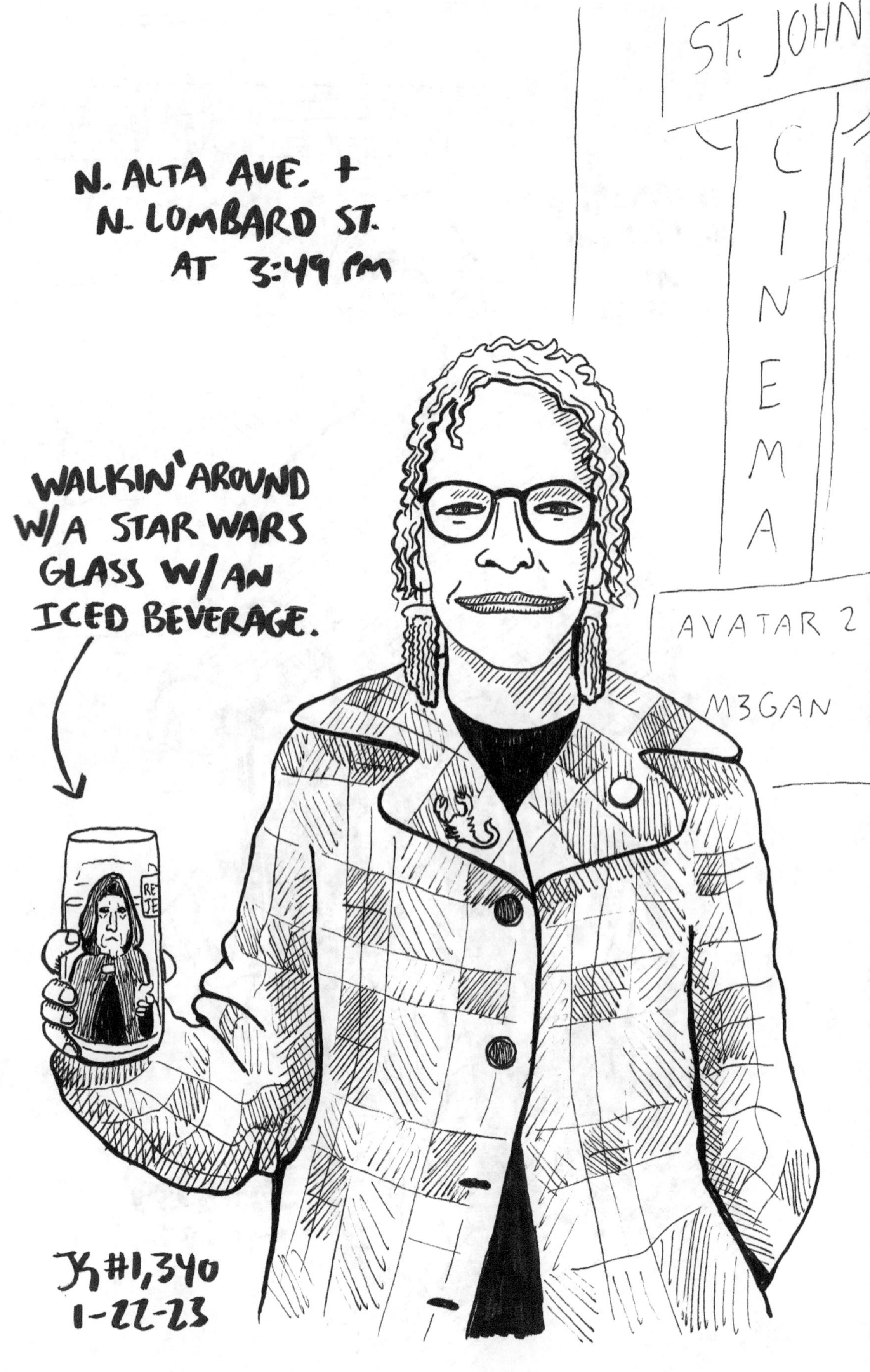

N. ALTA AVE. +
N. LOMBARD ST.
AT 3:49 PM
WALKIN' AROUND
W/ A STAR WARS
GLASS W/ AN
ICED BEVERAGE.
ST. JOHN
CINEMA
AVATAR 2
M3GAN
JK #1,340
1-22-23

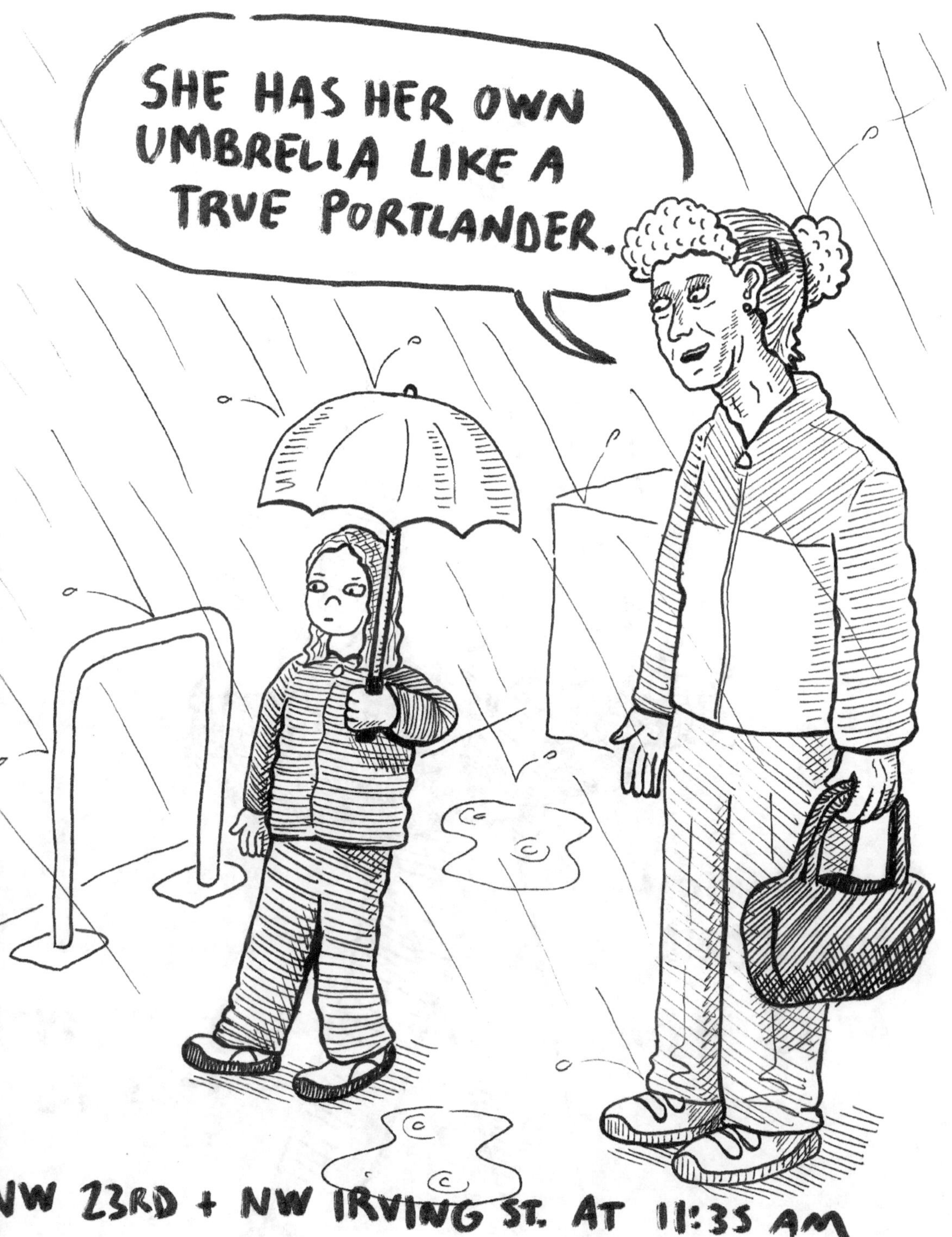

SHE HAS HER OWN
UMBRELLA LIKE A
TRUE PORTLANDER.
NW 23RD + NW IRVING ST. AT 11:35 AM
JK #1,341 1-22-23

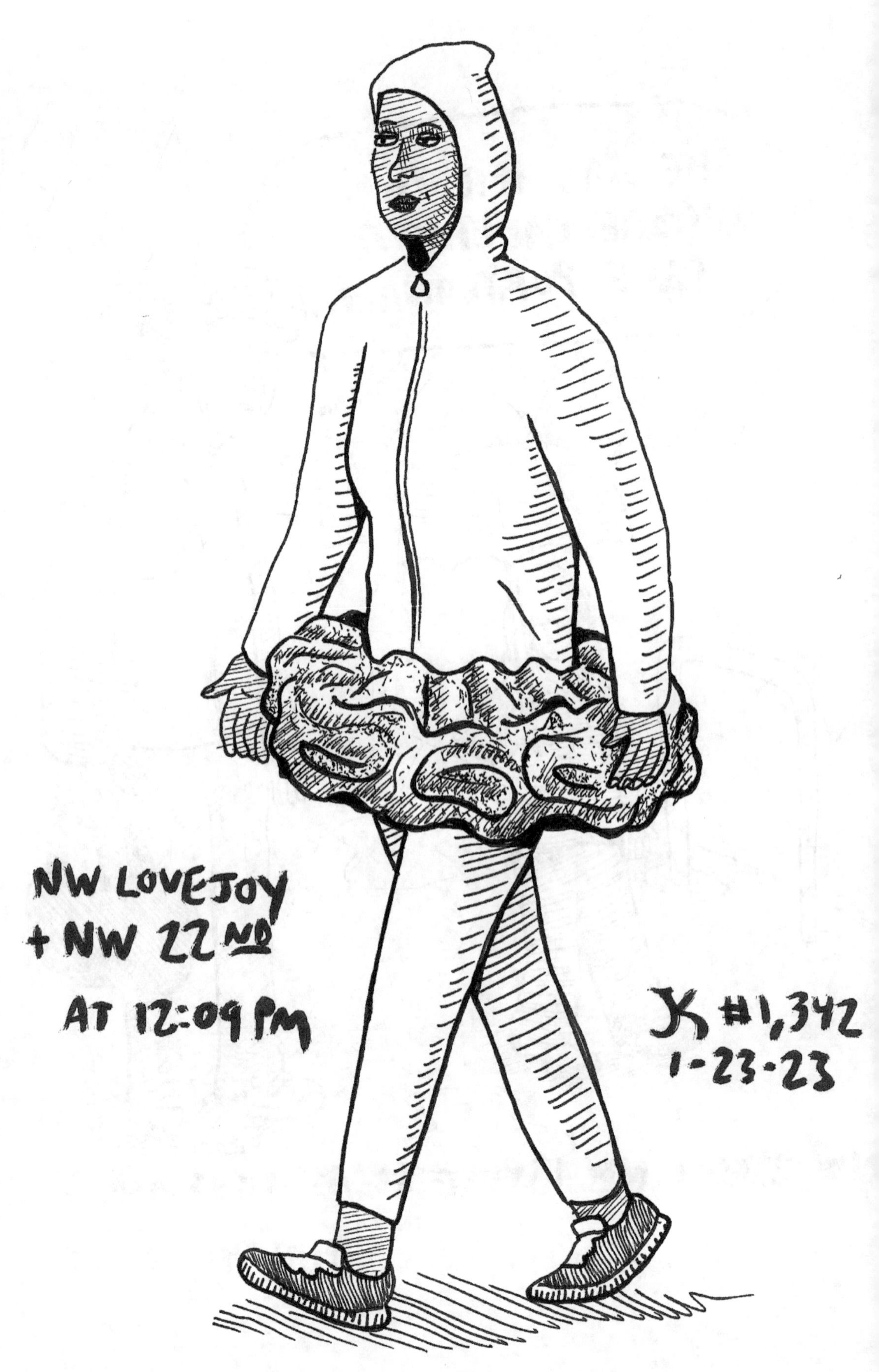

NW LOVEJOY
+ NW 22ND
AT 12:09 PM
JK #1,342
1-23-23

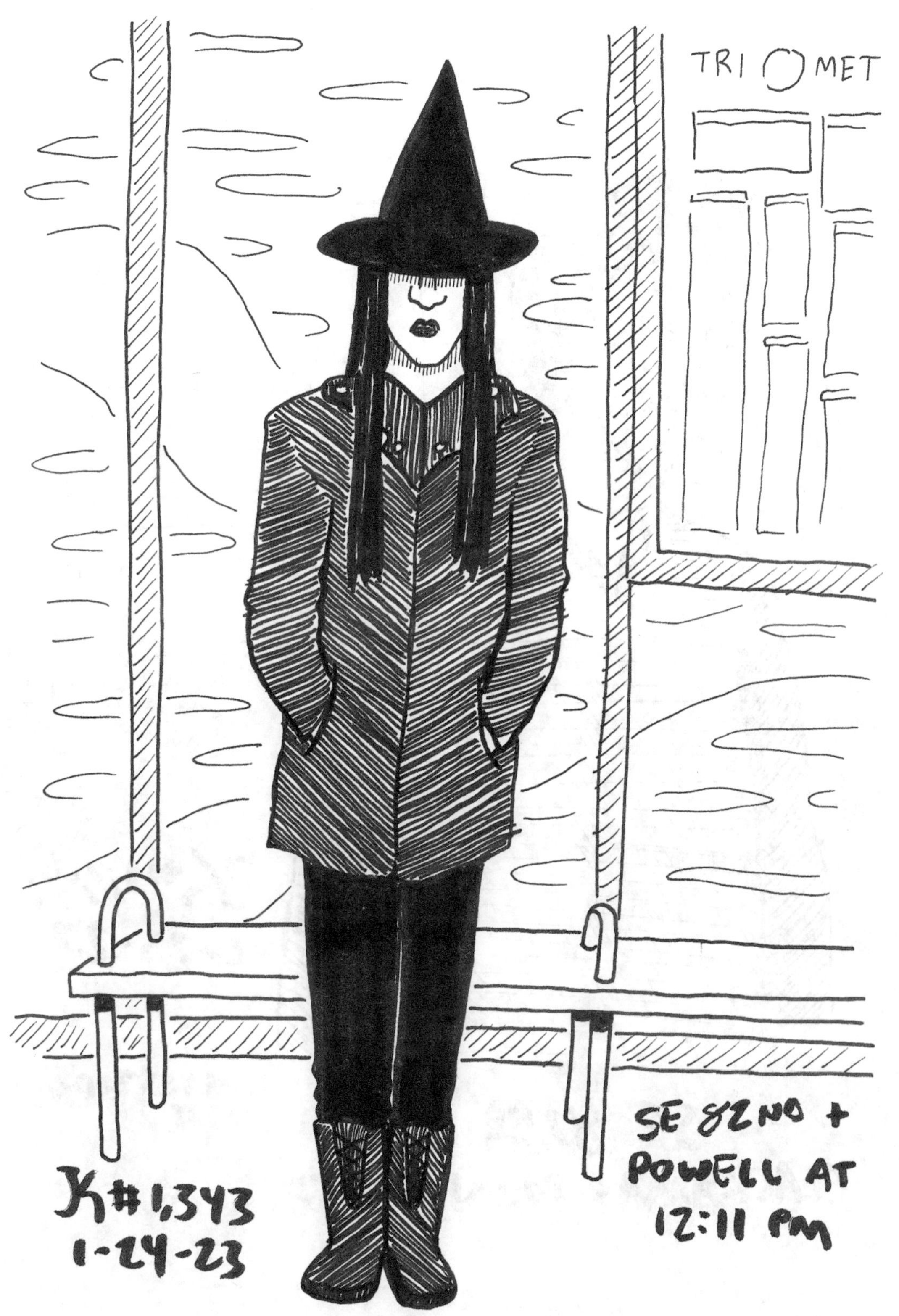

TRI O MET
SE 82ND +
POWELL AT
12:11 PM
K #1,343
1-24-23

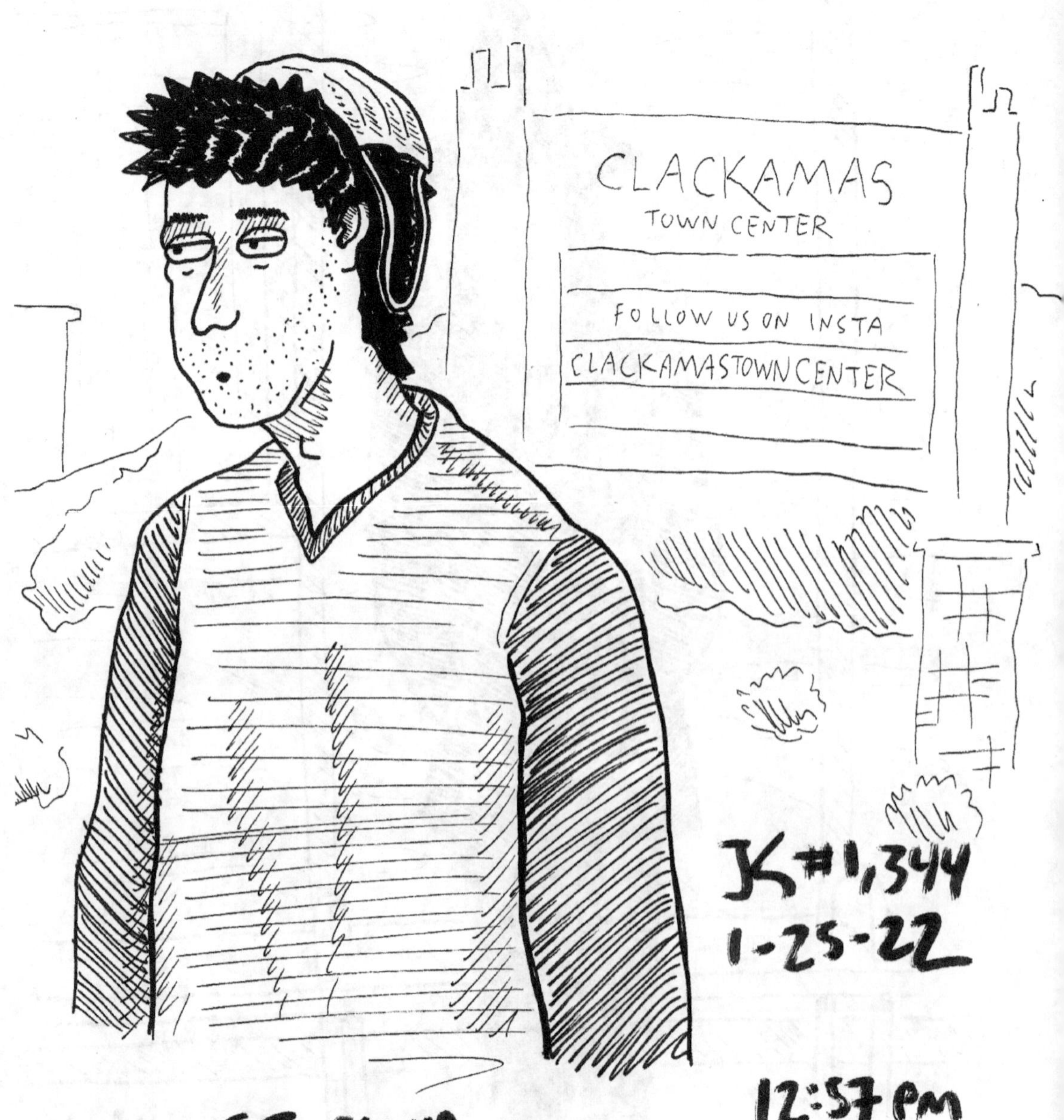

SE 82ND AT
CLACKAMAS TOWN CENTER

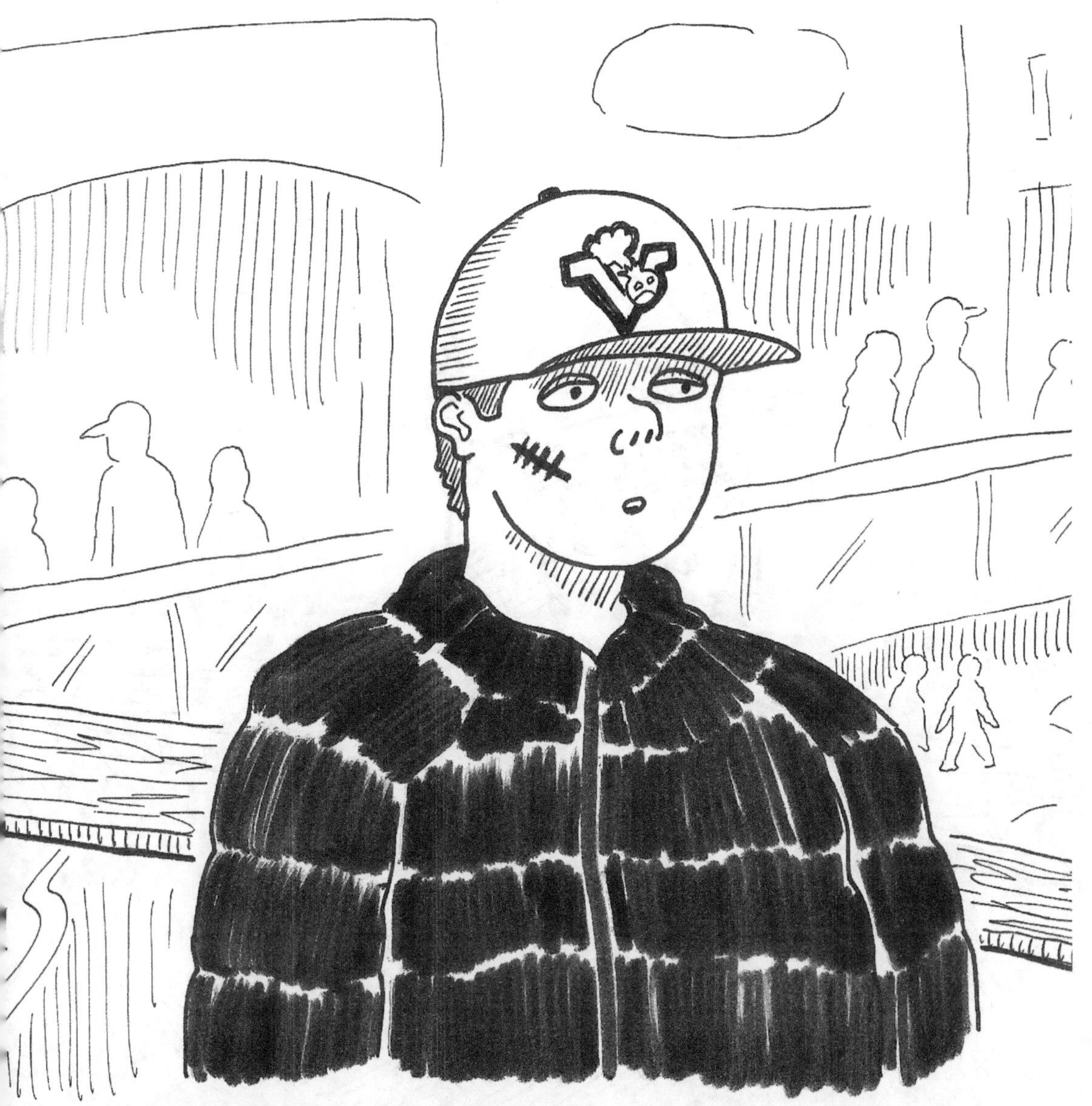

THE "SCAR" WAS DRAWN
ON W/ A SHARPIE.
CLACKAMAS TOWN CENTER
AT 1:22 PM
JS #1,345
1-26-23

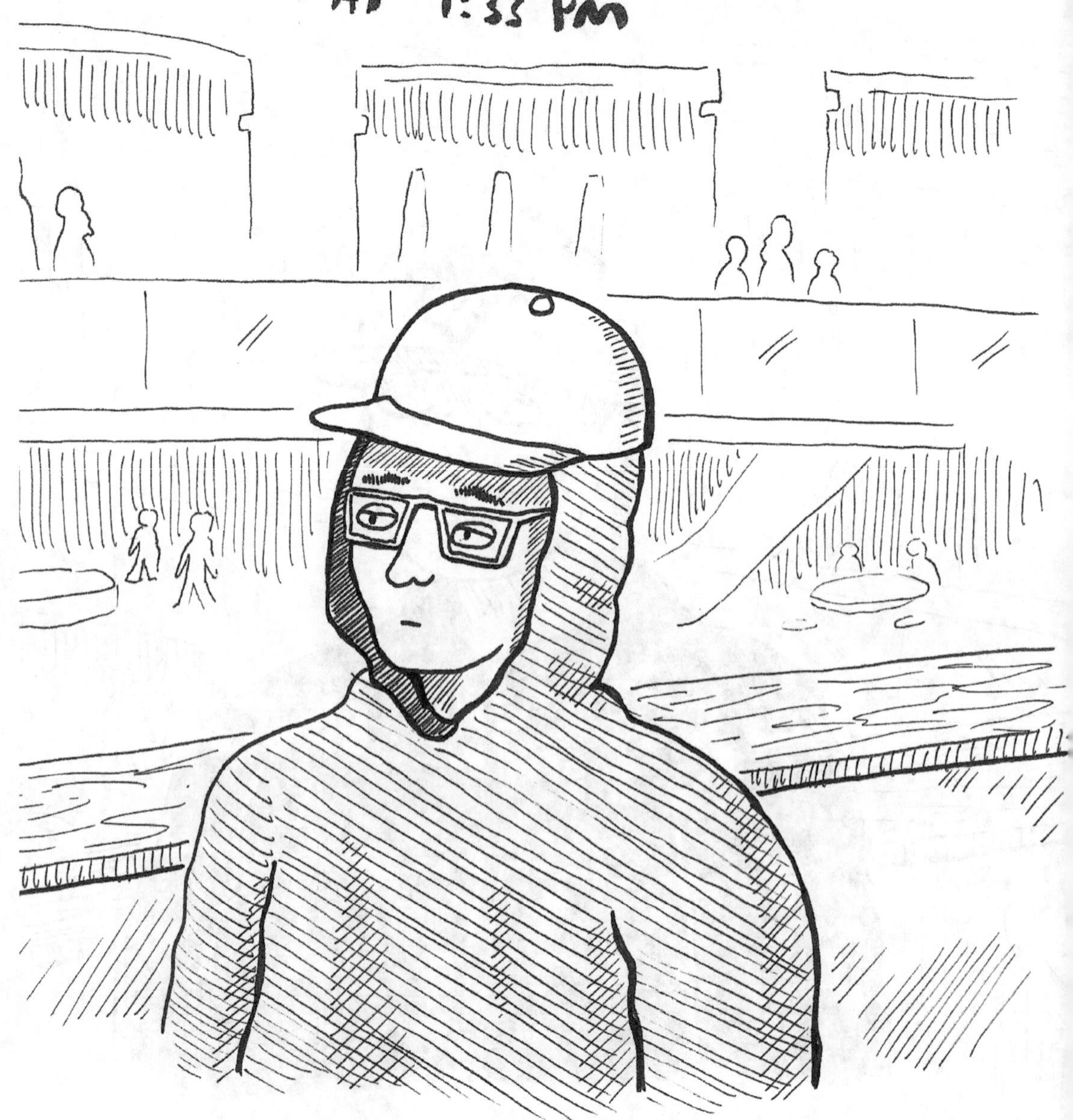

CLACKAMAS TOWN CENTER
AT 1:33 PM
JK #1,346 1-27-23

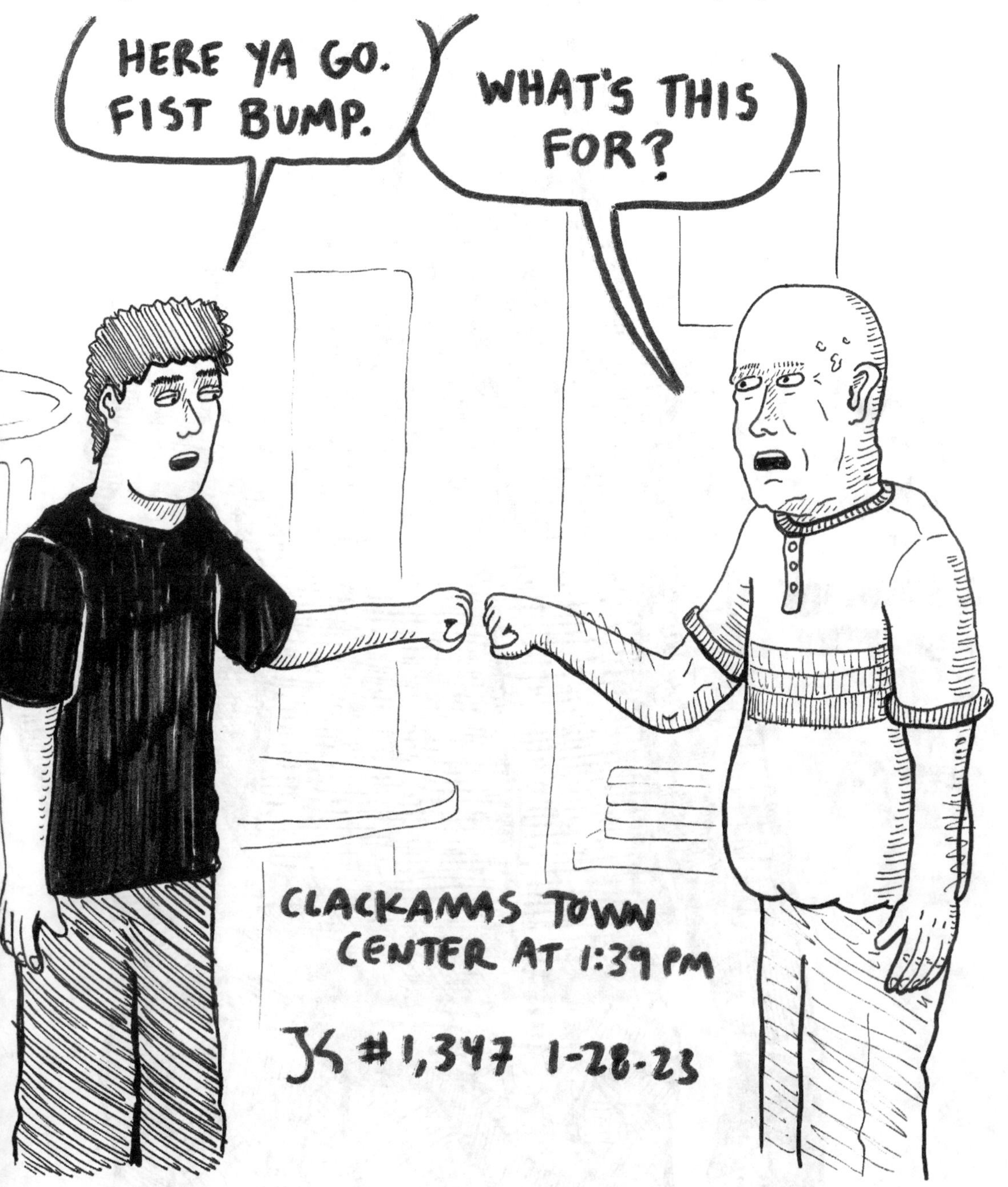

THESE TWO WERE STRANGERS.
HERE YA GO. FIST BUMP.
WHAT'S THIS FOR?
CLACKAMAS TOWN CENTER AT 1:39 PM
JS #1,347 1-28-23

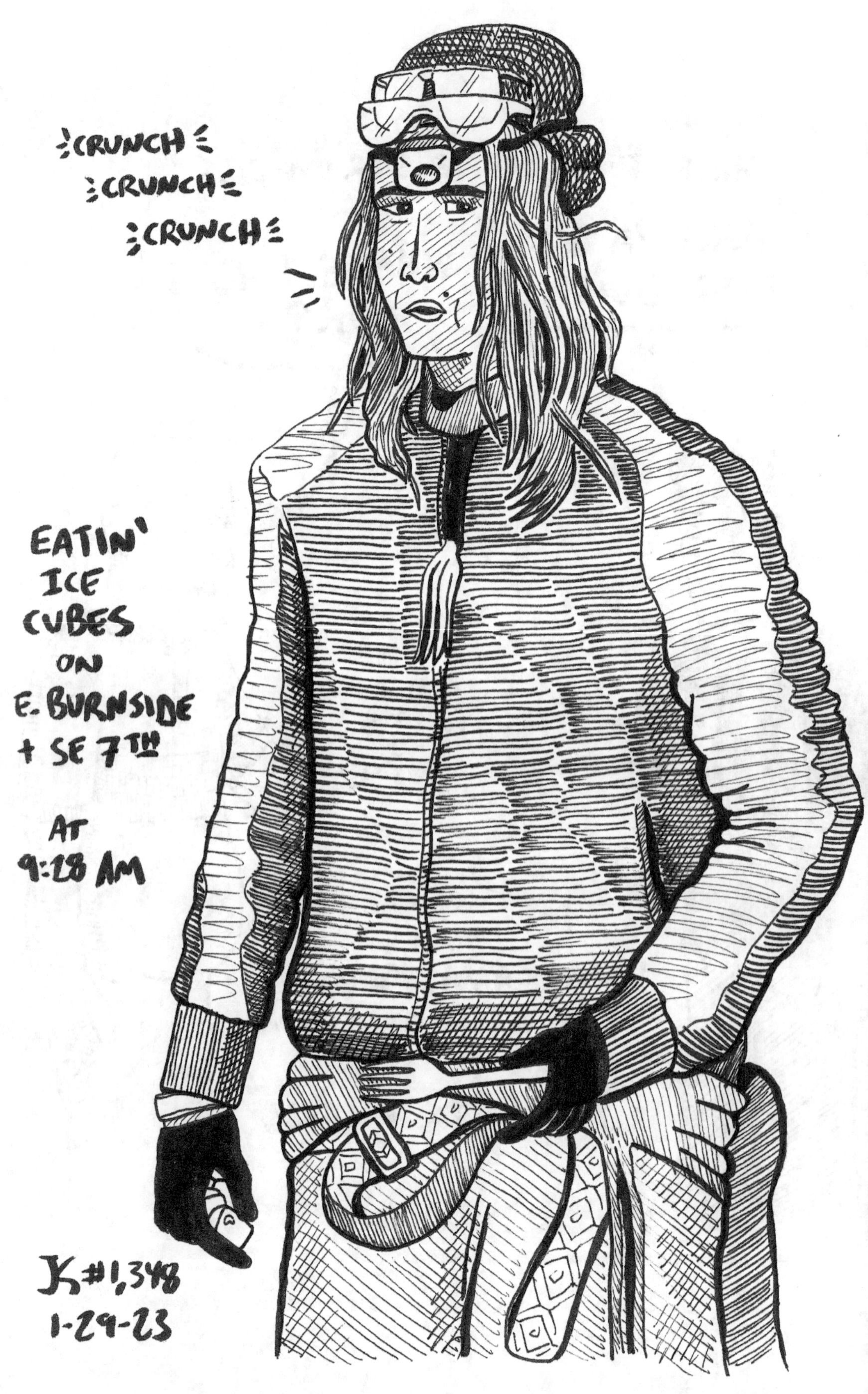

⫶CRUNCH⫶
⫶CRUNCH⫶
⫶CRUNCH⫶

EATIN'
ICE
CUBES
ON
E. BURNSIDE
+ SE 7TH

AT
9:28 AM

#1,348
1-29-23

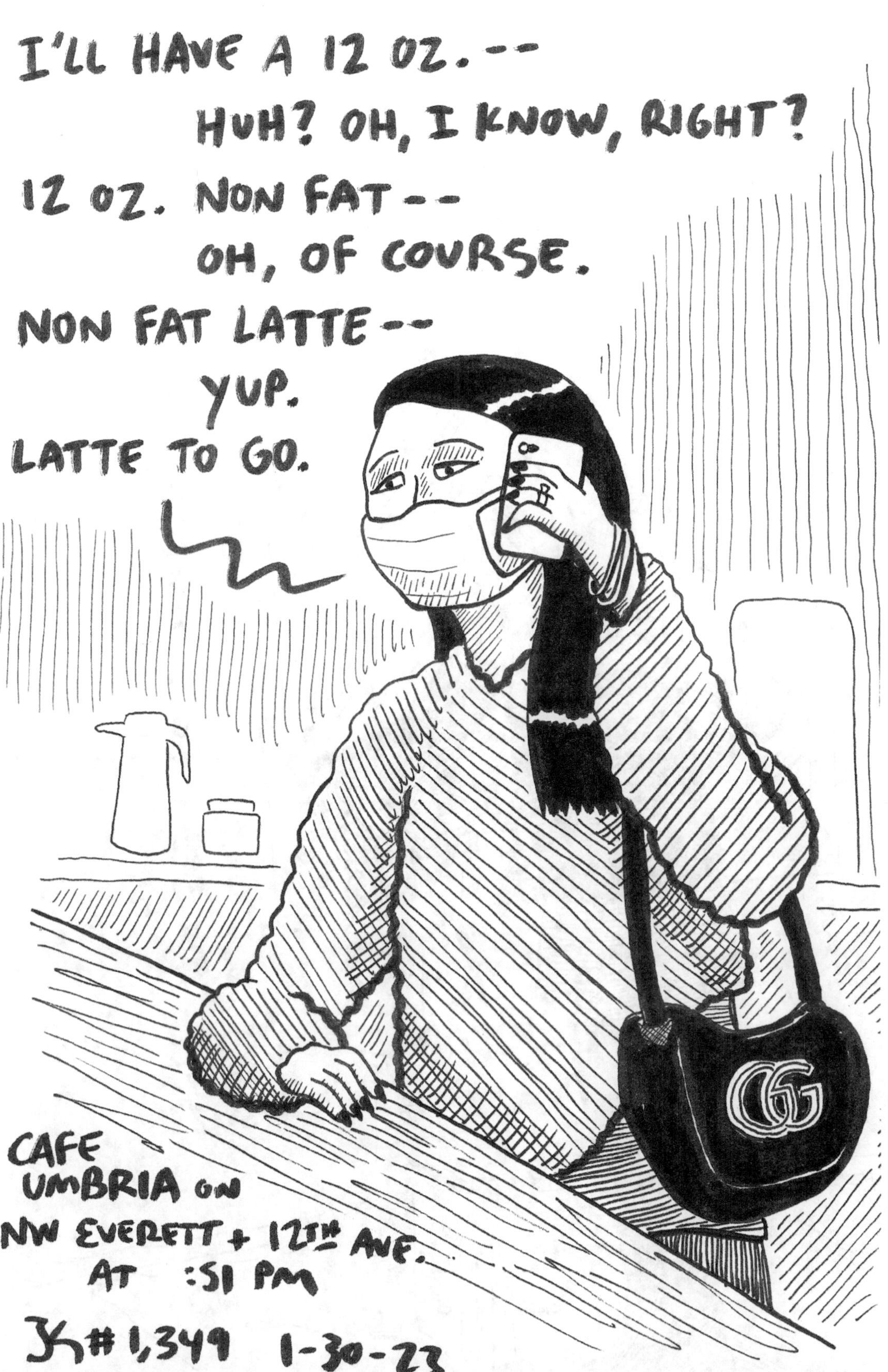

I'LL HAVE A 12 OZ. --
HUH? OH, I KNOW, RIGHT?
12 OZ. NON FAT --
OH, OF COURSE.
NON FAT LATTE --
YUP.
LATTE TO GO.
CAFE UMBRIA ON
NW EVERETT + 12TH AVE.
AT :51 PM
JK #1,349 1-30-23

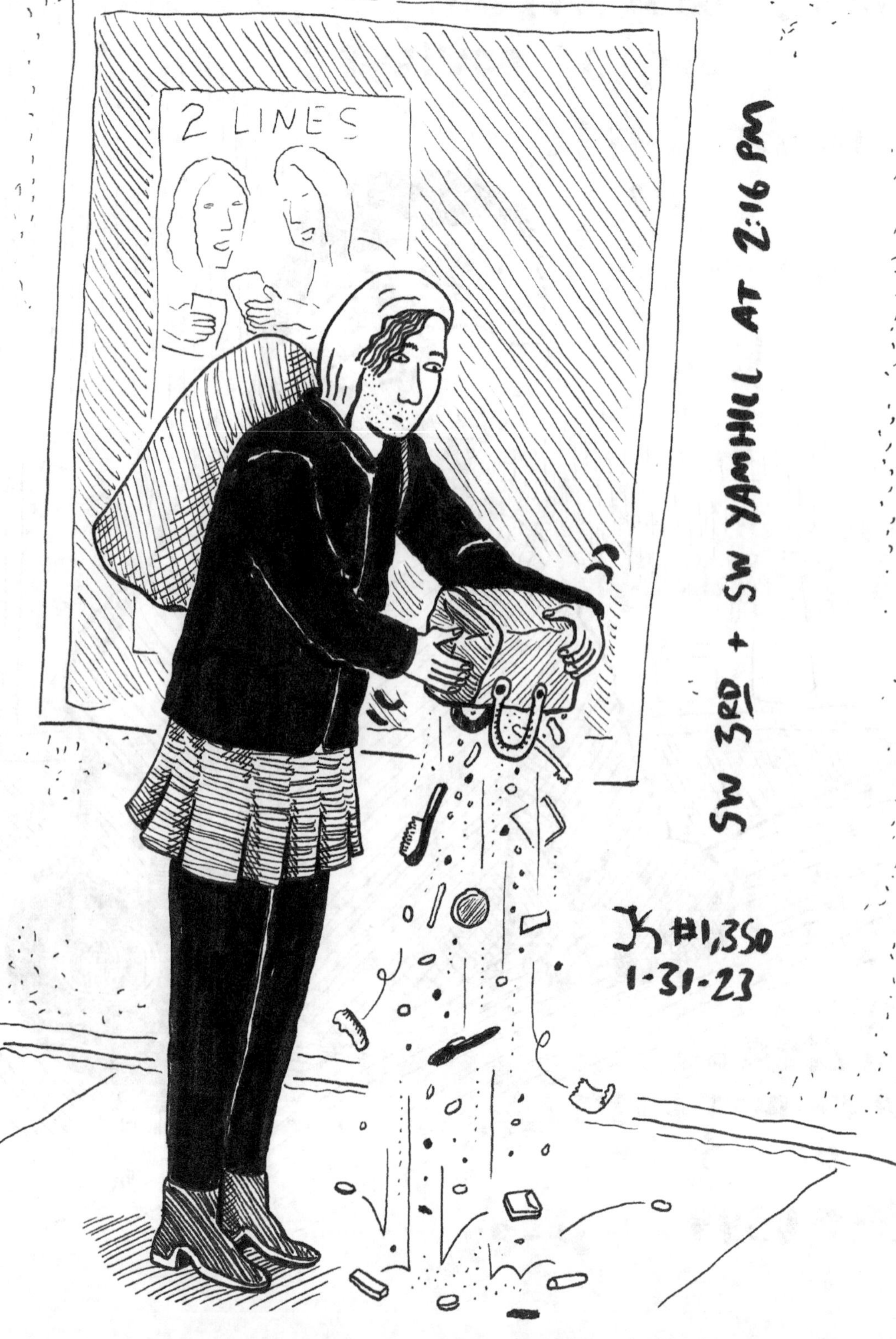

AT&T
2 LINES
SW 3RD + SW YAMHILL AT 2:16 PM
JK #1,350
1-31-23

HE'S ON THE LOOSE, ON THE LAM. THIS IS THE PERFECT PLACE TO BE ON THE LAM.
HE'S HOT.
#1,351 2-1-23
CASE STUDY COFFEE ON SW YAMHILL ST. + SW 10TH AVE. AT 10:35 AM

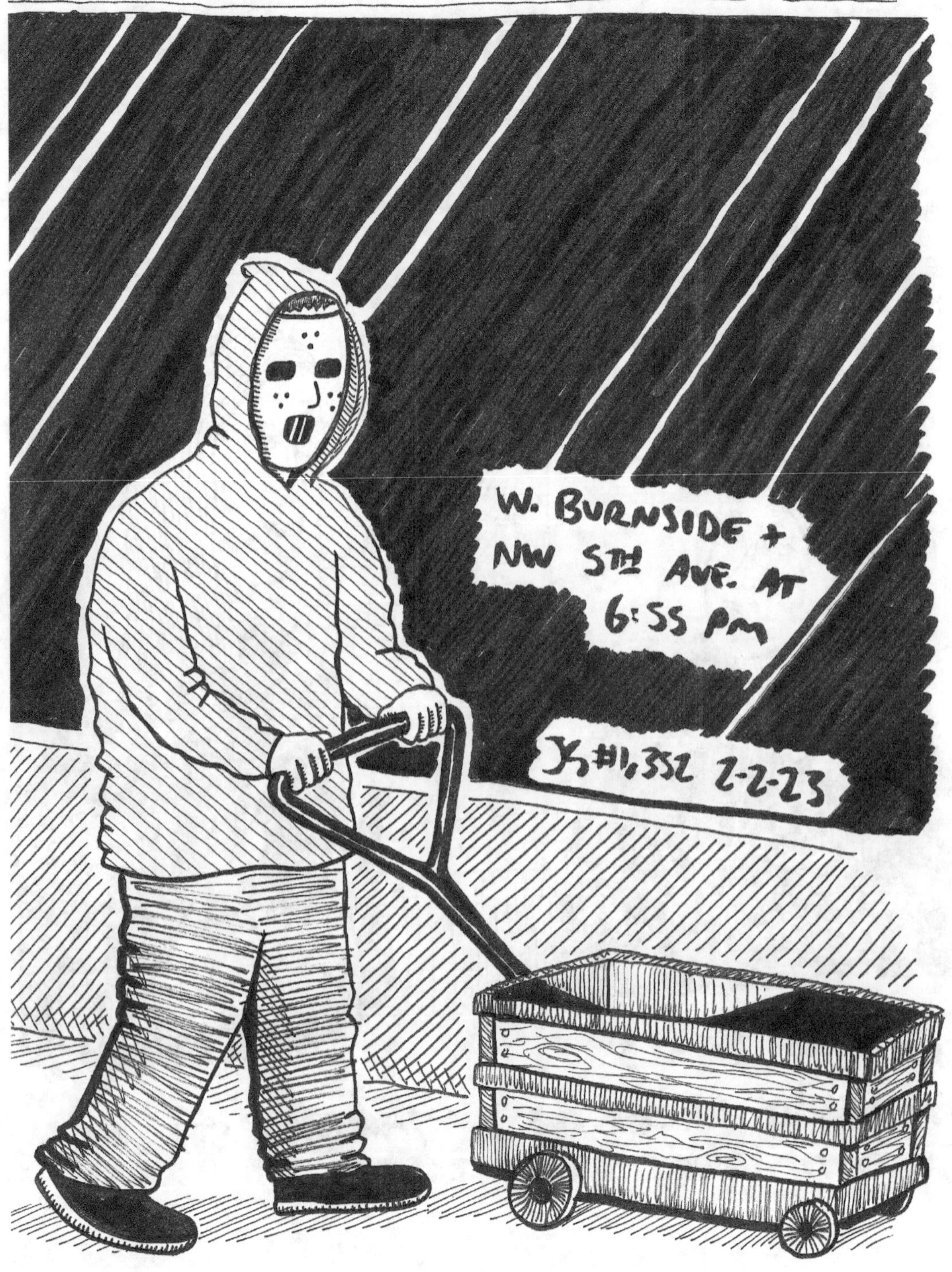

ALL NUDE REVIEW
W. BURNSIDE +
NW 5TH AVE. AT
6:55 PM
#1,352 2-2-23

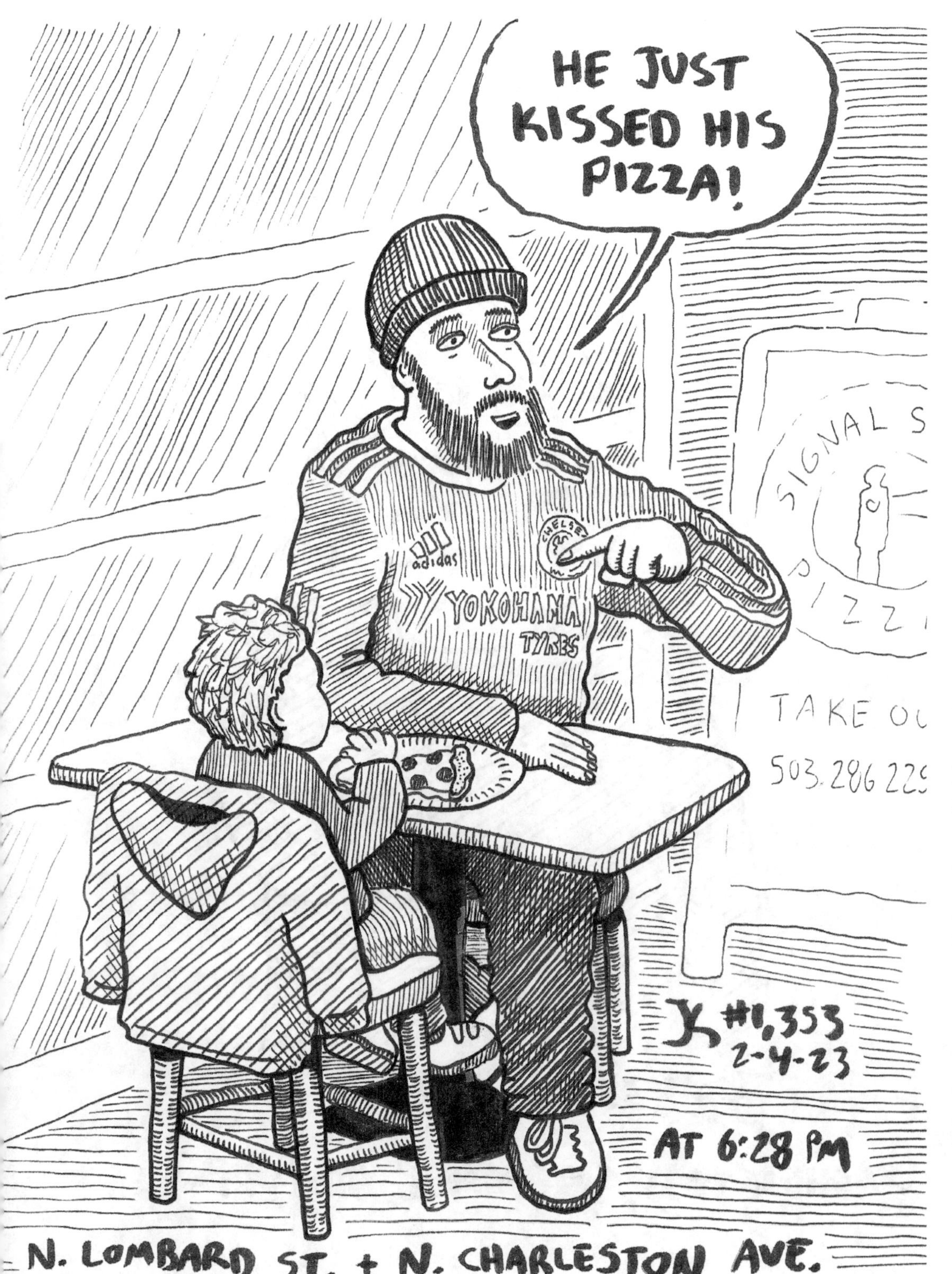

N. LOMBARD ST. + N. CHARLESTON AVE.

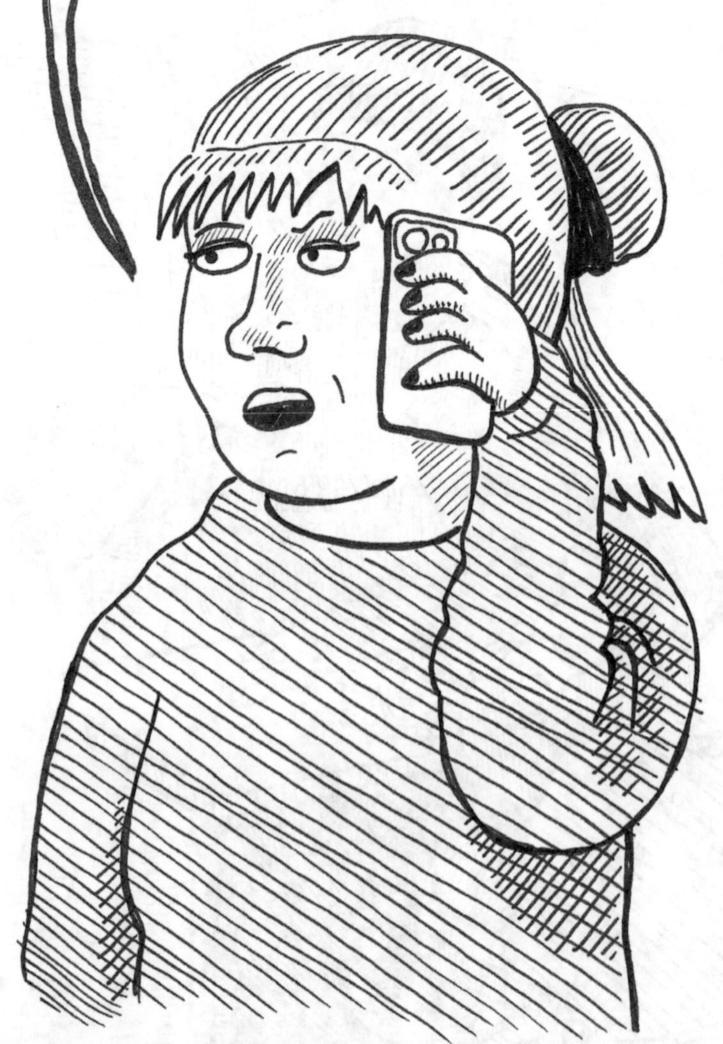

JK #1,354 2-5-23

WASHINGTON SQ. MALL AT 1:01 PM

COMPOST
#1,355 2-6-23
SW JEFFERSON + BROADWAY   AT 2:04 PM

BAG OF
CAP'N CRUNCH
W. BURNSIDE
+
NW KING AVE.
AT 12:35 PM
JS #1,356
2-10-23

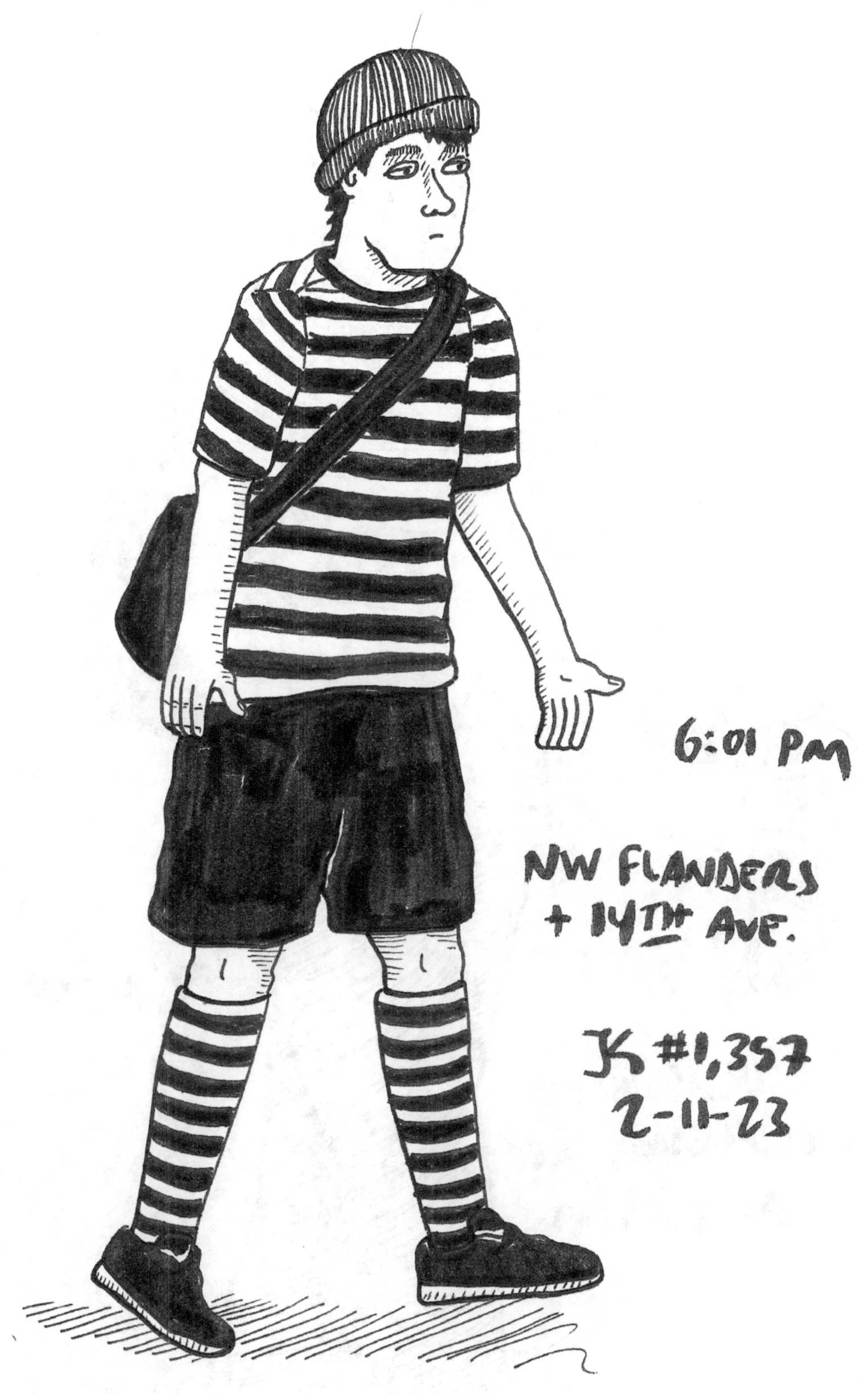

6:01 PM
NW FLANDERS
+ 14TH AVE.
JS #1,357
2-11-23

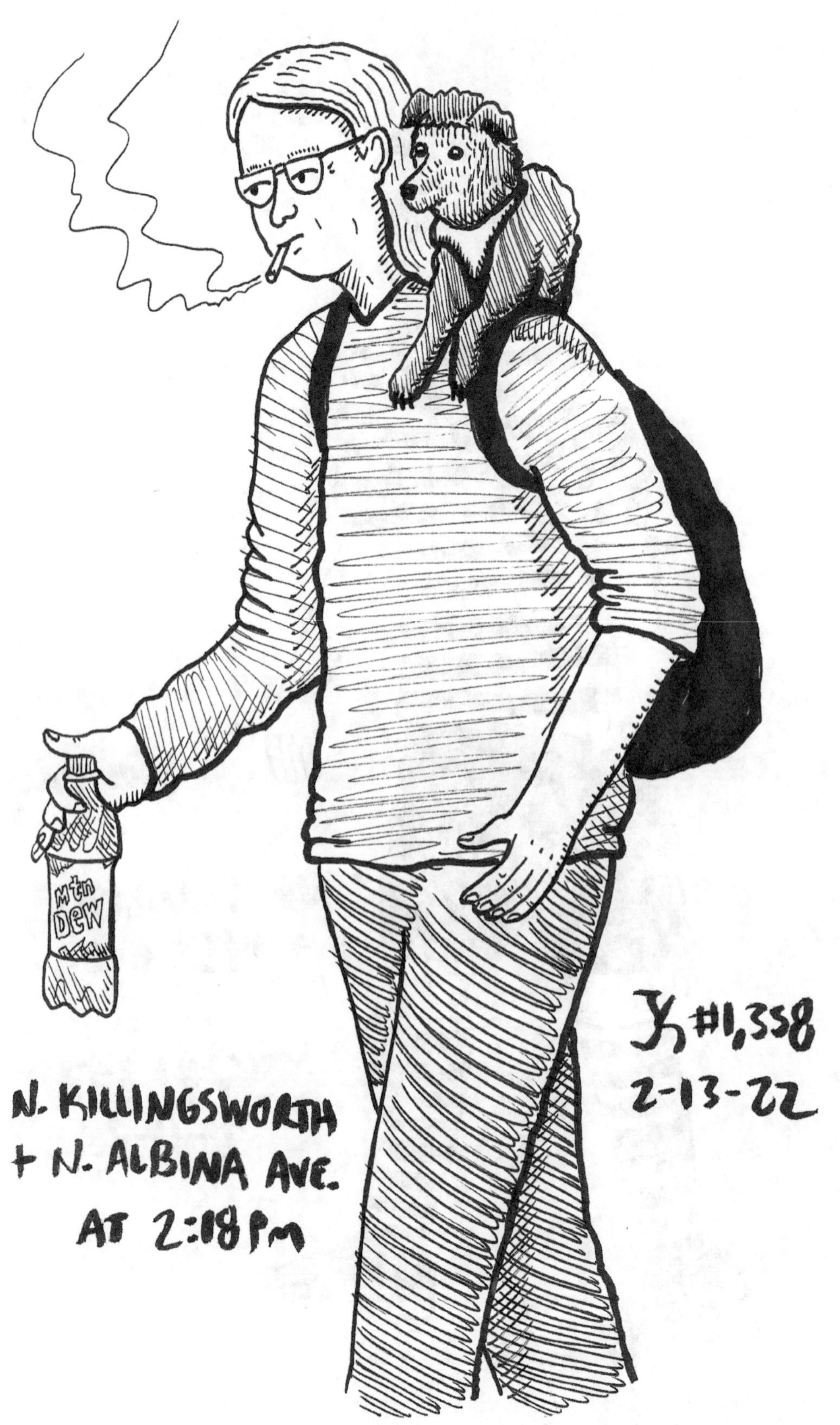

mtn Dew
N. KILLINGSWORTH
+ N. ALBINA AVE.
AT 2:18 PM
#1,358
2-13-22

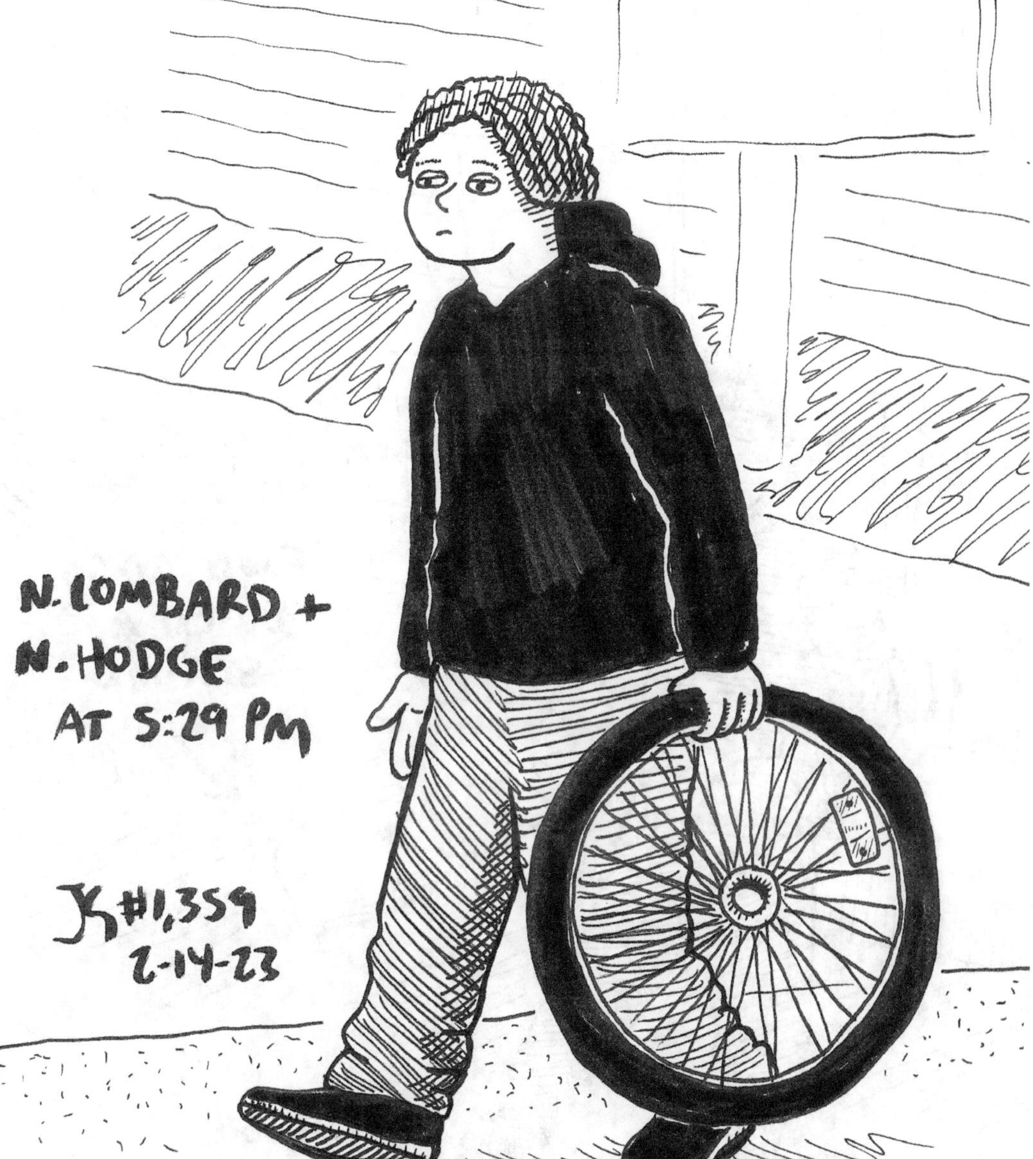

O'Reilly
AUTO PARTS
N. LOMBARD +
N. HODGE
AT 5:29 PM
JK #1,359
2-14-23

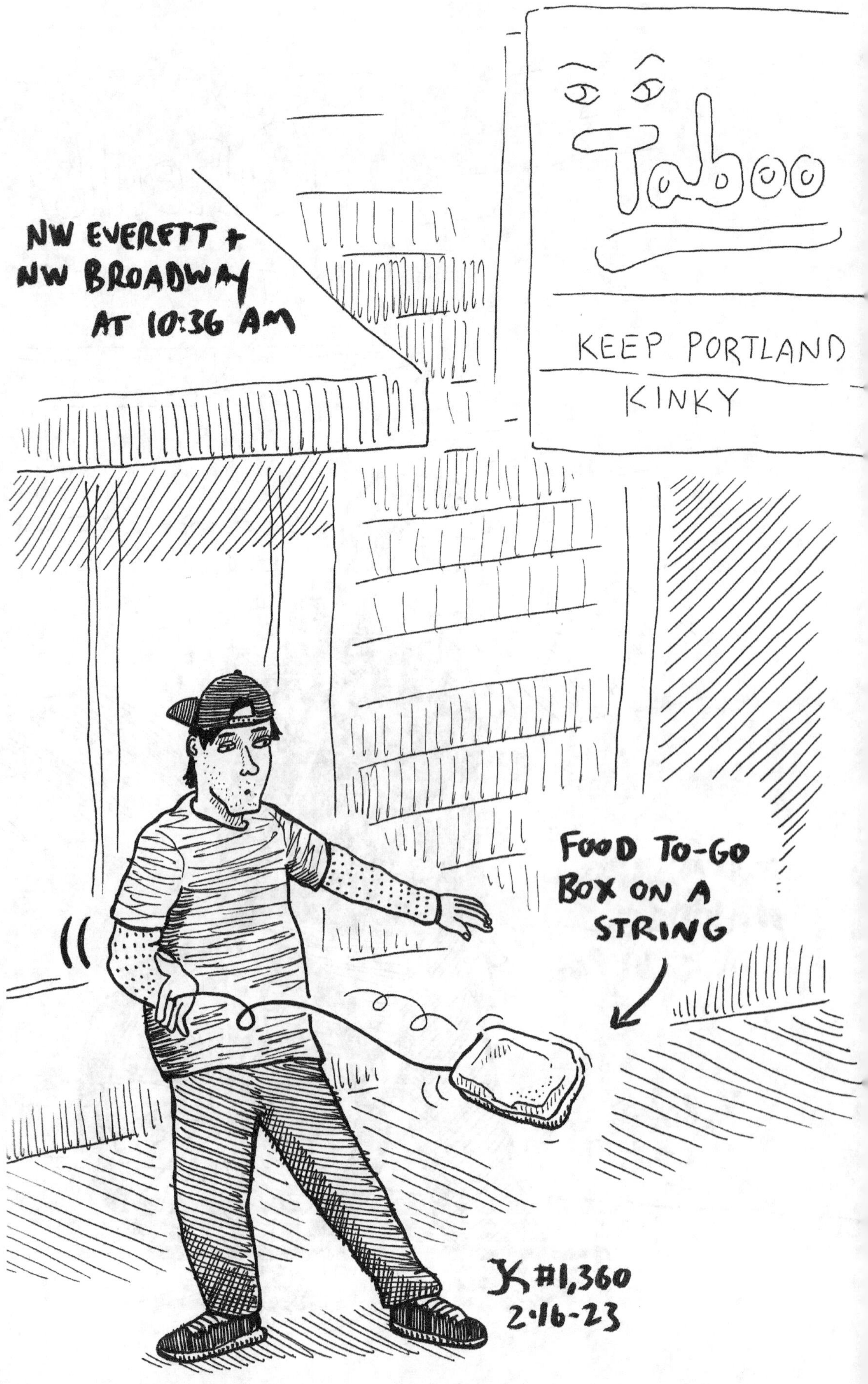

NW EVERETT +
NW BROADWAY
AT 10:36 AM
Taboo
KEEP PORTLAND
KINKY
FOOD TO-GO
BOX ON A
STRING
JK #1,360
2·16·23

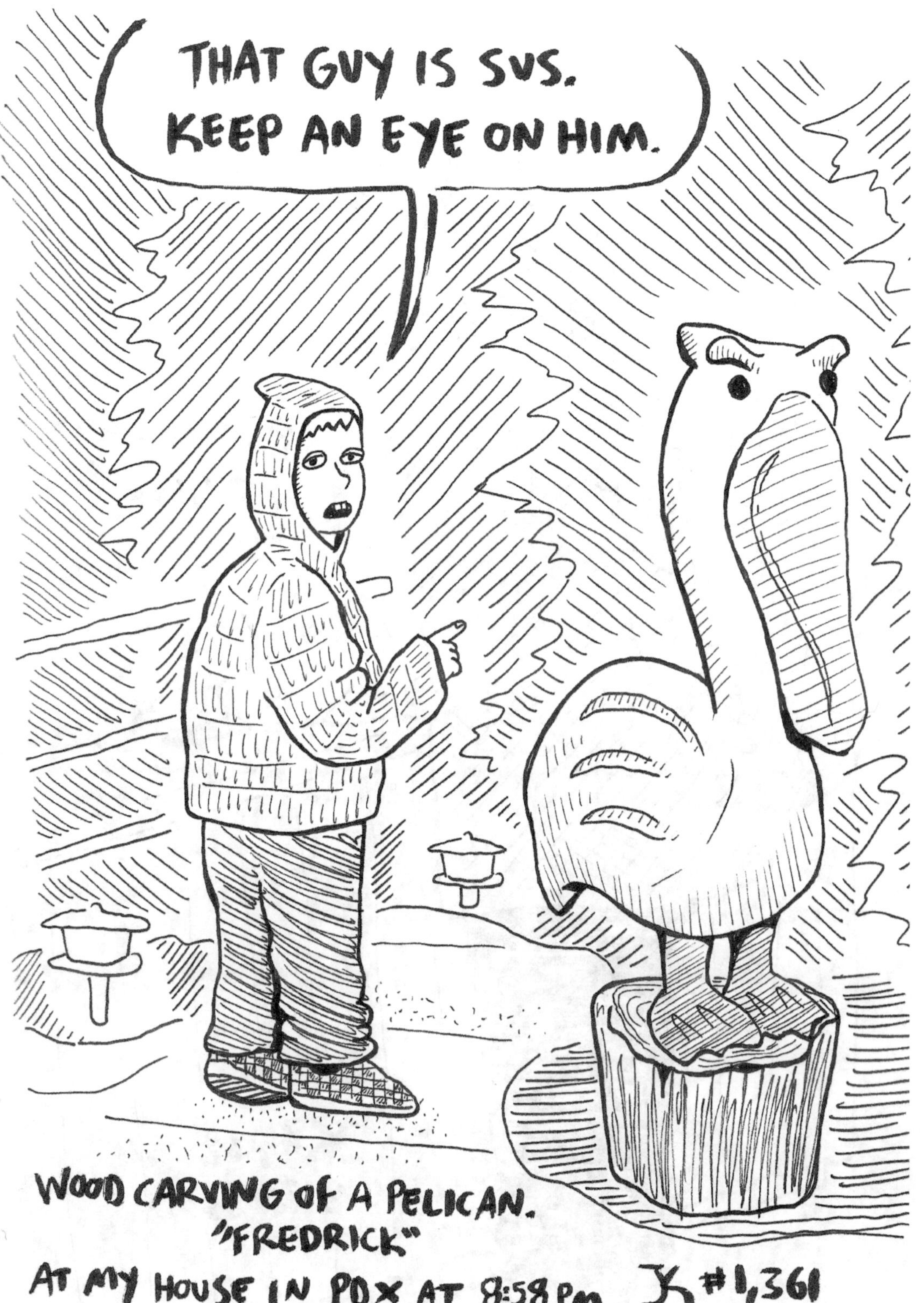

WOOD CARVING OF A PELICAN.
"FREDRICK"
AT MY HOUSE IN PDX AT 8:58 PM #1,361
2-19-23

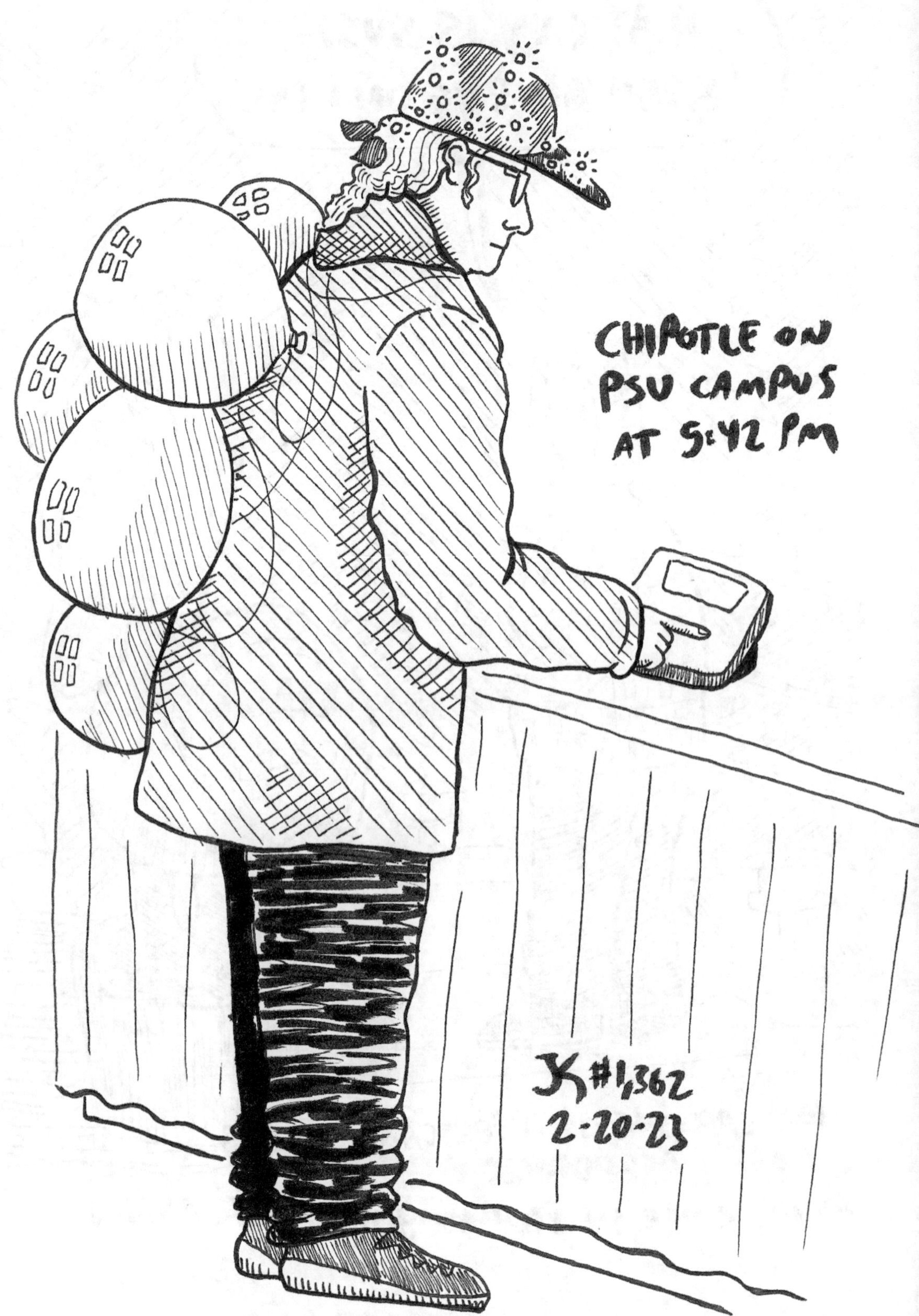

CHIPOTLE ON
PSU CAMPUS
AT 5:42 PM
JK #1,362
2-20-23

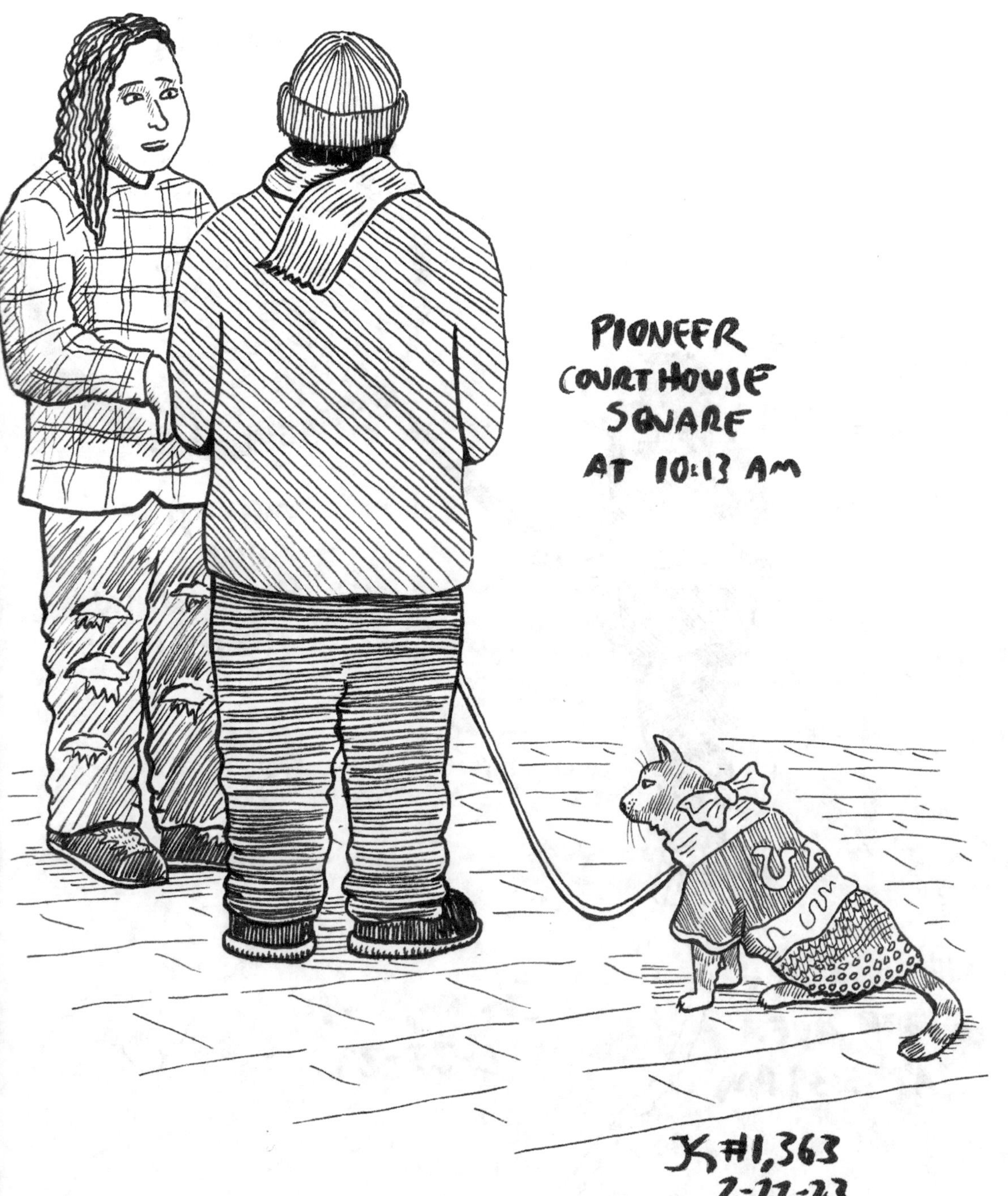

PIONEER
COURTHOUSE
SQUARE
AT 10:13 AM

JK #1,363
2-22-23

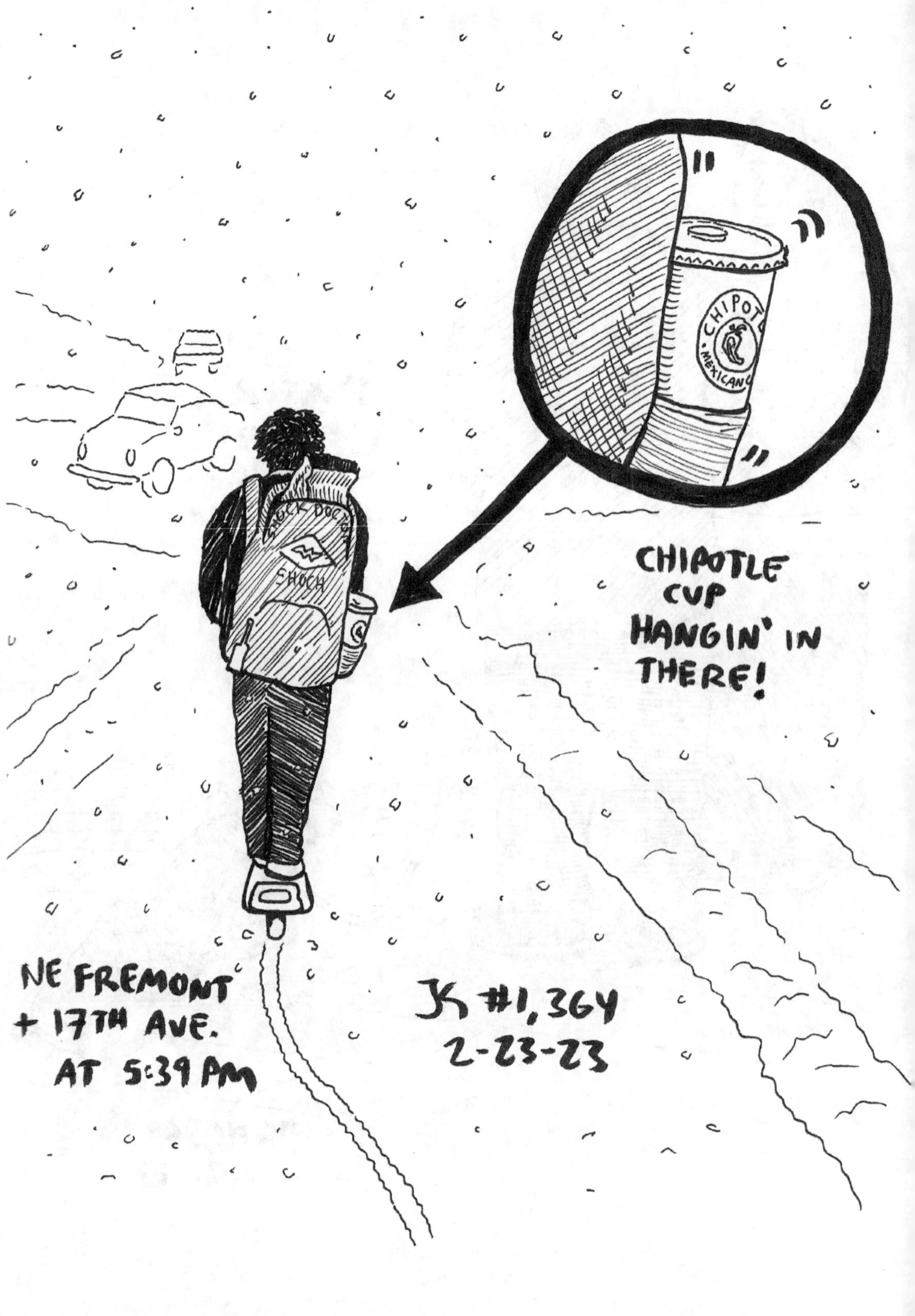

CHIPOTLE
CUP
HANGIN' IN
THERE!
NE FREMONT
+ 17TH AVE.
AT 5:39 PM
JS #1,364
2-23-23

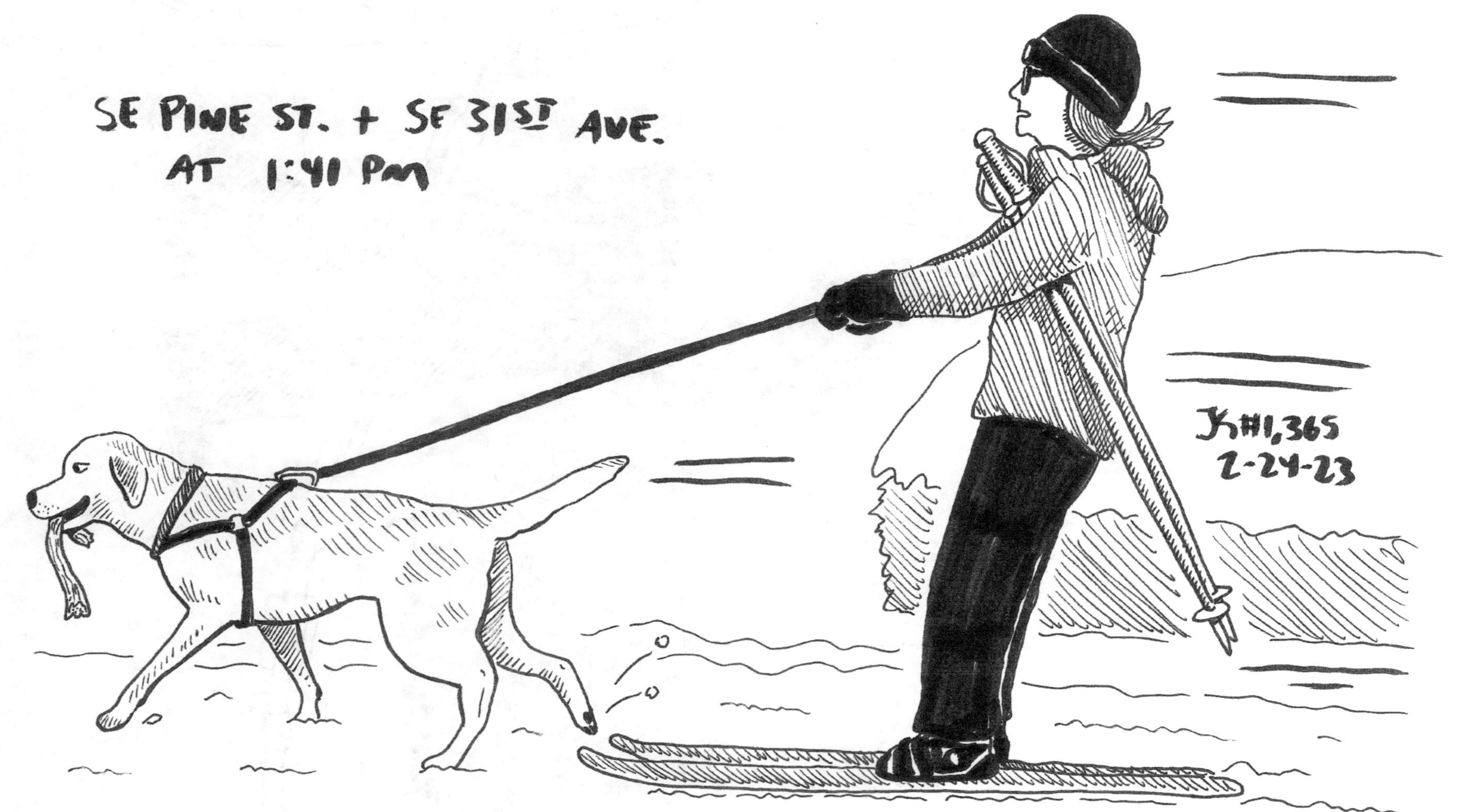

SE Pine St. + SE 31st Ave.
At 1:41 Pm
JK#1,365
2-24-23

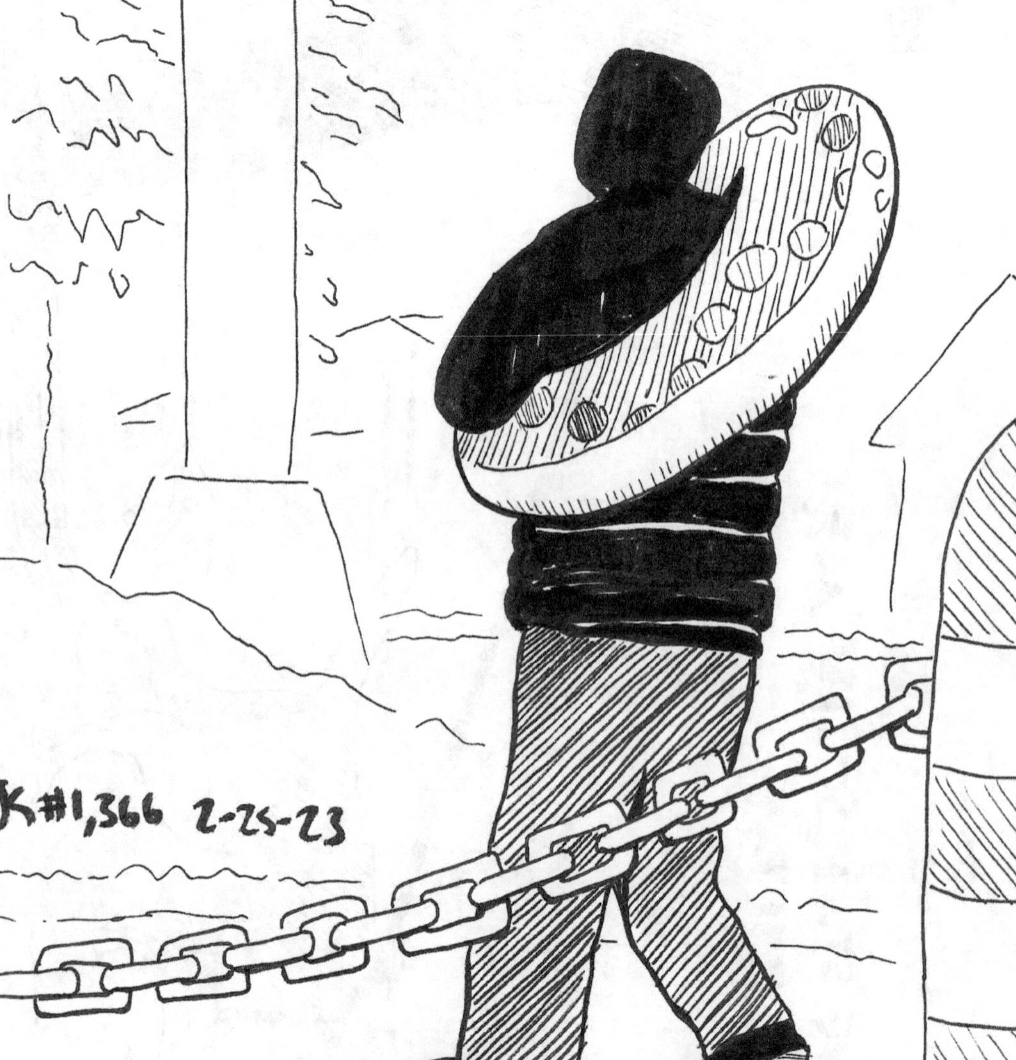

SOMEWHERE ALONG
INTERSTATE AVE.
MIDDAY

JK #1,366 2-25-23

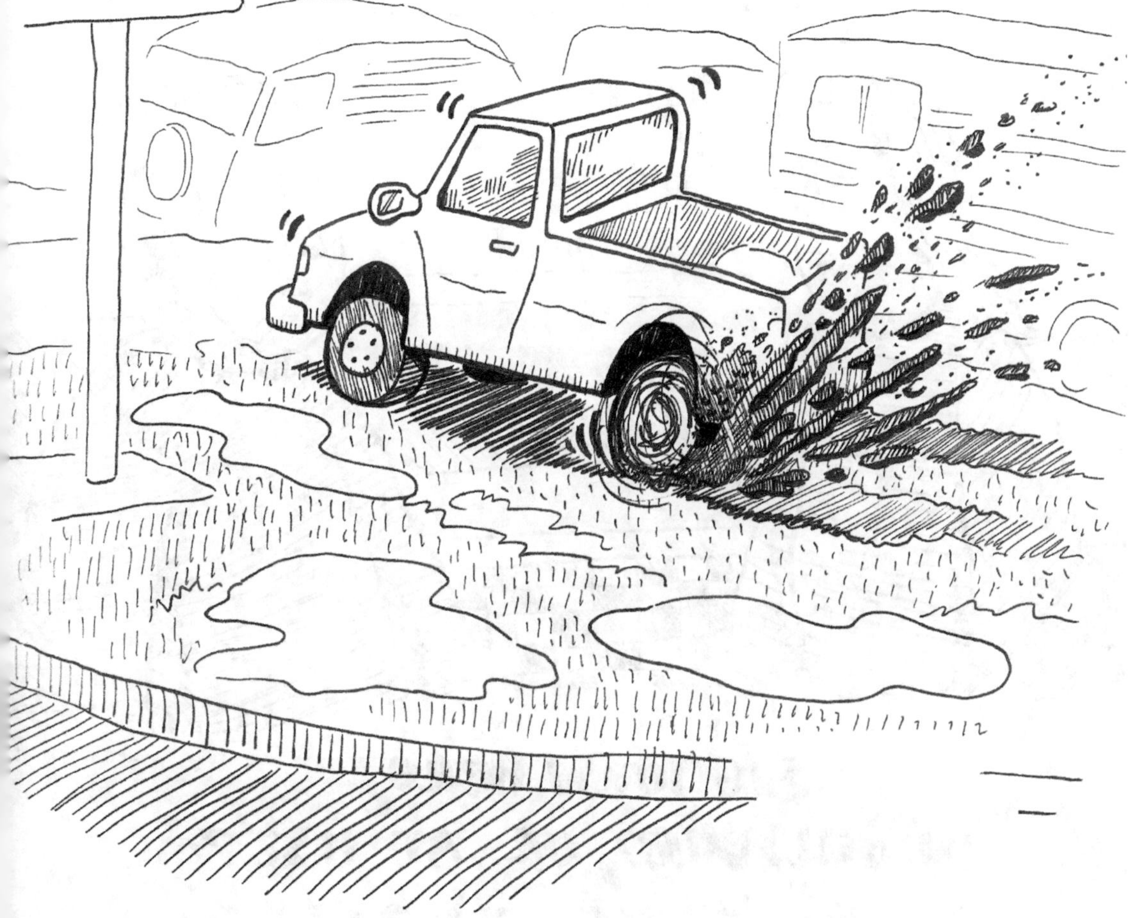

J5
SOUTH
Portland
Salem
I-205 EXIT & N. LOMBARD
1:55 PM   JK #1,367 2-27-23

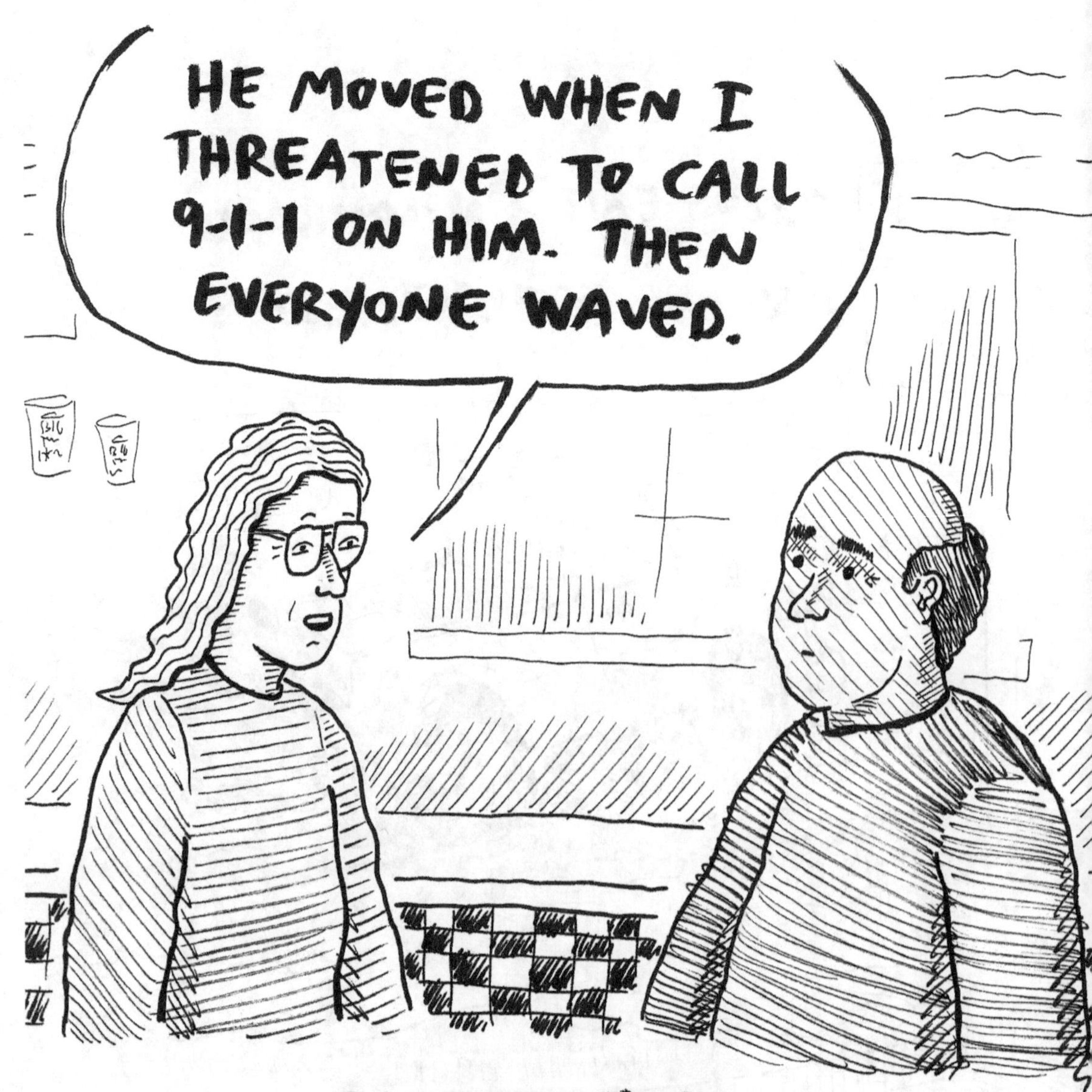

BIG TOWN HERO
IN HILLSBORO, OR AT 1:32 PM
#1,368 3-1-23

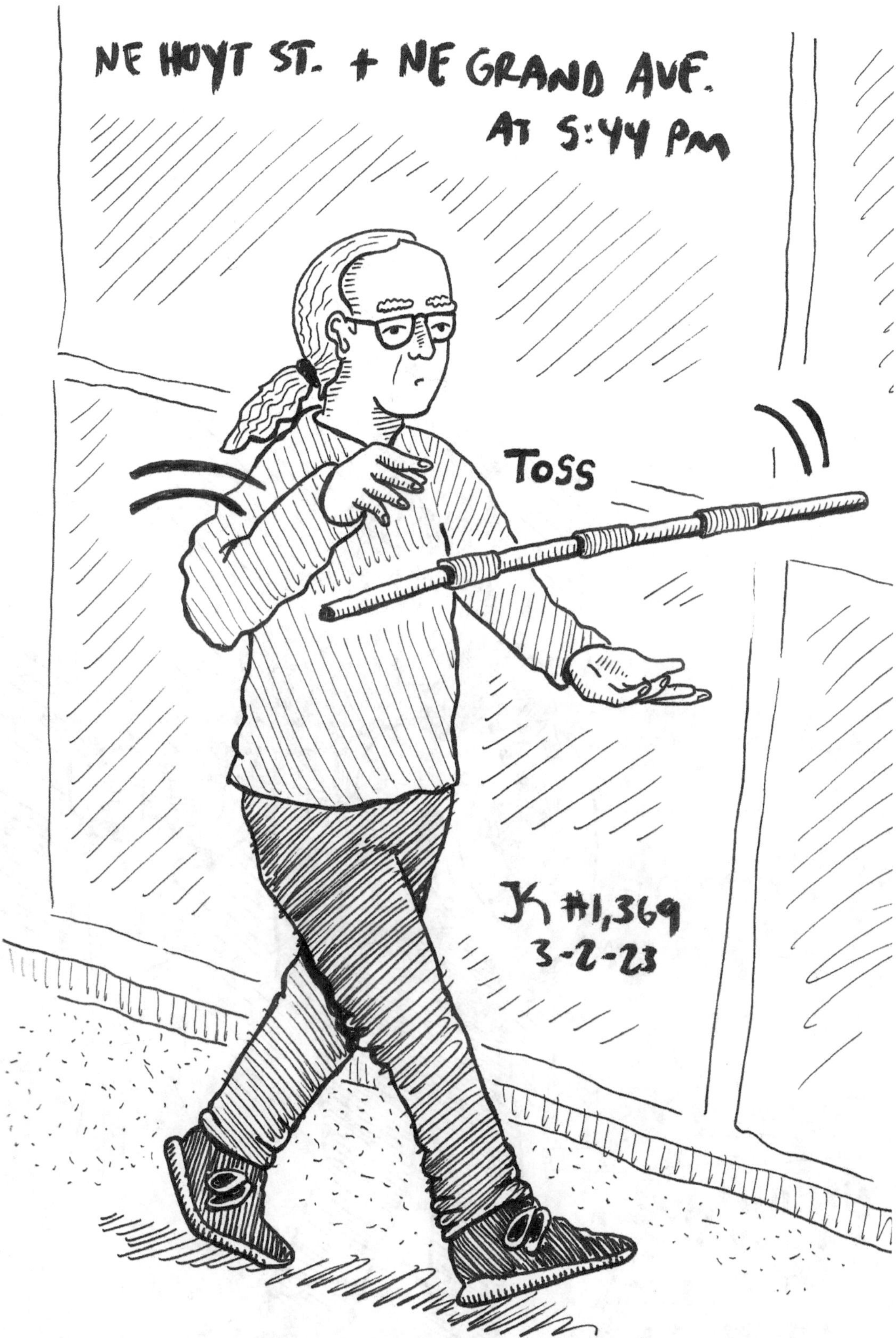

NE HOYT ST. + NE GRAND AVE.
AT 5:44 PM
TOSS
JK #1,369
3-2-23

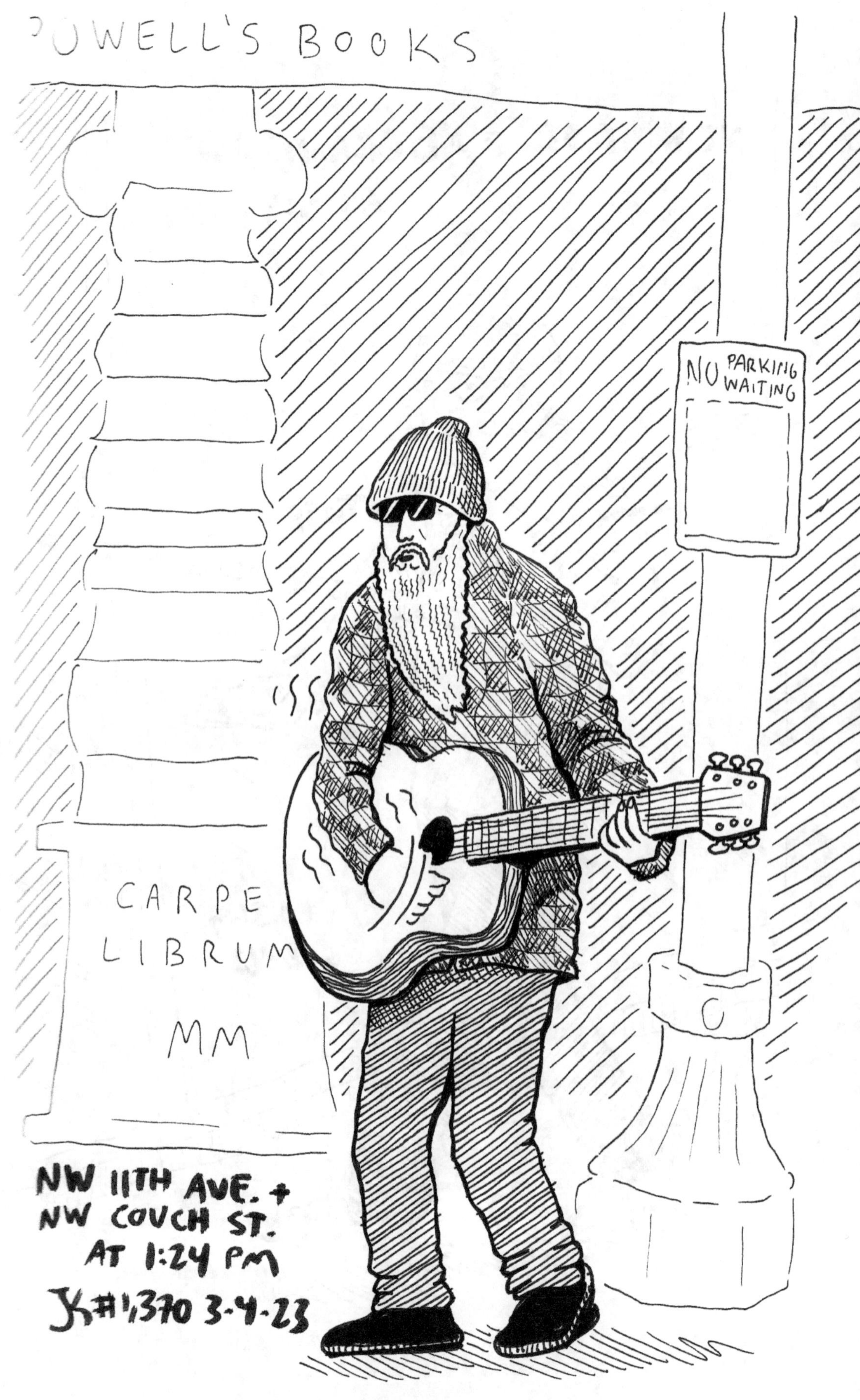
POWELL'S BOOKS
NO PARKING WAITING
CARPE
LIBRUM
MM
NW 11TH AVE. +
NW COUCH ST.
AT 1:24 PM
JK #1370 3-4-23

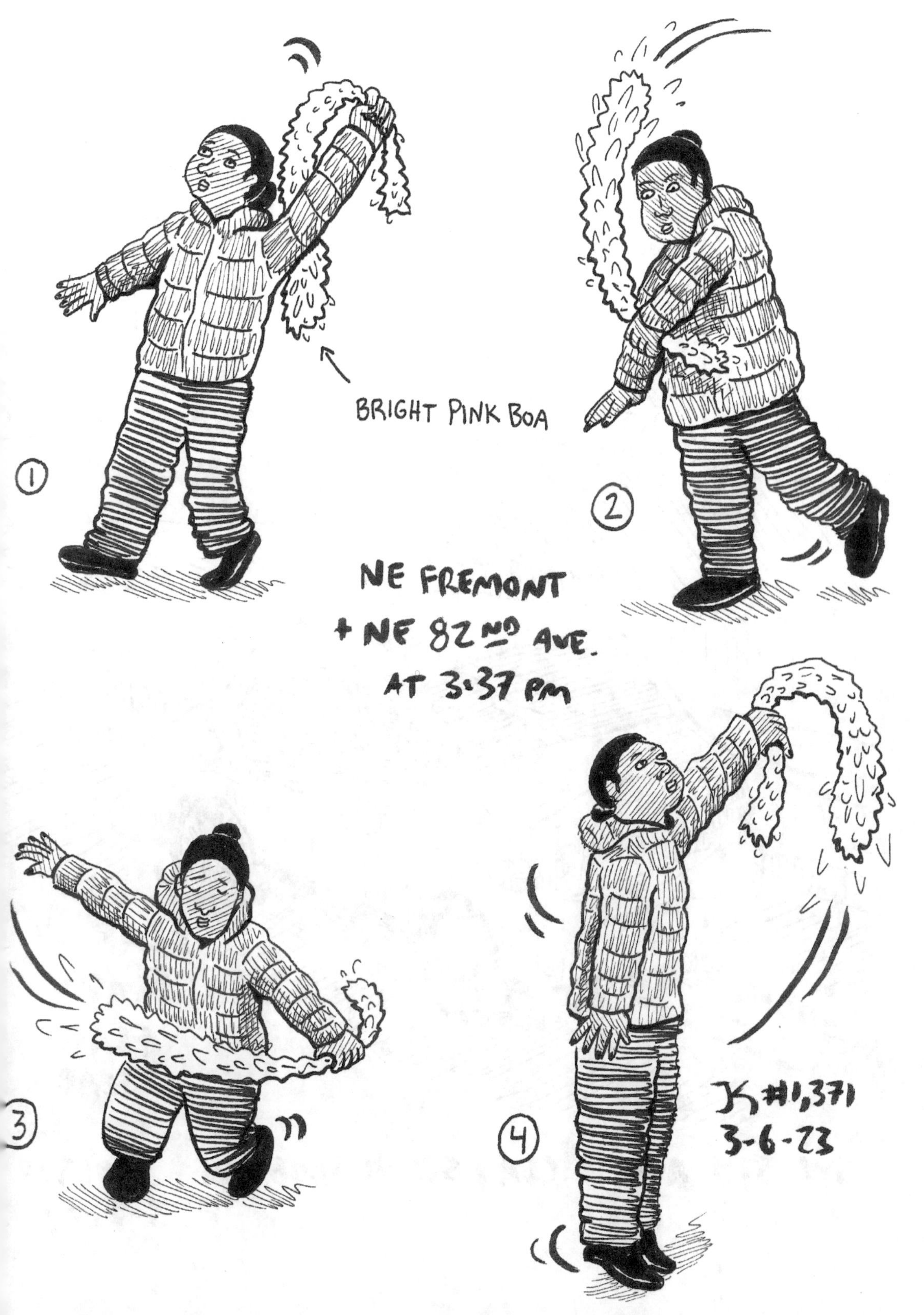

BRIGHT PINK BOA
NE FREMONT + NE 82ND AVE. AT 3:37 PM
①
②
③
④
JK #1,371
3-6-23

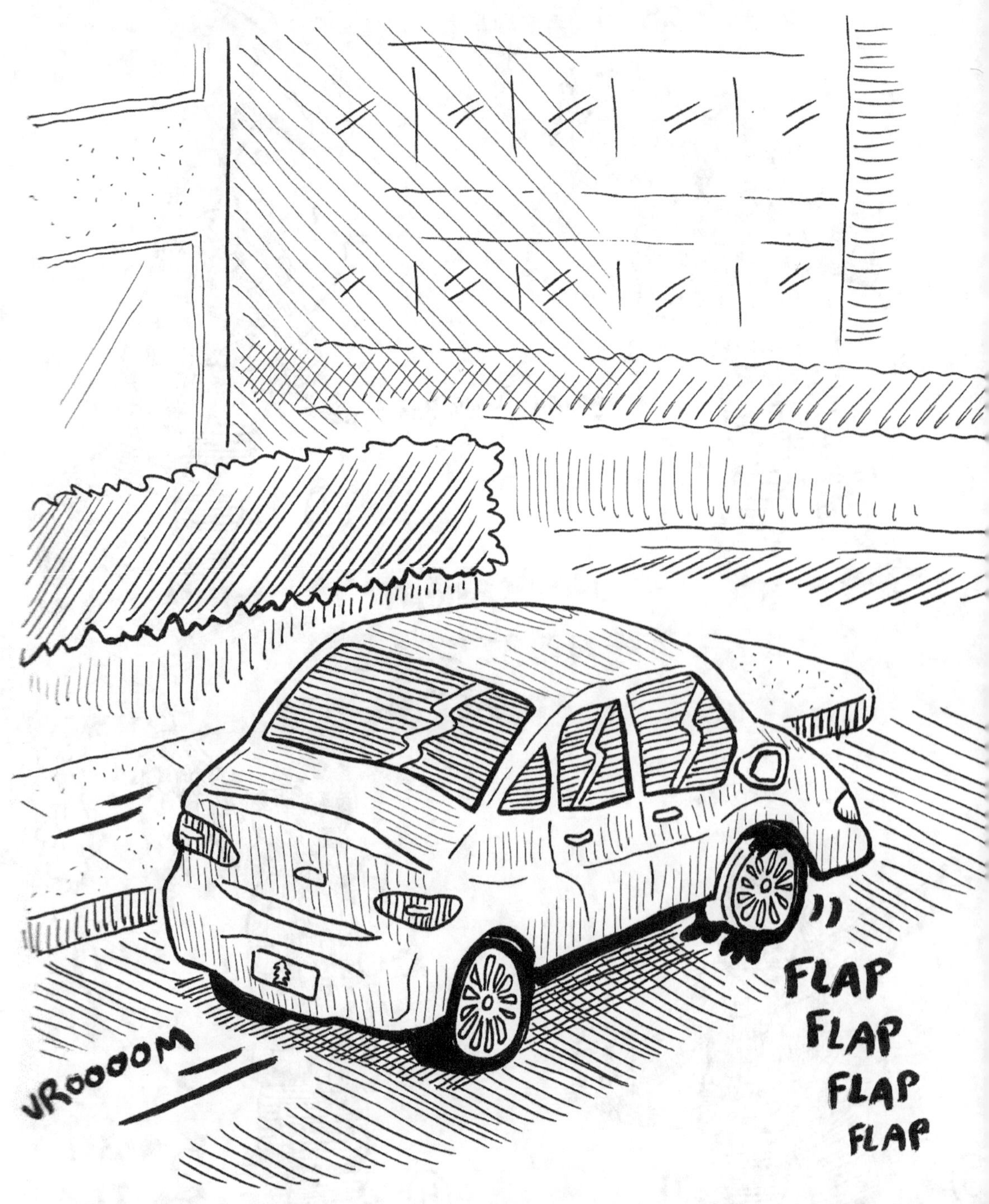

SW 5TH AVE. + CLAY ST. AT 4:06PM   JK #4,372
3-7-23

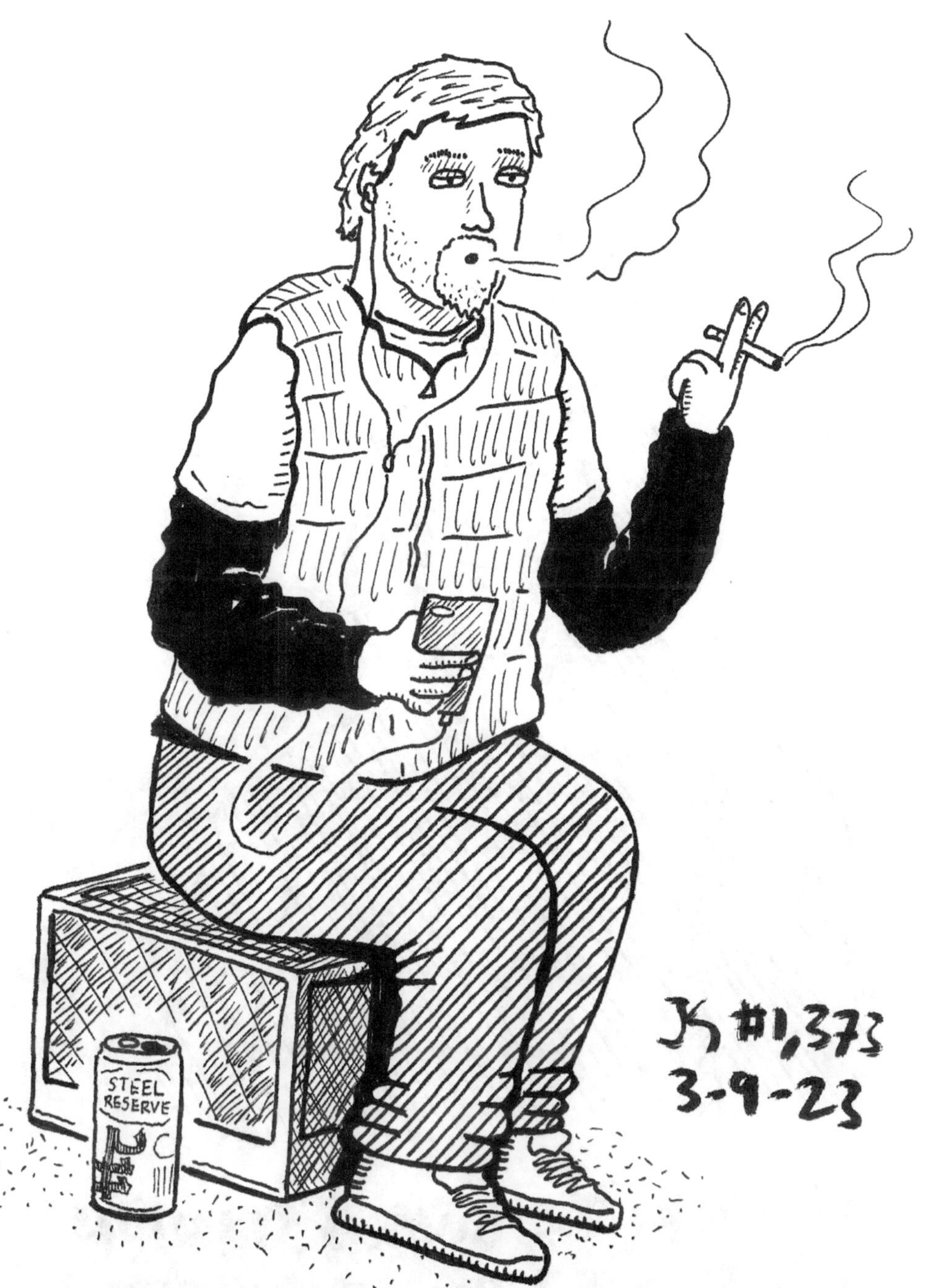

JS #1,373
3-9-23

NW 19TH AVE.
+ UPSHUR ST.   AT 5:32 PM

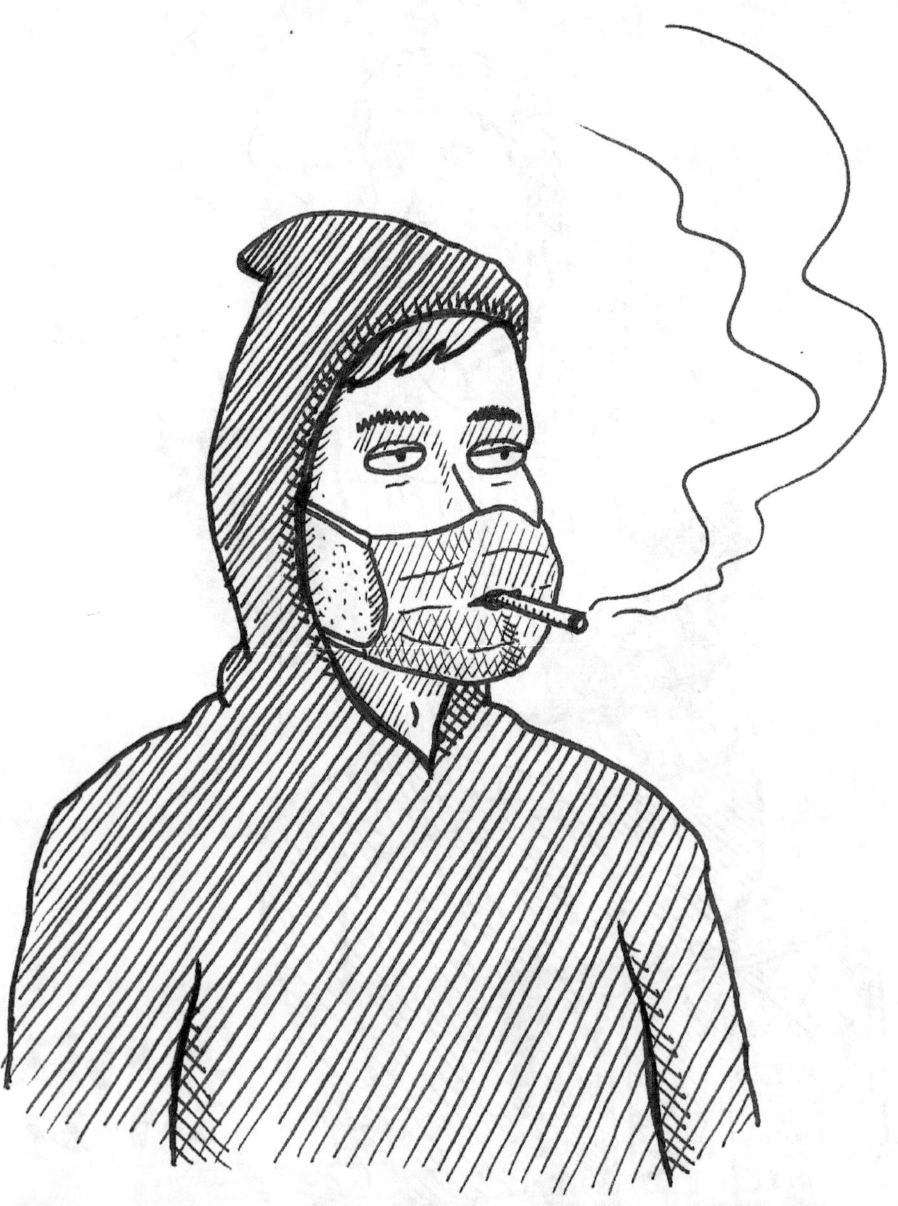

NE MLK JR. BLVD. + STANTON
AT 5:57 PM   JS#1,374
3-10-23

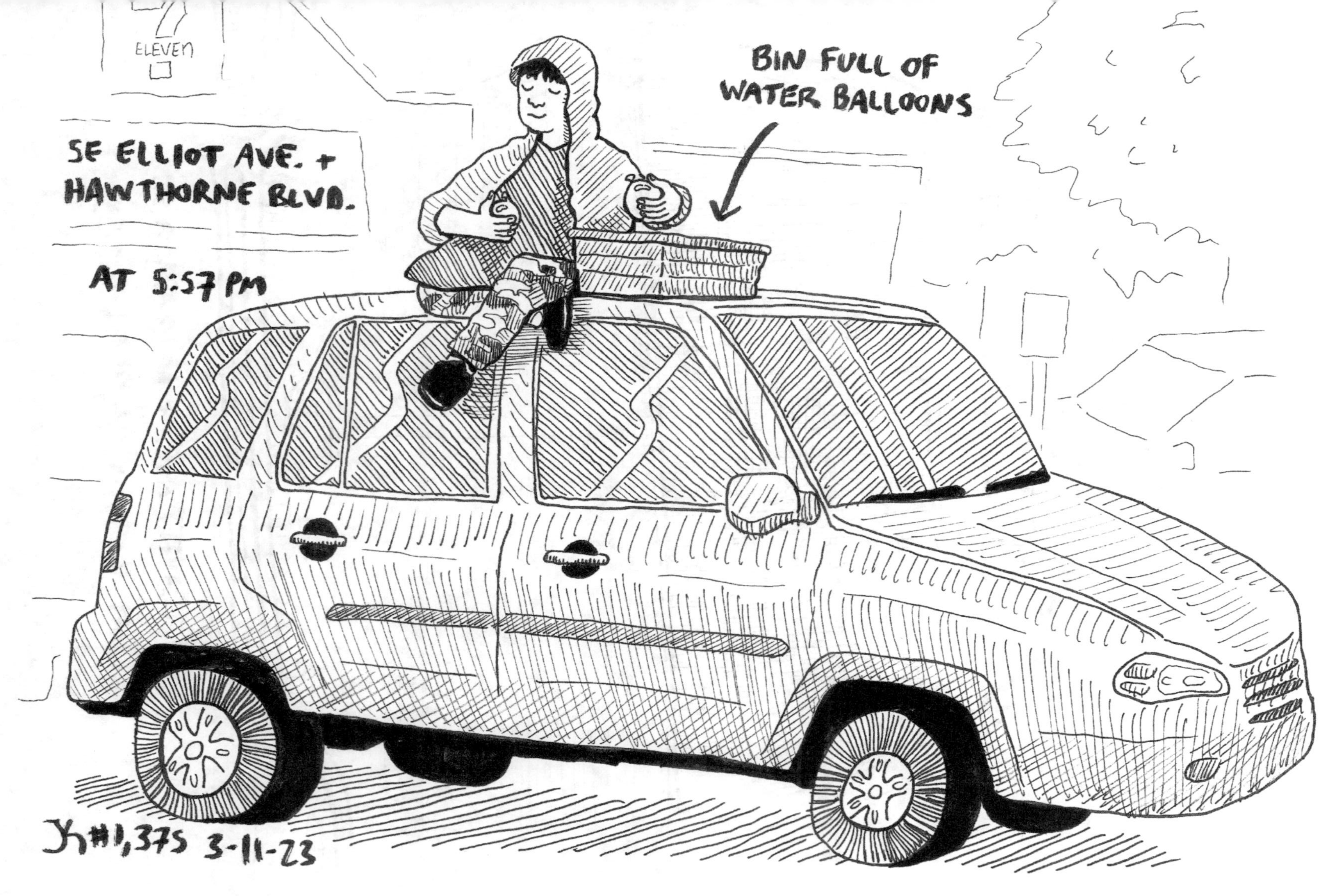

BIN FULL OF
WATER BALLOONS
SE ELLIOT AVE. +
HAWTHORNE BLVD.
AT 5:57 PM
ELEVEN
JJ #1,375 3-11-23

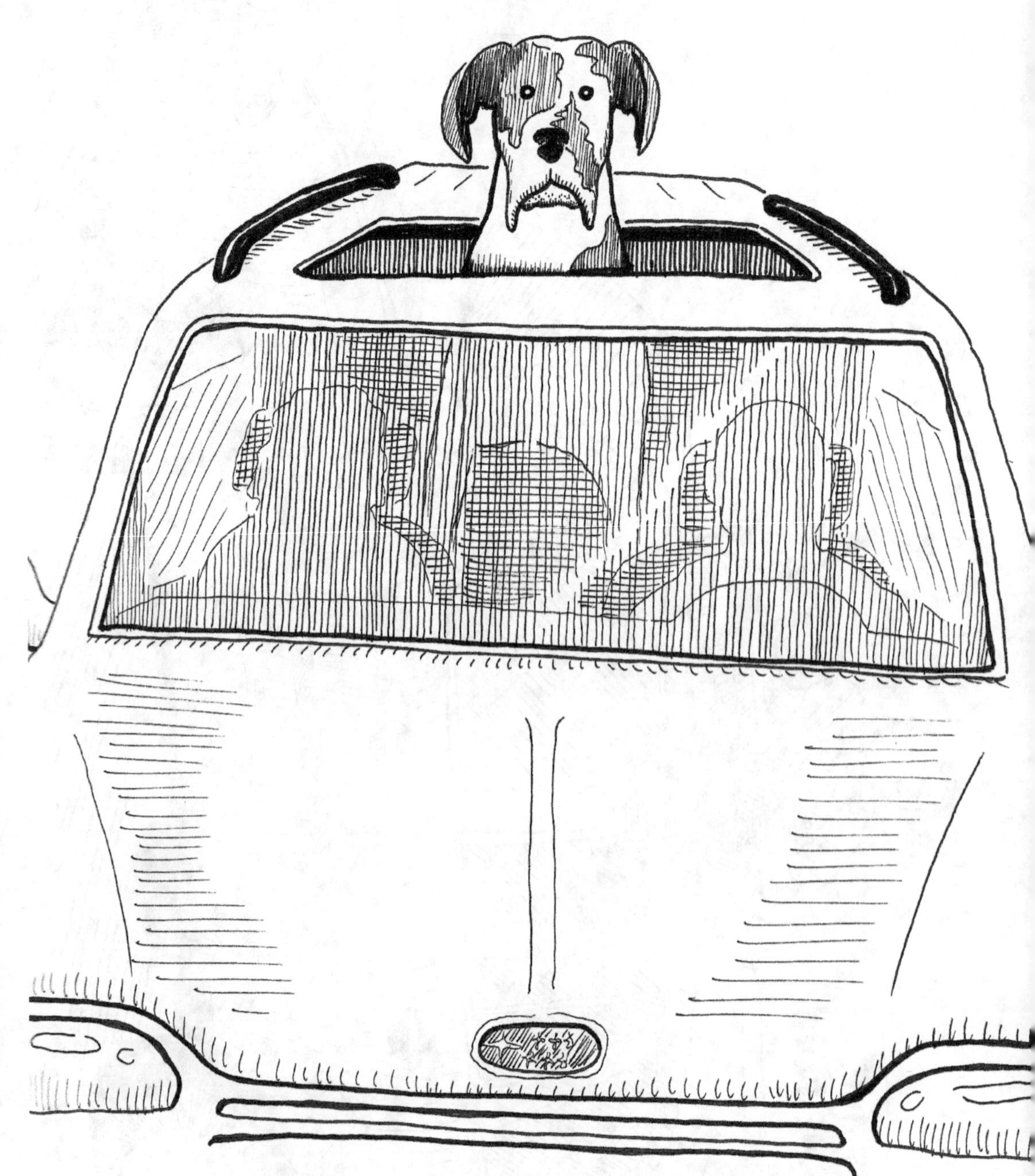

N. LEAVITT AVE. + N. LOMBARD ST.
AT 11:08 AM #1,376 3-12-23

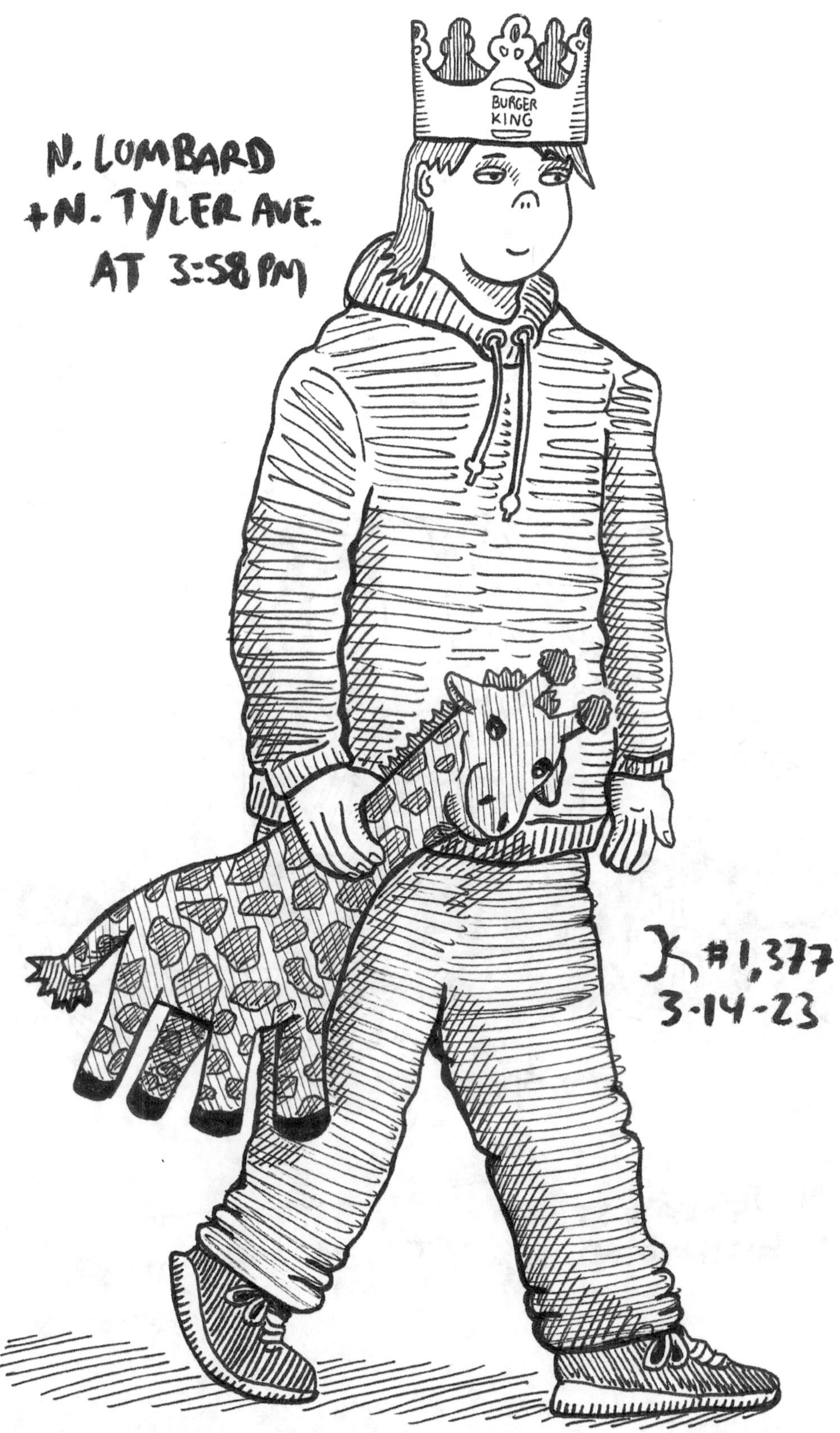

N. LOMBARD
+ N. TYLER AVE.
AT 3:58 PM

#1,377
3-14-23

BEFORE GETTING OUT OF THE CAR--

-- TESTS PUDDLE DEPTH BY LIGHTLY TAPPING JUST THE SHOE SOLE ON THE SURFACE, DISAPPROVES OF PUDDLE DEPTH + PARKS ELSEWHERE.

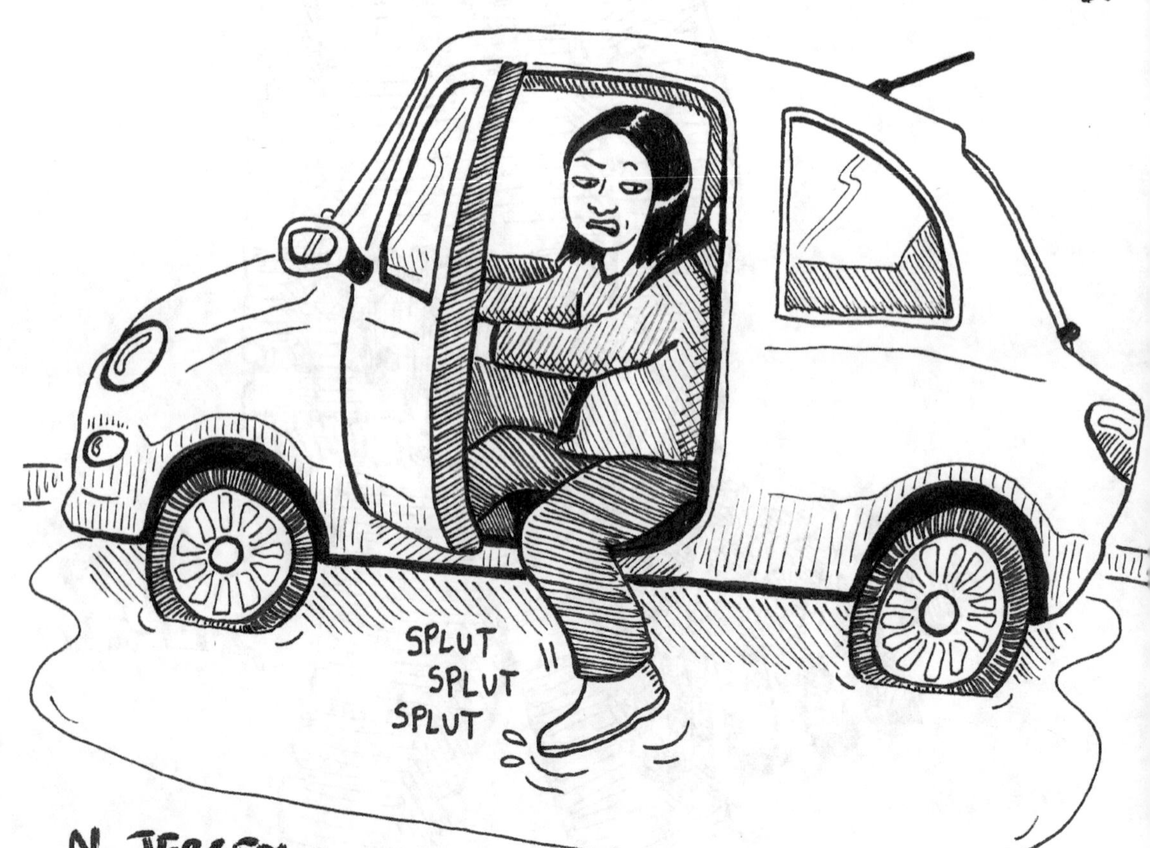

N. JERSEY ST. +
N. RICHMOND AVE.   AT 11:24 AM

#1,378
3-16-23

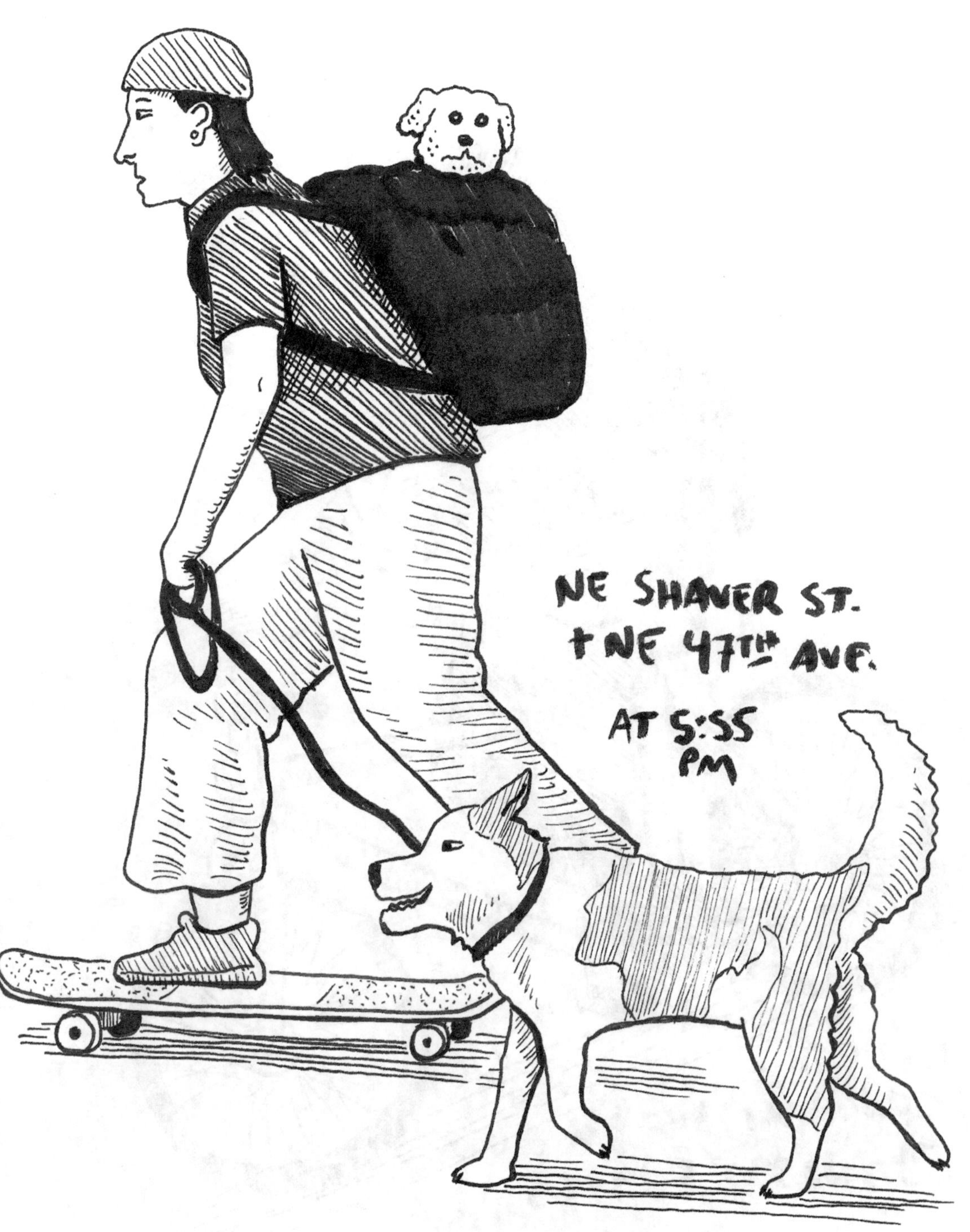

NE SHAVER ST.
+ NE 47TH AVE.

AT 5:55
PM

#1,379 3-18-23

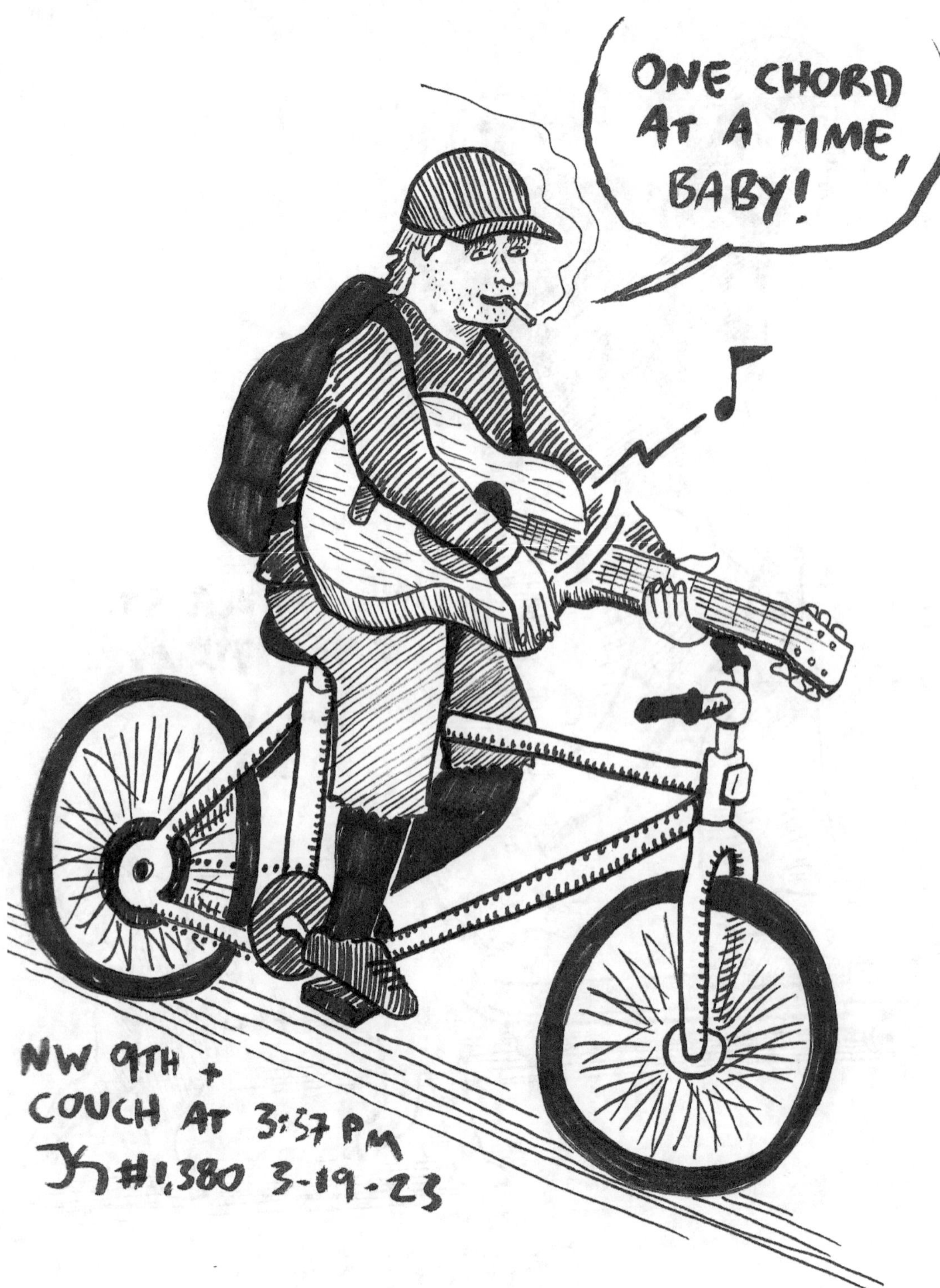

ONE CHORD AT A TIME, BABY!
NW 9TH + COUCH AT 3:57 PM
#1,380 3-19-23

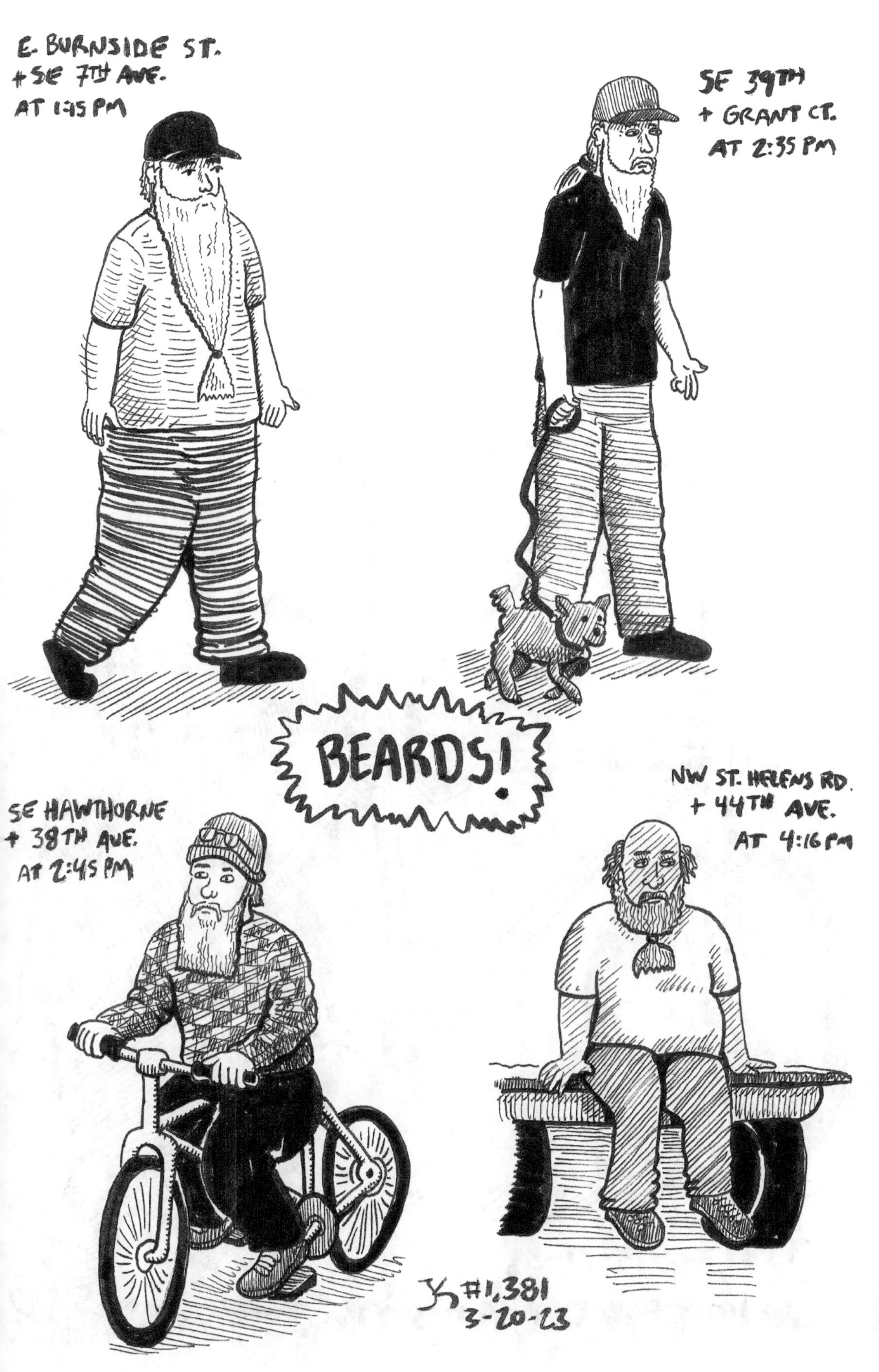

E. BURNSIDE ST.
+ SE 7TH AVE.
AT 1:35 PM

SE 39TH
+ GRANT CT.
AT 2:35 PM

BEARDS!

SE HAWTHORNE
+ 38TH AVE.
AT 2:45 PM

NW ST. HELENS RD.
+ 44TH AVE.
AT 4:16 PM

#1,381
3-20-23

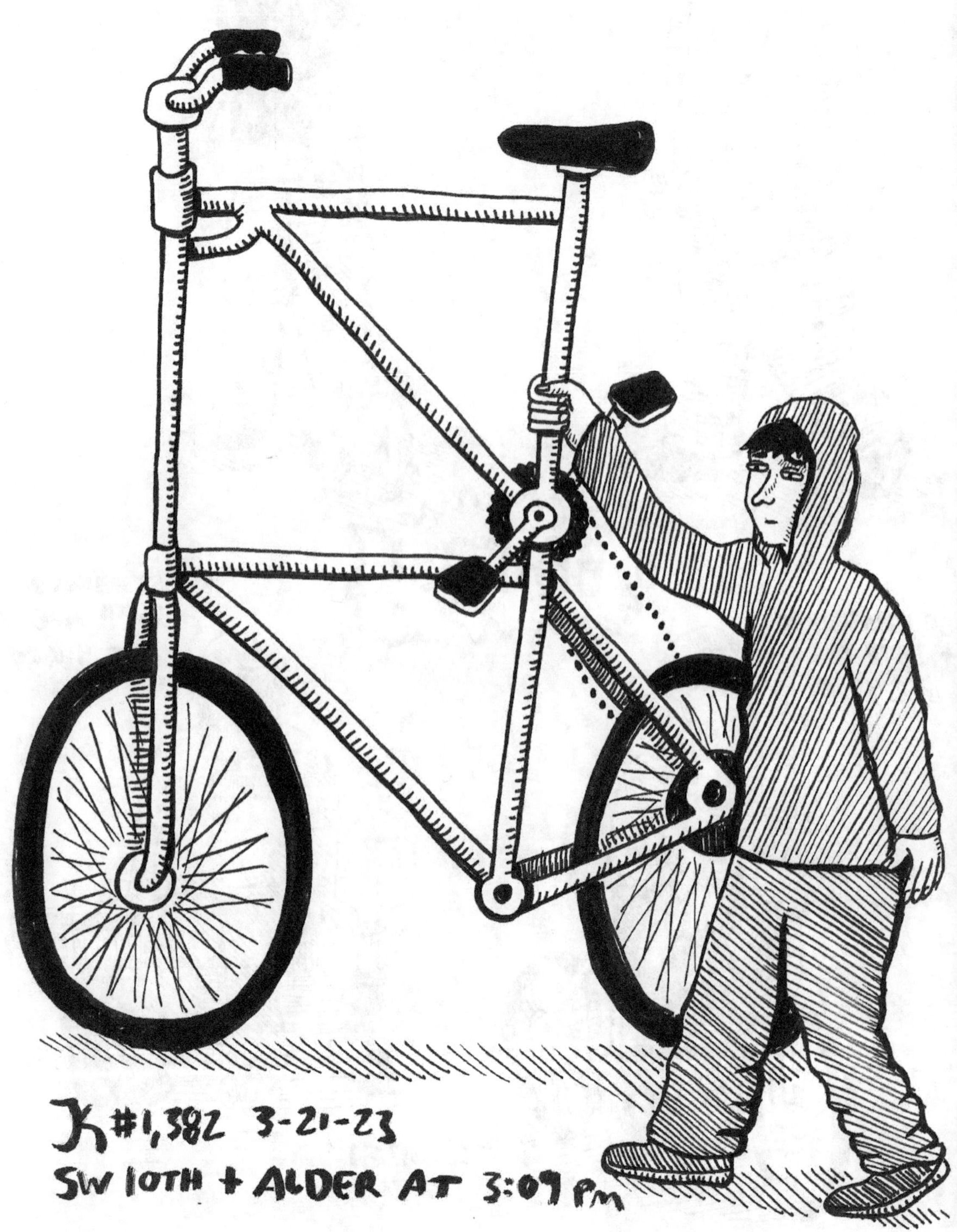

JK #1,382 3-21-23
SW 10TH + ALDER AT 3:09 PM

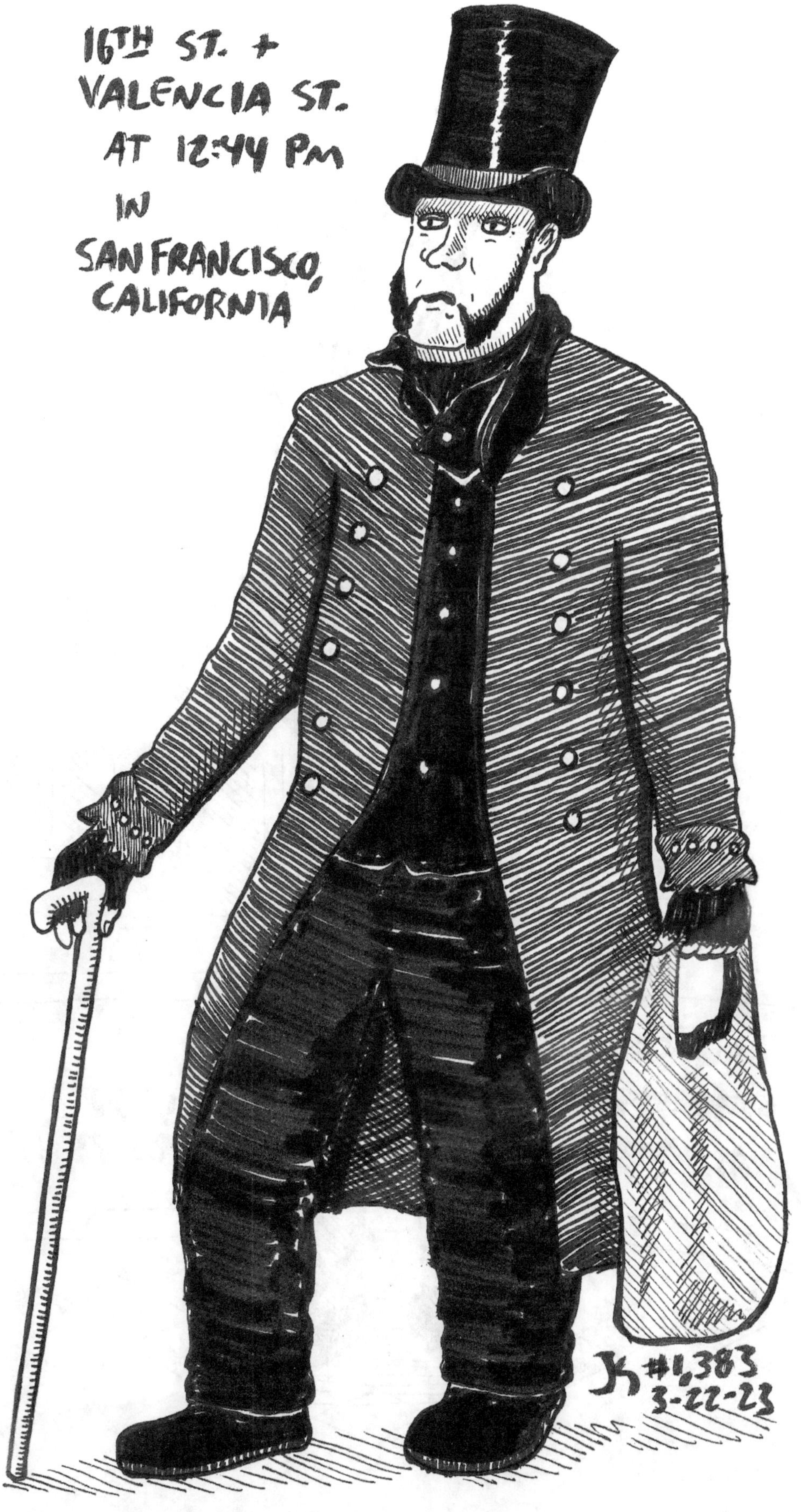

16TH ST. +
VALENCIA ST.
AT 12:44 PM
IN
SAN FRANCISCO,
CALIFORNIA
JS #4,383
3-22-23

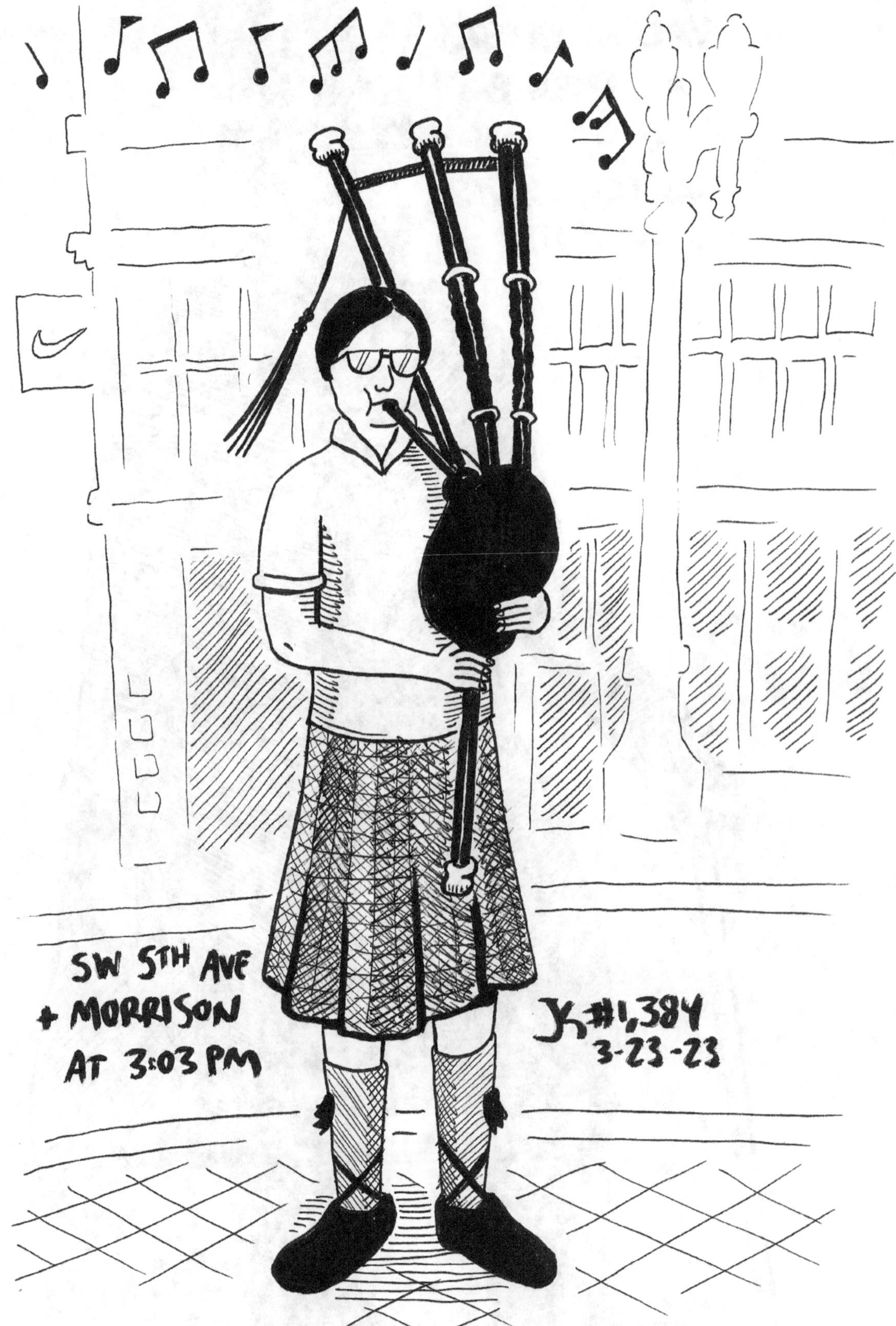

SW 5TH AVE
+ MORRISON
AT 3:03 PM
JK #1,384
3-23-23

THIS WAS A TOME!
ADIDAS CAMPUS ON N. GREELEY AVE. AT 5:54 PM
#1,385
3-24-23

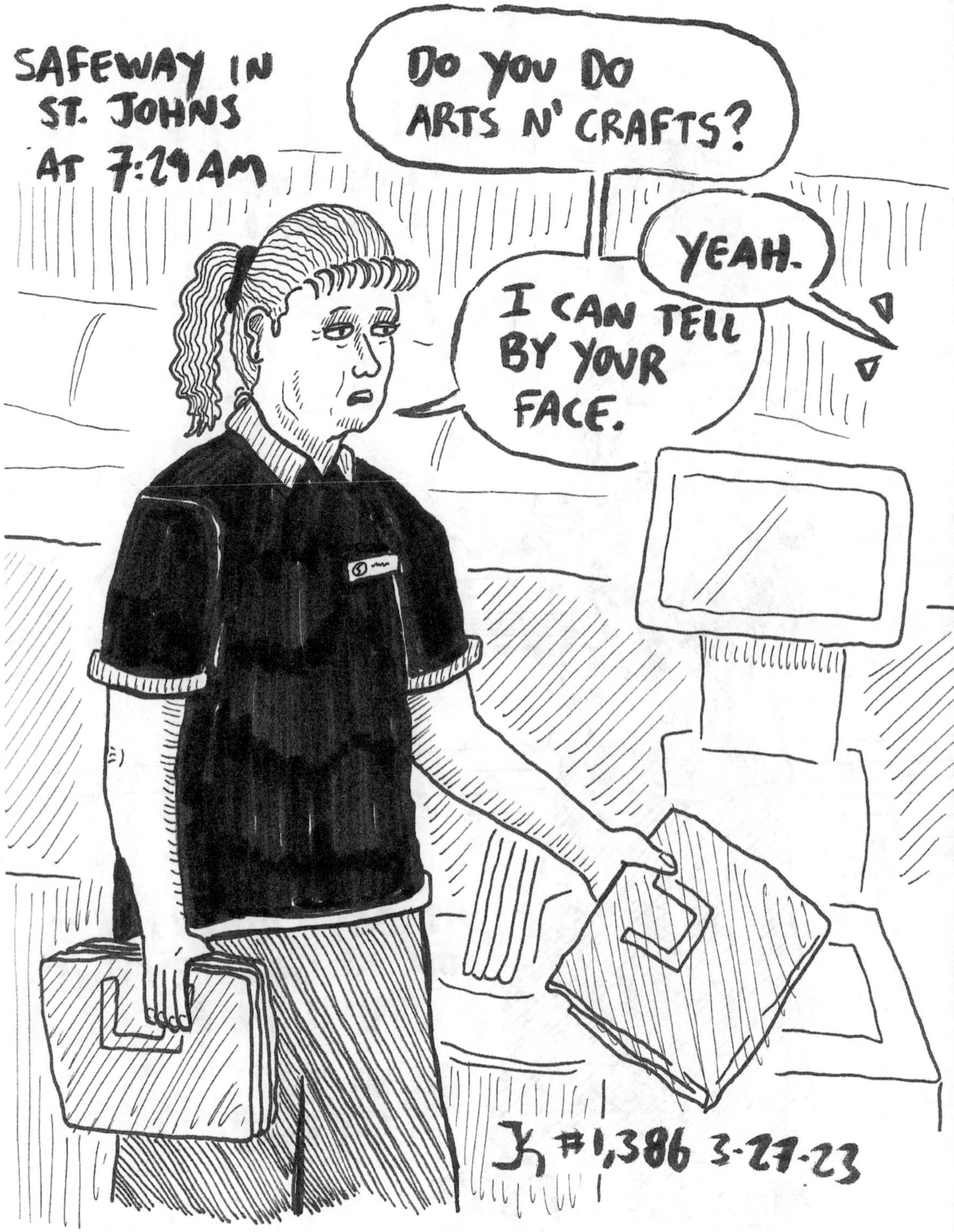

SAFEWAY IN ST. JOHNS AT 7:29 AM
DO YOU DO ARTS N' CRAFTS?
YEAH.
I CAN TELL BY YOUR FACE.
#1,386 3-27-23

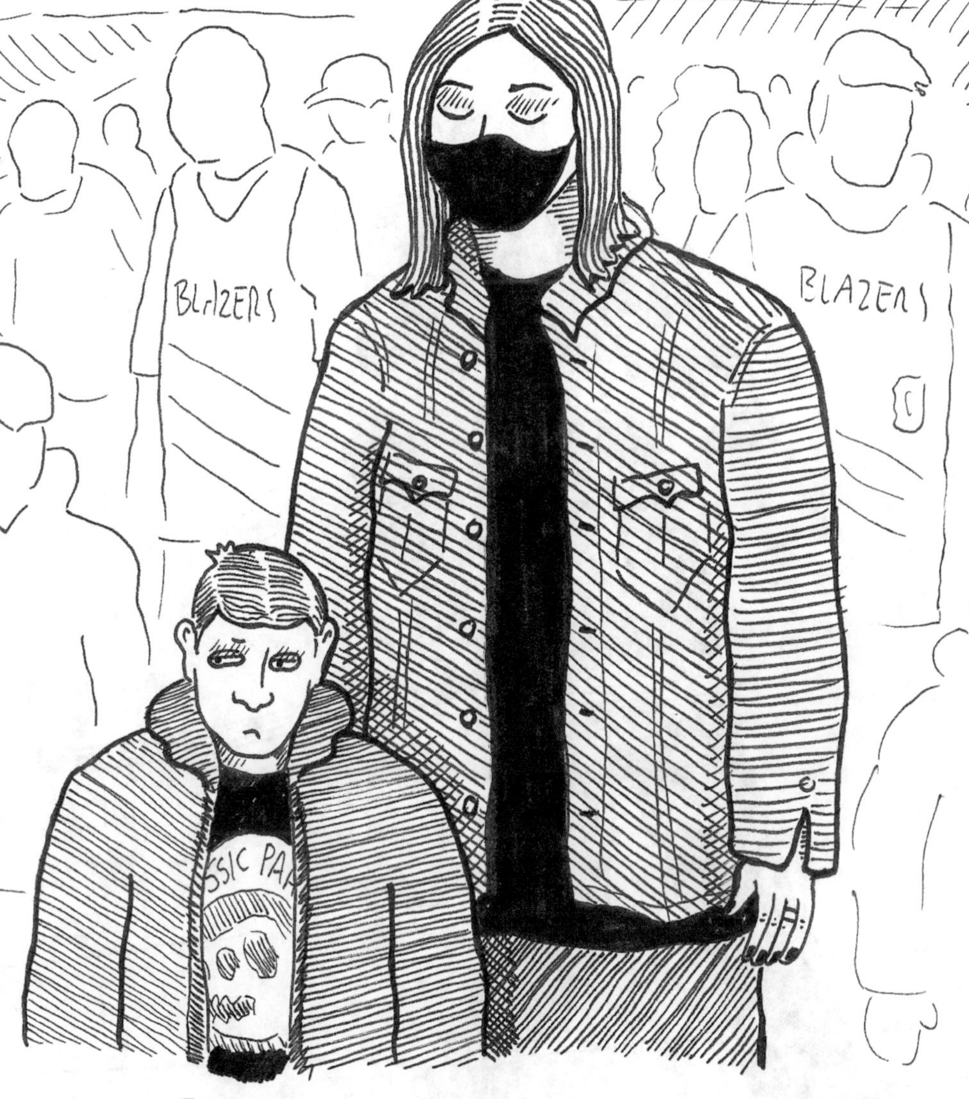

GOING INTO THE BLAZERS / THUNDER GAME

#1,387
3-28-23

3:15 PM

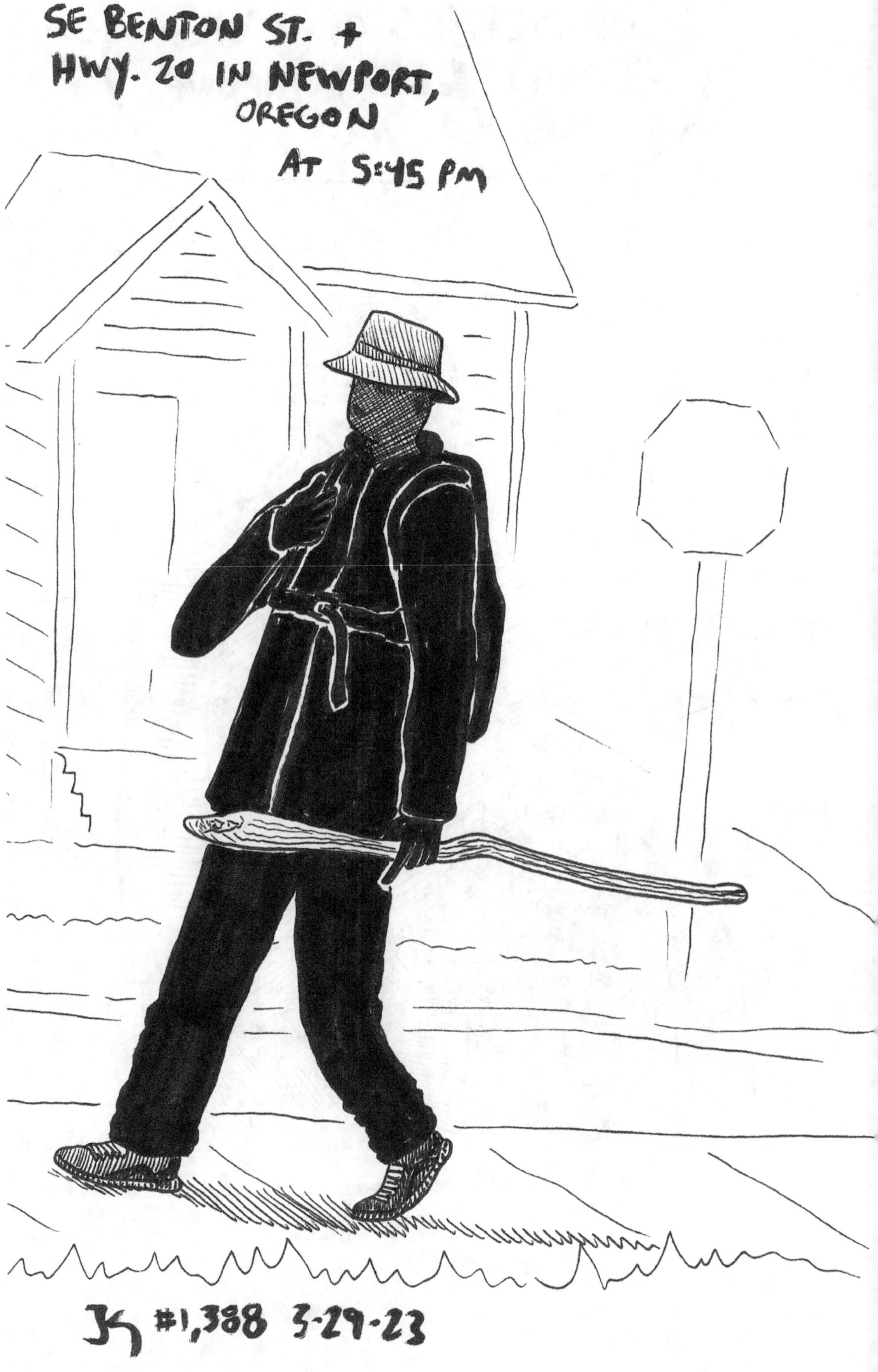

SE BENTON ST. &
HWY. 20 IN NEWPORT,
OREGON
AT 5:45 PM

JK #1,388 3-29-23

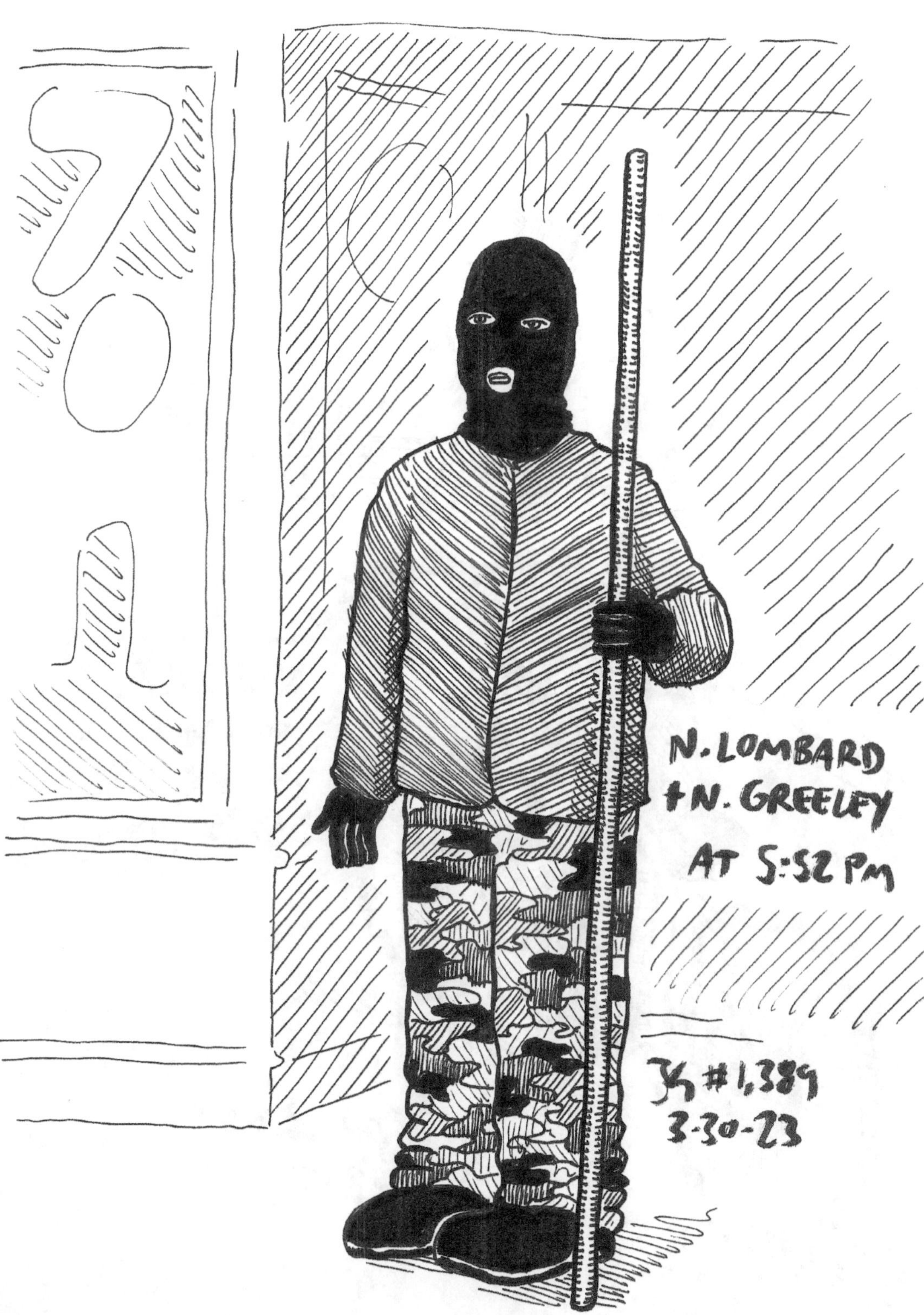

BUUM BUUMS
BALLOONS
N. LOMBARD
+ N. GREELEY
AT 5:52 PM
#1,389
3-30-23

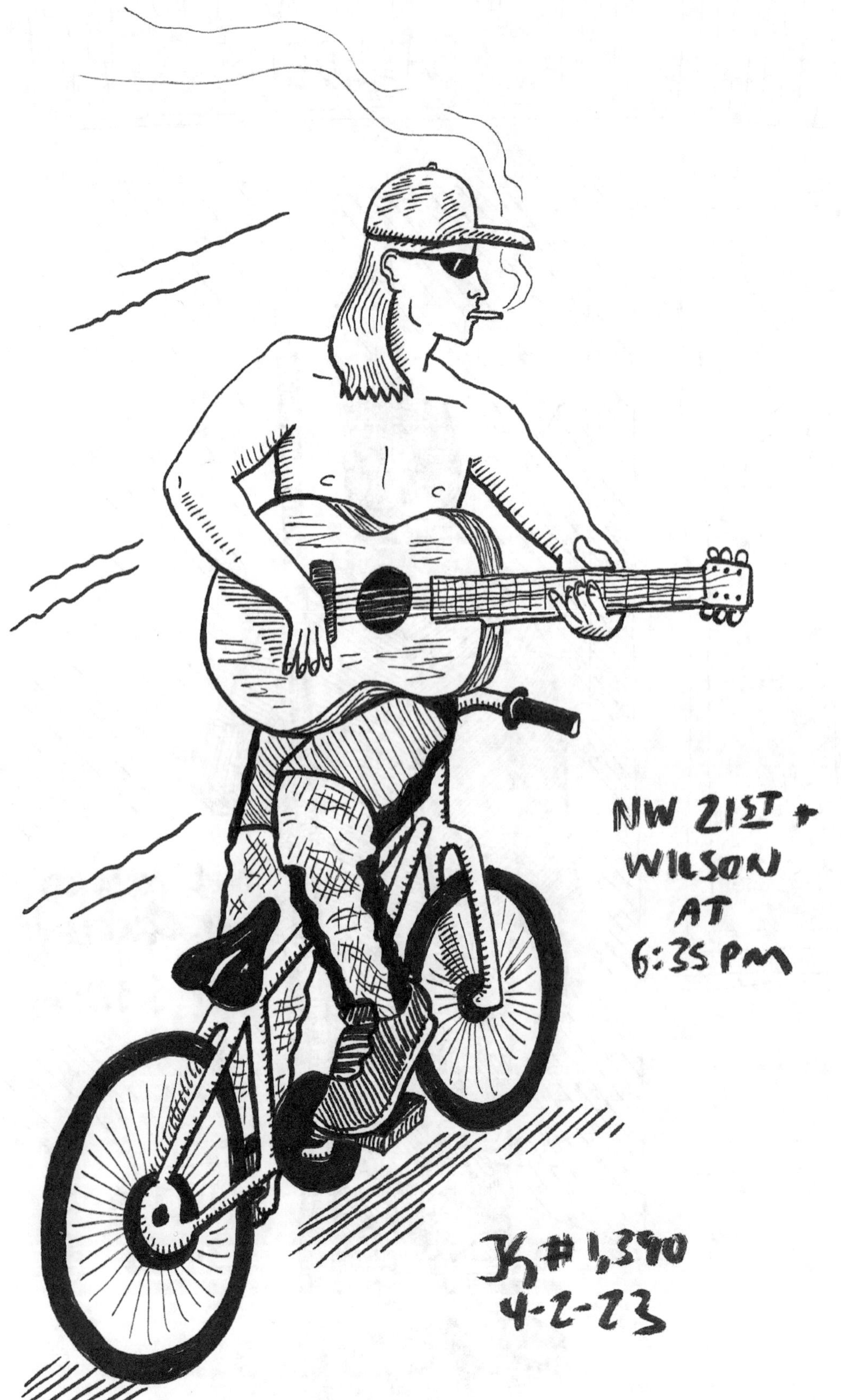

NW 21ST +
WILSON
AT
6:35 PM

JG #1,390
4-2-23

THIS IS OSCAR.
JS #1,391
4-3-23
SAFEWAY
IN ST. JOHNS
AT 12:32 PM

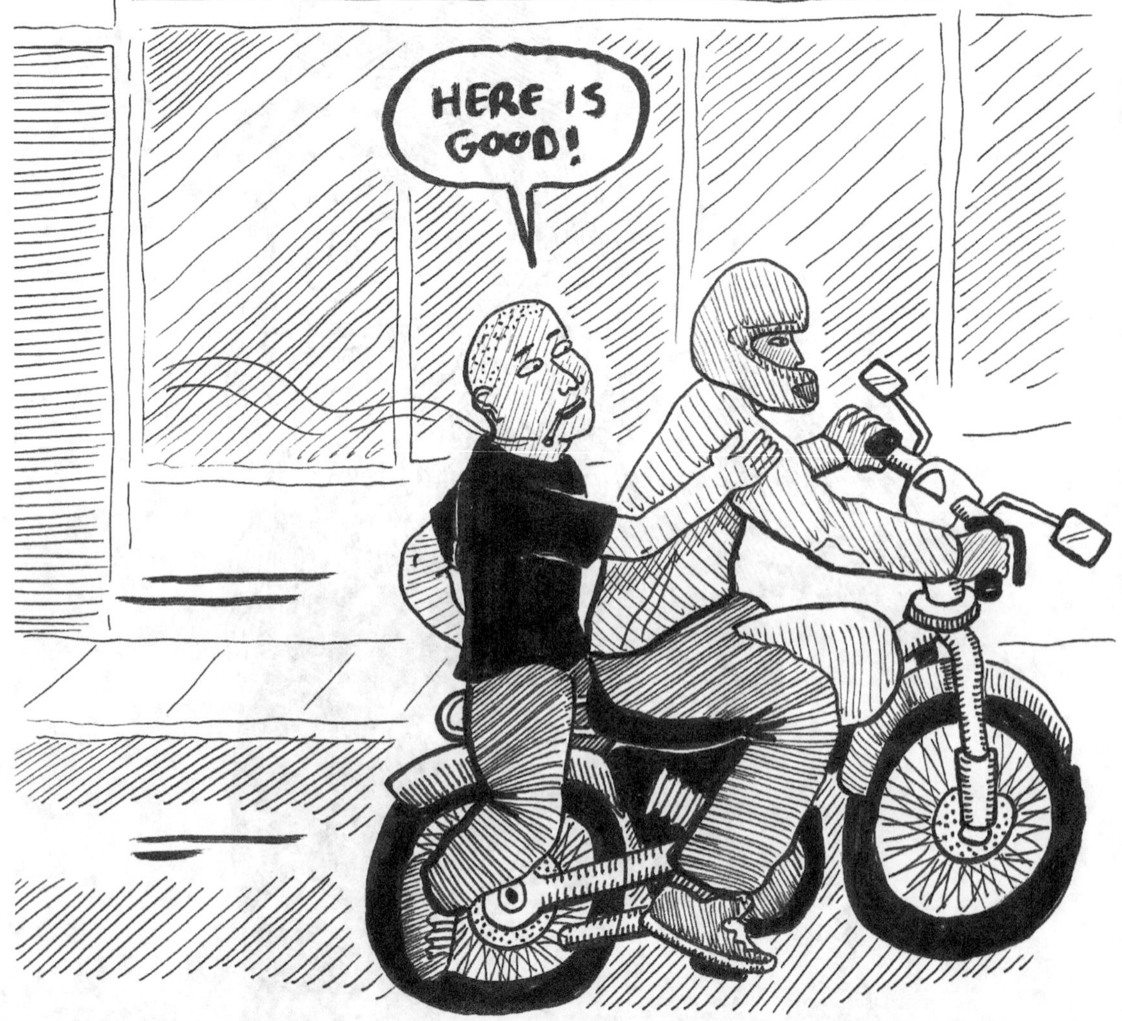

NW 12TH +
NW EVERETT
AT 3:30 PM

1,342
4-4-23

BEFORE THE BIKE CAME TO
A COMPLETE STOP, THE
PASSENGER JUMPED OFF INTO
A RUN THAT TURNED INTO A
WALK AS HE JOINED
PEDESTRIANS ON THE SIDEWALK.

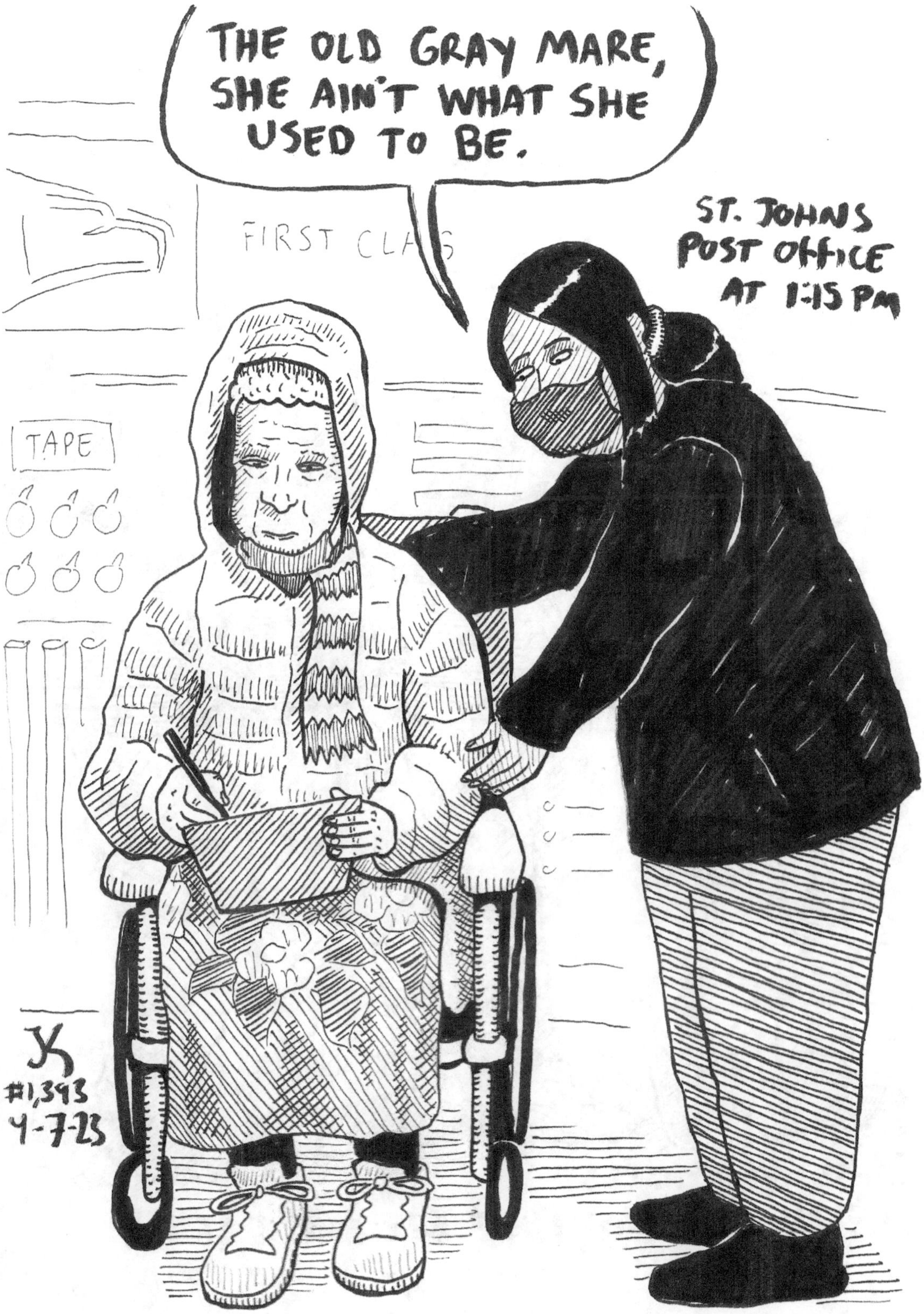

THE OLD GRAY MARE, SHE AIN'T WHAT SHE USED TO BE.
FIRST CLASS
ST. JOHNS POST OFFICE AT 1:15 PM
TAPE
#1,393
4-7-23

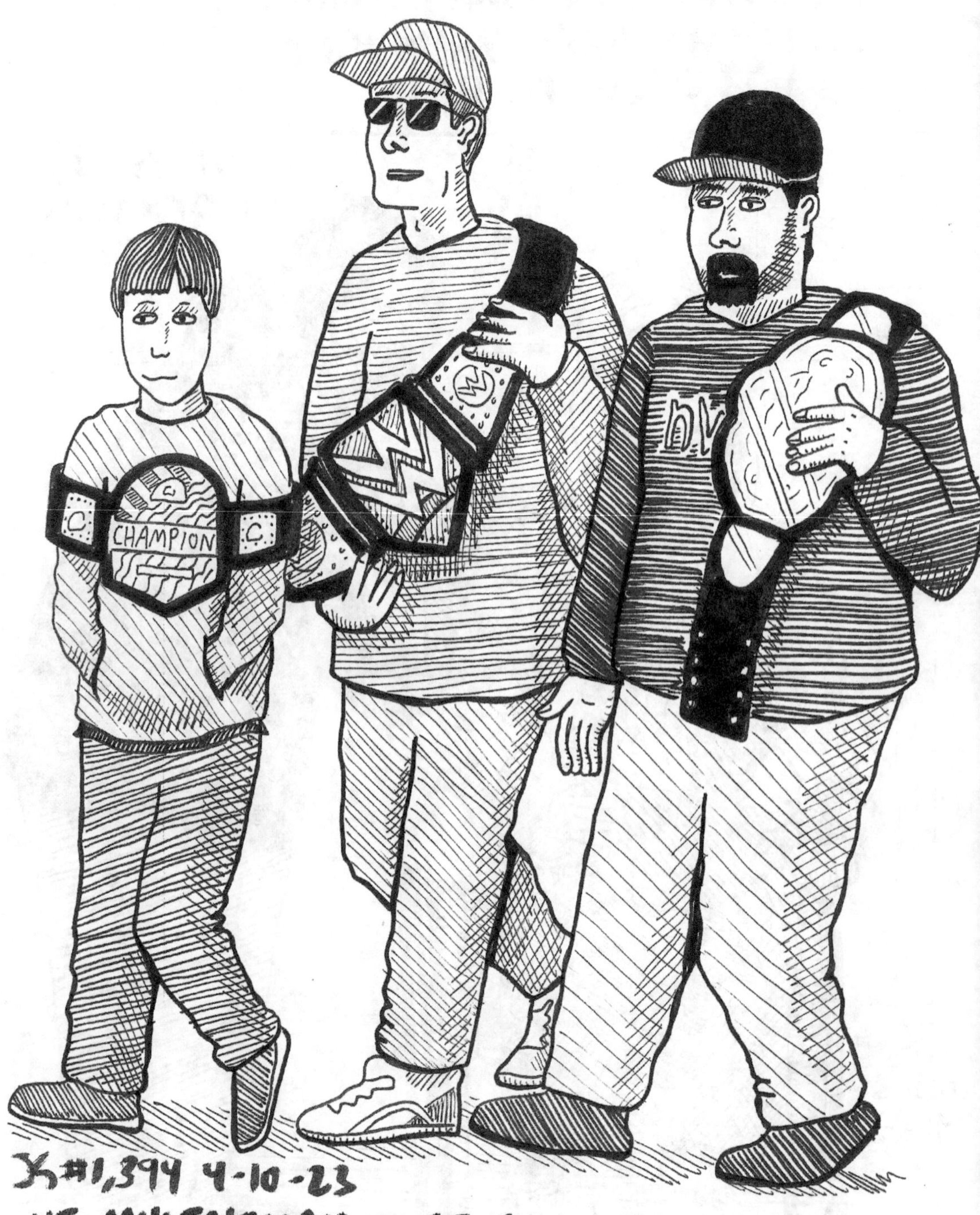

#1,394 4-10-23
NE MULTNOMAH + NE 6TH AT 3:56 PM

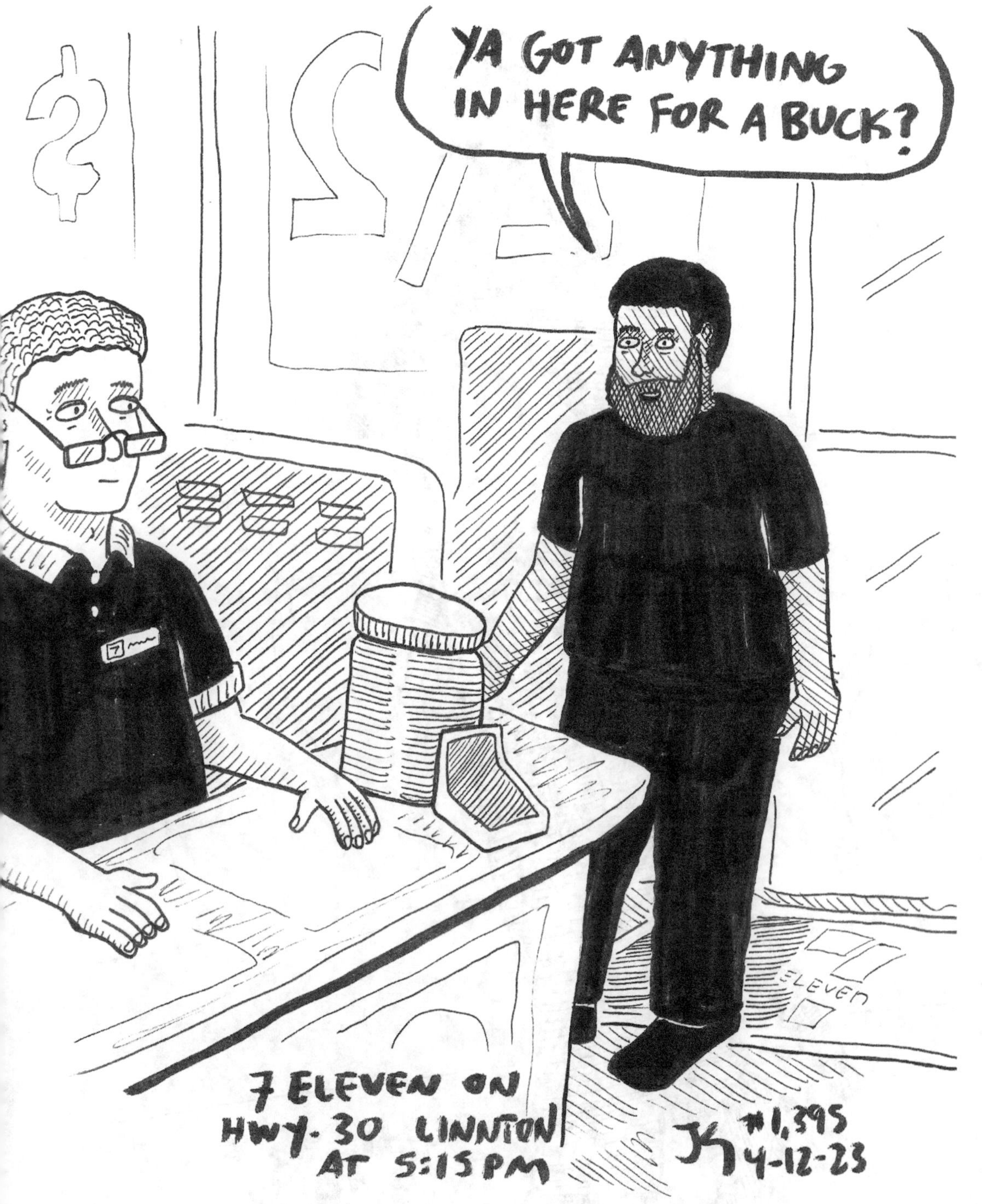

YA GOT ANYTHING
IN HERE FOR A BUCK?
7 ELEVEN ON
HWY. 30 LINNTON
AT 5:15 PM
#1,395
4-12-23

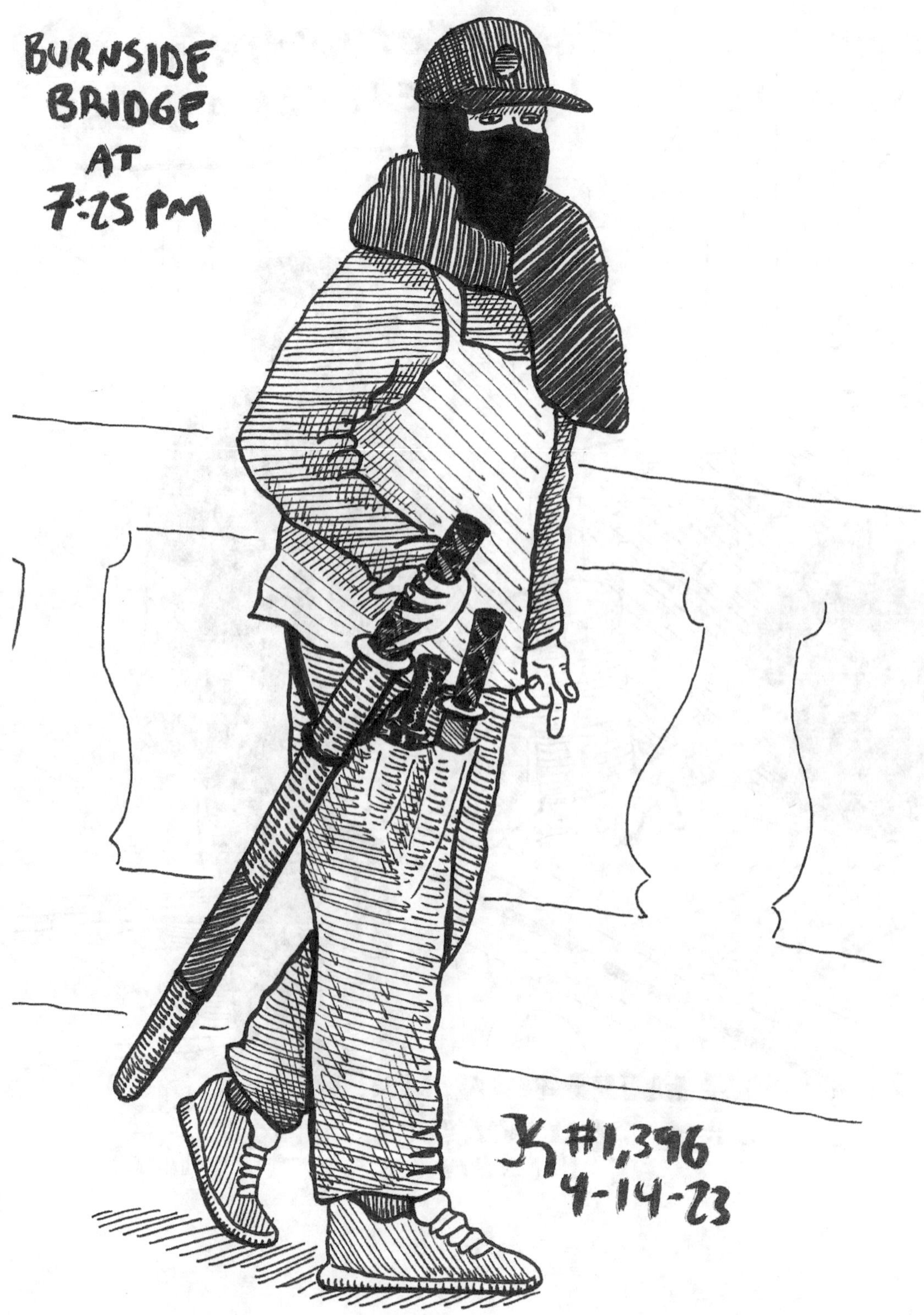

BURNSIDE
BRIDGE
AT
7:25 PM
#1,396
4-14-23

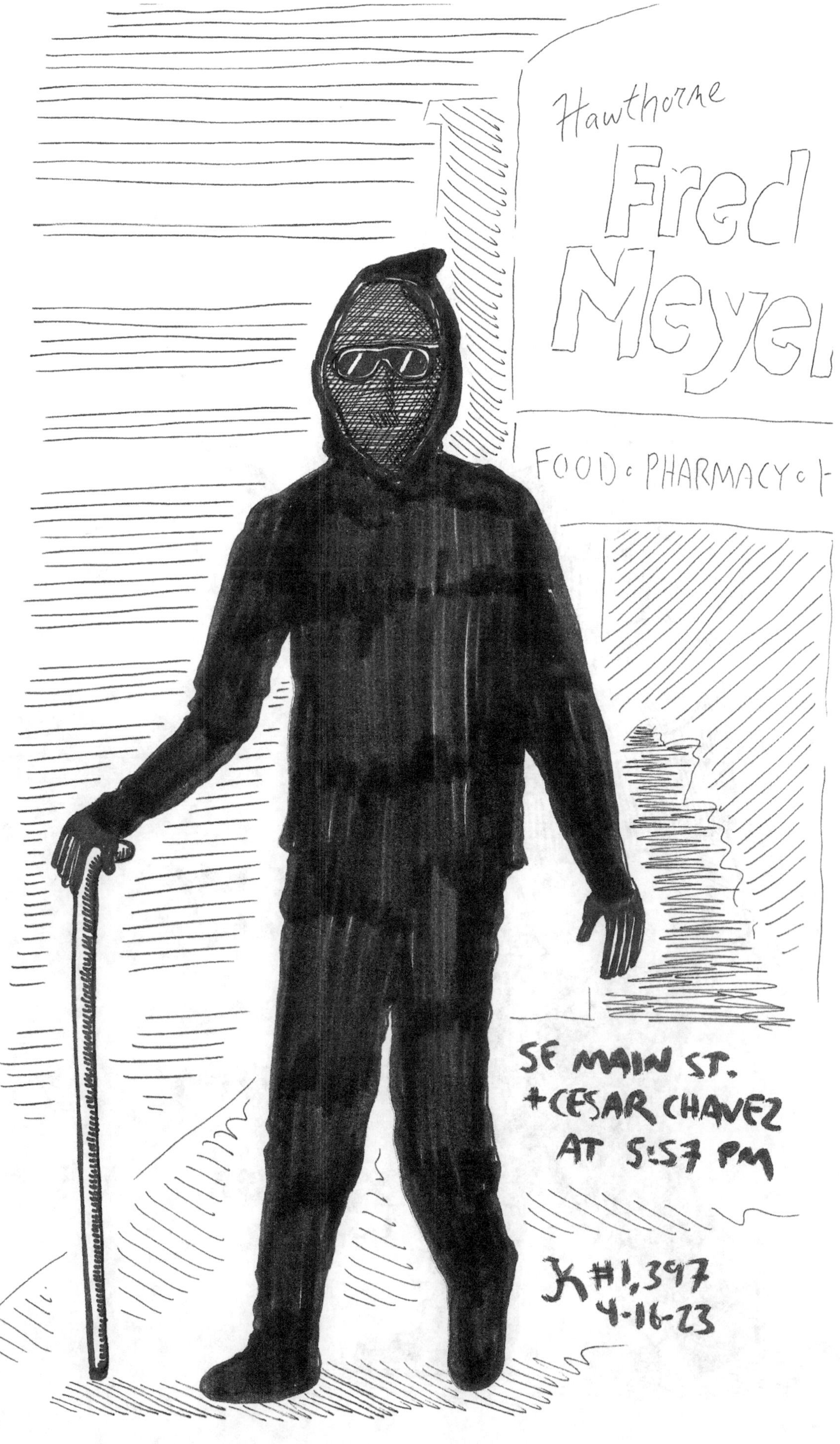

Hawthorne
Fred
Meyer
FOOD • PHARMACY •
SE MAIN ST.
CESAR CHAVEZ
AT 5:57 PM
JK #1,397
4-16-23

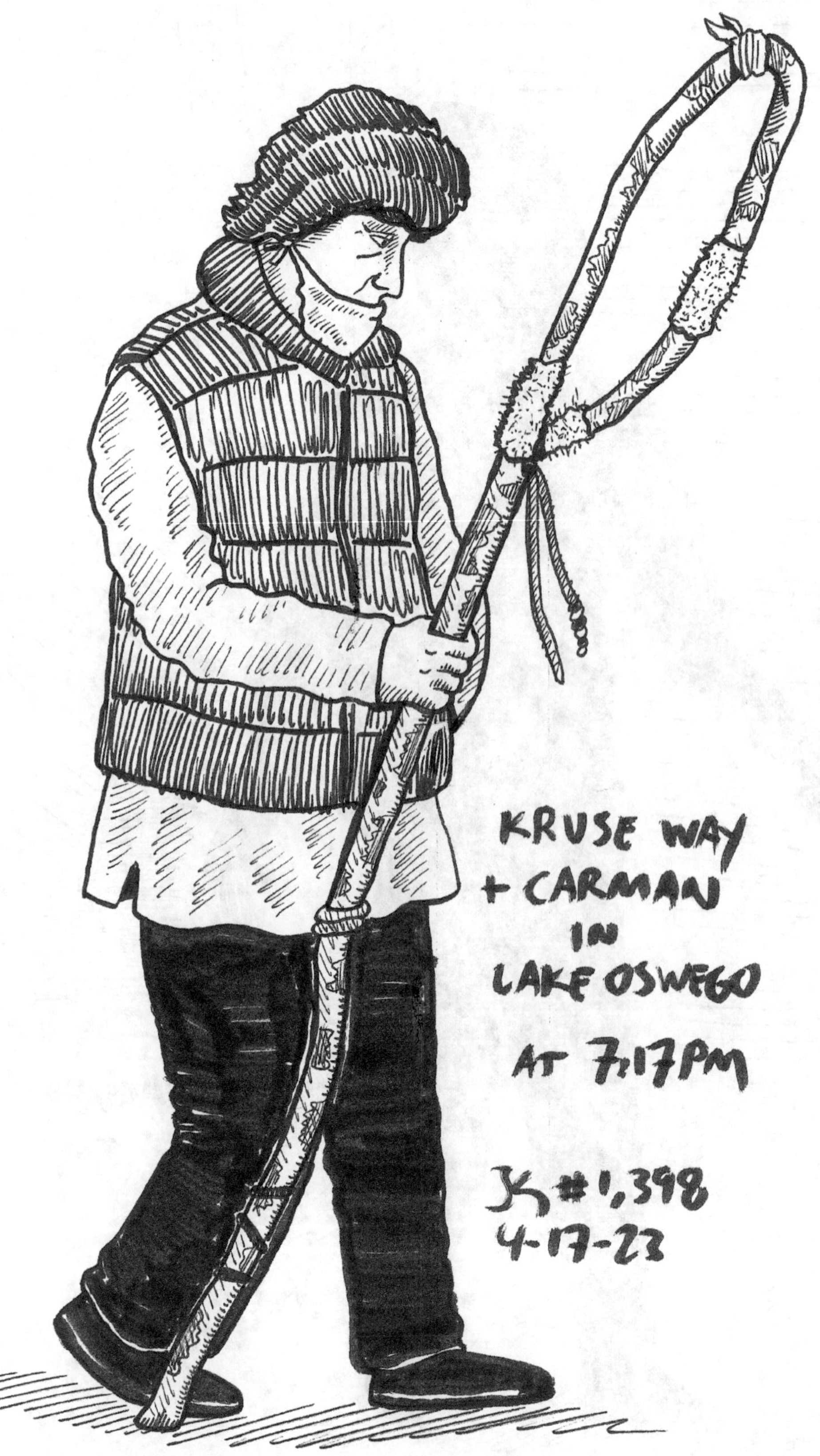

KRUSE WAY
+ CARMAN
IN
LAKE OSWEGO
AT 7:17 PM

JK #1,398
4-17-23

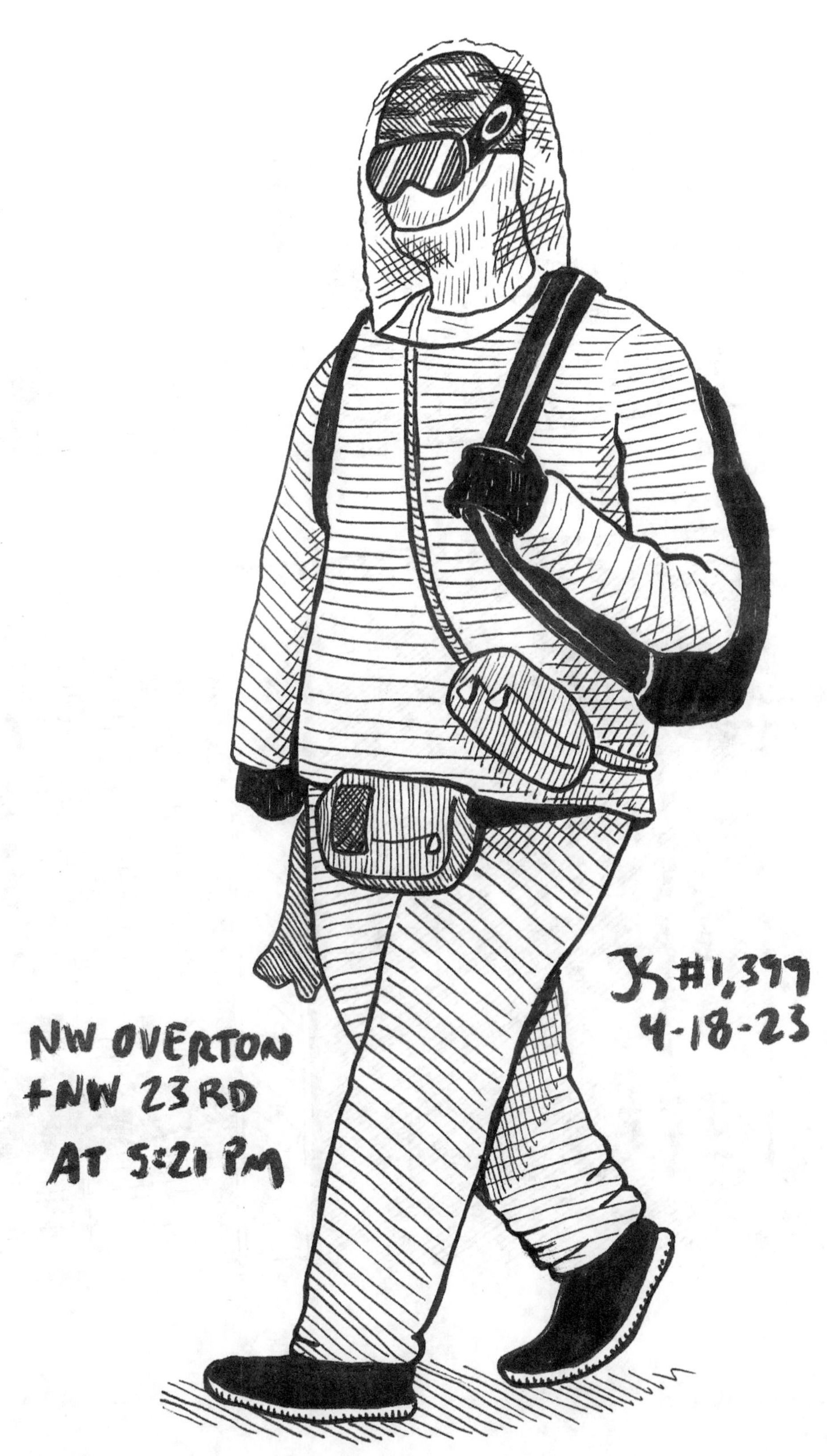

NW OVERTON
+NW 23RD
AT 5:21 PM
JS #1,399
4-18-23

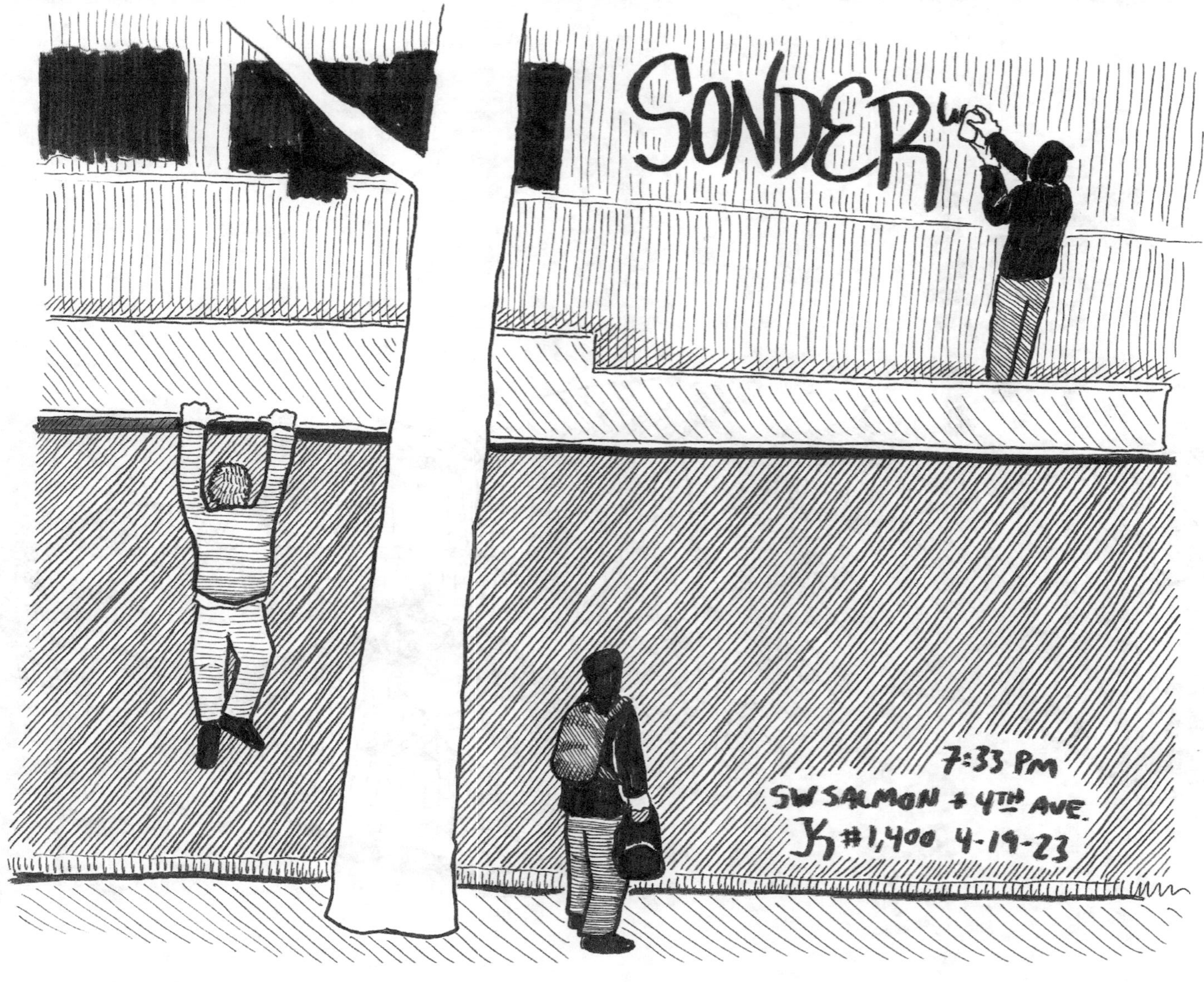

SONDER
7:33 PM
SW SALMON & 4TH AVE.
#1,400 4-19-23

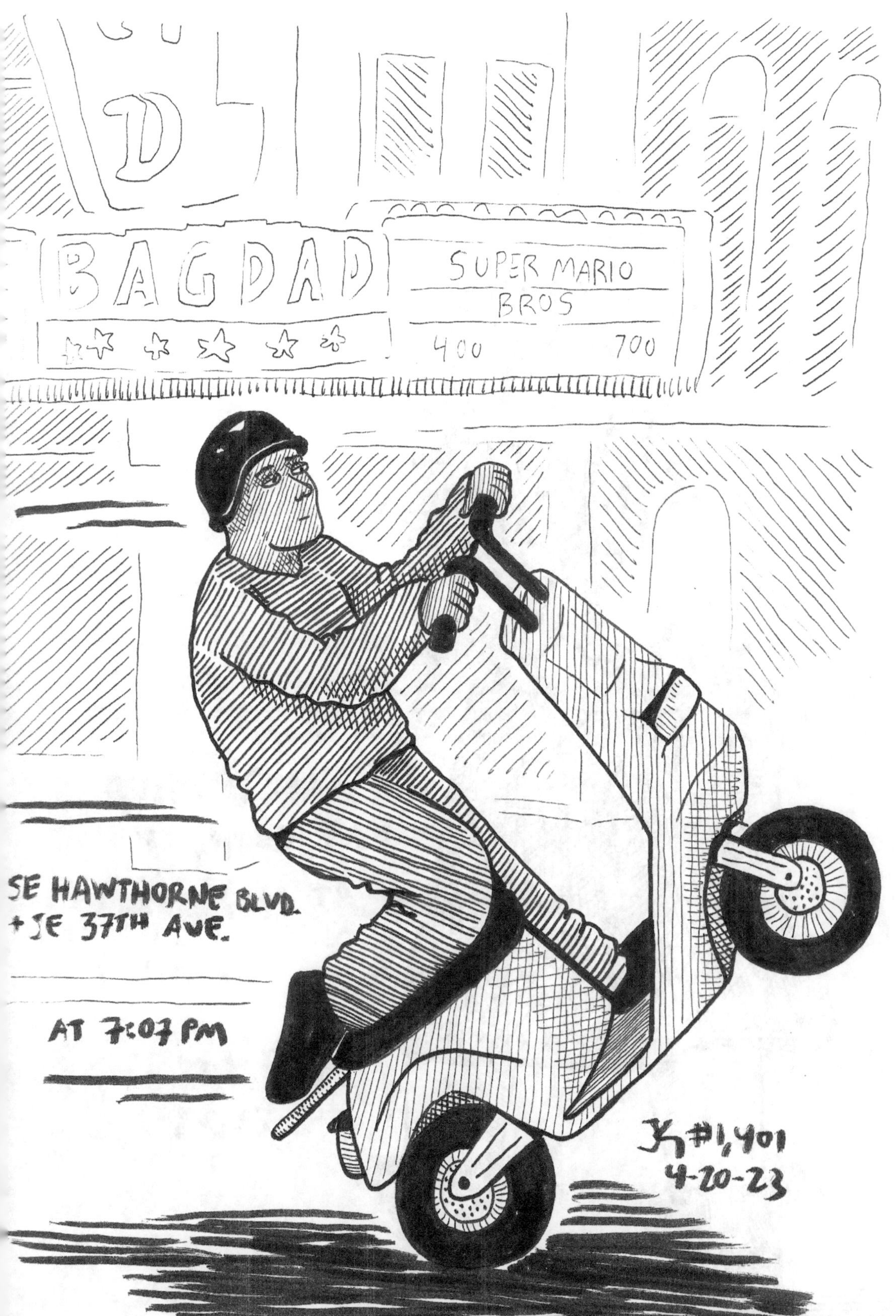
BAGDAD
SUPER MARIO
BROS
400   700
SE HAWTHORNE BLVD.
+ SE 37TH AVE.
AT 7:07 PM
K #1,401
4-20-23

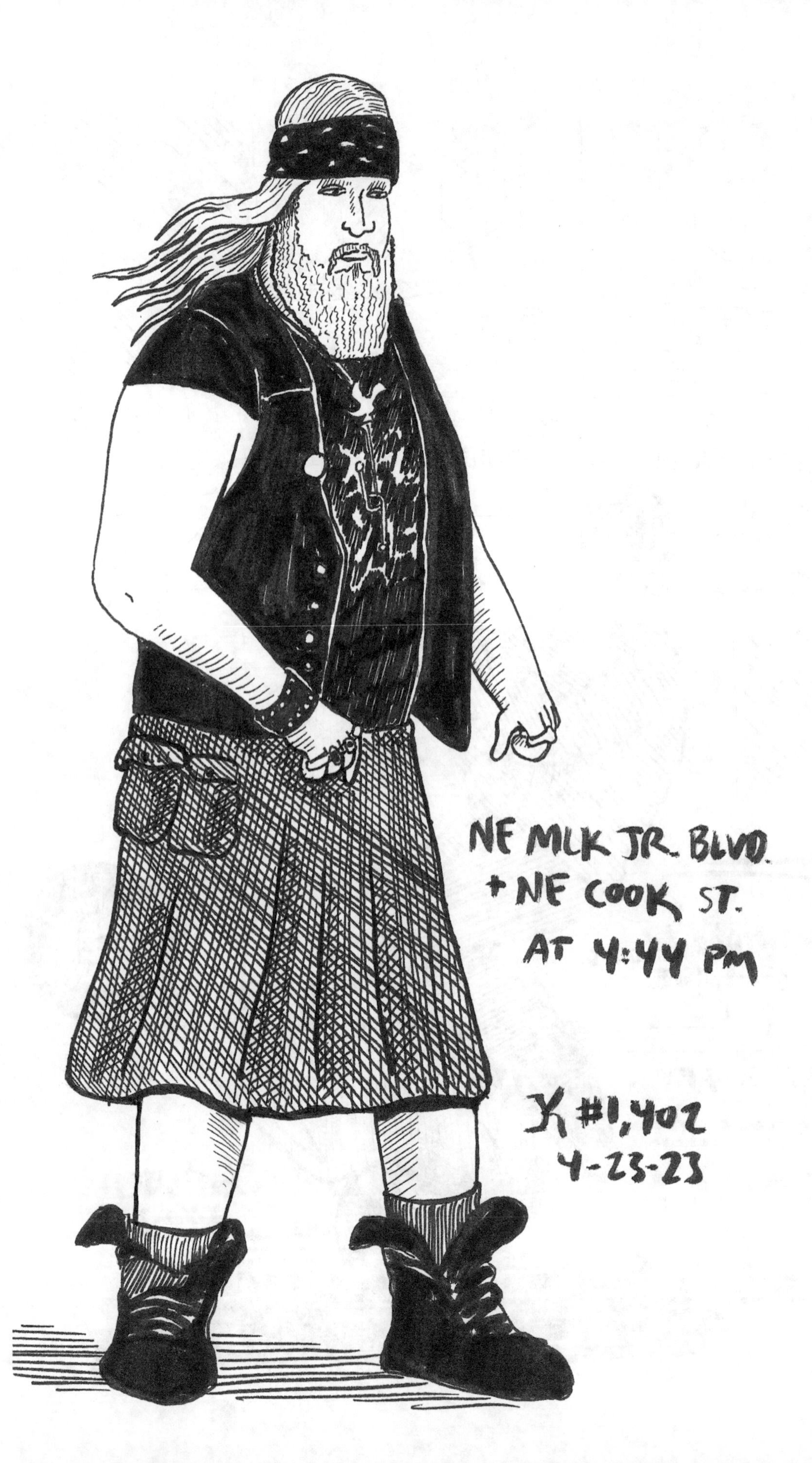

NE MLK JR. BLVD.
+ NE COOK ST.
AT 4:44 PM

#1,402
4-23-23

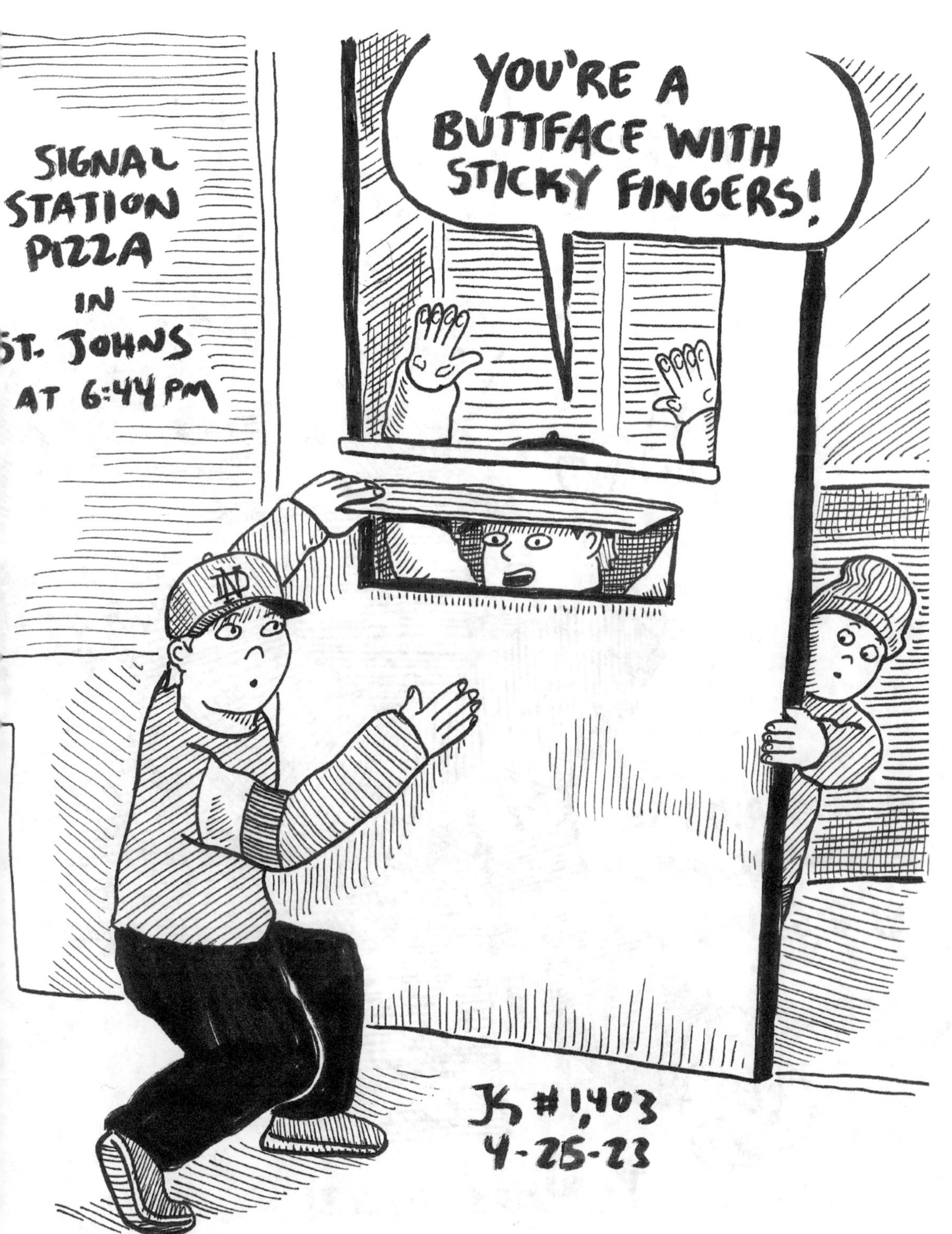

SIGNAL STATION PIZZA IN ST. JOHNS AT 6:44 PM
YOU'RE A BUTTFACE WITH STICKY FINGERS!
JK #1,403
4-25-23

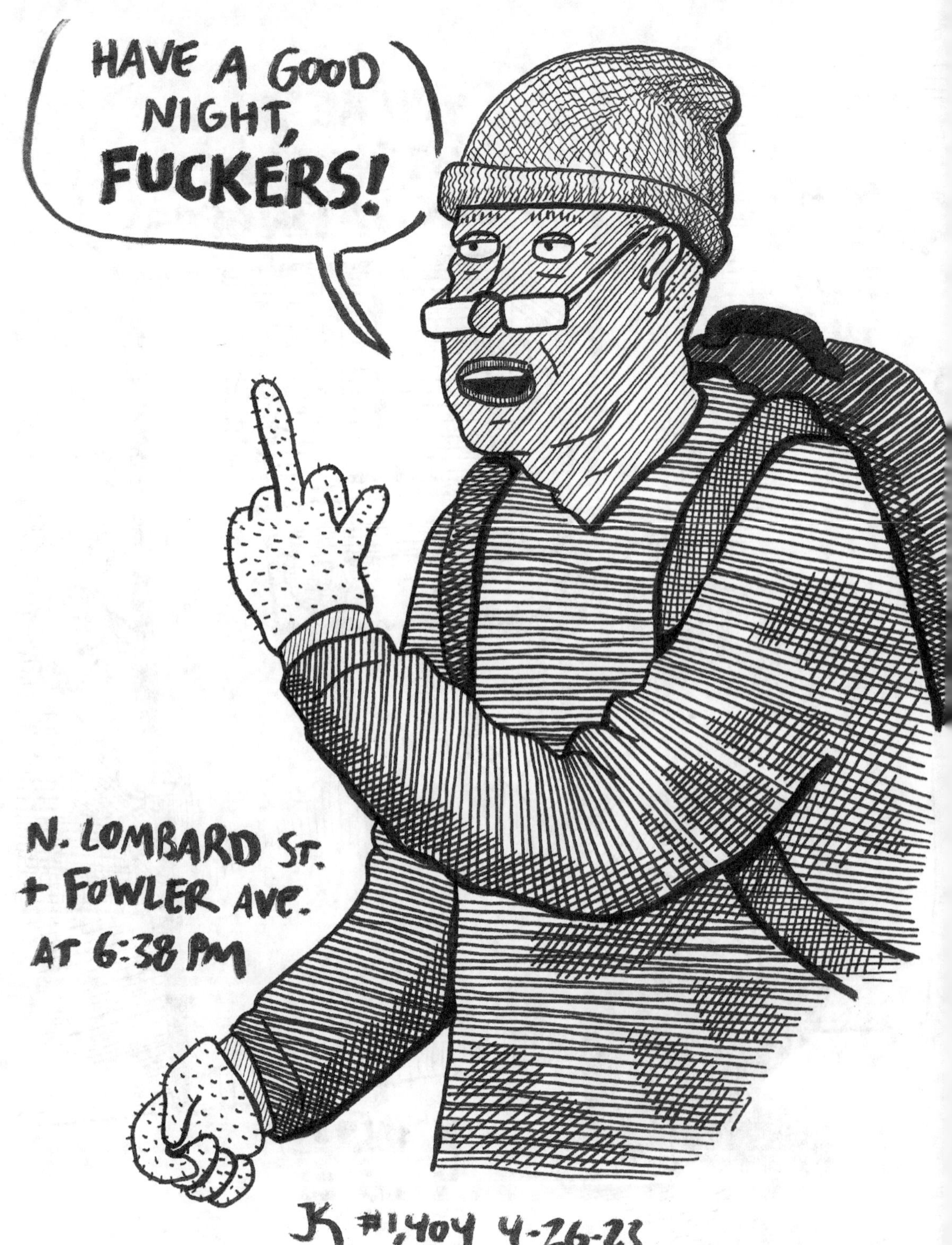

HAVE A GOOD NIGHT, FUCKERS!
N. LOMBARD ST. + FOWLER AVE. AT 6:38 PM
JK #1,404 4-26-23

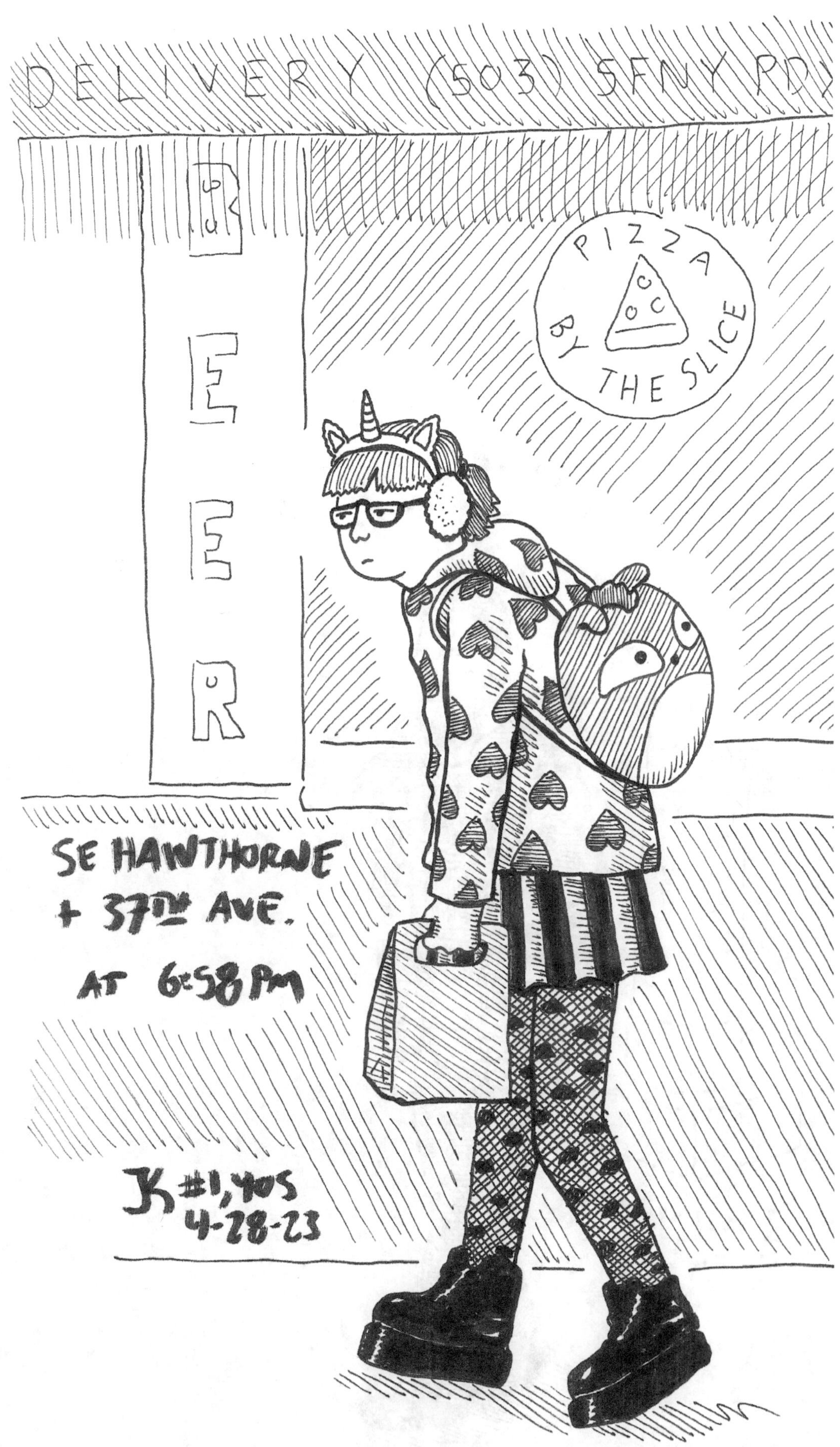
DELIVERY (503) 5FNY RD
BEER
PIZZA
BY THE SLICE
SE HAWTHORNE
+ 37TH AVE.
AT 6:58 PM
JK #1,405
4-28-23

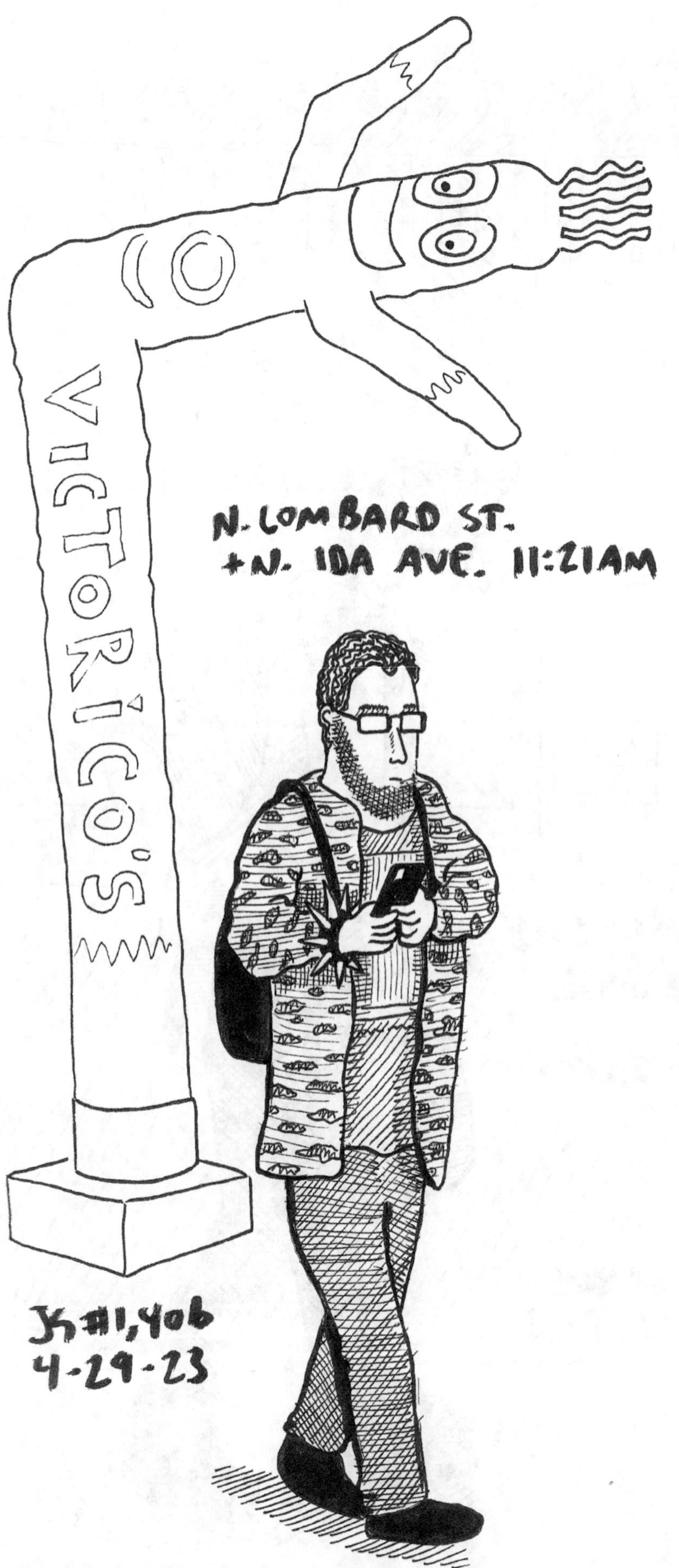

VICTORICO'S
N. LOMBARD ST.
+ N. IDA AVE. 11:21AM
JS #1,406
4-29-23

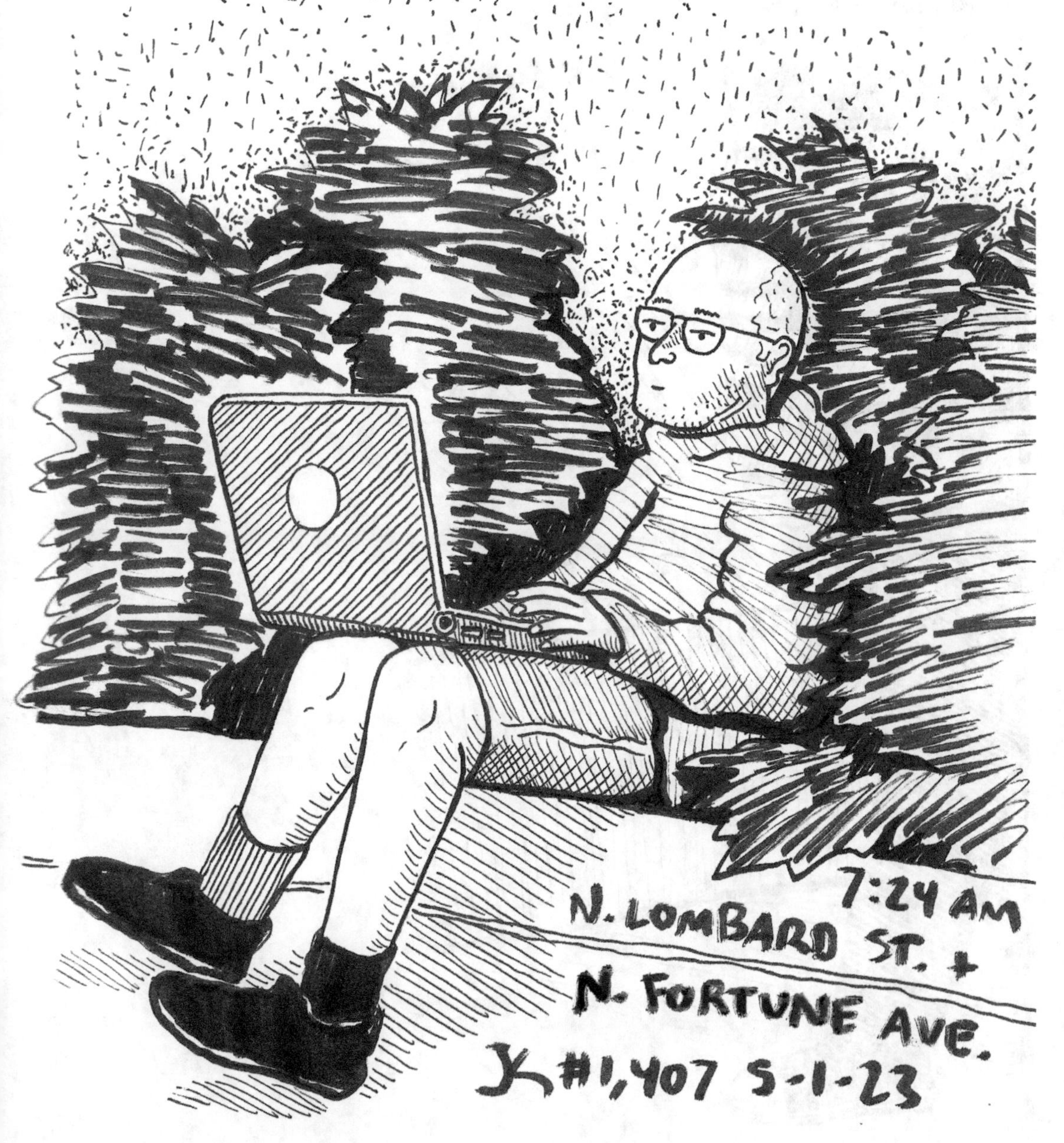

7:24 AM
N. LOMBARD ST. +
N. FORTUNE AVE.
#1,407 5-1-23

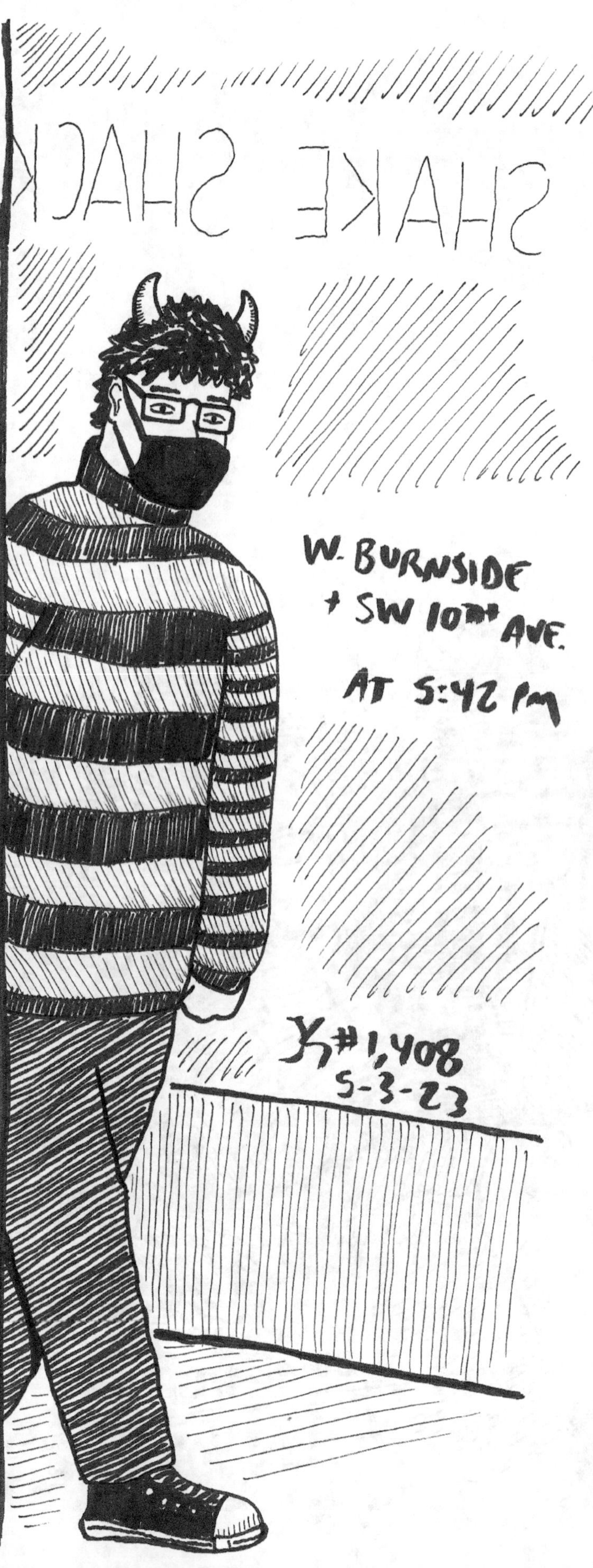
SHAKE SHACK
W. BURNSIDE
+ SW 10TH AVE.
AT 5:42 PM
#1,408
5-3-23

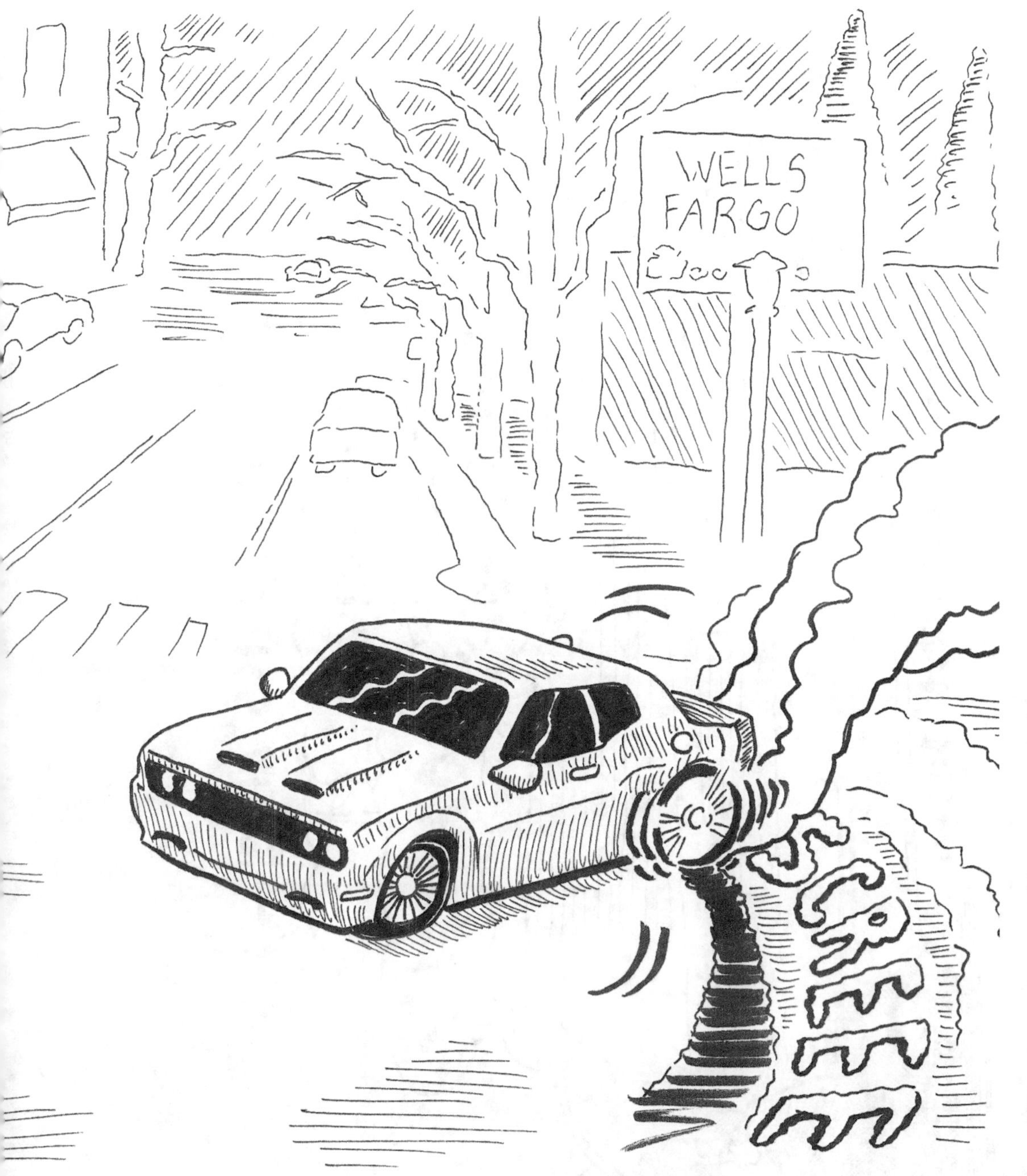

WELLS
FARGO
SCREE
N. DENVER +
N. McCLELLAN AT 5:01PM
#1,404 5-4-23

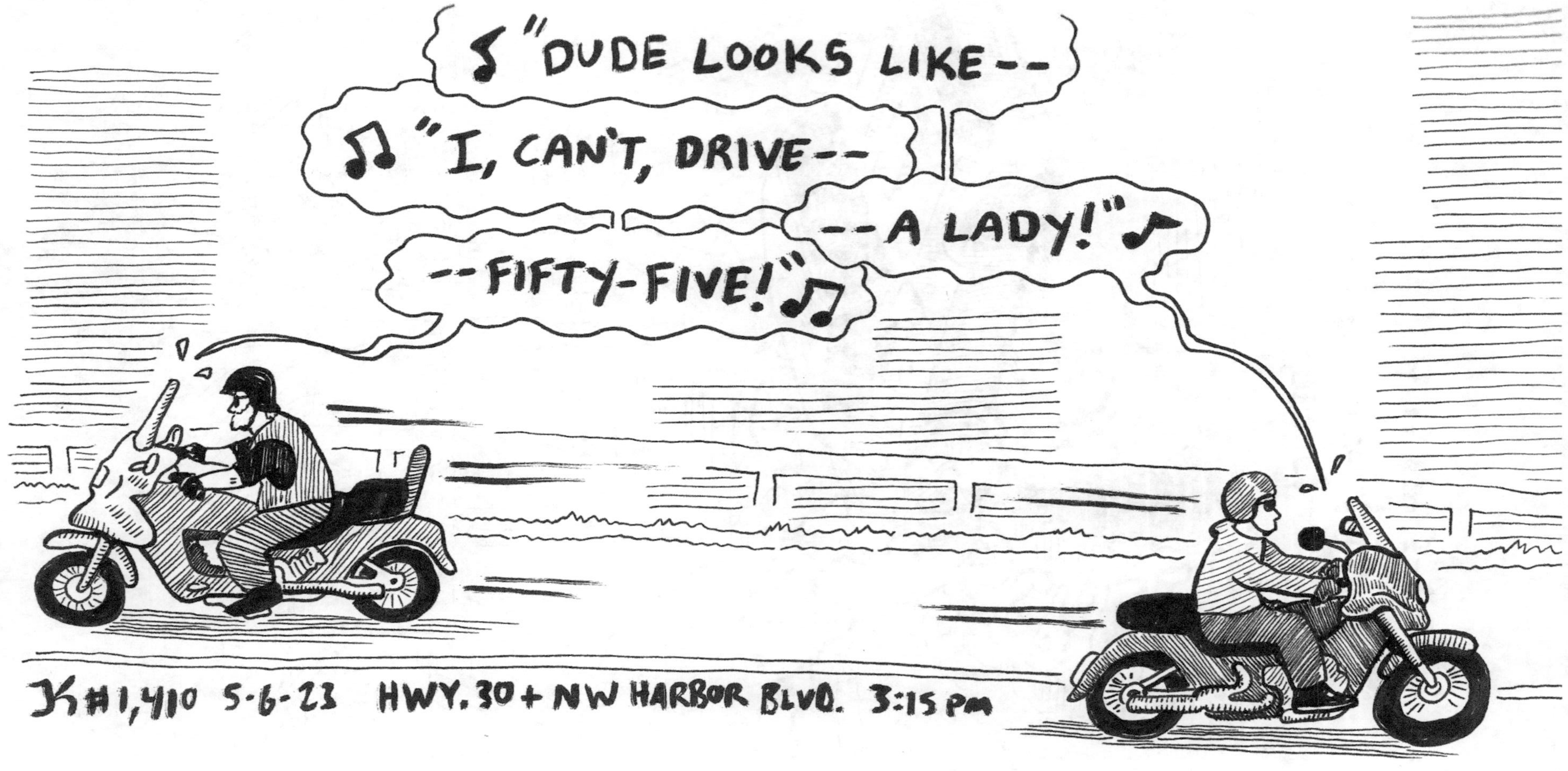

♪ "DUDE LOOKS LIKE--
♫ "I, CAN'T, DRIVE--
--A LADY!" ♪
--FIFTY-FIVE!" ♫
JK #1,410 5-6-23 HWY. 30 + NW HARBOR BLVD. 3:15 PM

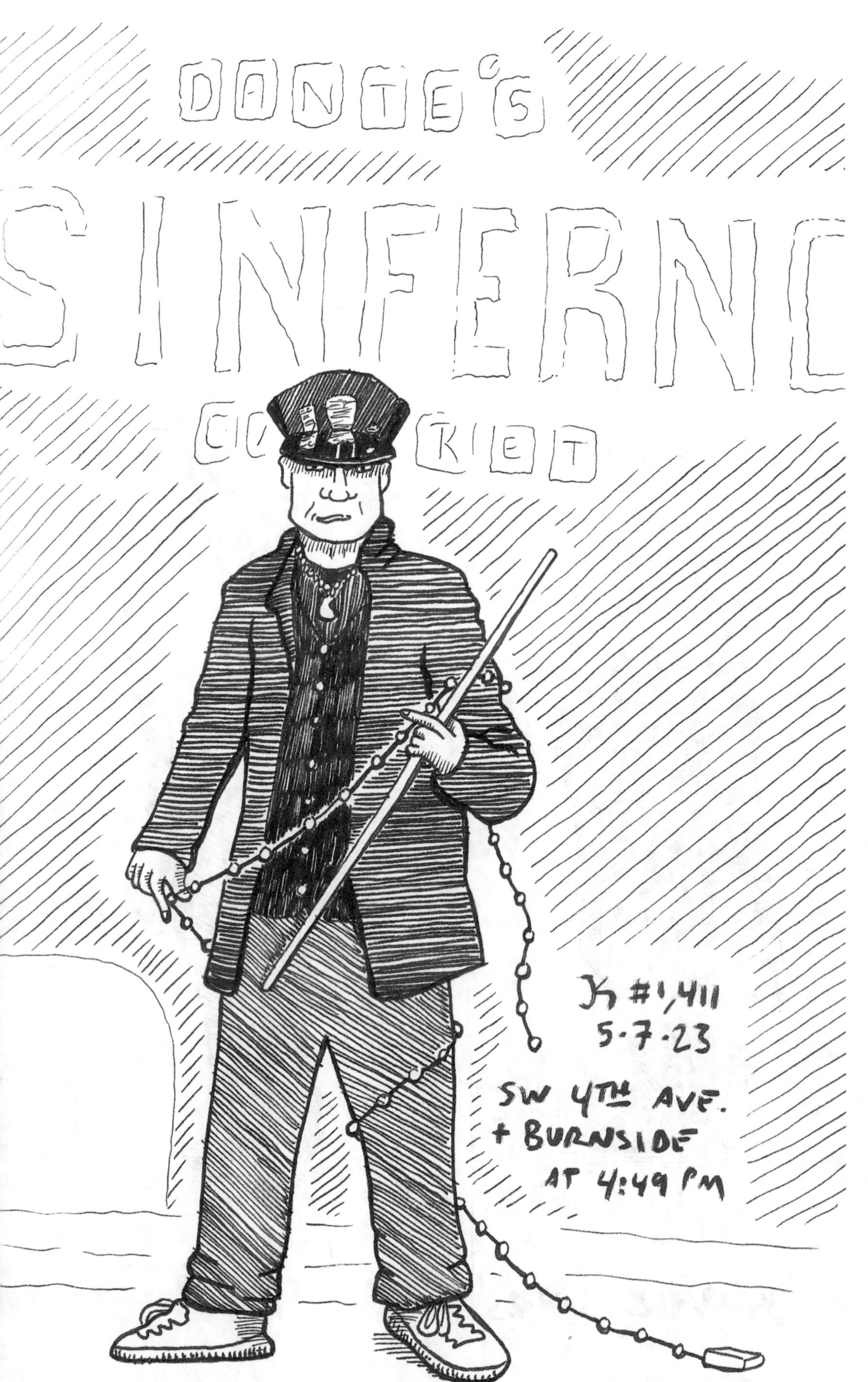

DANTE'S
SINFERNO
CONCERT RIOT
JS #1,411
5-7-23
SW 4TH AVE.
+ BURNSIDE
AT 4:49 PM

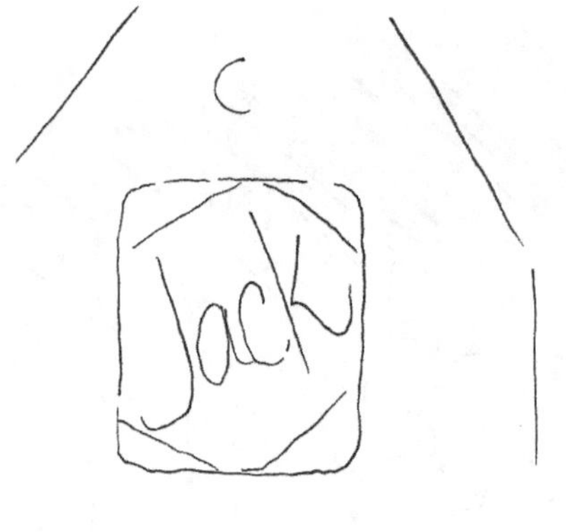

Jack

NE SANDY BLVD.
+ 57TH AVE.
AT 2:52 PM

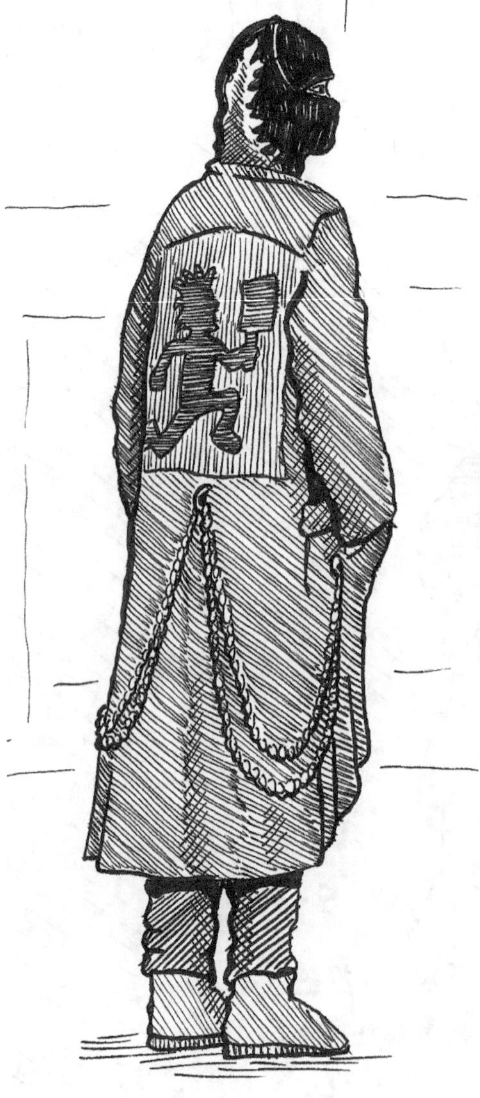

BACK

JK #1,412   5-9-23

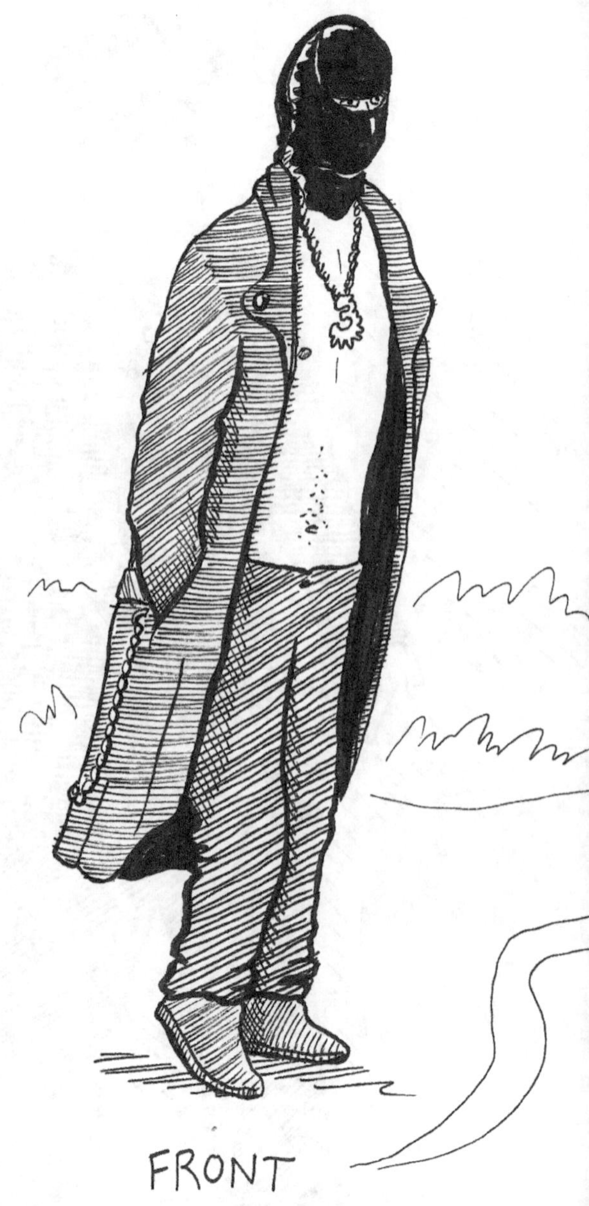

FRONT

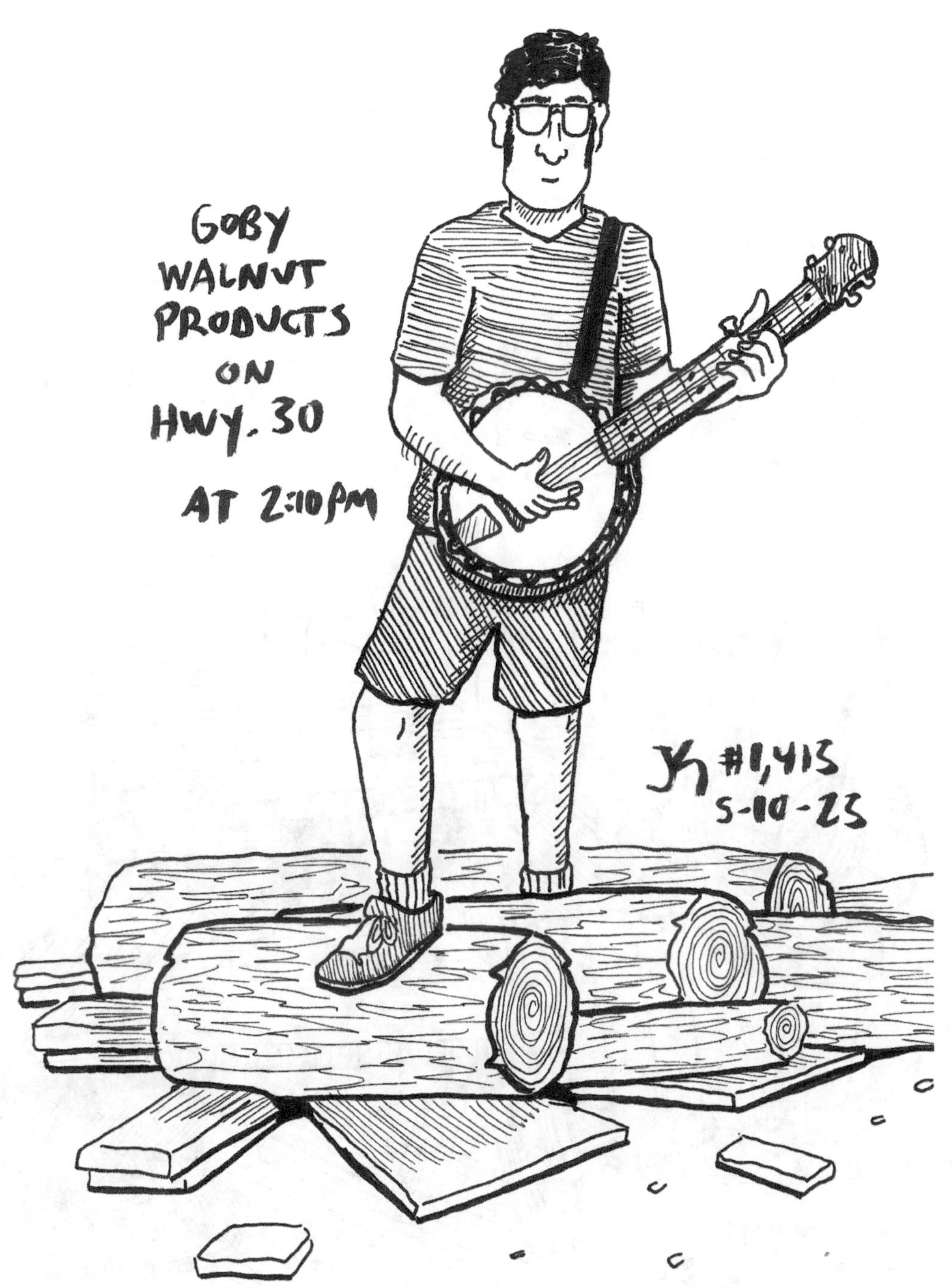

GOBY
WALNUT
PRODUCTS
ON
HWY. 30
AT 2:10 PM

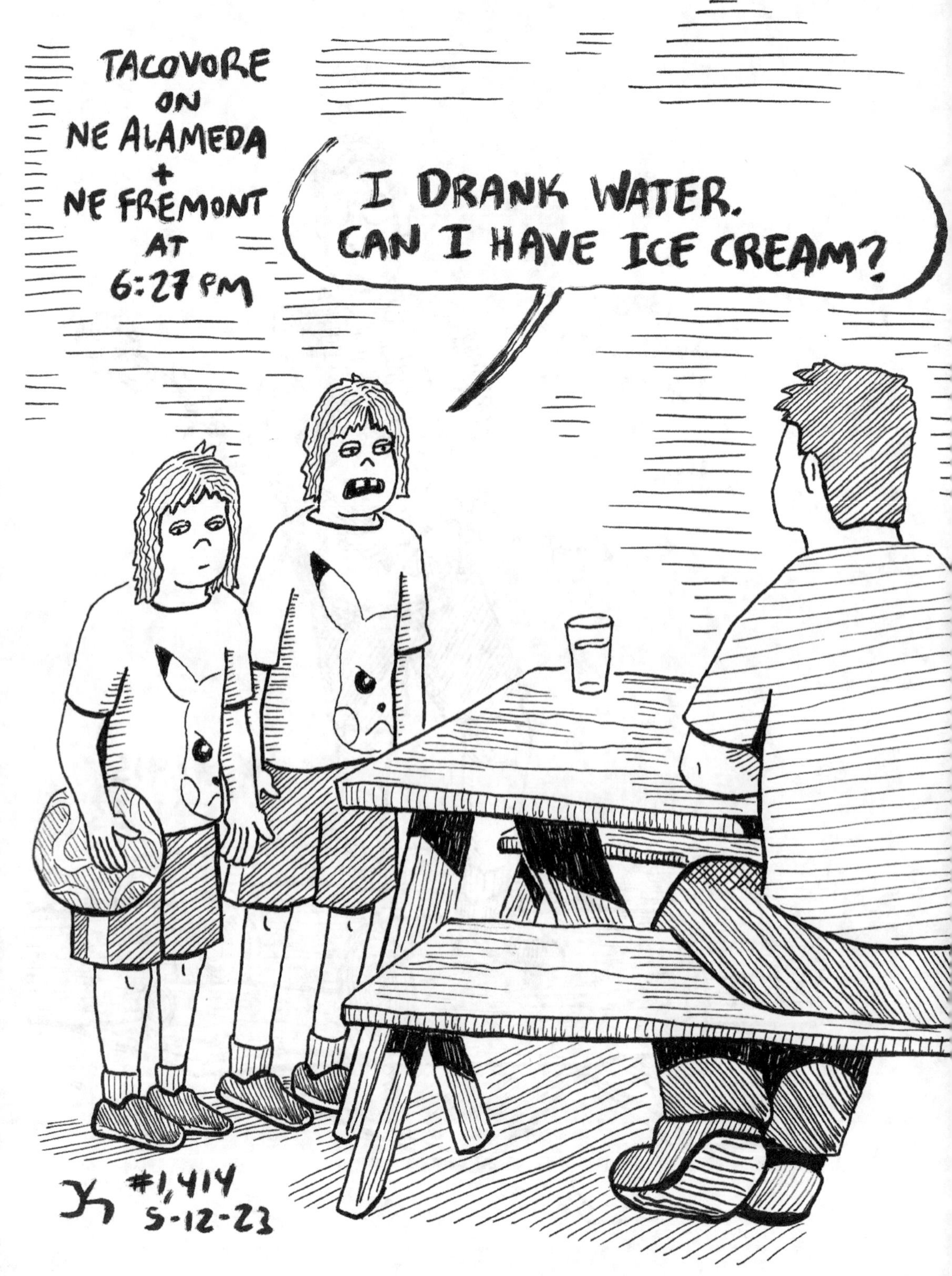

TACOVORE
ON
NE ALAMEDA
+
NE FREMONT
AT
6:27 PM
I DRANK WATER.
CAN I HAVE ICE CREAM?
#1,414
5-12-23

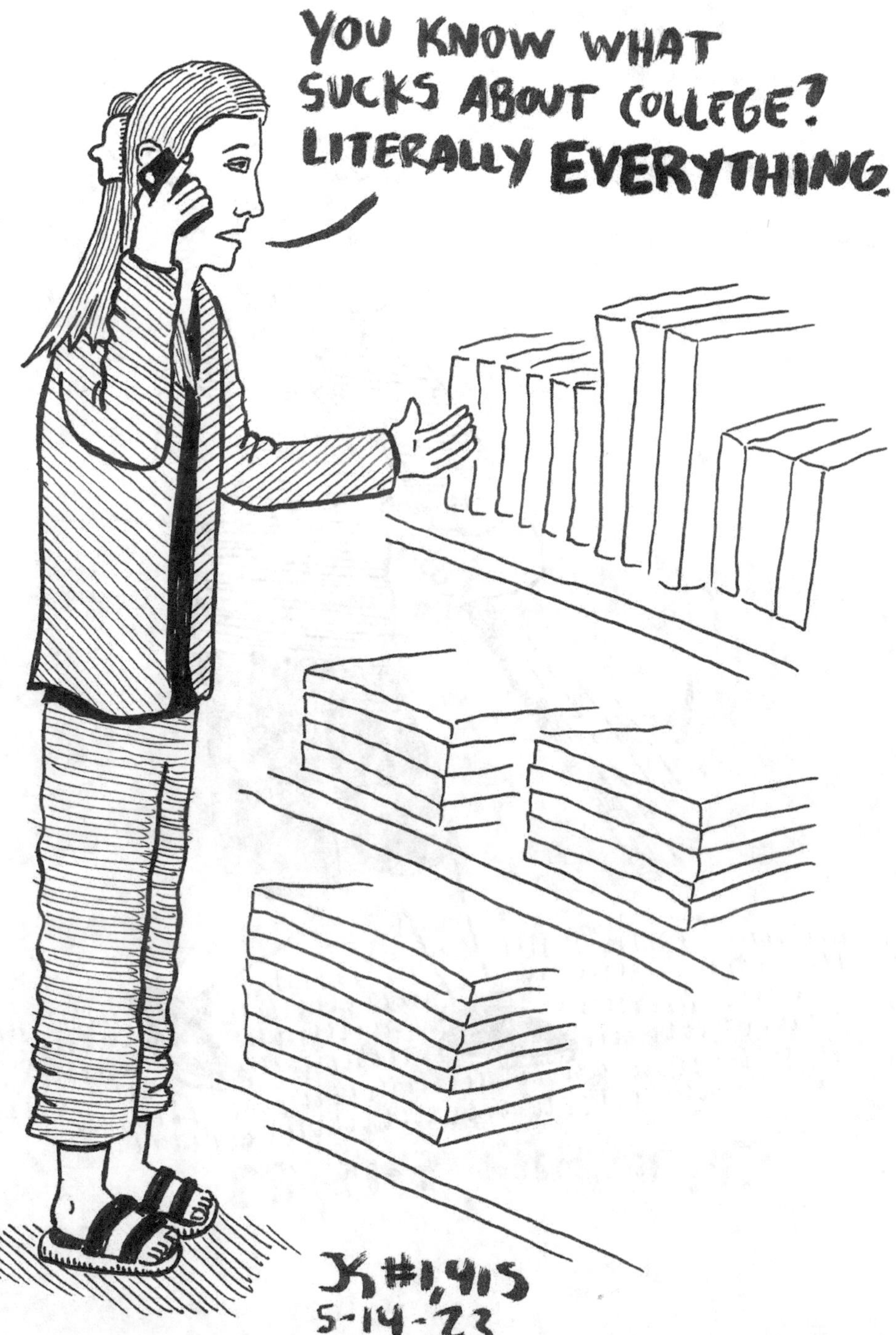

COLUMBIA ART &
DRAFTING AT 2:48 PM
YOU KNOW WHAT
SUCKS ABOUT COLLEGE?
LITERALLY EVERYTHING.
JK #1,415
5-14-23

NE LIBERTY ST.
+ HIGH ST.
SALEM, OR
AT 7:52 PM
#1,416   5-15-23

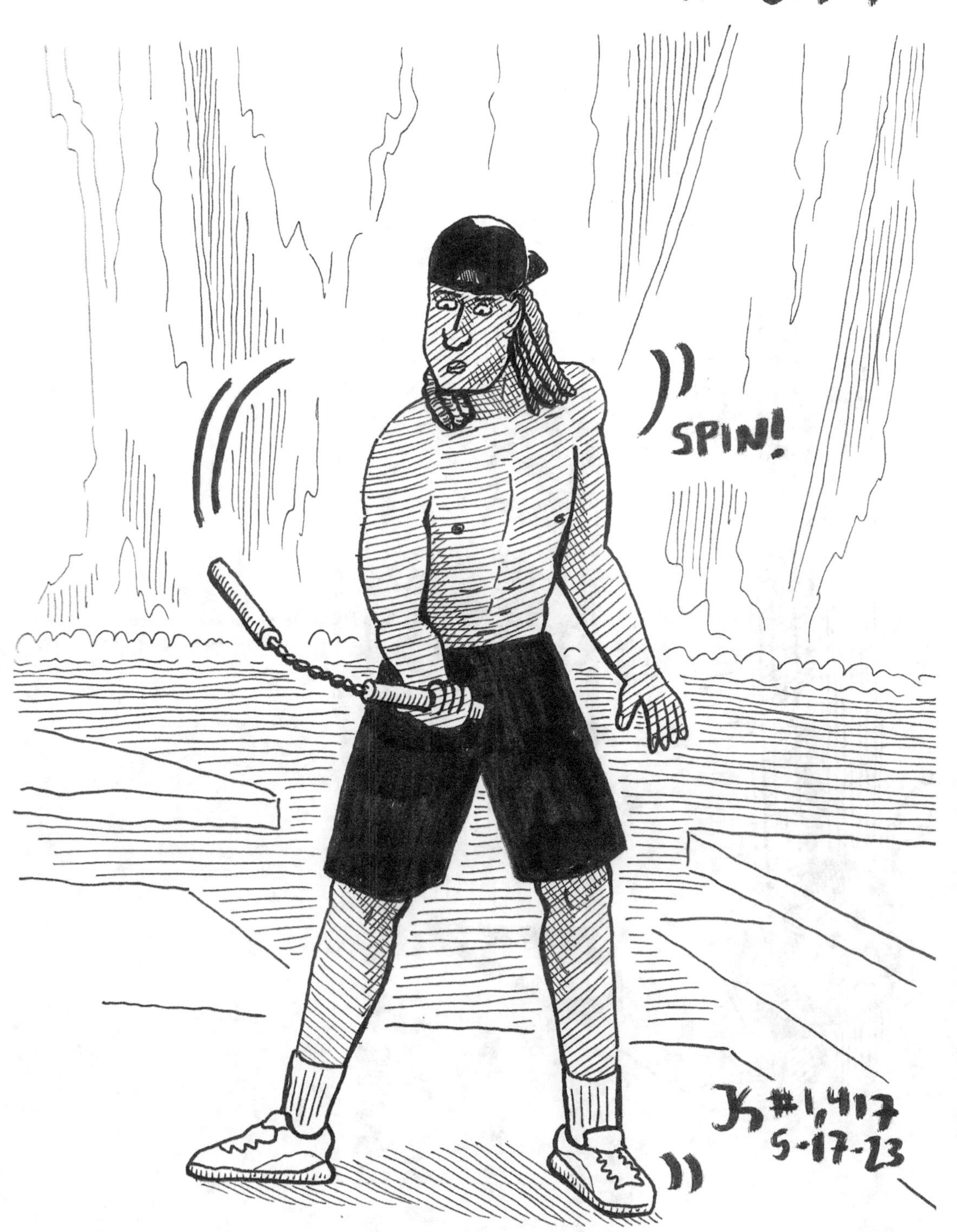
KELLER FOUNTAIN PARK
AT 11:08 AM
SPIN!
JS #1,417
5-17-23

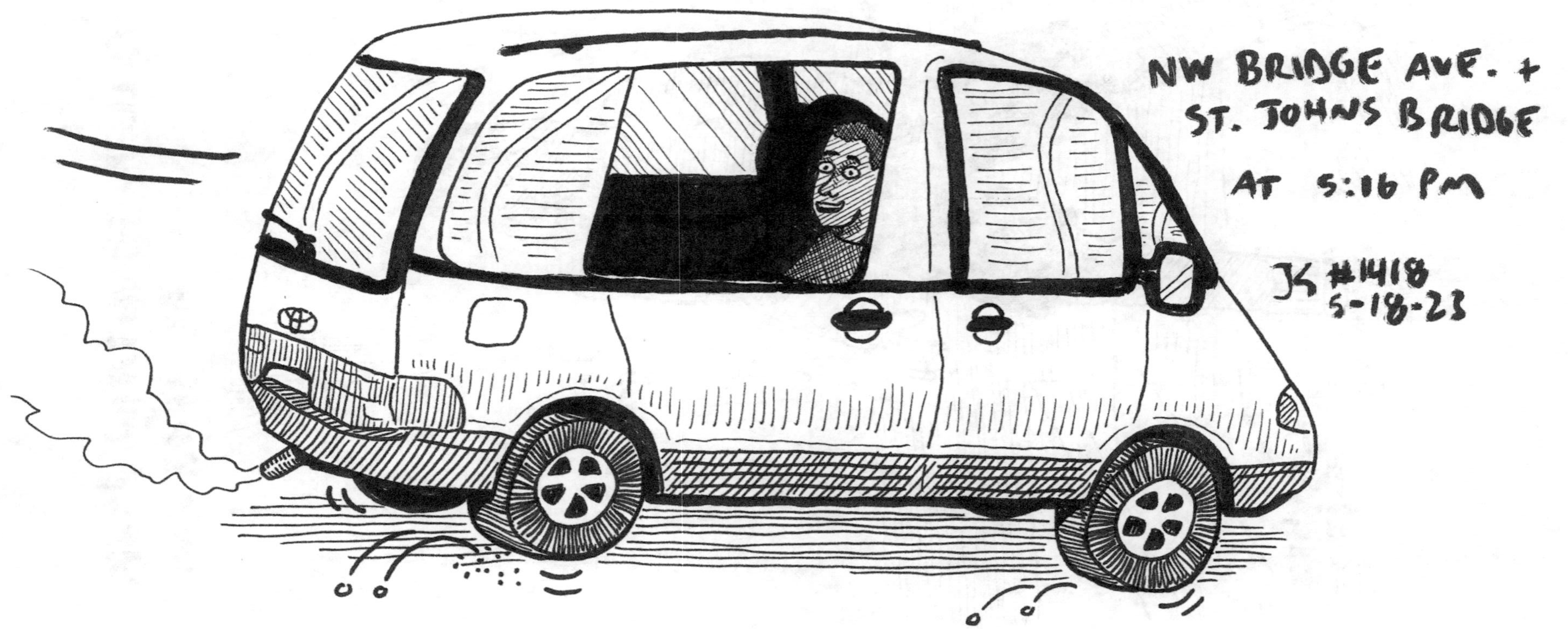

NW BRIDGE AVE. +
ST. JOHNS BRIDGE
AT 5:16 PM
JS #1418
5-18-23

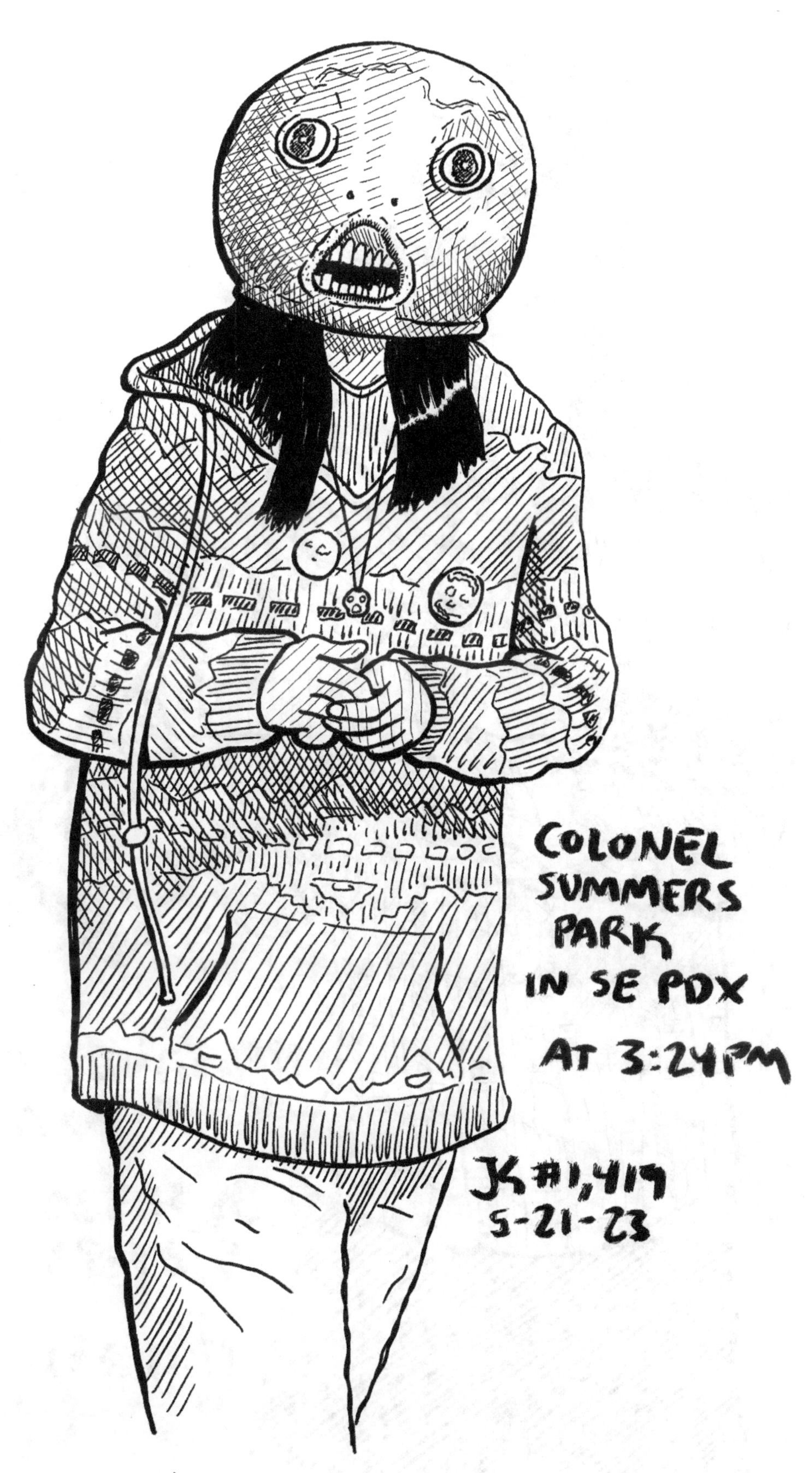

COLONEL
SUMMERS
PARK
IN SE PDX
AT 3:24PM

JK #1,419
5-21-23

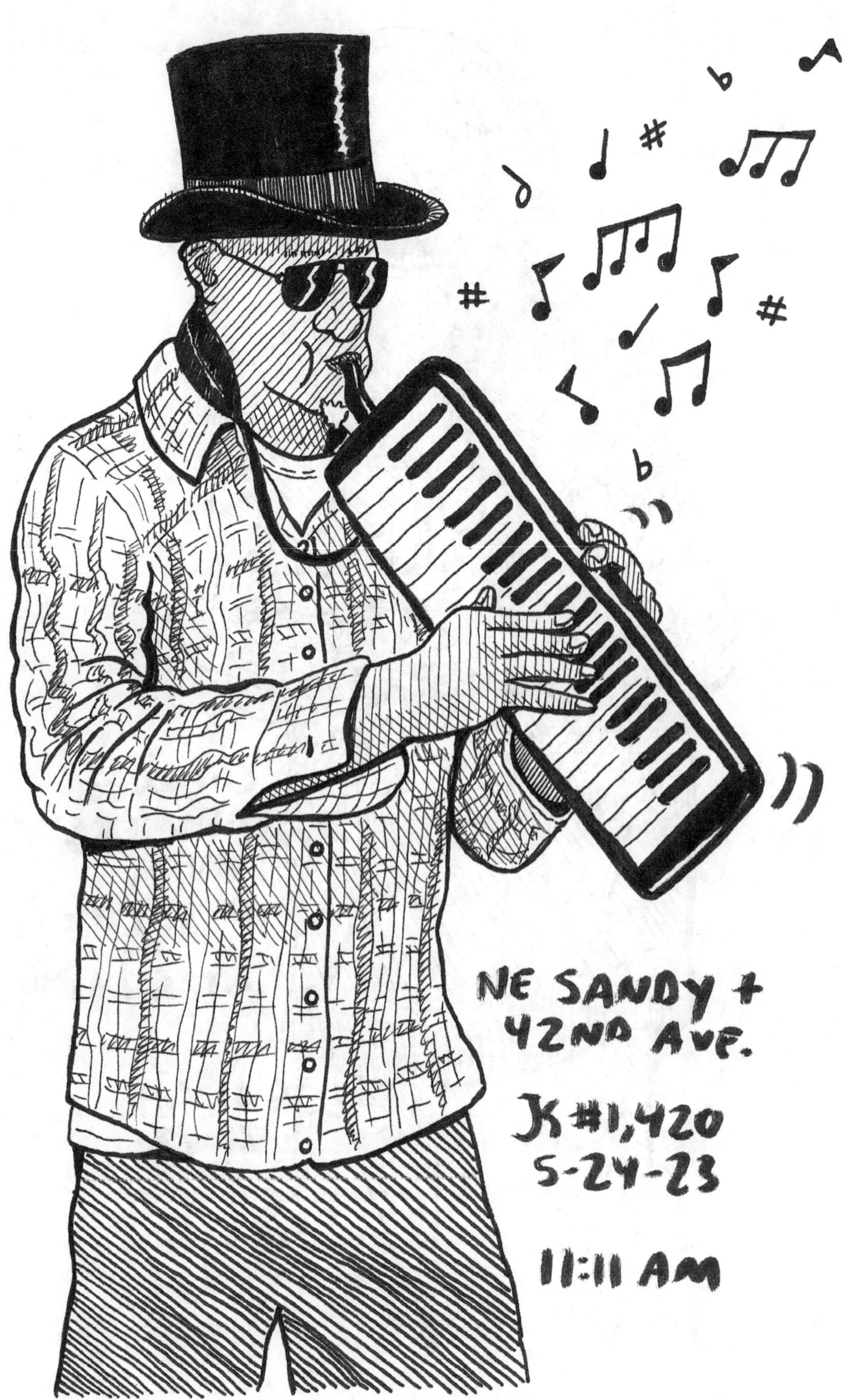

NE SANDY +
42ND AVE.
JK #1,420
5-24-23
11:11 AM

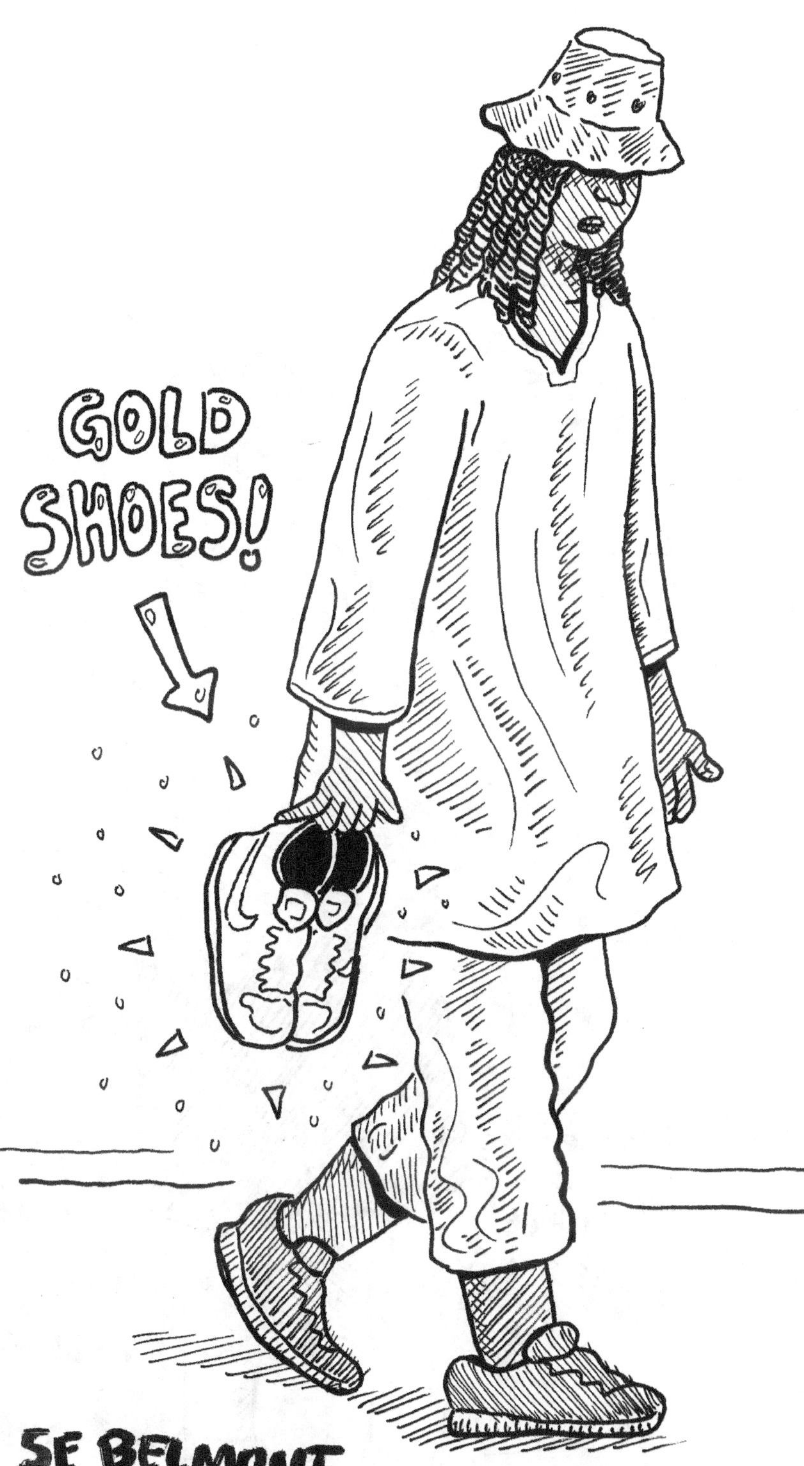

GOLD
SHOES!
SE BELMONT
+ C. CHÁVEZ BLVD.
AT 4:10 PM
JK #1,421
5-25-23

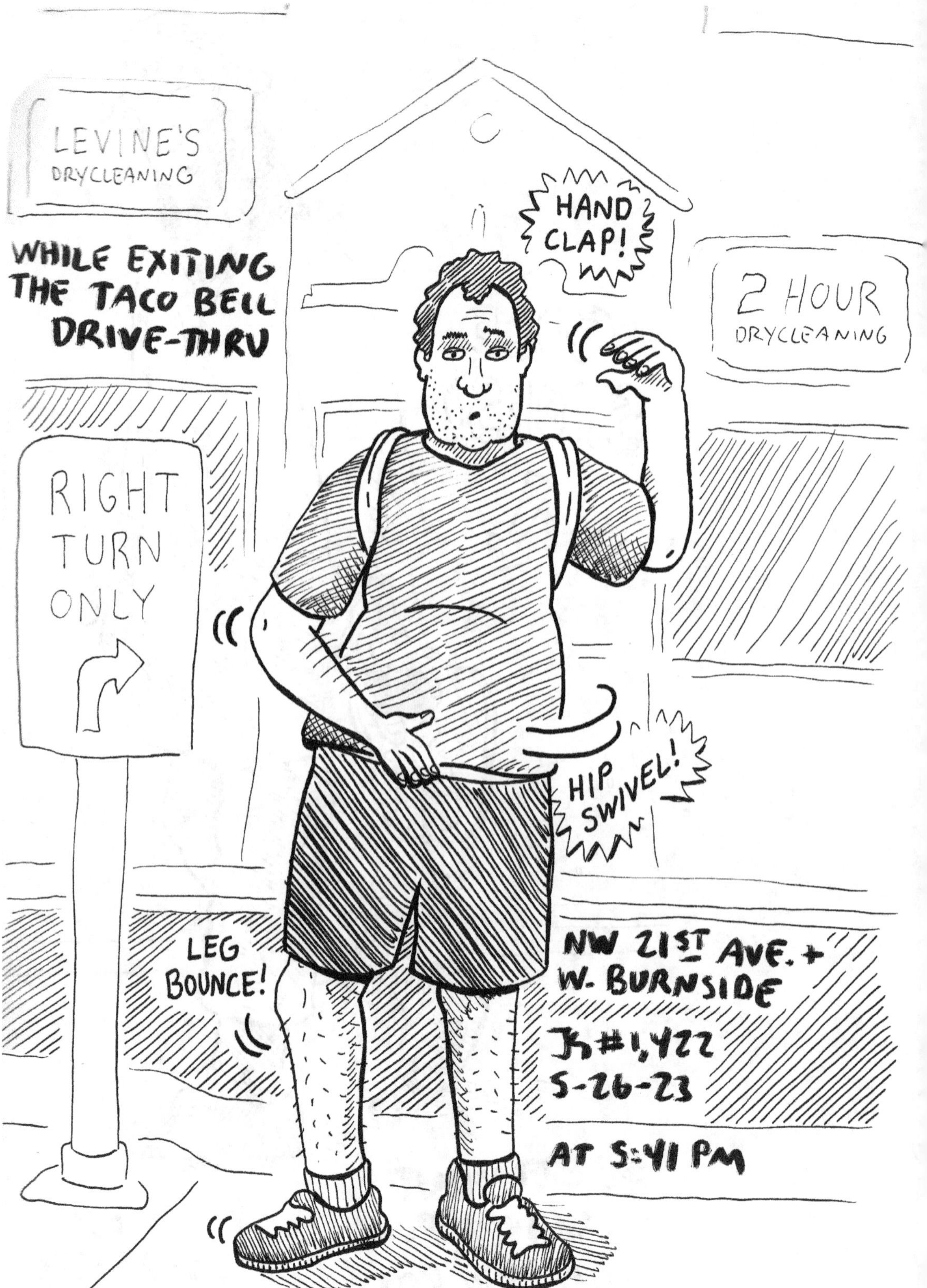

LEVINE'S DRYCLEANING
WHILE EXITING THE TACO BELL DRIVE-THRU
RIGHT TURN ONLY
HAND CLAP!
2 HOUR DRYCLEANING
HIP SWIVEL!
LEG BOUNCE!
NW 21ST AVE. + W. BURNSIDE
JS #1,422
5-26-23
AT 5:41 PM

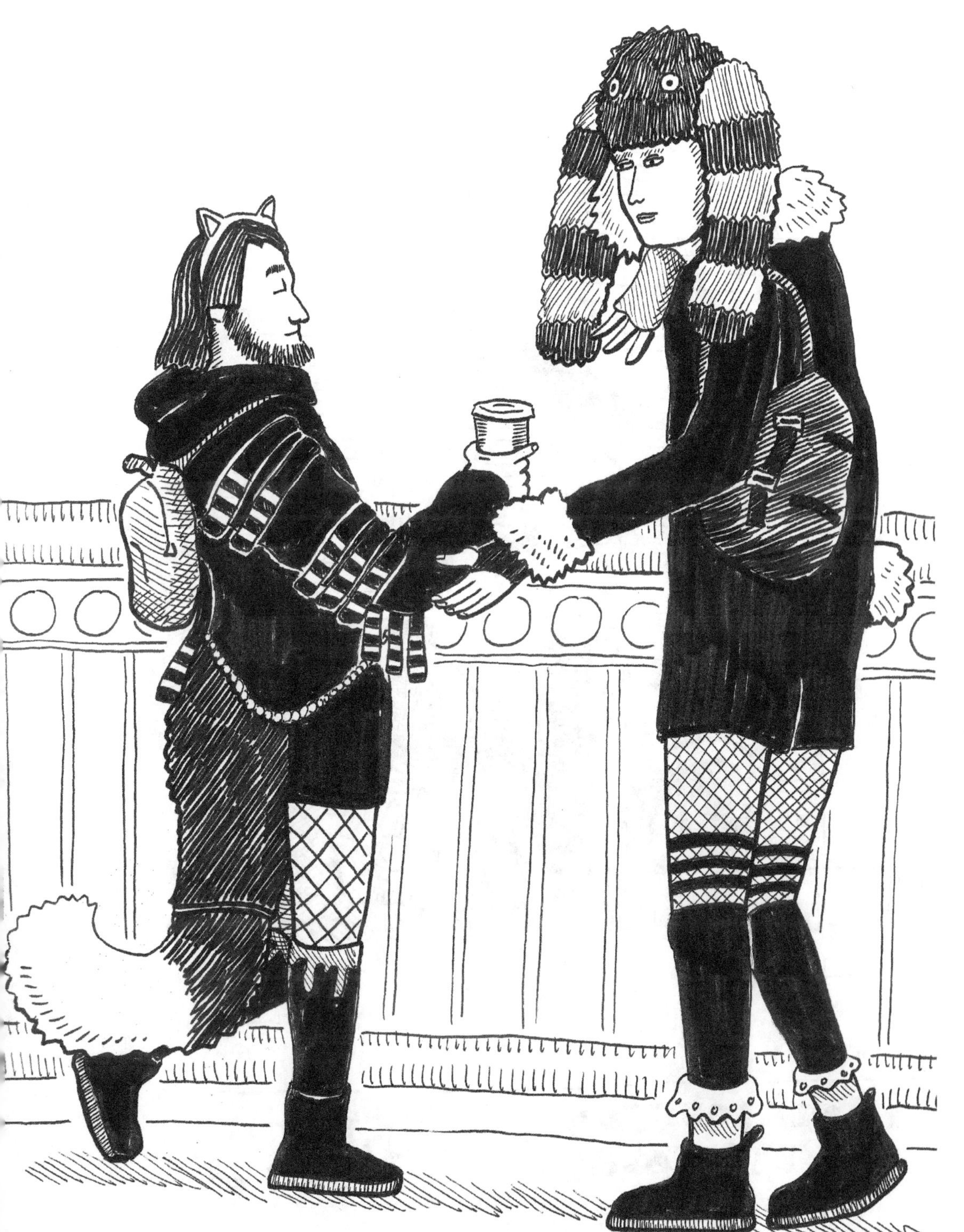

ST. JOHNS BRIDGE
AT 10:41 AM

JK #1,423
5-28-23

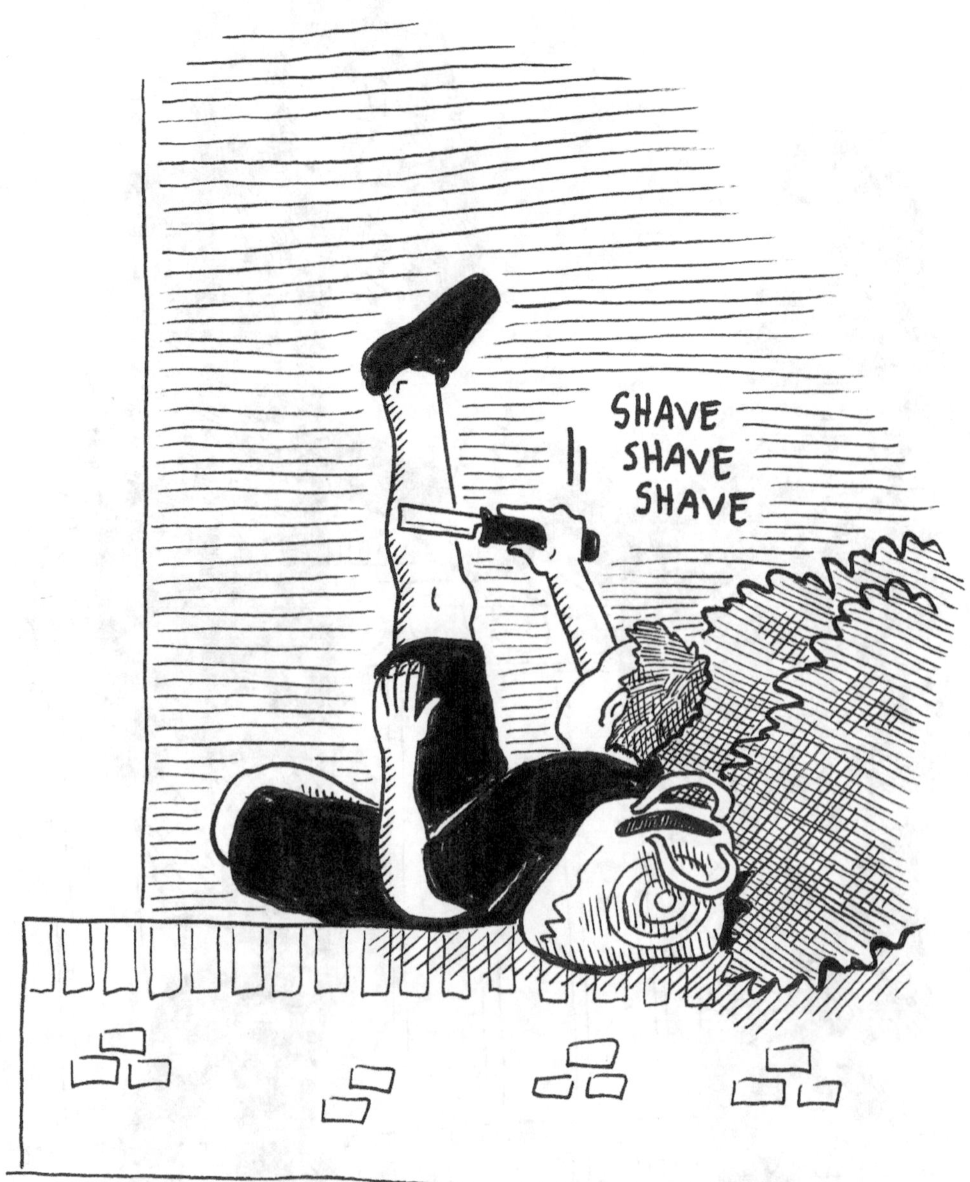

NW LOVEJOY
+ 23RD AVE.
AT 2:05 PM

JS #1,424
5-29-23

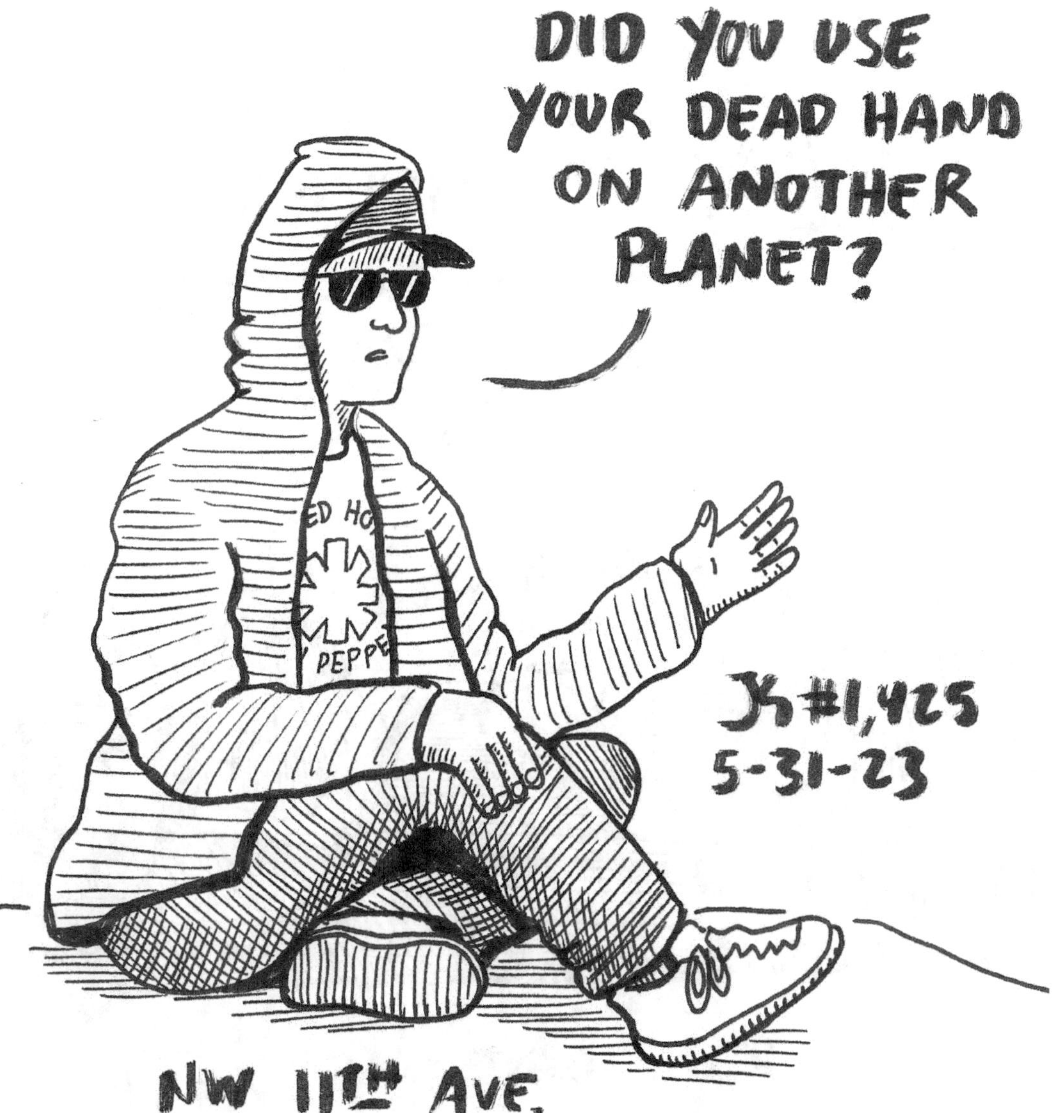
DID YOU USE
YOUR DEAD HAND
ON ANOTHER
PLANET?
RED HO
PEPPE
JK #1,425
5-31-23
NW 11TH AVE.
+ NW COUCH ST.
AT 1:55 PM

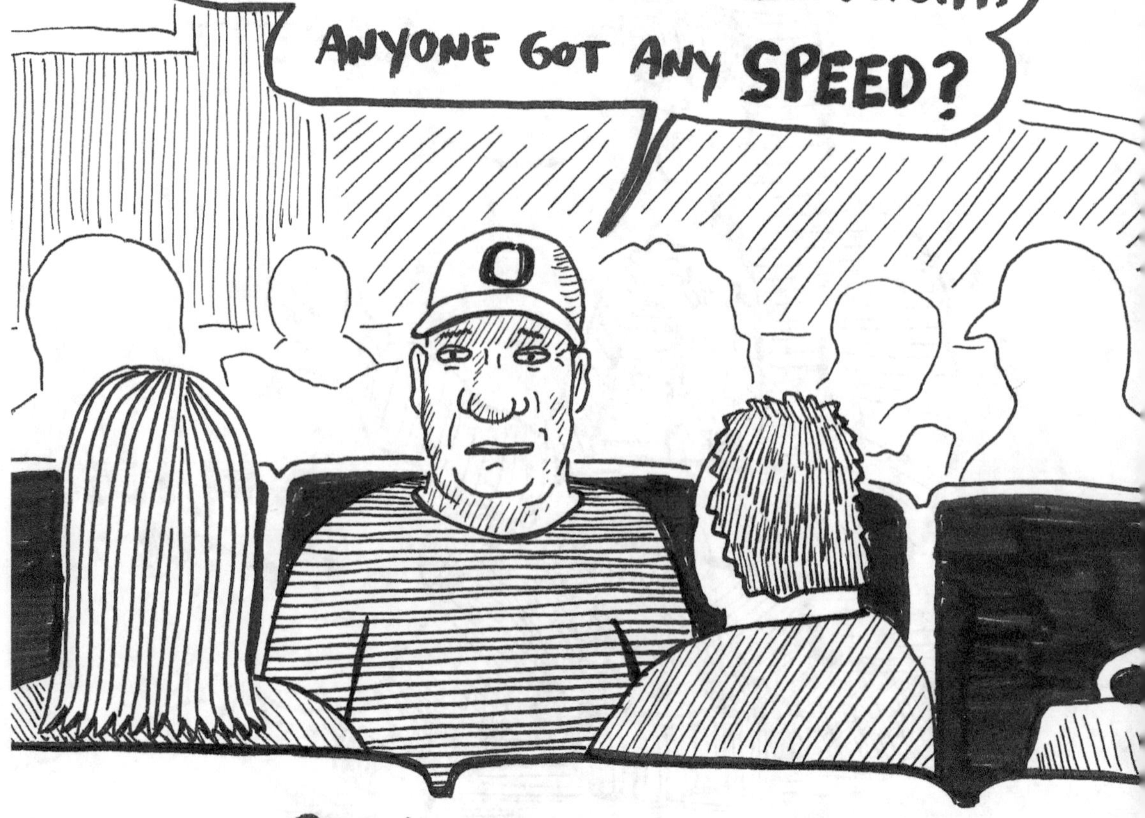

WE'RE GONNA FLY ALL NIGHT, THEN HAVE A TWO HOUR LAYOVER, THEN ANOTHER FLIGHT. ANYONE GOT ANY SPEED?
O
PDX GATE D14 AT 6:10 PM
K #1,426
6-2-23

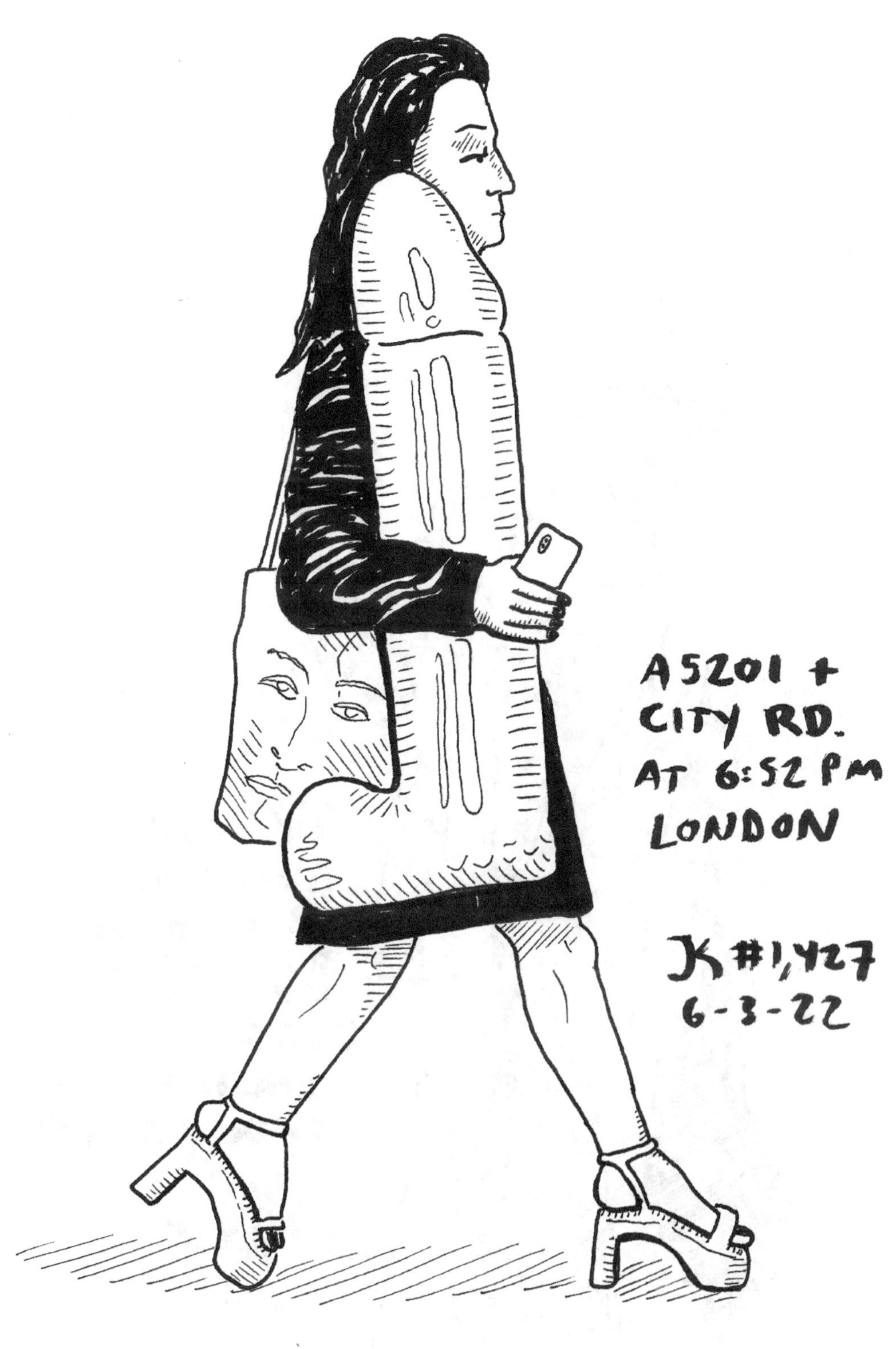

A5201 +
CITY RD.
AT 6:52 PM
LONDON

JK #1,427
6-3-22

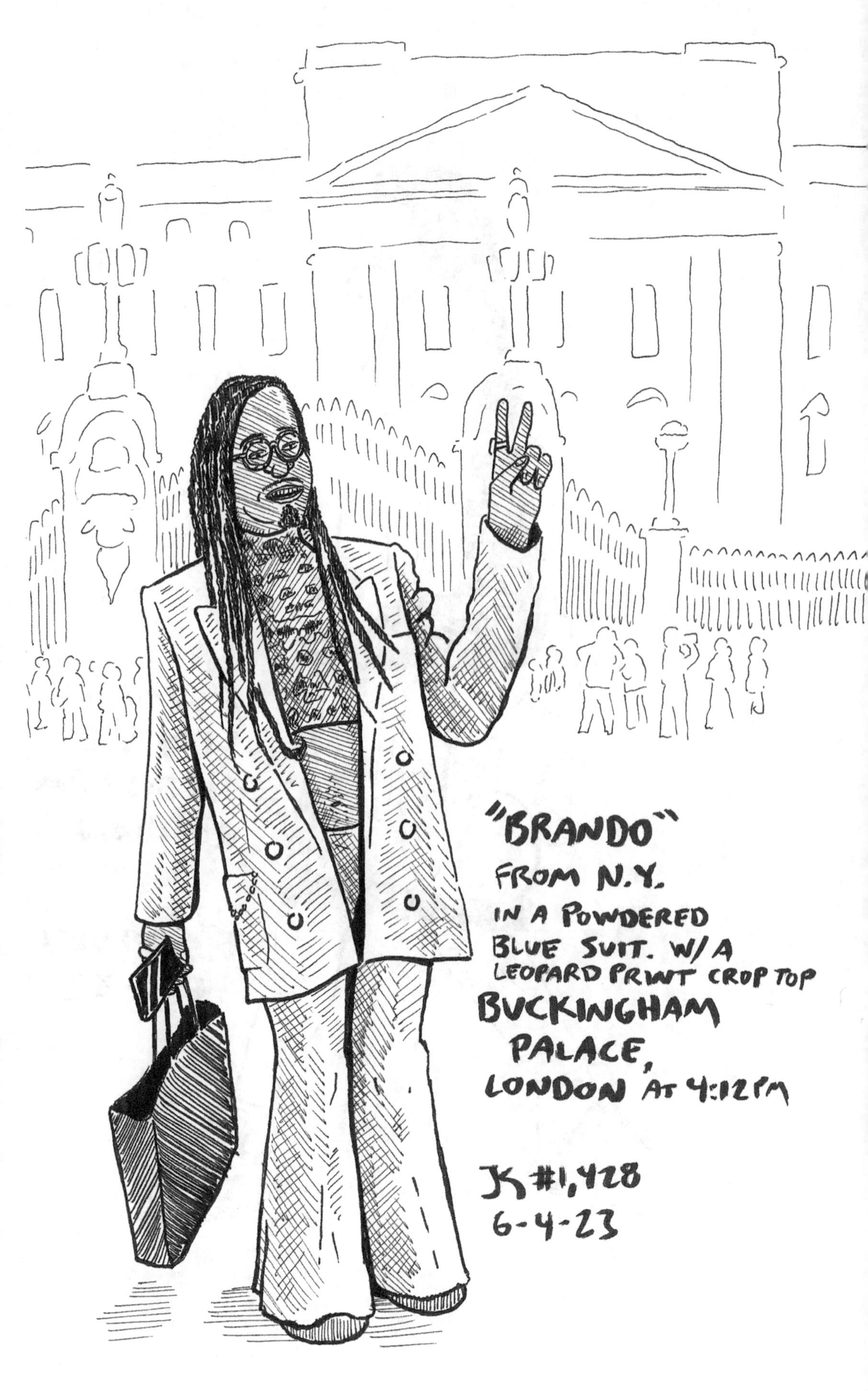

"BRANDO"
FROM N.Y.
IN A POWDERED
BLUE SUIT. W/ A
LEOPARD PRINT CROP TOP
BUCKINGHAM
PALACE,
LONDON AT 4:12 PM

JK #1,428
6-4-23

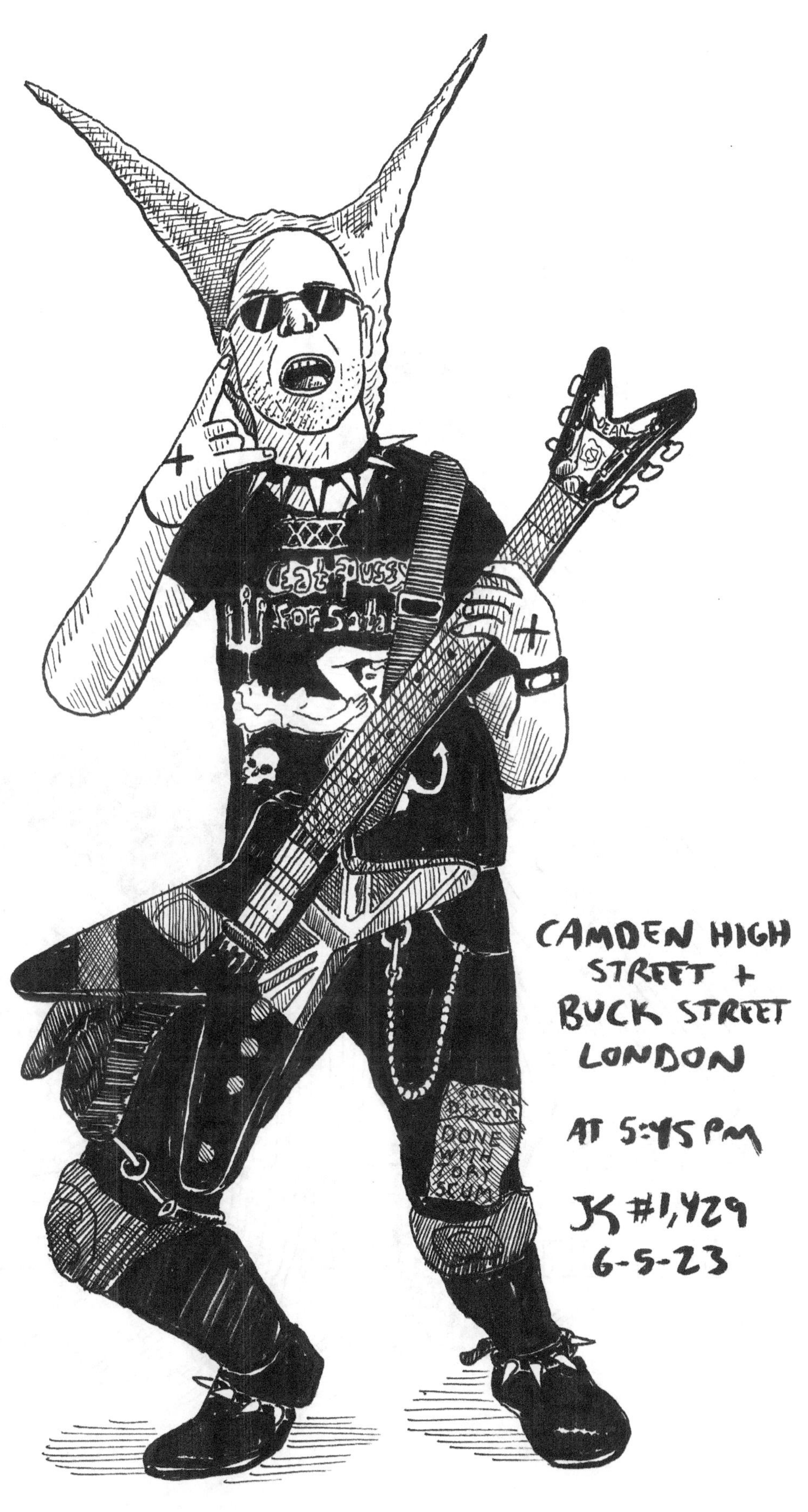

CAMDEN HIGH
STREET +
BUCK STREET
LONDON

AT 5:45 PM

JS #1,429
6-5-23

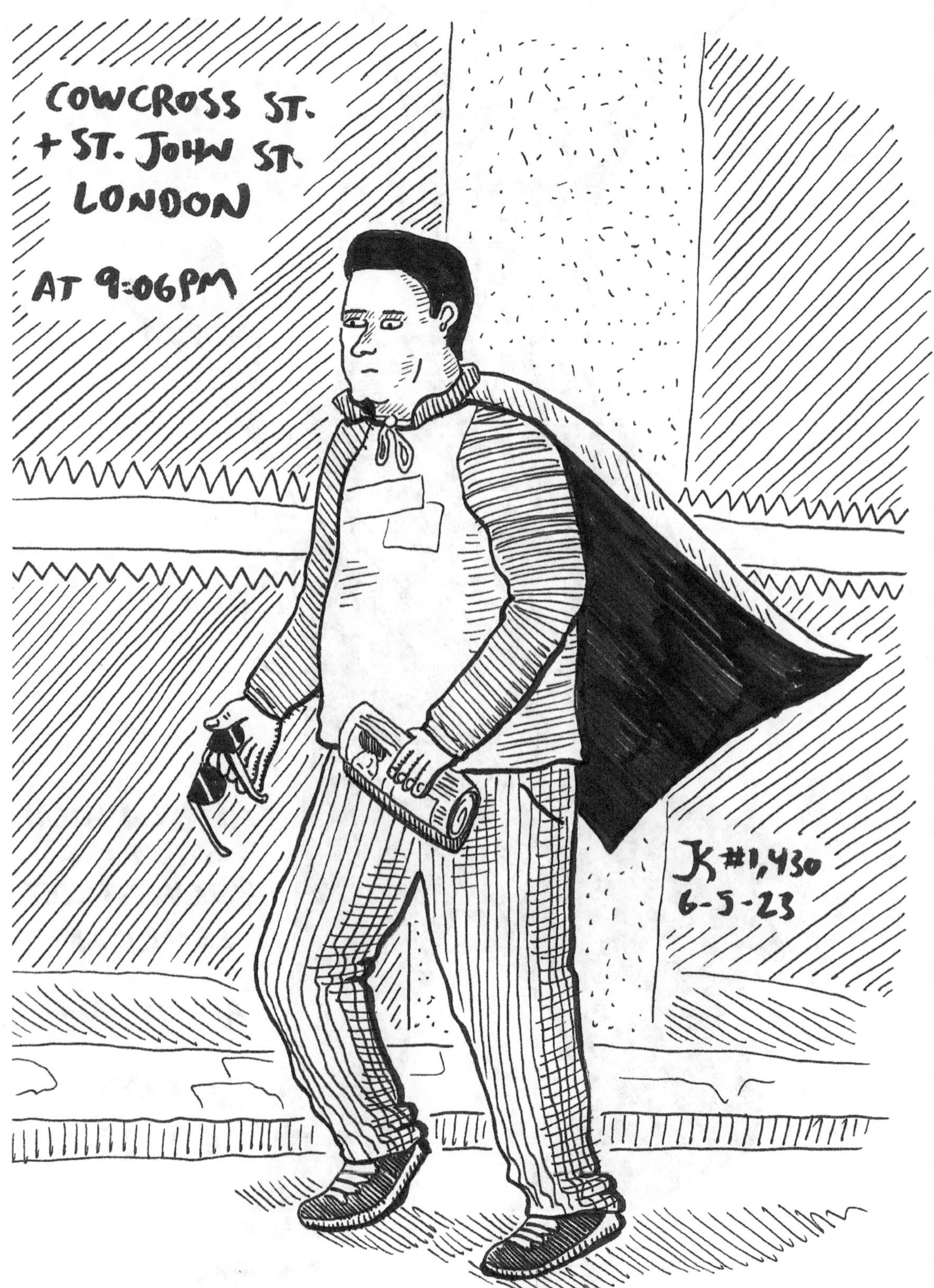

COWCROSS ST.
+ ST. JOHN ST.
LONDON

AT 9:06PM

JK #1,430
6-5-23

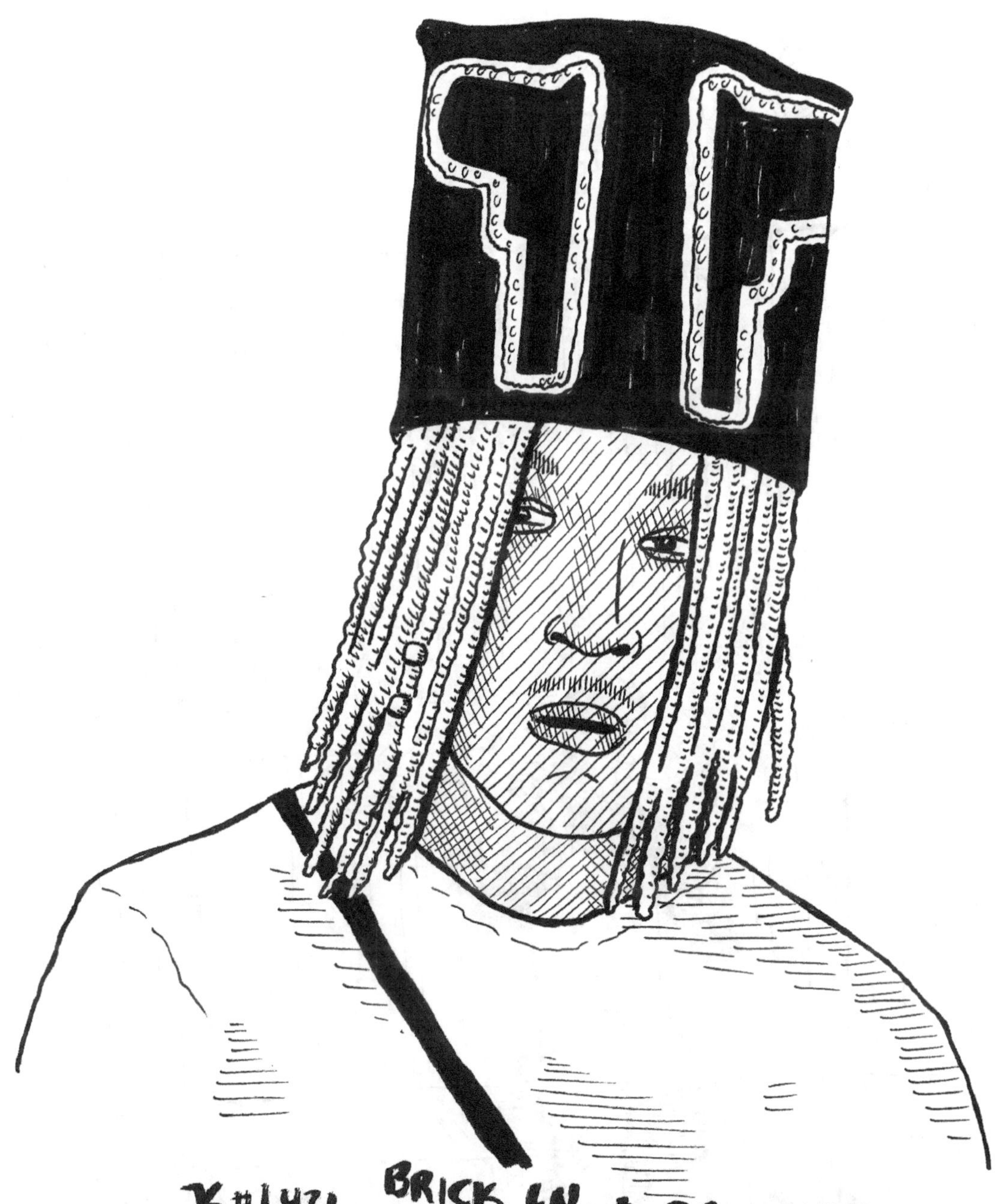
K. #1,431
6-6-23
BRICK LN. # BACON ST.
LONDON
AT 7:45 PM

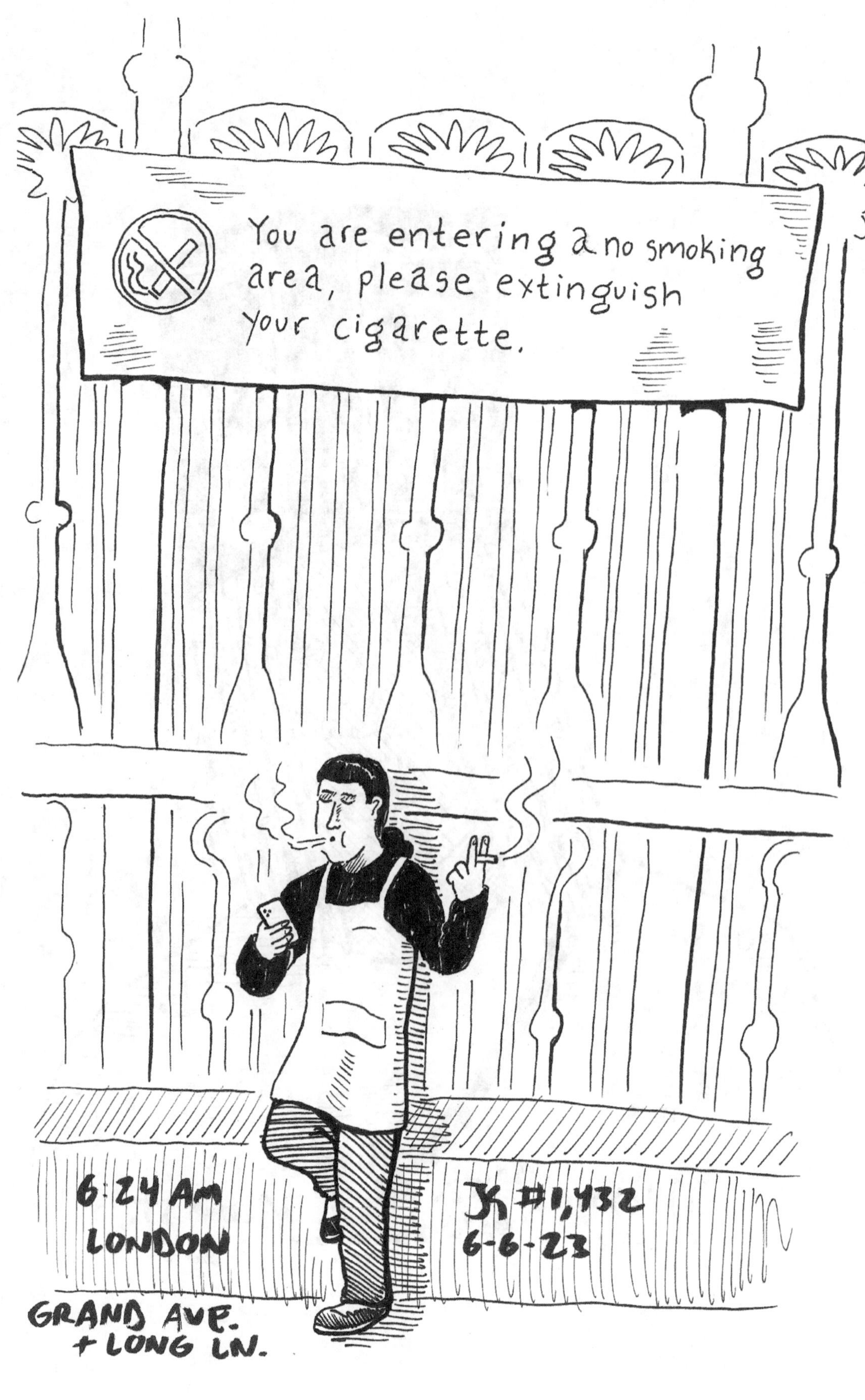

You are entering a no smoking area, please extinguish your cigarette.
6:24 AM
LONDON
GRAND AVE. + LONG LN.
#1,432
6-6-23

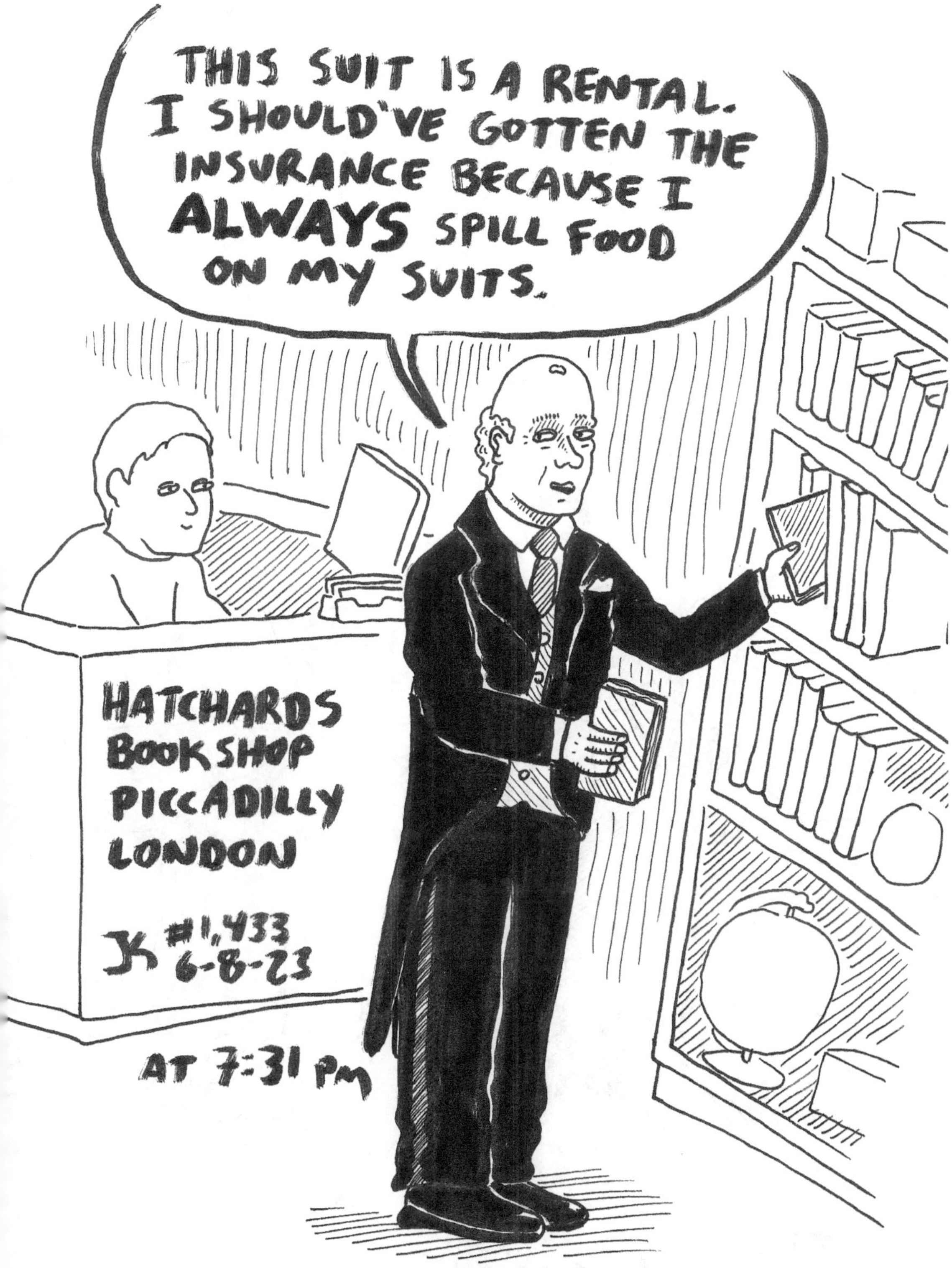

THIS SUIT IS A RENTAL. I SHOULD'VE GOTTEN THE INSURANCE BECAUSE I ALWAYS SPILL FOOD ON MY SUITS.
HATCHARDS BOOKSHOP PICCADILLY LONDON
#1,433
6-8-23
AT 7:31 PM

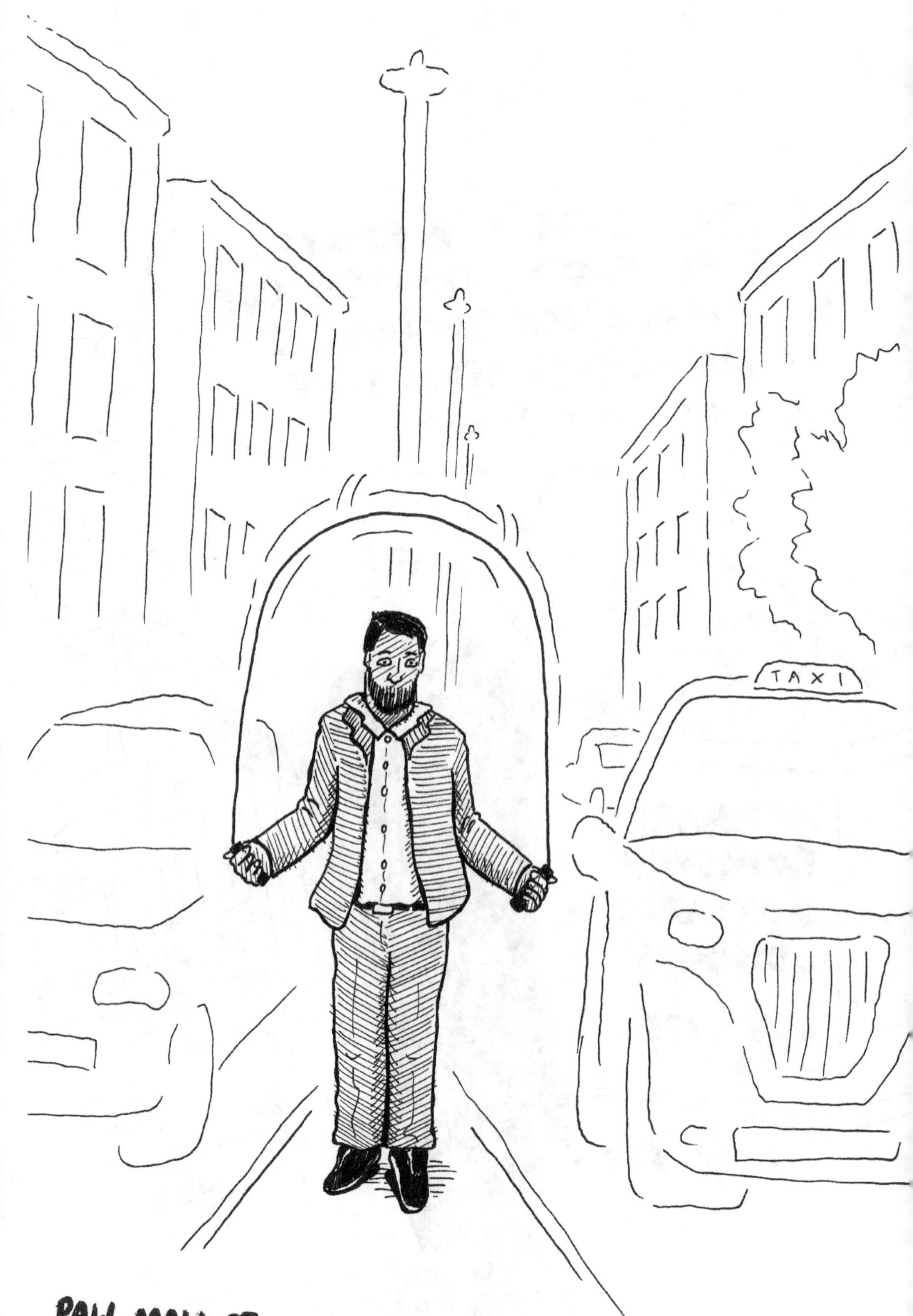

PALL MALL ST.
+ ST. JAMES'S
SQUARE
AT 2:37 PM
LONDON
#1,434 6-9-23

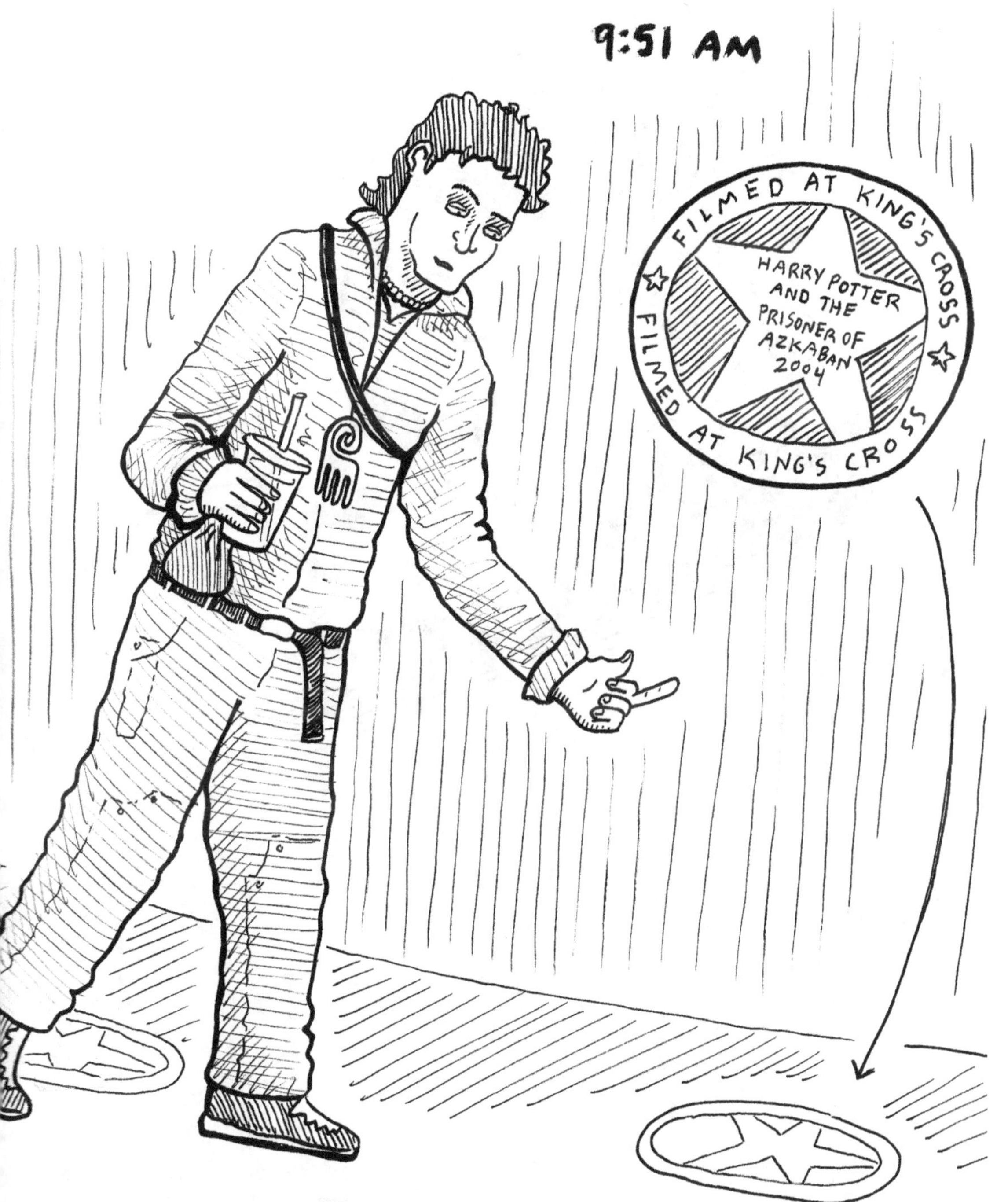

THERE WERE STARS ON THE GROUND NOTING THE MOVIES FILMED AT KING'S CROSS STATION IN LONDON.

THIS GUY FLIPPED THE BIRD TO ALL THE HARRY POTTER STARS.

9:51 AM

FILMED AT KING'S CROSS
FILMED AT KING'S CROSS
HARRY POTTER AND THE PRISONER OF AZKABAN 2004

JS #1,435 6-9-23

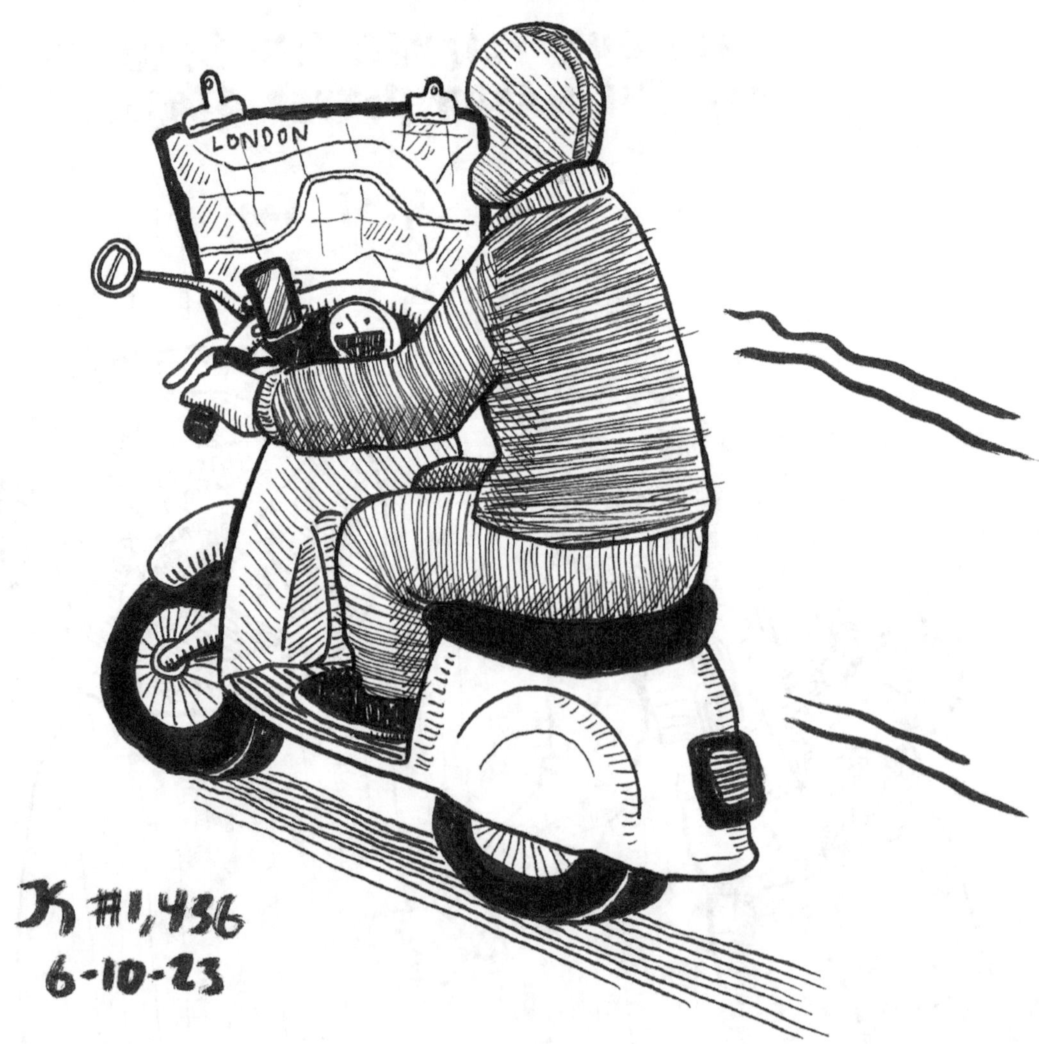

JK #1,436
6-10-23

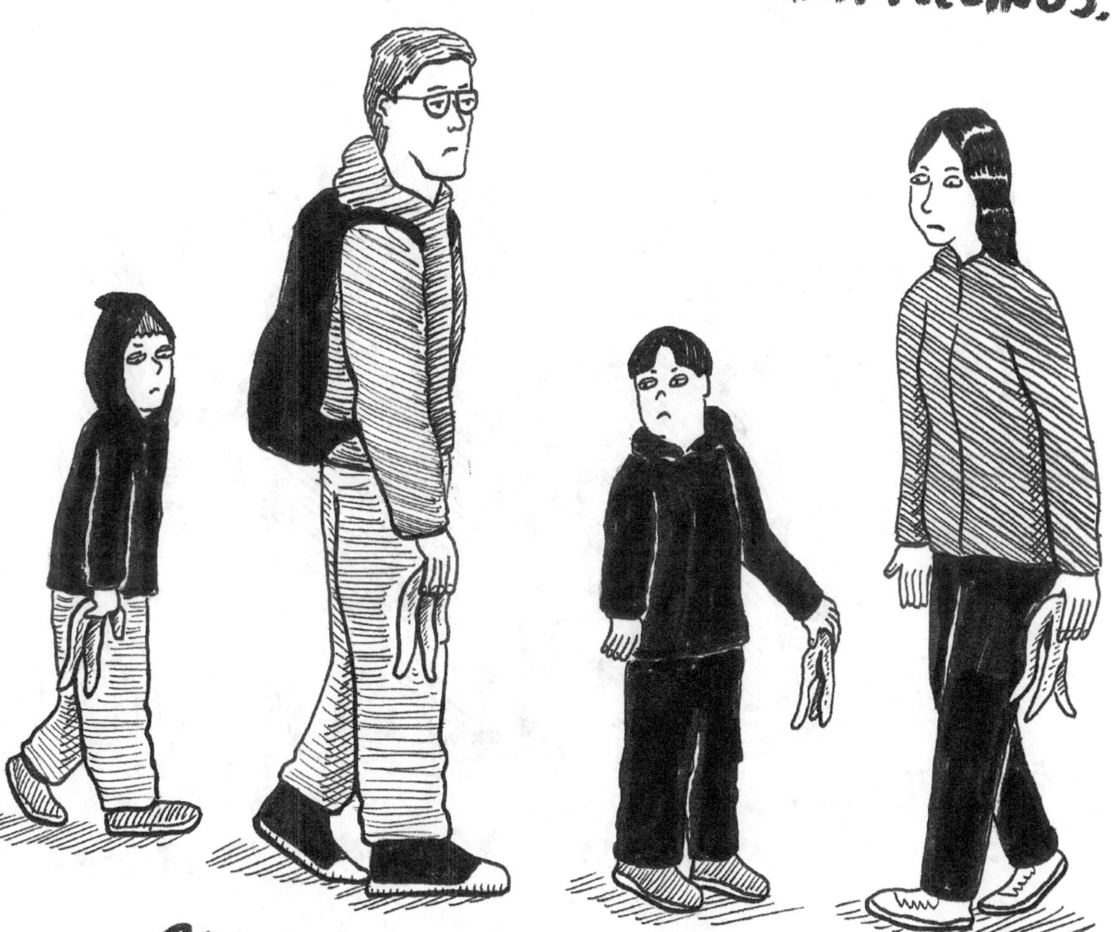
BAD FEELINGS
'BOUT BANANA PEELINGS.

BAYSWATER RD. +
WESTBOURNE ST.
HYDE PARK LONDON

JS #1,437 6-10-23
11:03AM

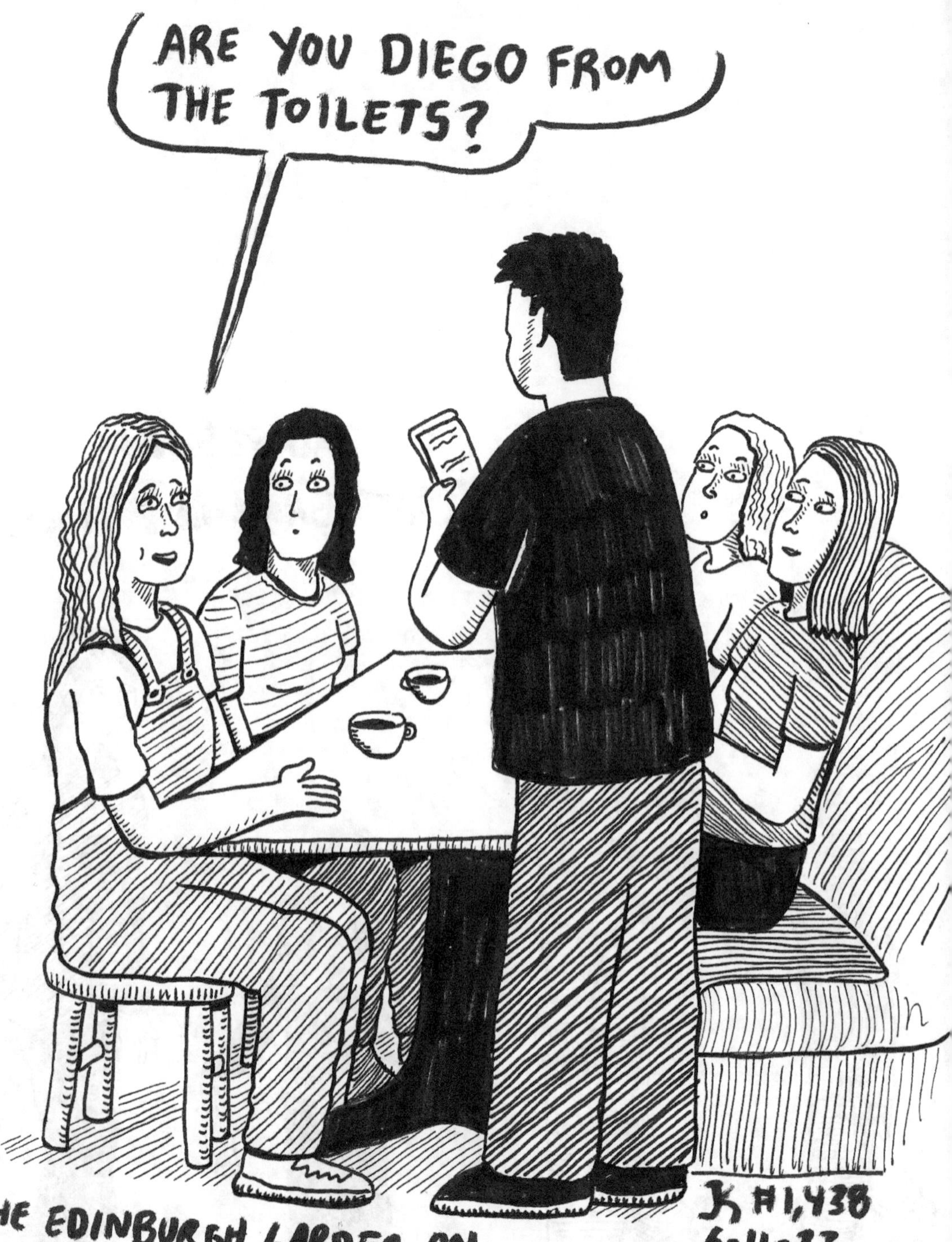

ARE YOU DIEGO FROM THE TOILETS?
THE EDINBURGH LARDER ON HIGH ST. + BLACKFRIAR ST.   SCOTLAND
#1,438
6-11-23
AT 12:30 PM

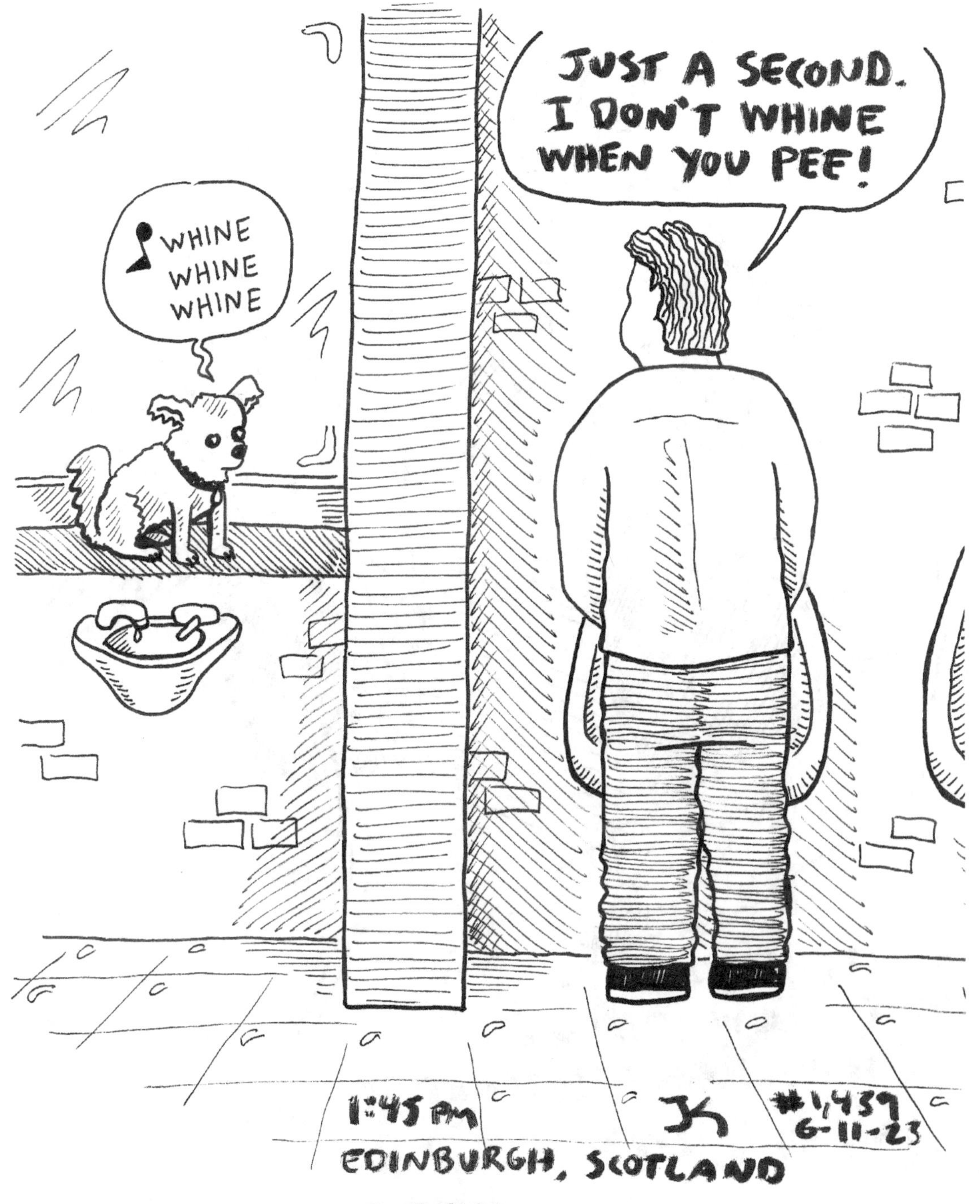

JUST A SECOND. I DON'T WHINE WHEN YOU PEE!
WHINE WHINE WHINE
1:45 PM
EDINBURGH, SCOTLAND
THE RED COCKEREL CAFE ON PRINCES ST.
#1,437
6-11-23

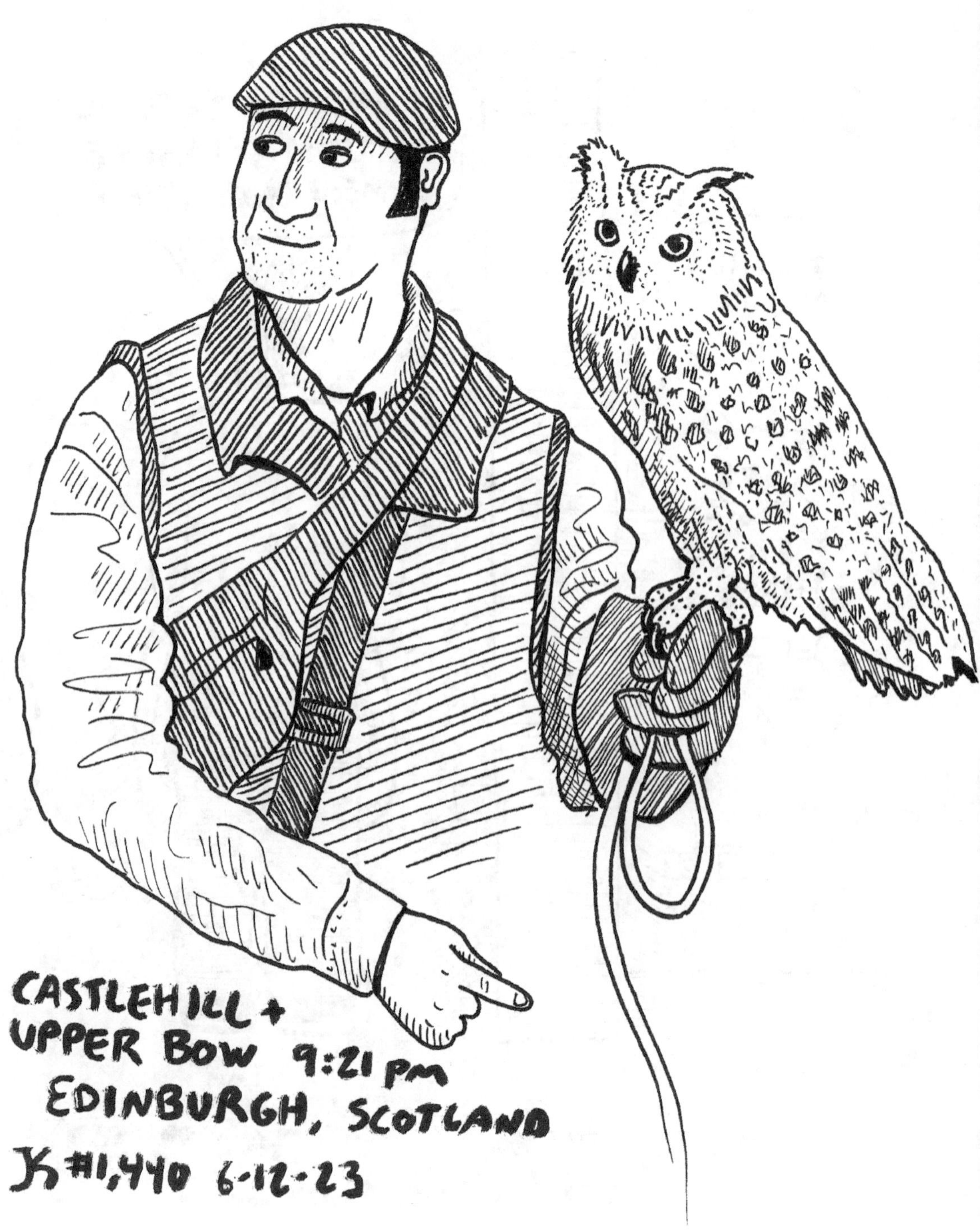

CASTLEHILL +
UPPER BOW 9:21 PM
EDINBURGH, SCOTLAND
JS #1,440 6-12-23

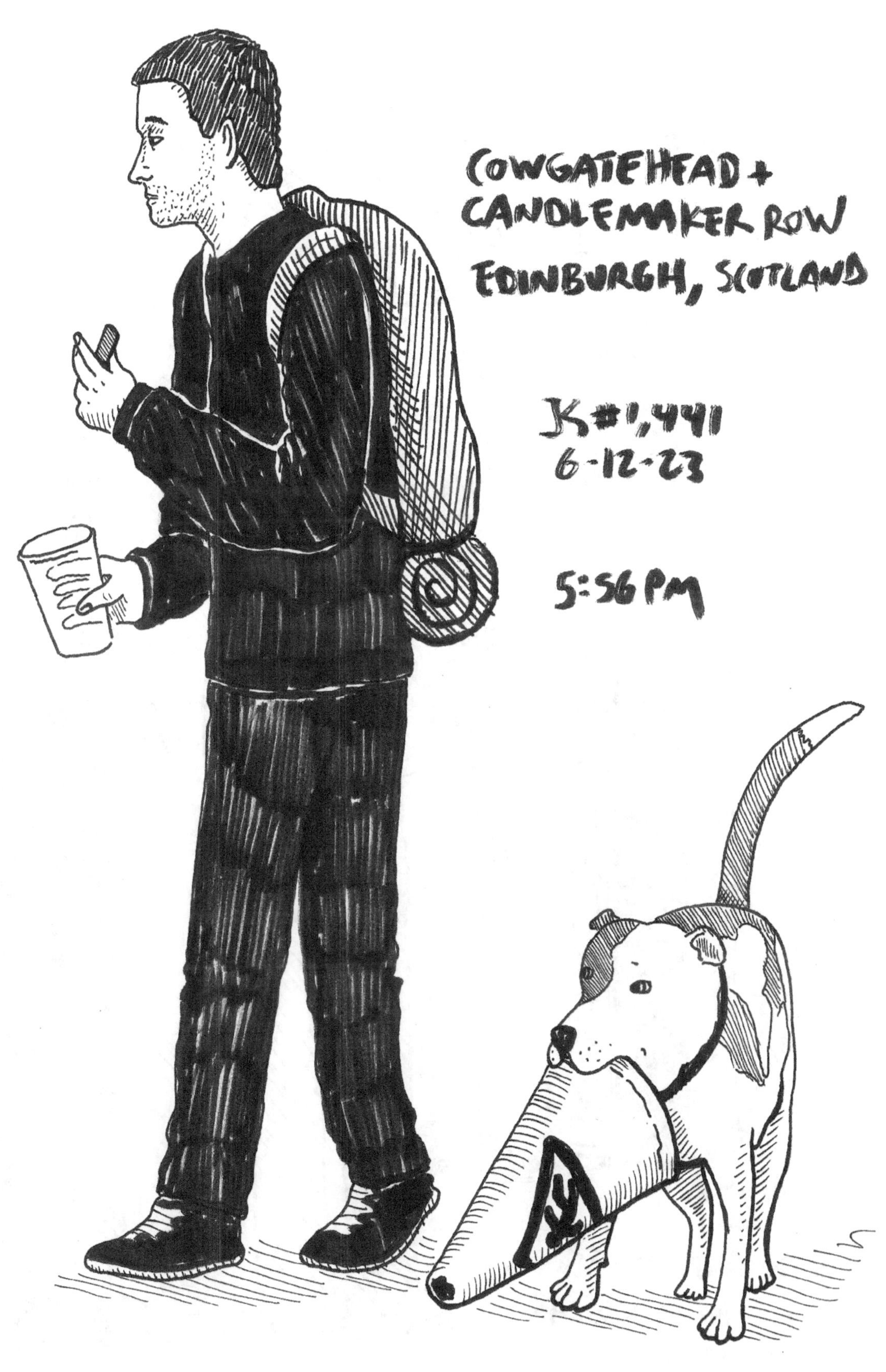

COWGATEHEAD +
CANDLEMAKER ROW
EDINBURGH, SCOTLAND

JK #1,441
6-12-23

5:56 PM

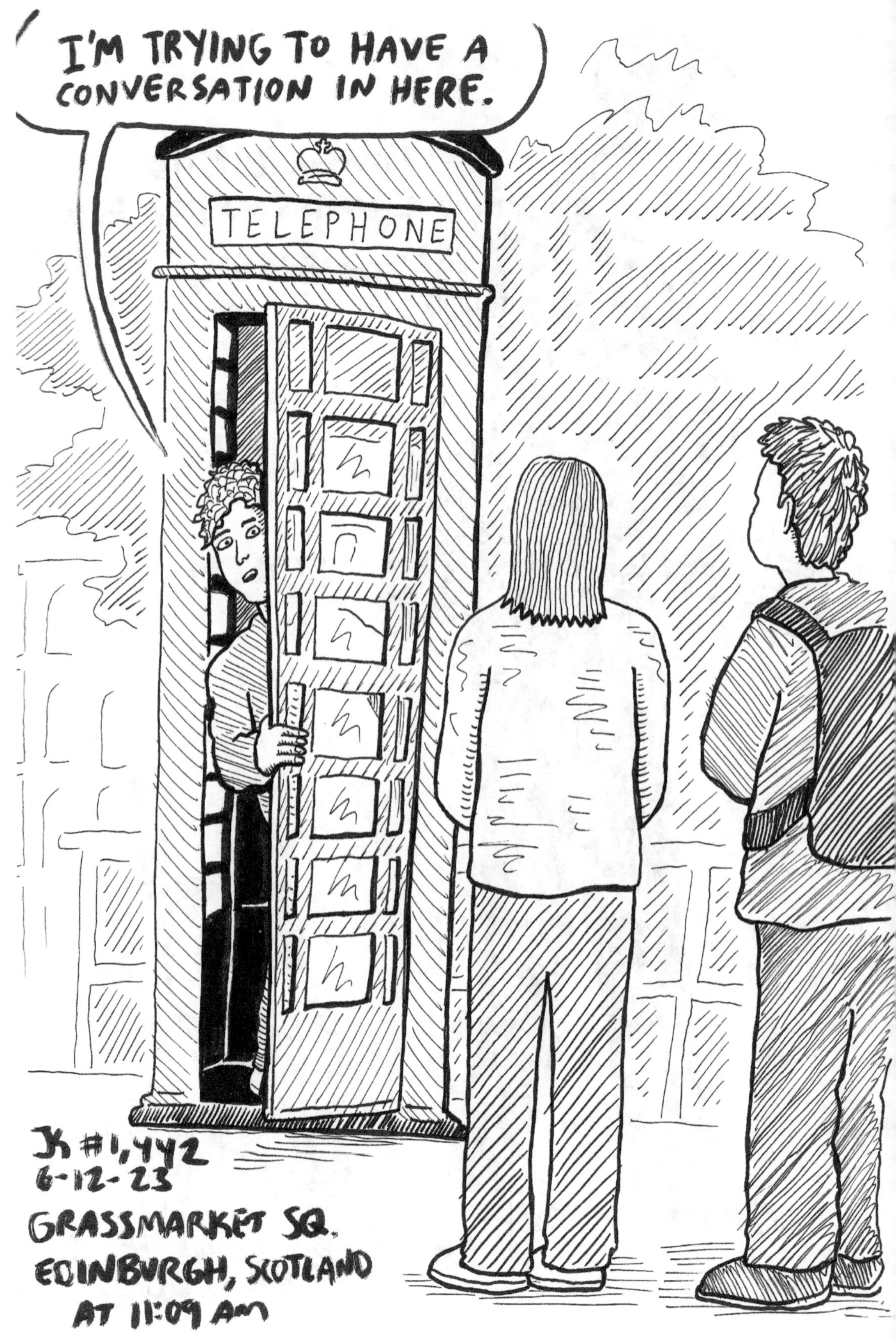

I'M TRYING TO HAVE A CONVERSATION IN HERE.
TELEPHONE
JK #1,442
6-12-23
GRASSMARKET SQ.
EDINBURGH, SCOTLAND
AT 11:09 AM

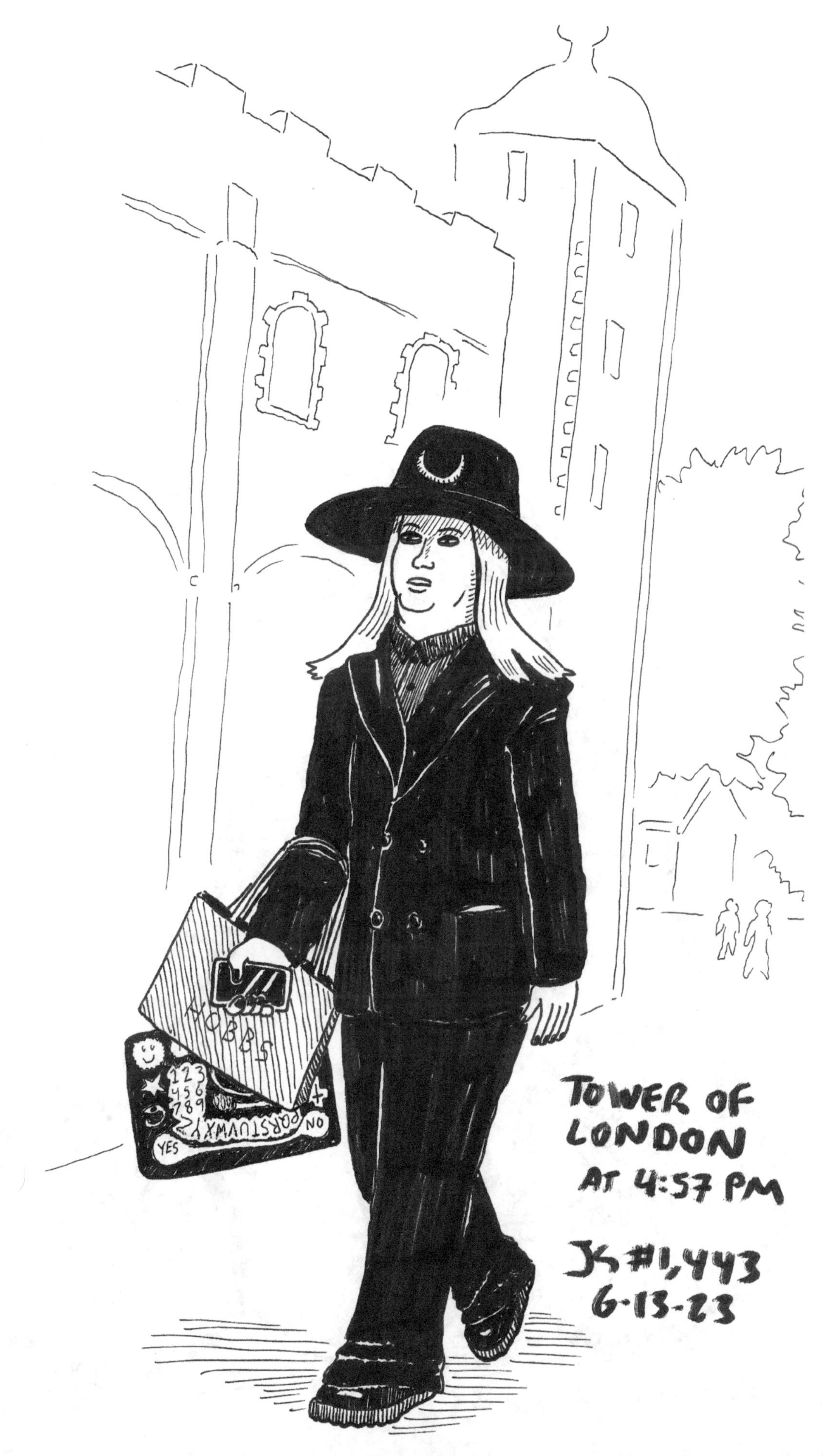

HOBBS
123
456
789
PQRSTUVWXYZ
NO
YES
TOWER OF
LONDON
AT 4:57 PM
JS #1,443
6-13-23

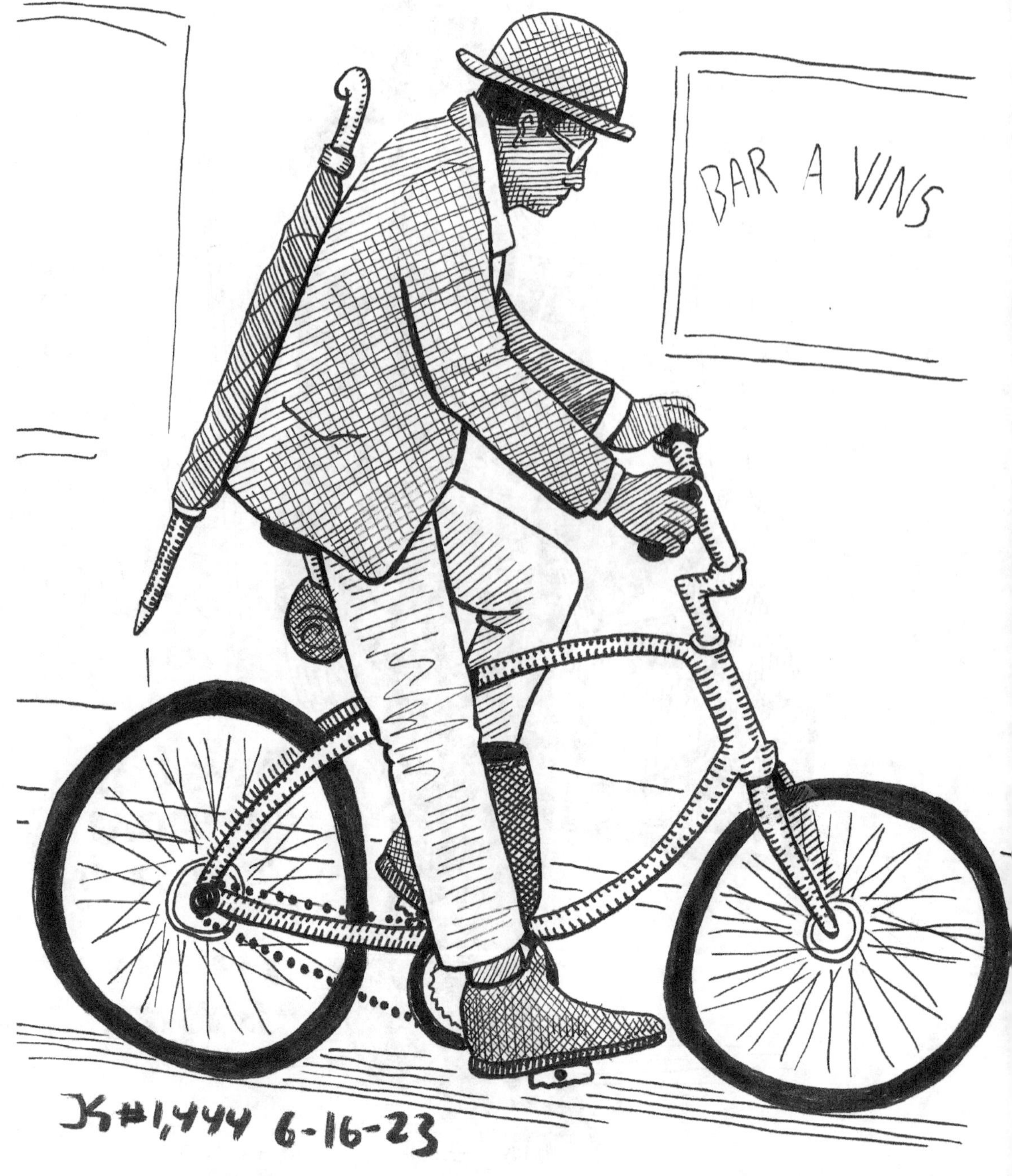

PORTOBELLO RD. LONDON AT 2:37 PM
BAR A VINS
JG #1,444 6-16-23

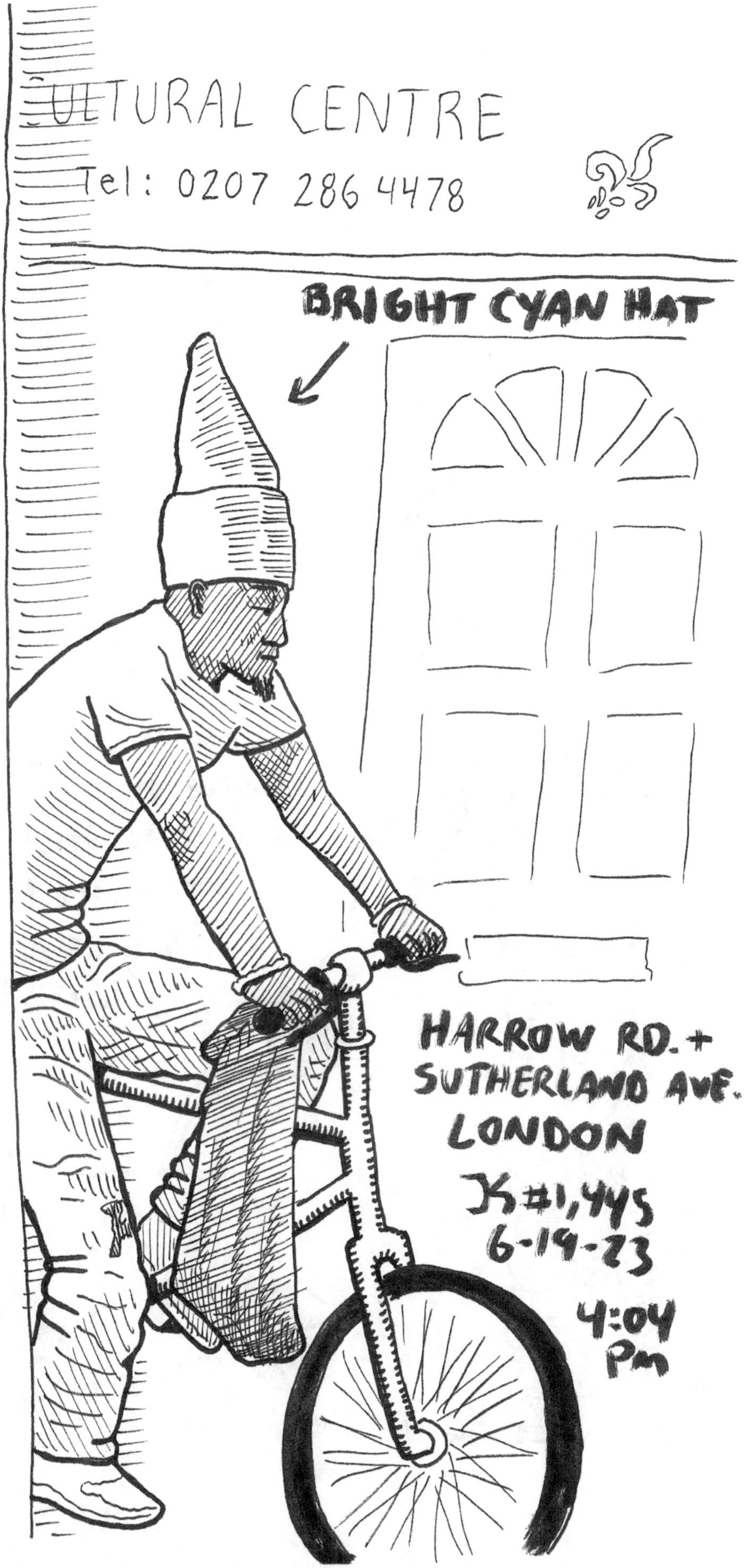

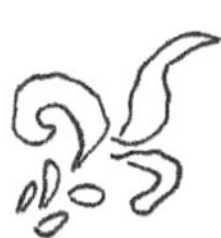

ULTURAL CENTRE
Tel: 0207 286 4478

BRIGHT CYAN HAT

HARROW RD. +
SUTHERLAND AVE.
LONDON
JS #1,445
6-19-23

4:04
PM

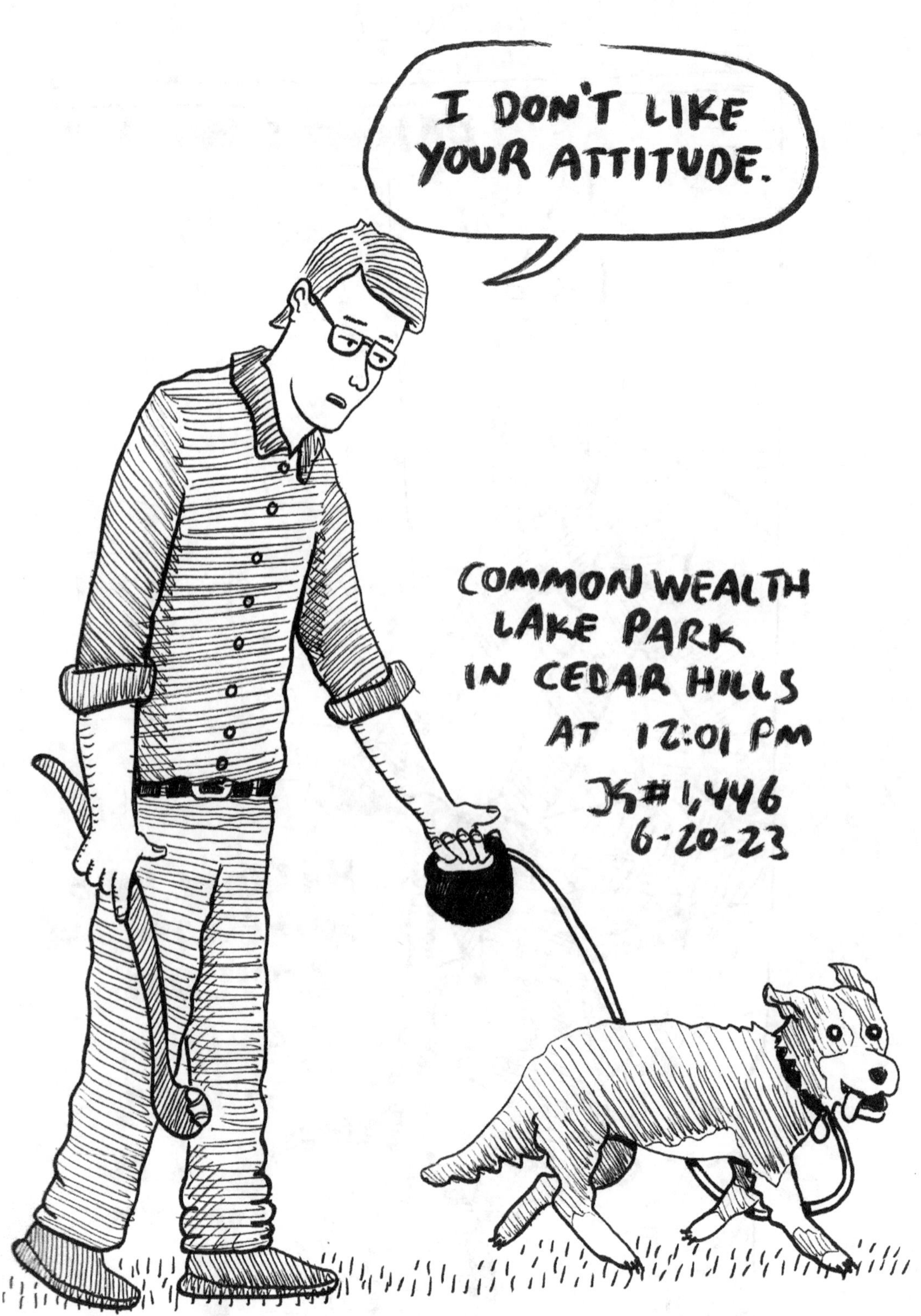

I DON'T LIKE YOUR ATTITUDE.
COMMONWEALTH LAKE PARK IN CEDAR HILLS AT 12:01 PM
JS #1,446
6-20-23

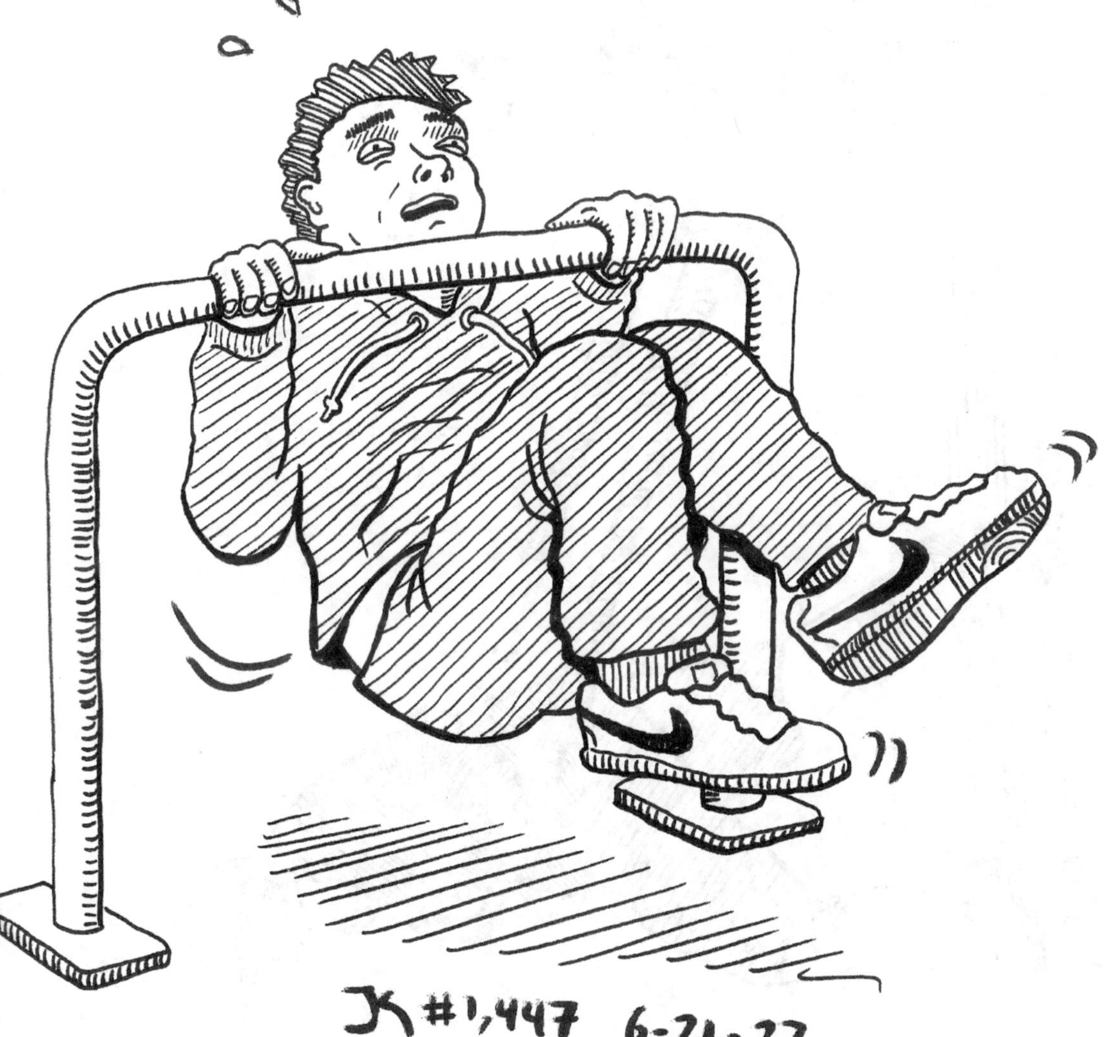

JK #1,447 6-21-23
SW 11TH AVE. + MORRISON ST.
AT 10:30 AM

JK #1,448 6-22-23 SW 21ST. AVE. + W. BURNSIDE AT 6:PM

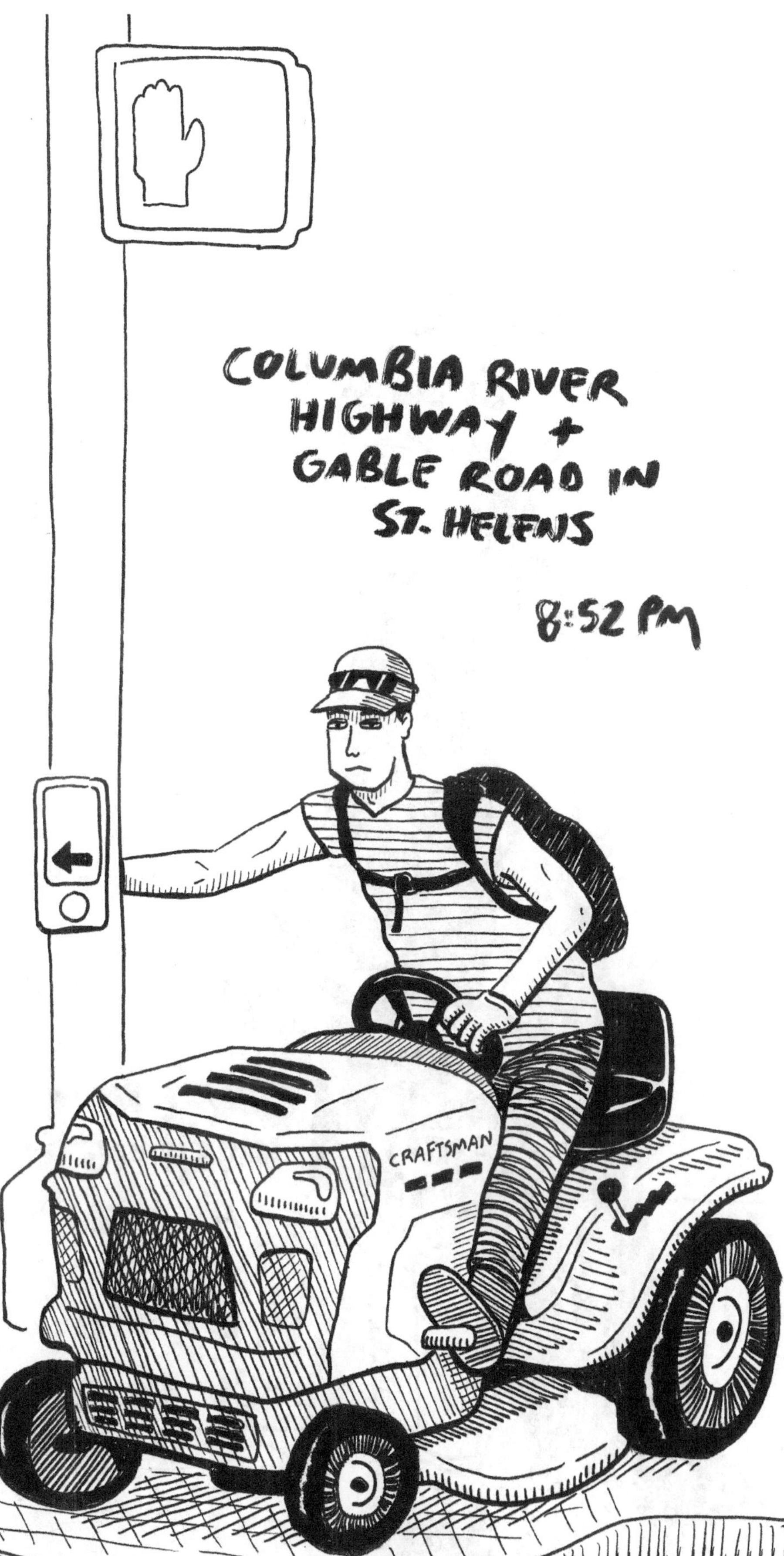

COLUMBIA RIVER
HIGHWAY +
GABLE ROAD IN
ST. HELENS

8:52 PM

CRAFTSMAN

JK #1,449 6-24-23

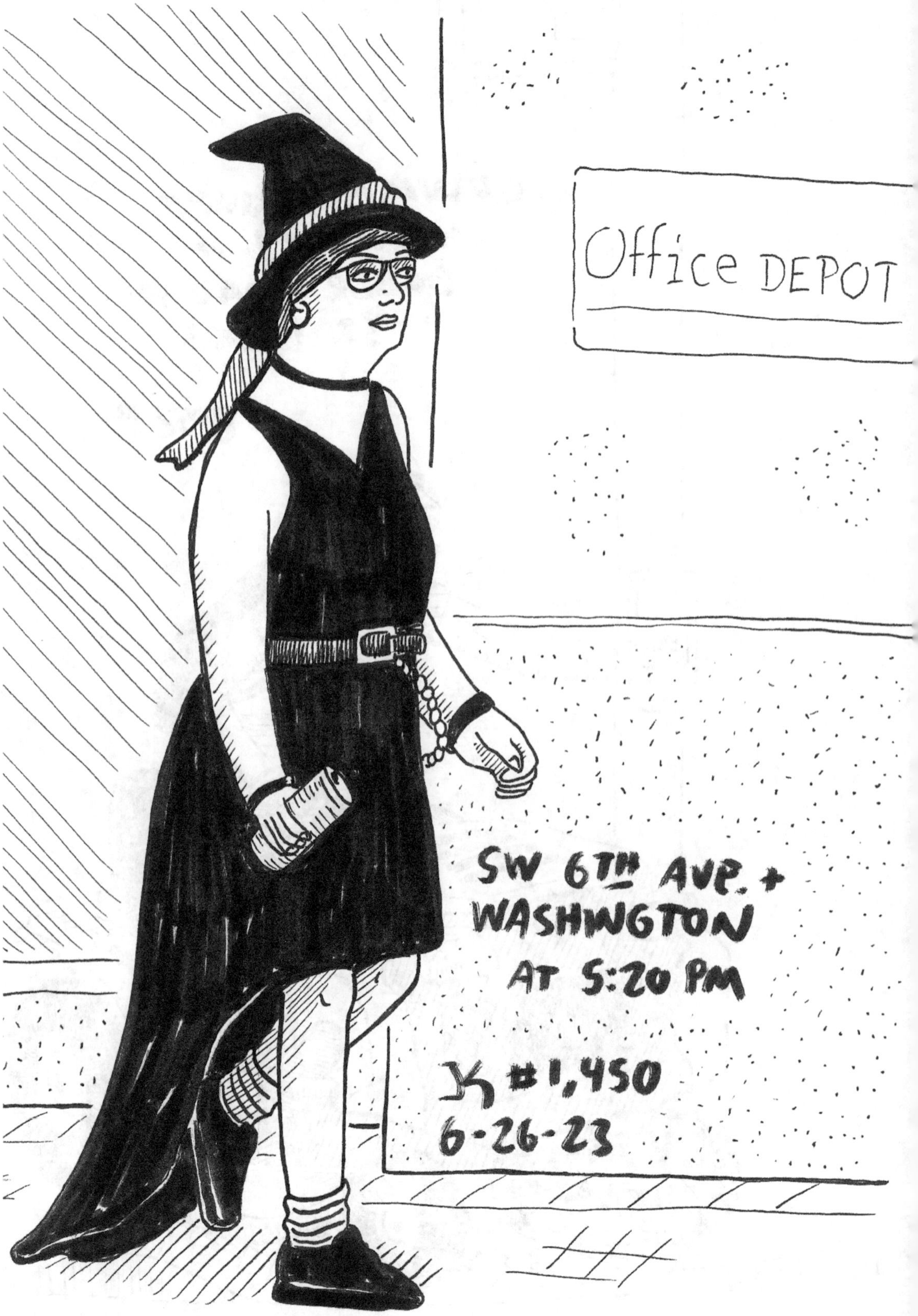

Office DEPOT
SW 6TH AVE. +
WASHINGTON
AT 5:20 PM
#1,450
6-26-23

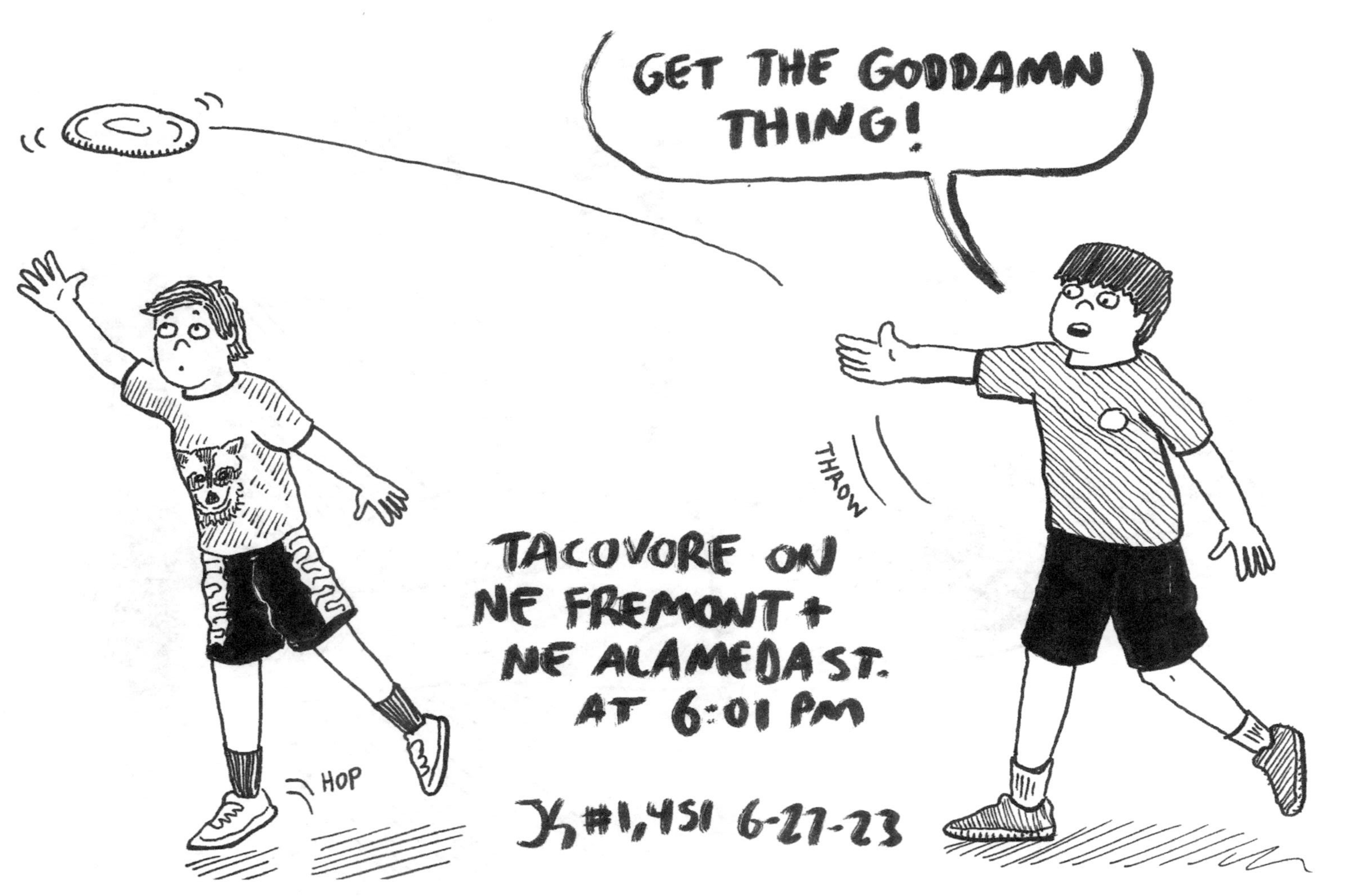

GET THE GODDAMN THING!
THROW
HOP
TACOVORE ON NE FREMONT + NE ALAMEDA ST. AT 6:01 PM
#1,451 6-27-23

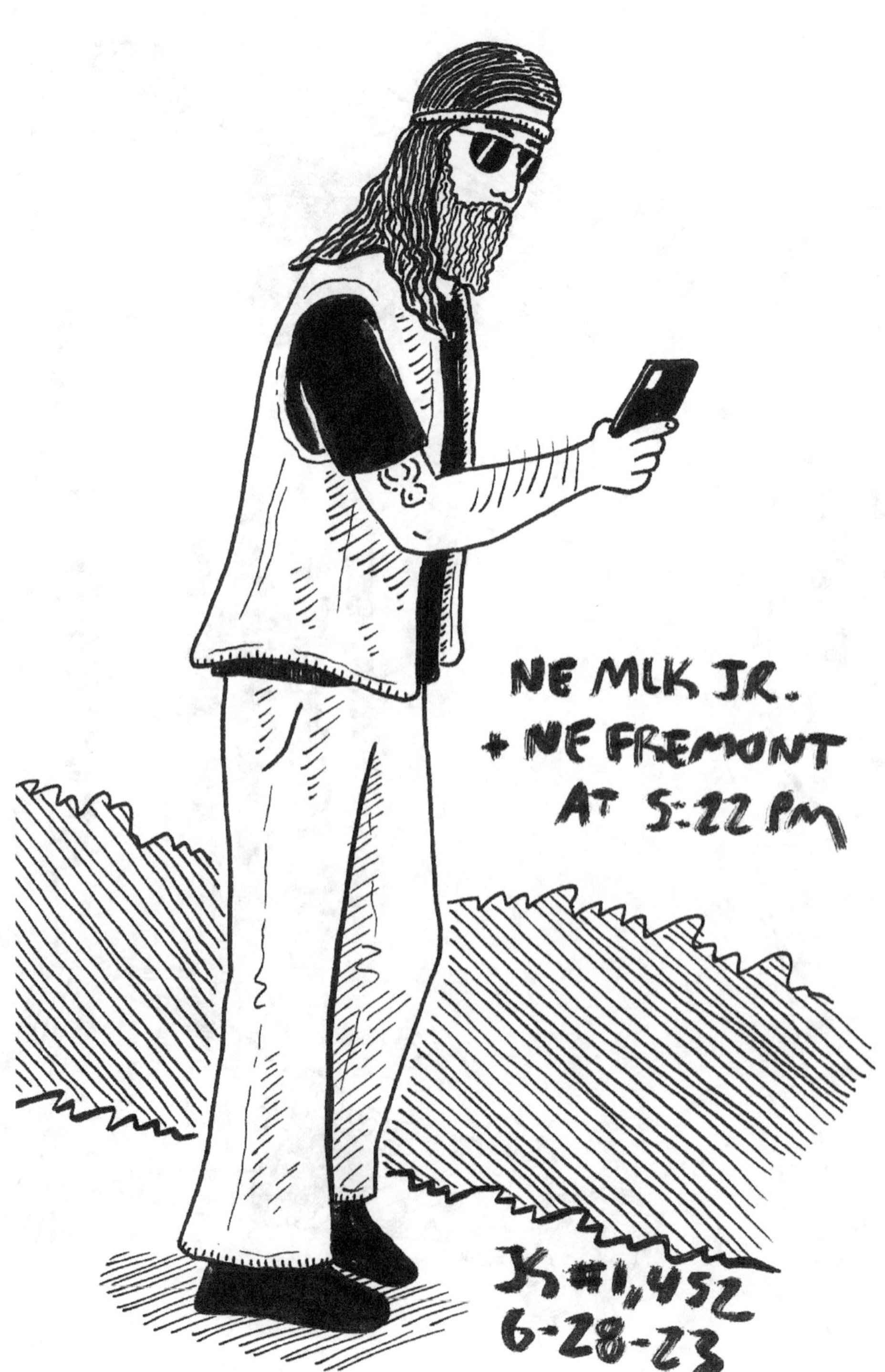

NE MLK JR.
+ NE FREMONT
AT 5:22 PM
JK #1,452
6-28-23

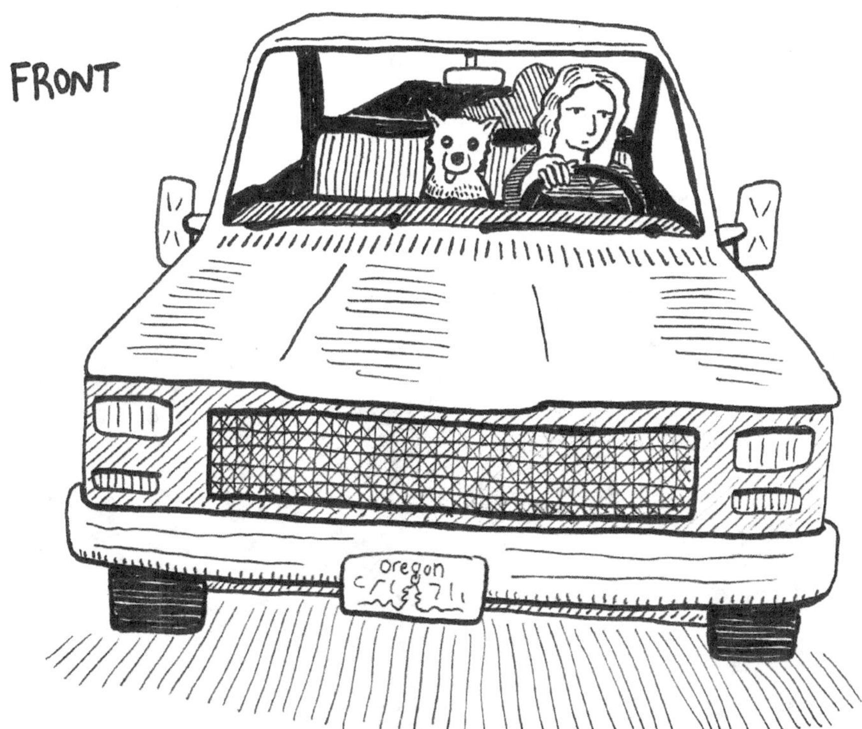

N. LOMBARD + N. WESTANNA AT 2:44 PM
#1,453 6-30-23

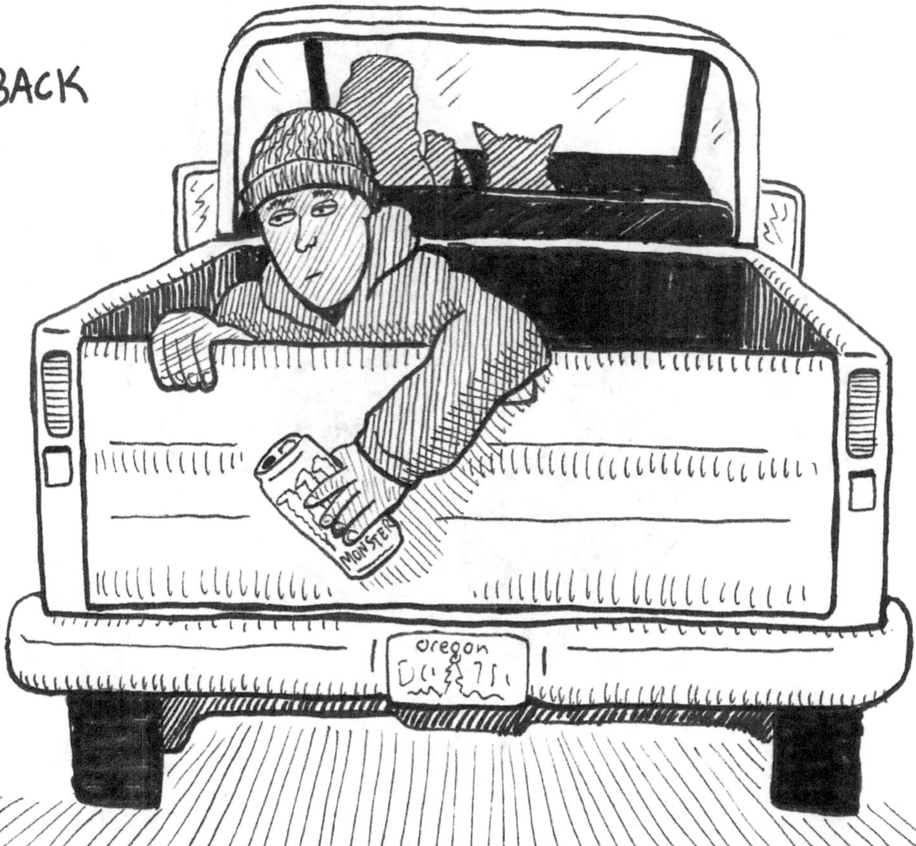

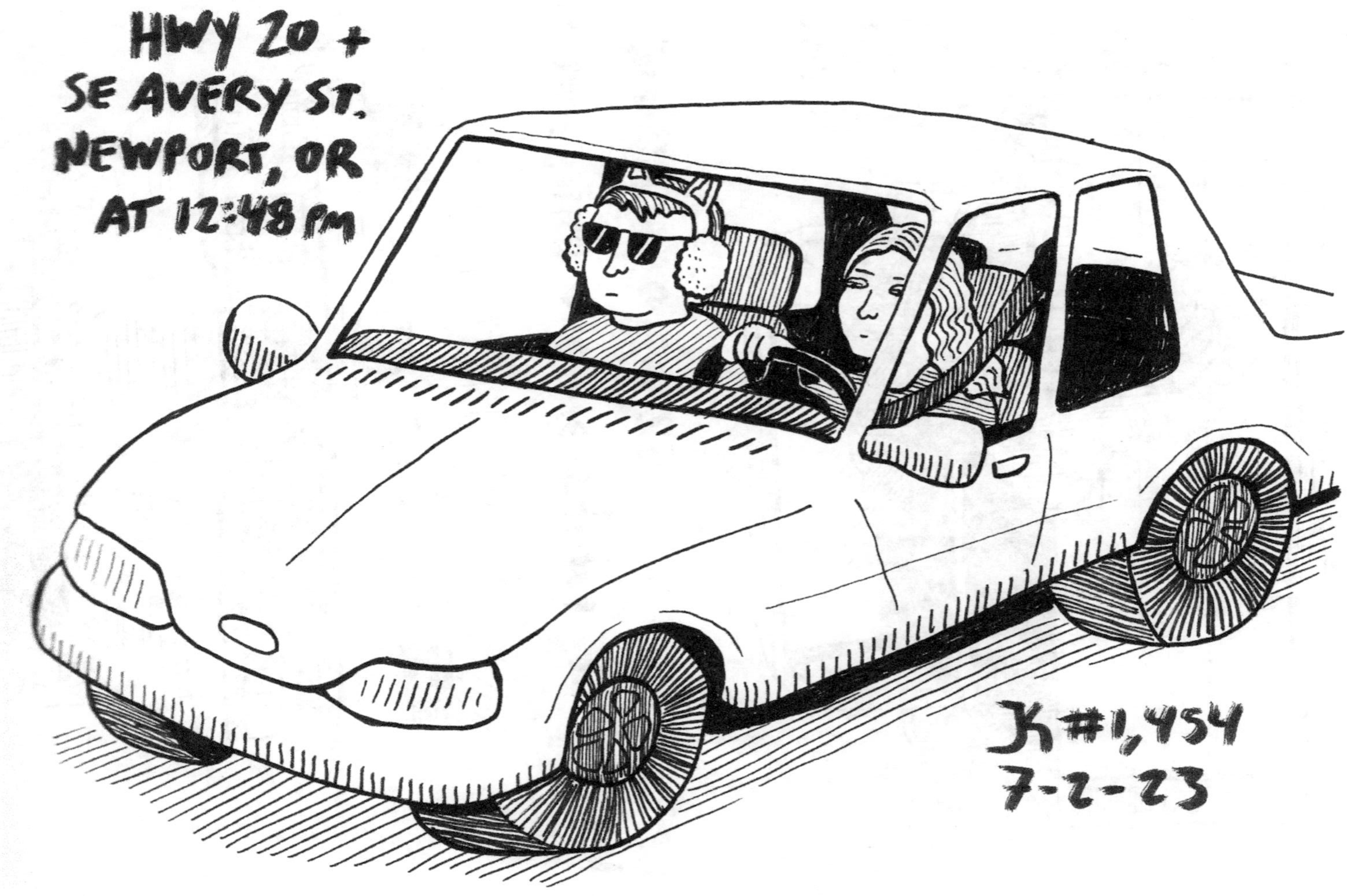

HWY 20 +
SE AVERY ST,
NEWPORT, OR
AT 12:48 PM
JK #1,454
7-2-23

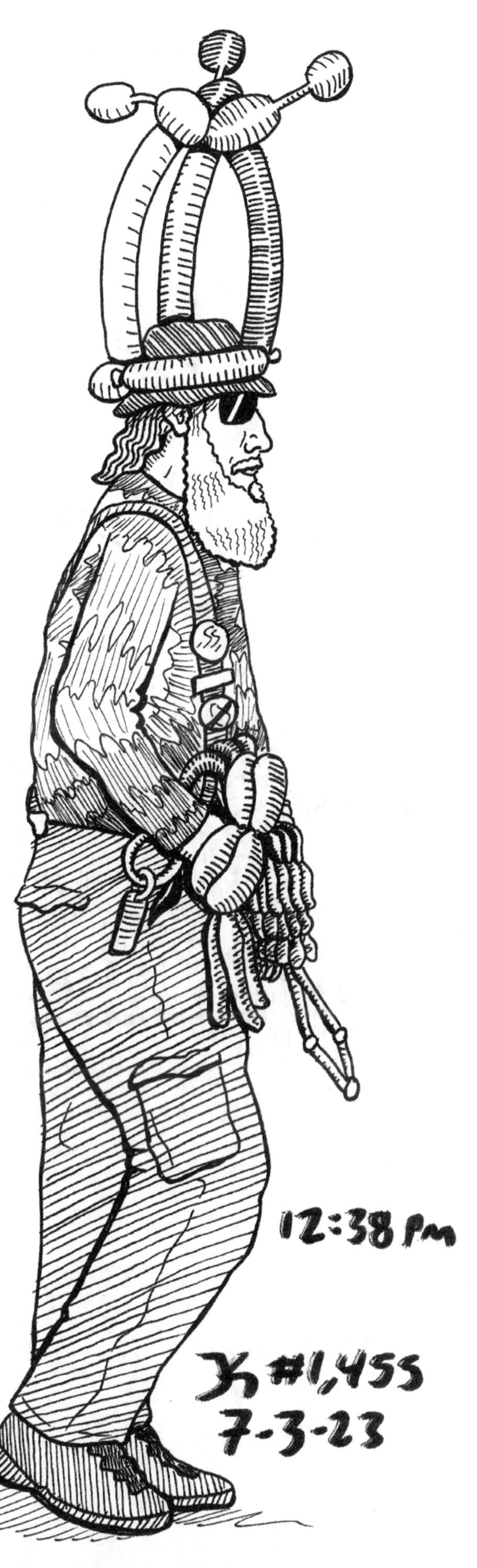

THE
BAYFRONT
IN
NEWPORT,
OREGON
12:38 PM
#1,455
7-3-23

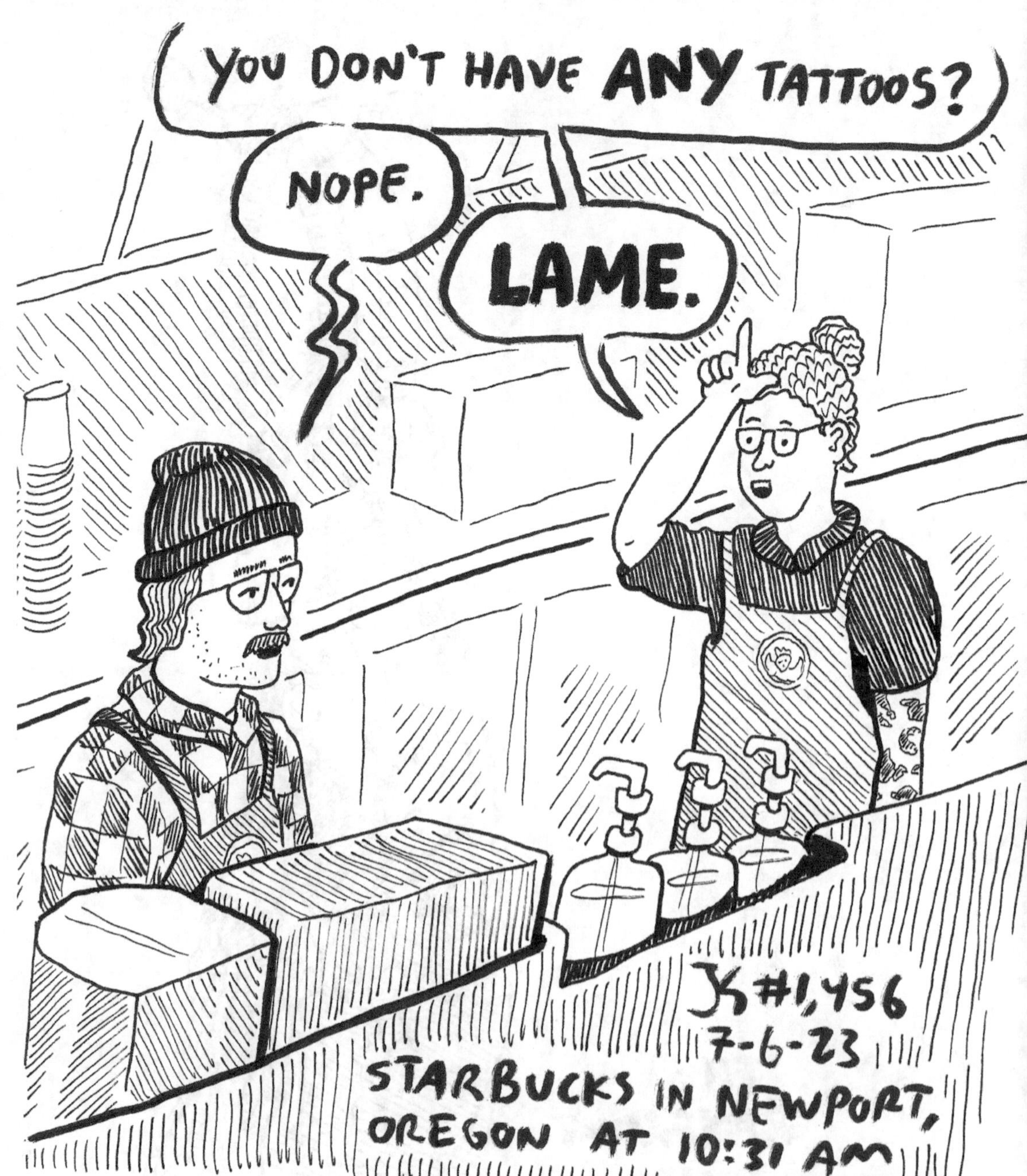

YOU DON'T HAVE ANY TATTOOS?
NOPE.
LAME.
JS #1,456
7-6-23
STARBUCKS IN NEWPORT,
OREGON AT 10:31 AM

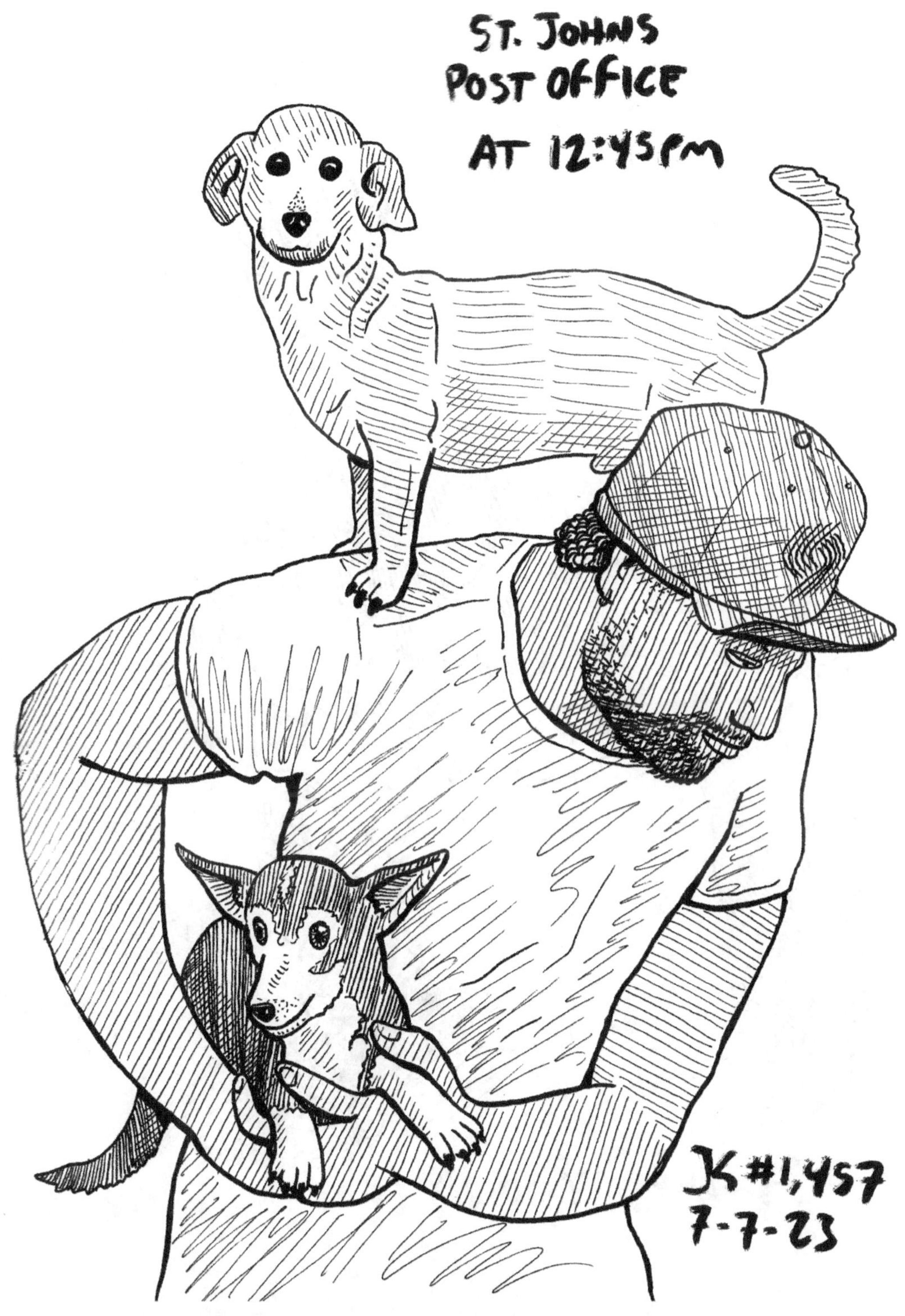

ST. JOHNS
POST OFFICE
AT 12:45 PM
JG #1,457
7-7-23

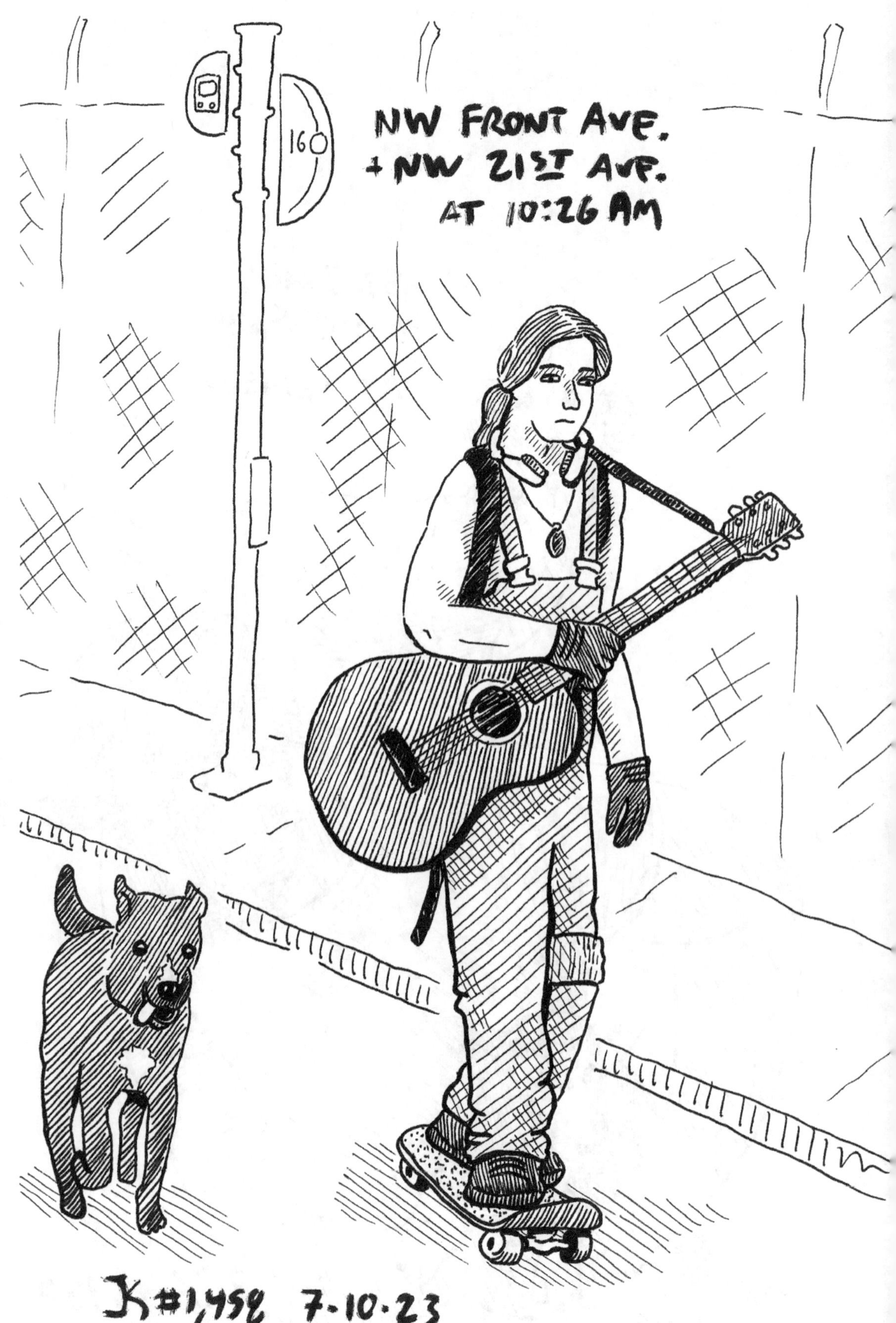

16
NW FRONT AVE.
+ NW 21ST AVE.
AT 10:26 AM
K #1,458 7-10-23

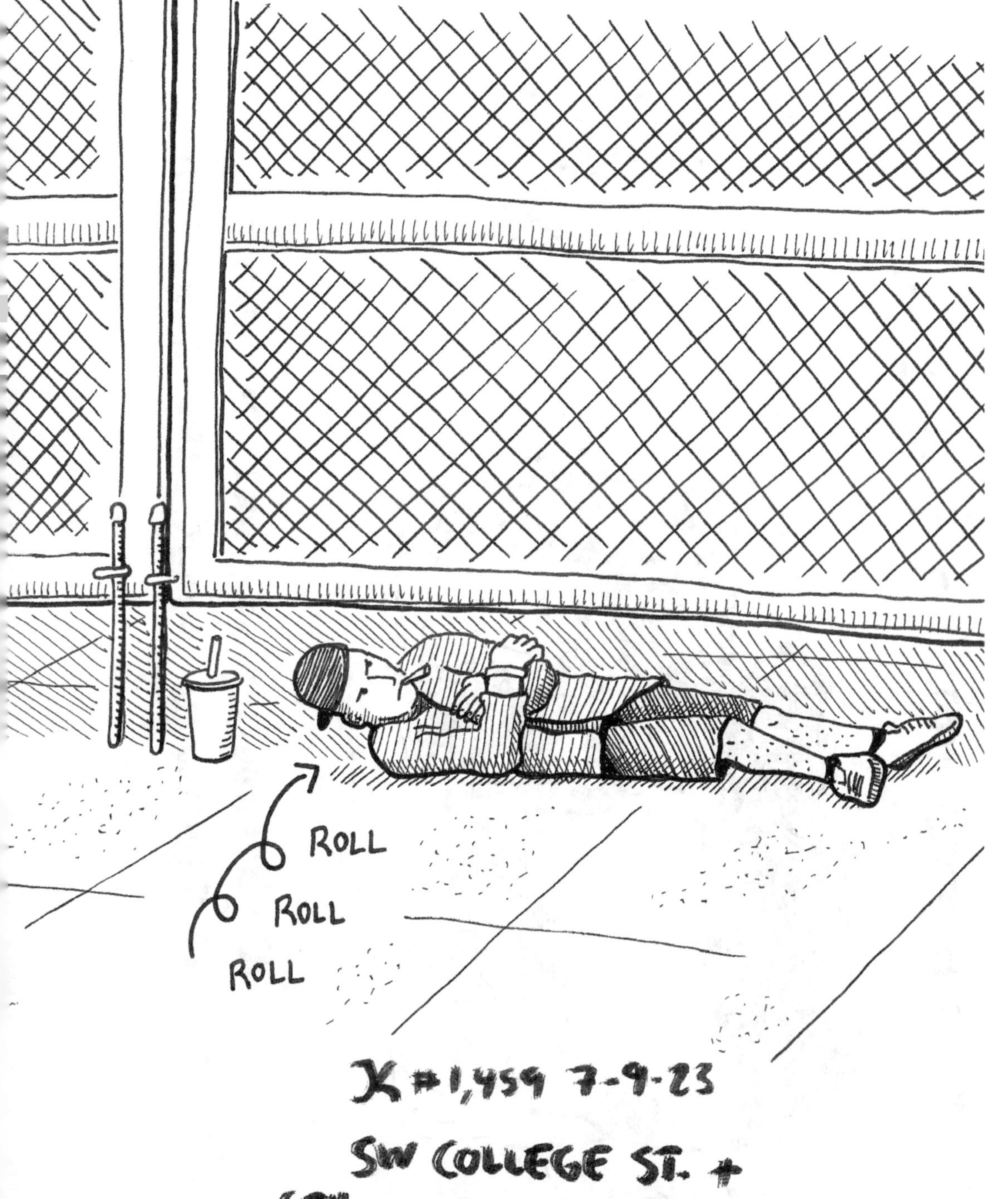

ROLL
ROLL
ROLL
X #1,459 7-9-23
SW COLLEGE ST. &
6TH AVE. AT 3:08 PM
NOTE: GATE WAS UNLOCKED.
ABOUT A MINUTE LATER
SOMEONE OPENED IT
AND WALKED THROUGH.

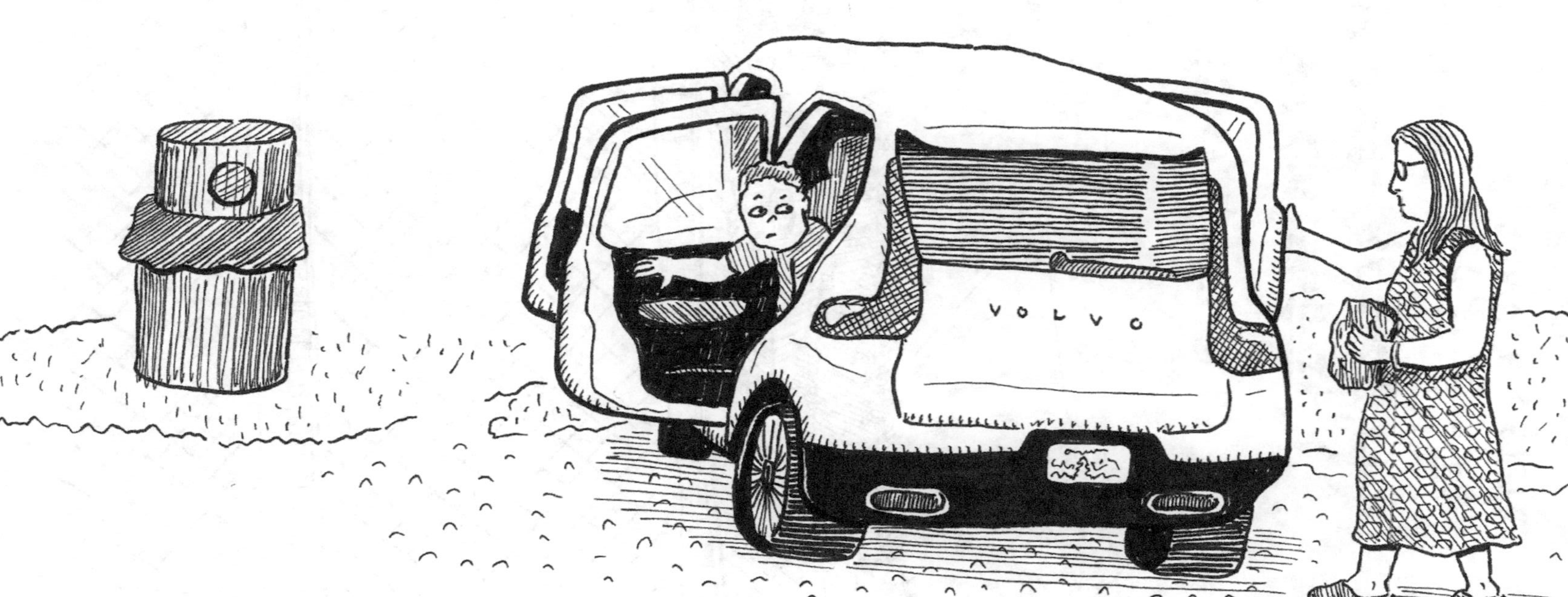

THIS LADY TOOK SEVEN ARMLOADS OF GARBAGE FROM HER CAR TO THE PARK GARBAGE CAN.

JK #1,460 7-10-23 CATHEDRAL PARK IN ST. JOHNS 4:05PM

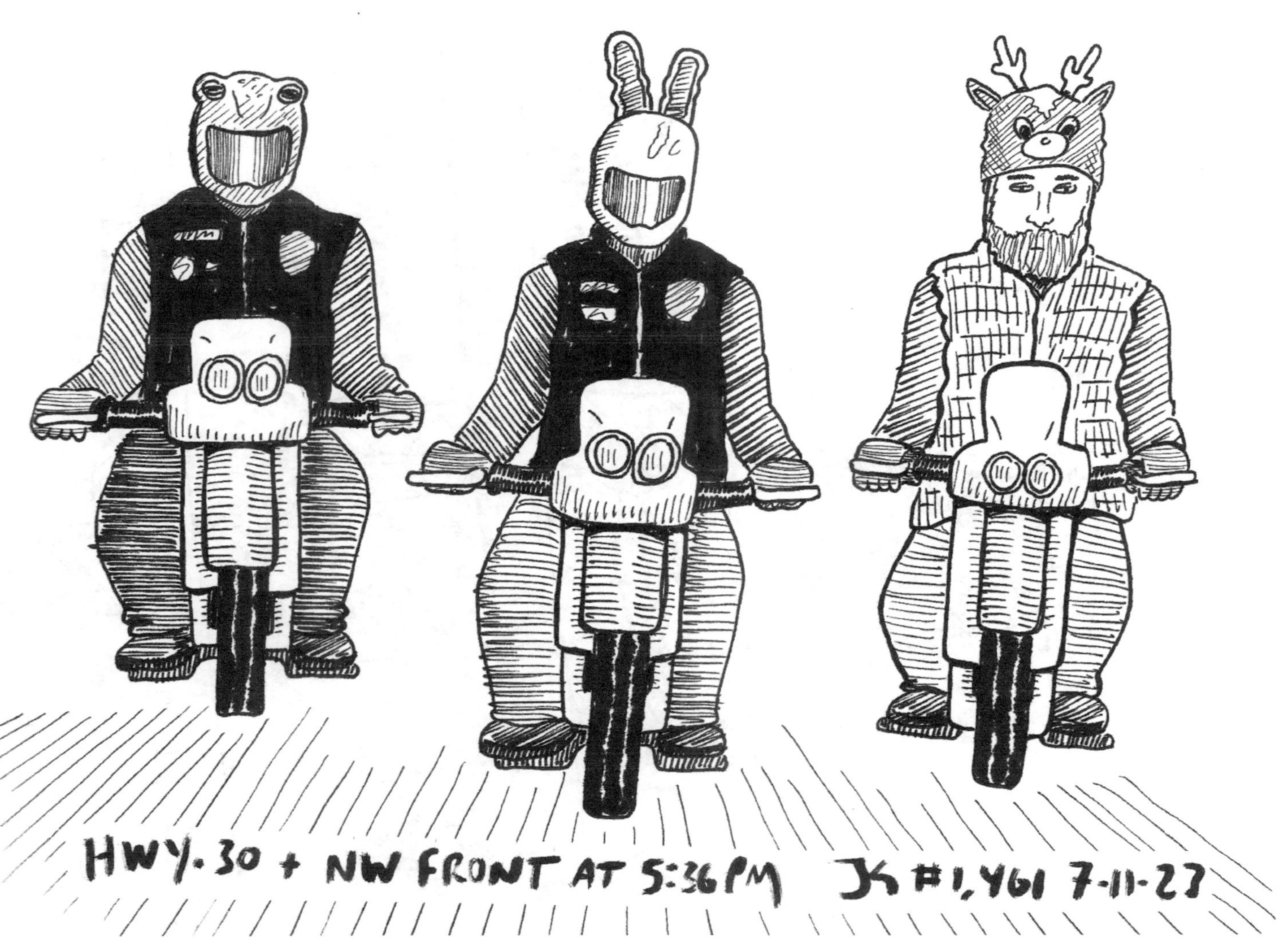

HWY. 30 + NW FRONT AT 5:36 PM   JS #1,461 7-11-27

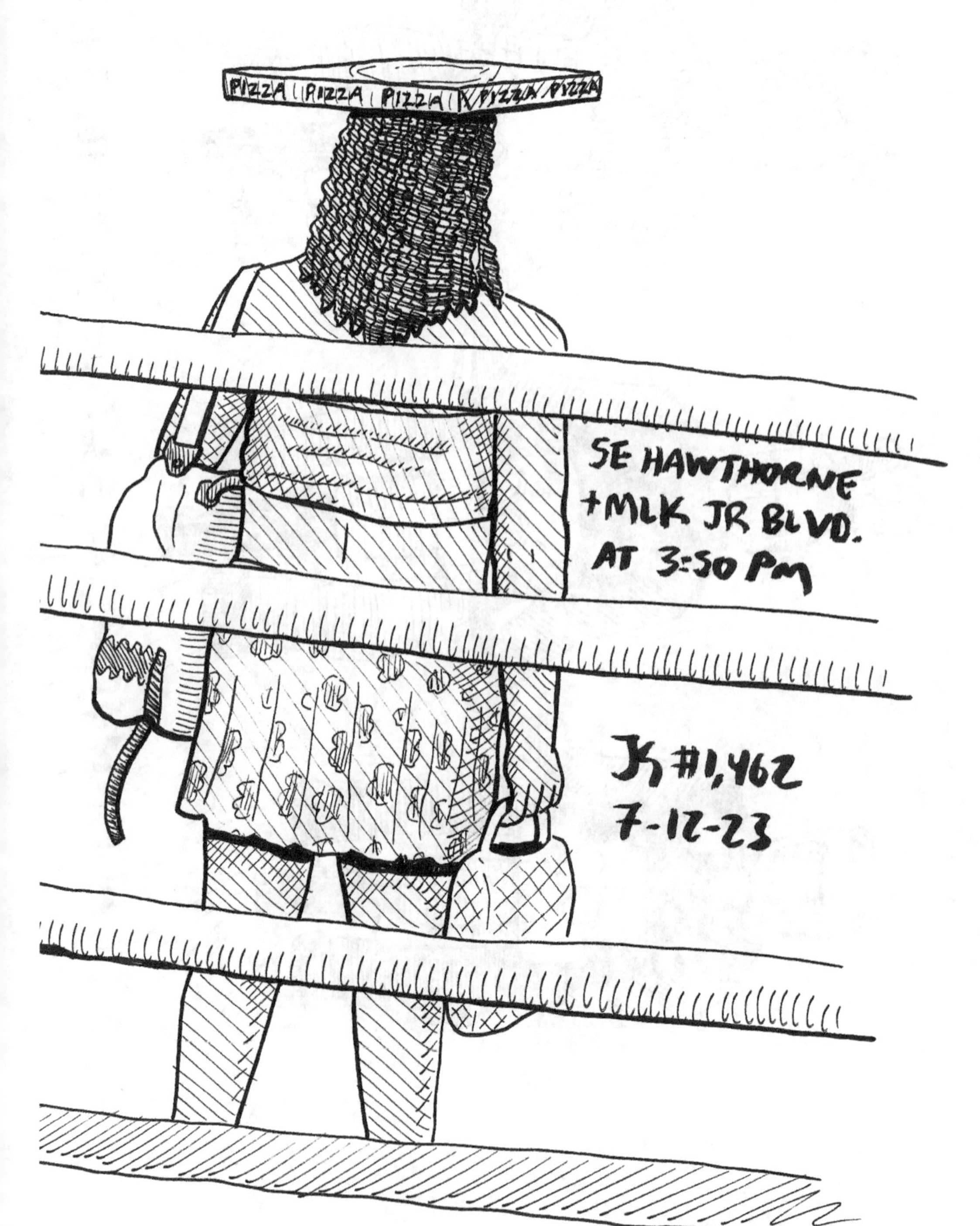

PIZZA | PIZZA | PIZZA | PIZZA | PIZZA
SE HAWTHORNE
+ MLK JR BLVD.
AT 3:50 PM
JK #1,462
7-12-23

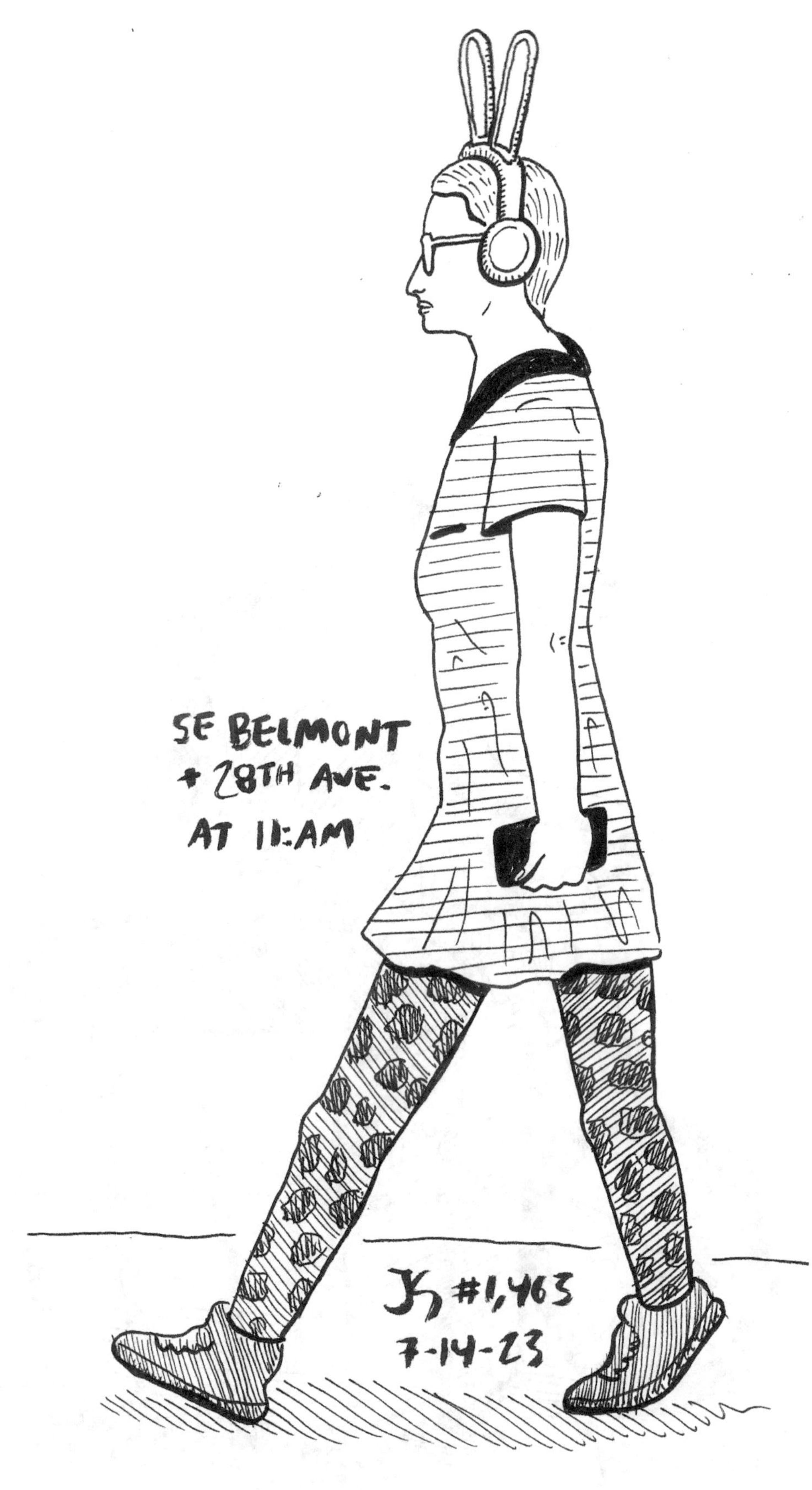

SE BELMONT
+ 28TH AVE.
AT 11:AM

#1,463
7-14-23

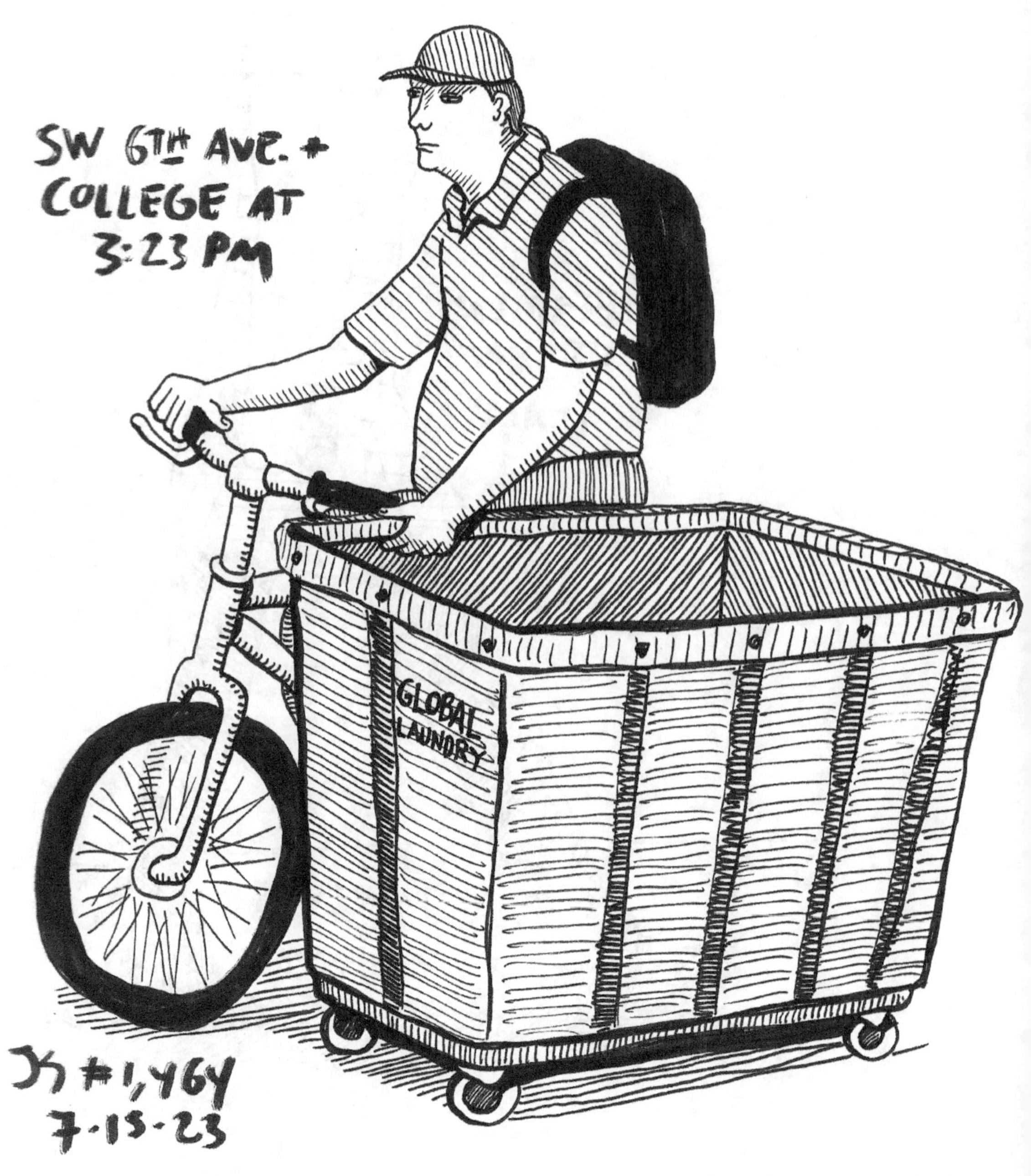

SW 6TH AVE. +
COLLEGE AT
3:23 PM
GLOBAL
LAUNDRY
JS #1,464
7-15-23

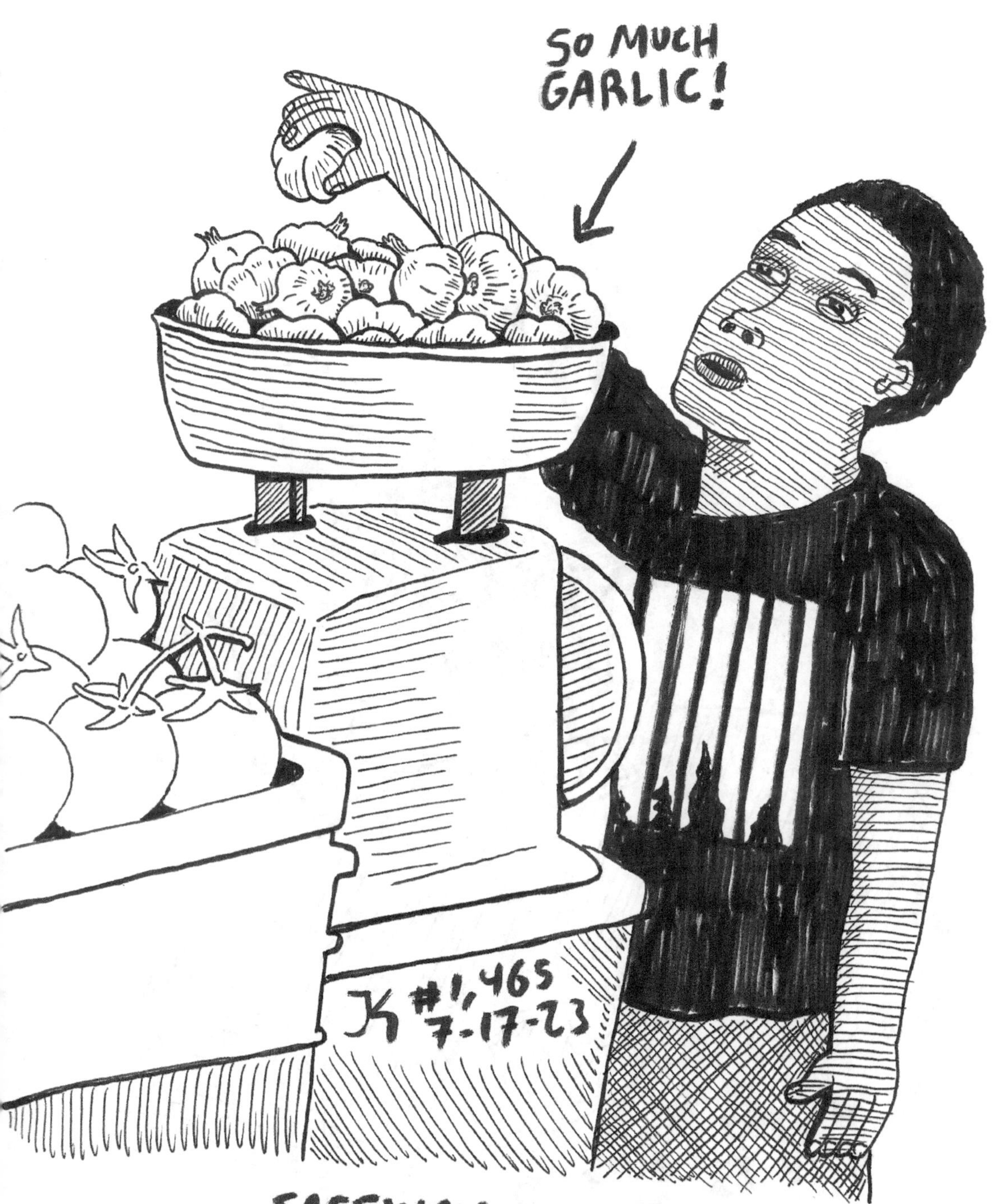
SO MUCH
GARLIC!
JS #1,465
7-17-23
SAFEWAY IN ST. JOHNS
AT 4:31 PM

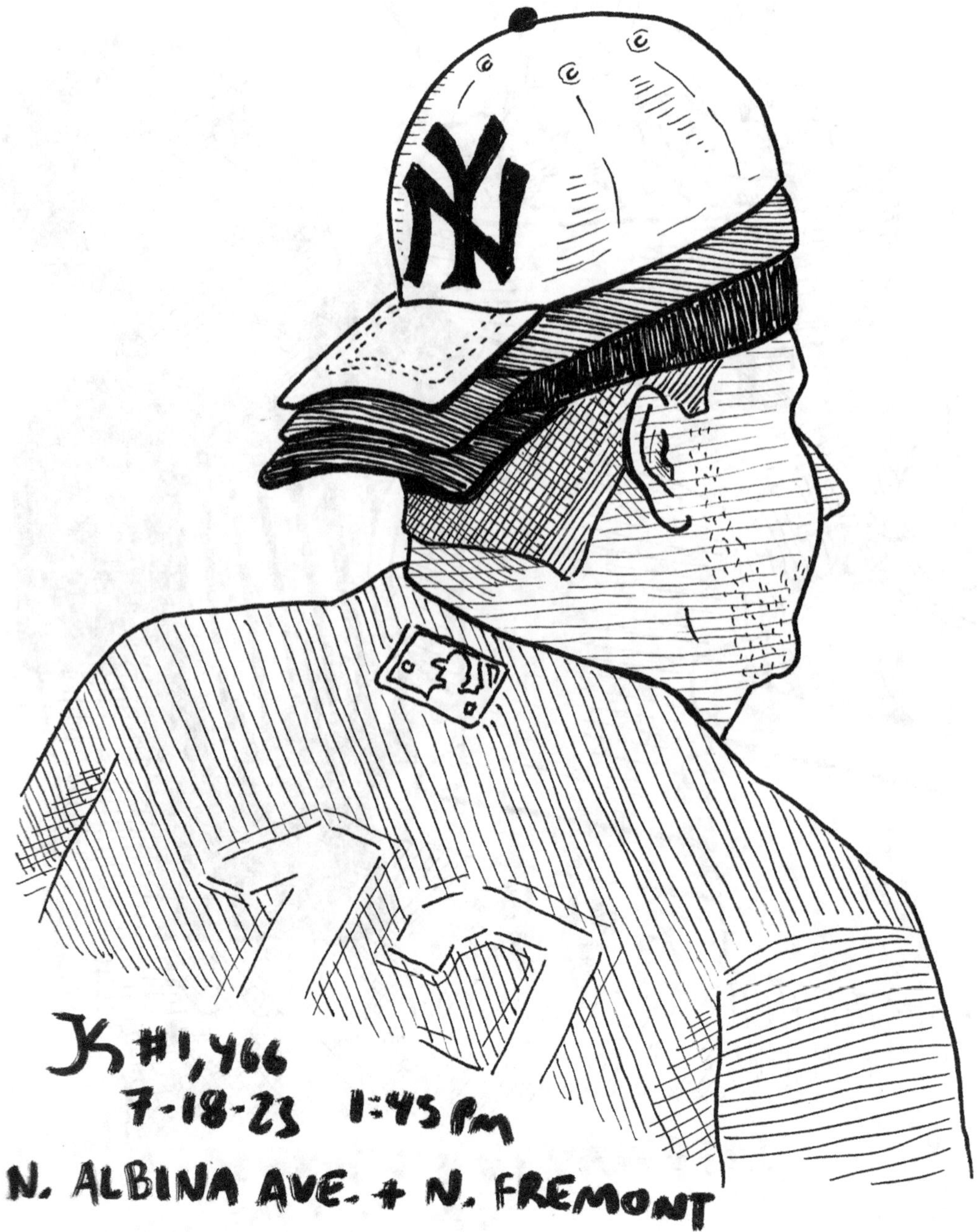

JK #1,466
7-18-23   1:45 PM
N. ALBINA AVE. + N. FREMONT

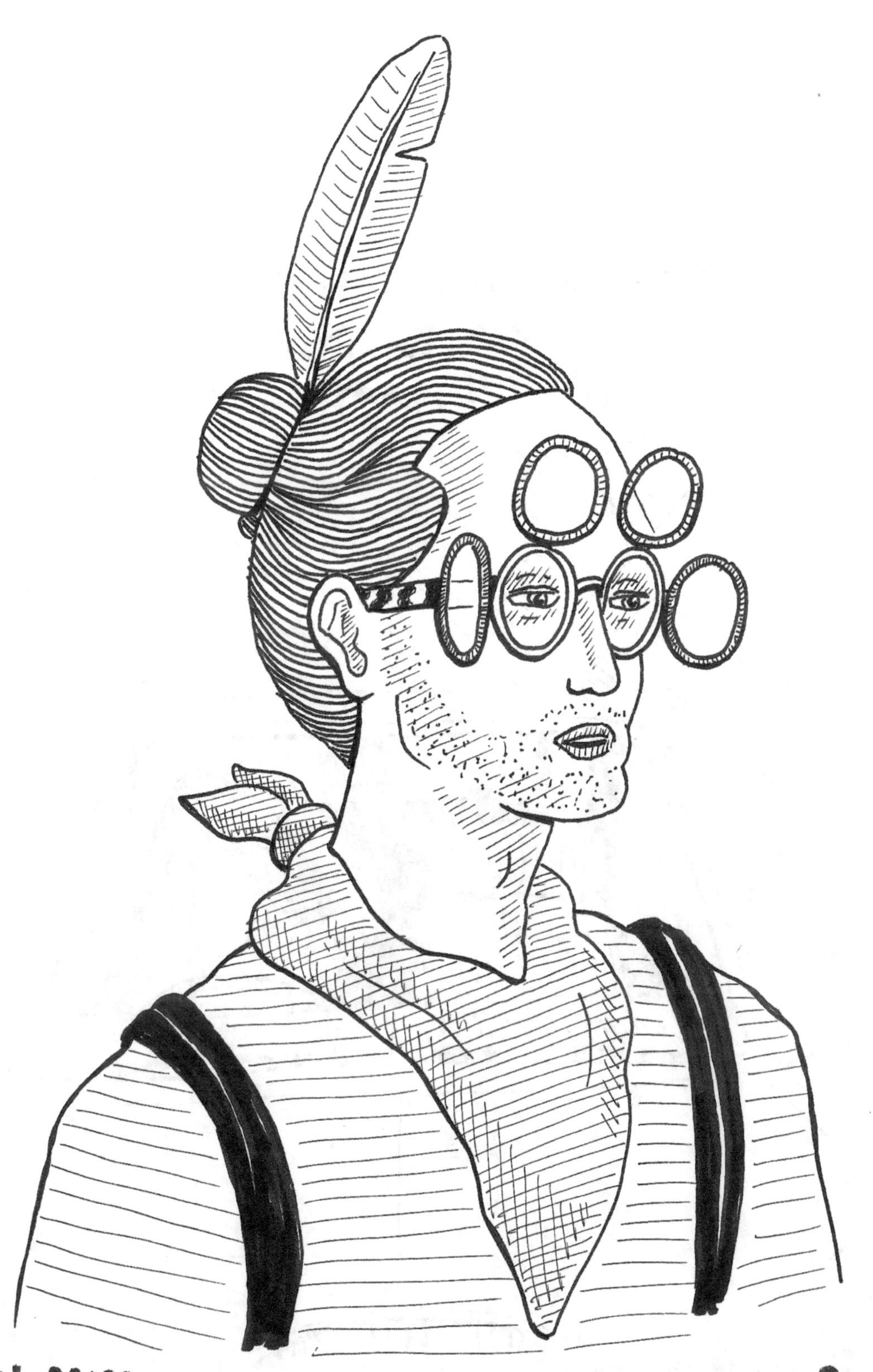

N. MISSISSIPPI + FREMONT ST. AT 8:29 PM
#1,467 7-19-23

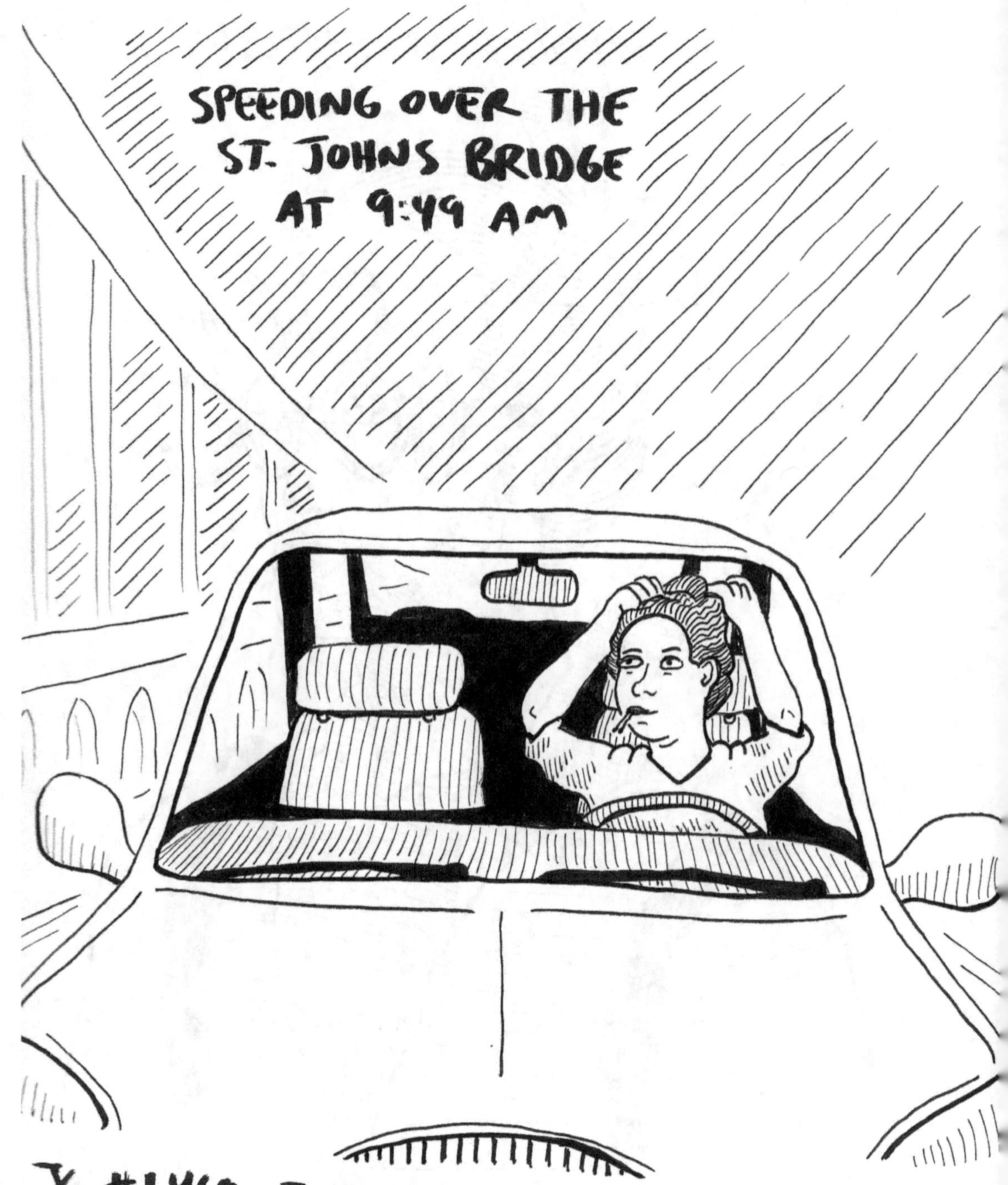

SPEEDING OVER THE
ST. JOHNS BRIDGE
AT 9:49 AM

#1,468 7-20-23

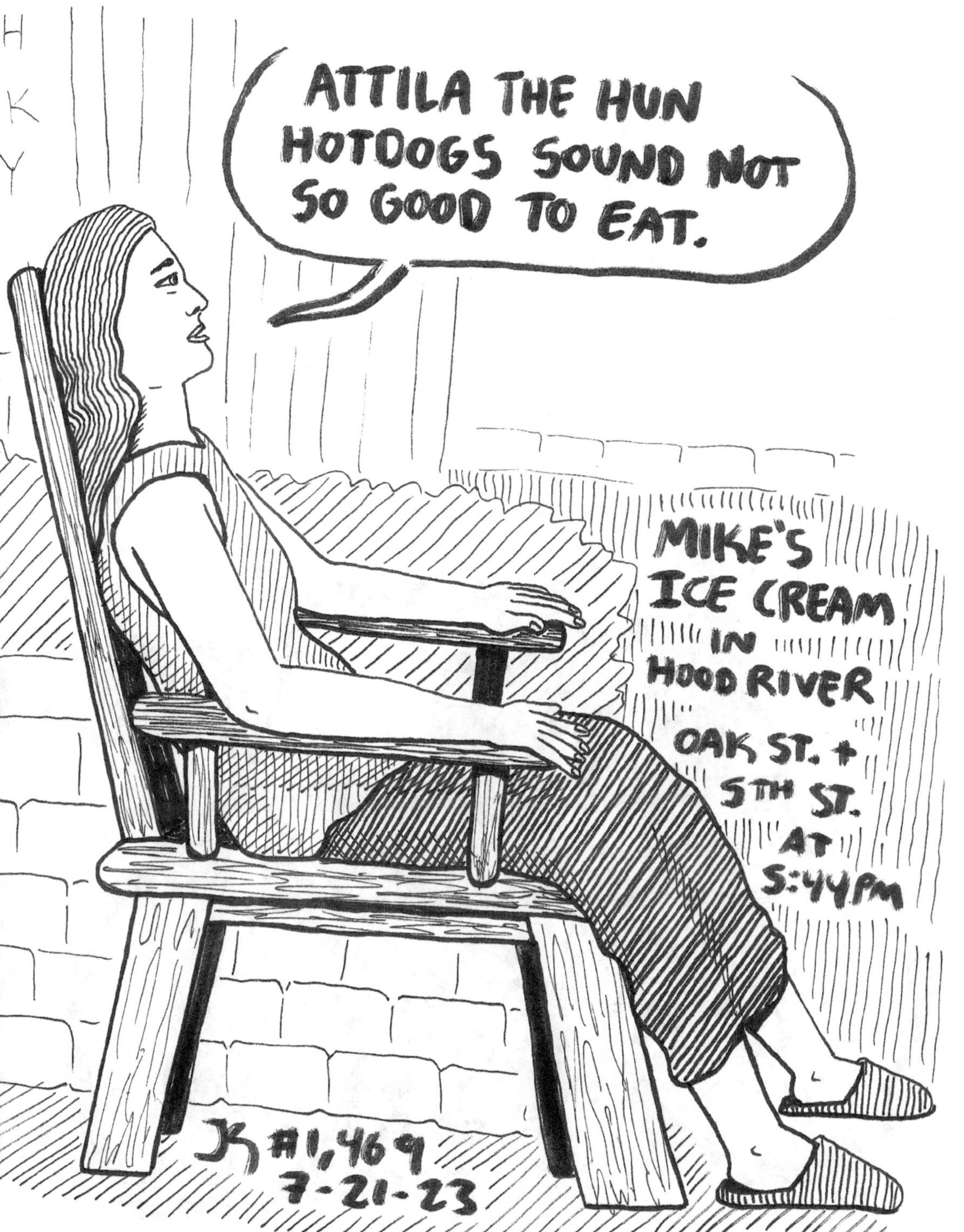

ATTILA THE HUN HOTDOGS SOUND NOT SO GOOD TO EAT.
MIKE'S ICE CREAM IN HOOD RIVER
OAK ST. + 5TH ST.
AT 5:44 PM

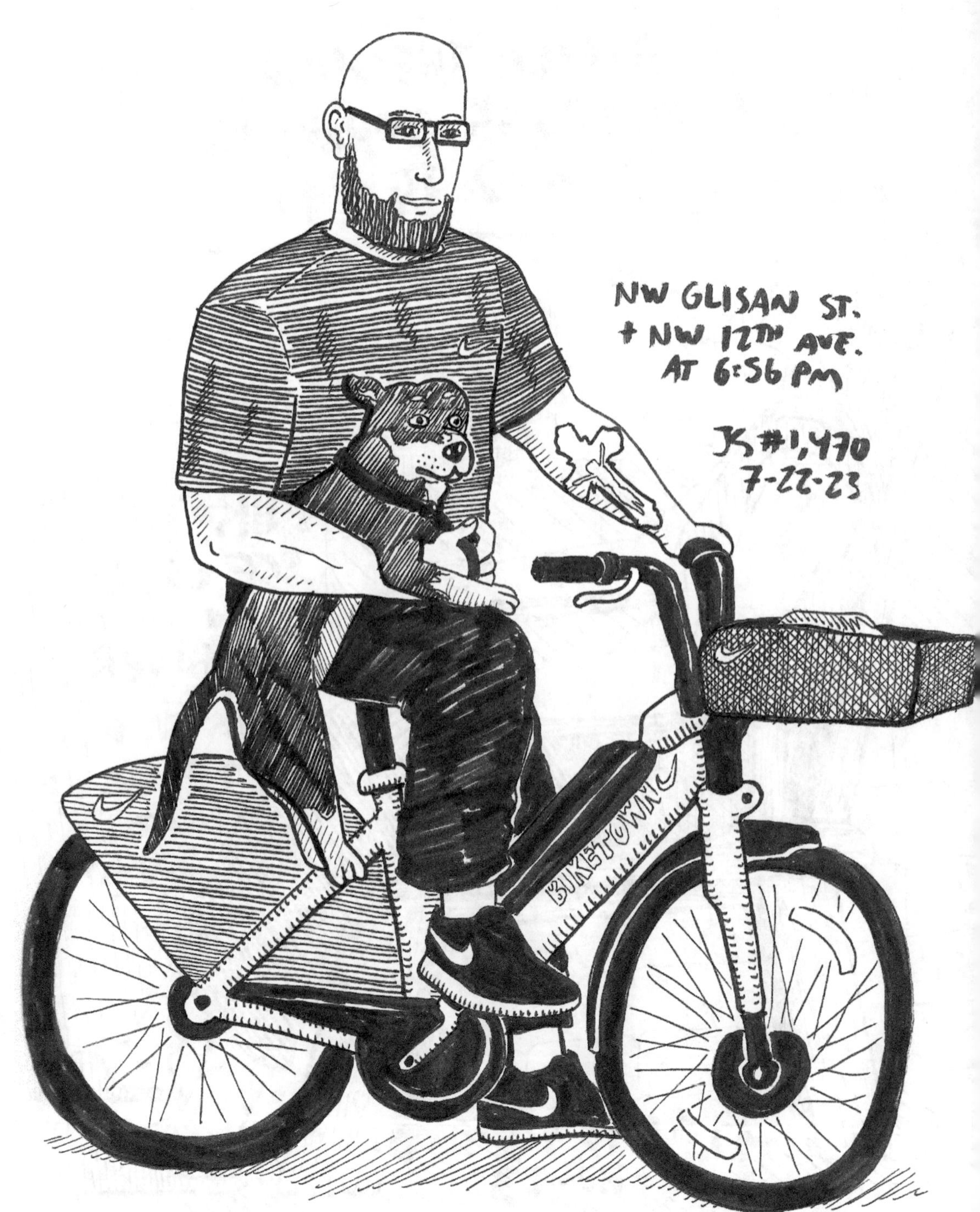

NW GLISAN ST.
+ NW 12TH AVE.
AT 6:56 PM

JS #1,470
7-22-23

BIKETOWN

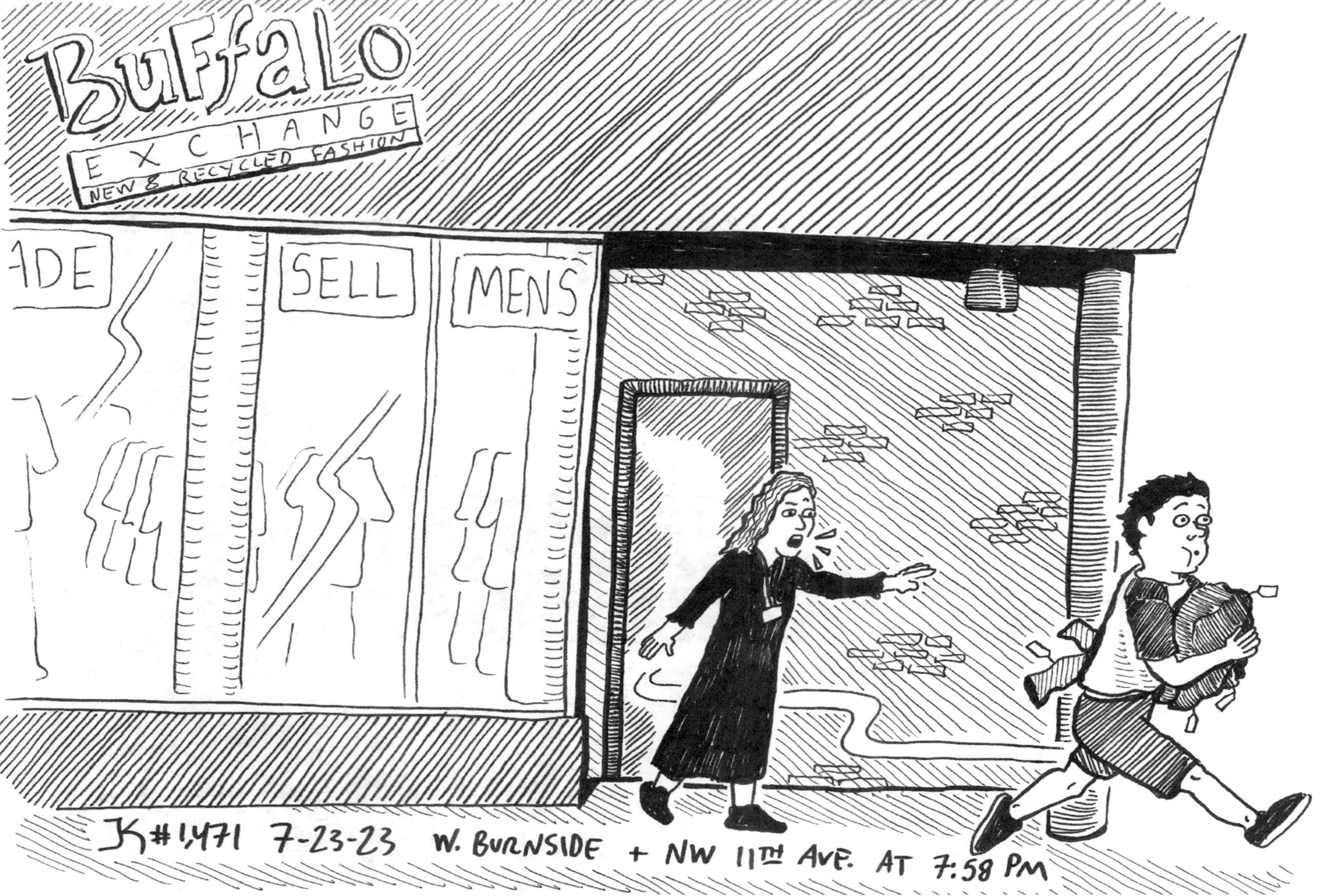

BuFFaLo
EXCHANGE
NEW & RECYCLED FASHION
ADE
SELL
MENS
JK #1,471 7-23-23 W. BURNSIDE + NW 11TH AVE. AT 7:58 PM

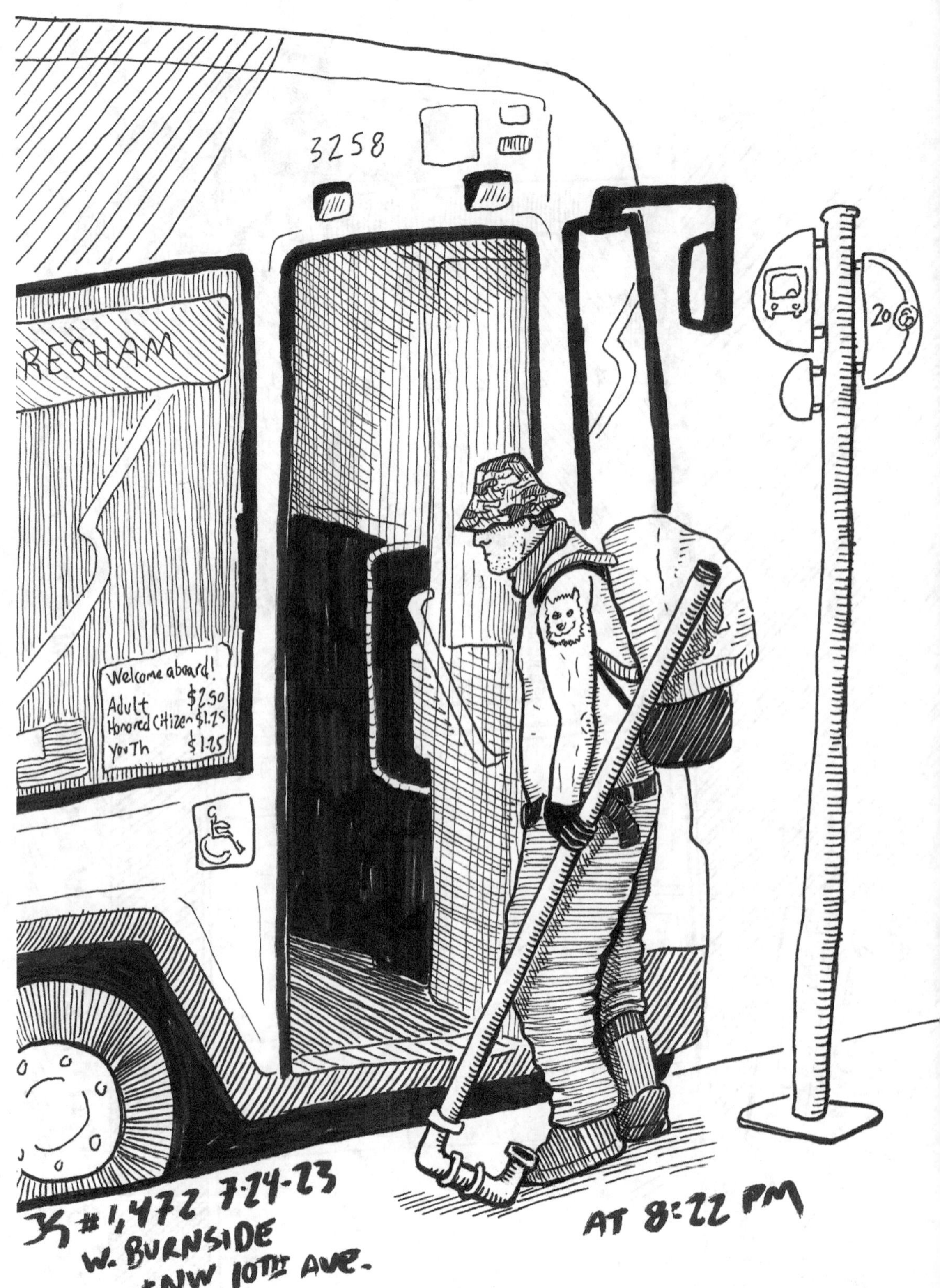
3258
RESHAM
Welcome aboard!
Adult $2.50
Honored Citizen $1.25
Youth $1.25
20
JS #1,472 7·24·23
W. BURNSIDE
+ NW 10TH AVE.
AT 8:22 PM

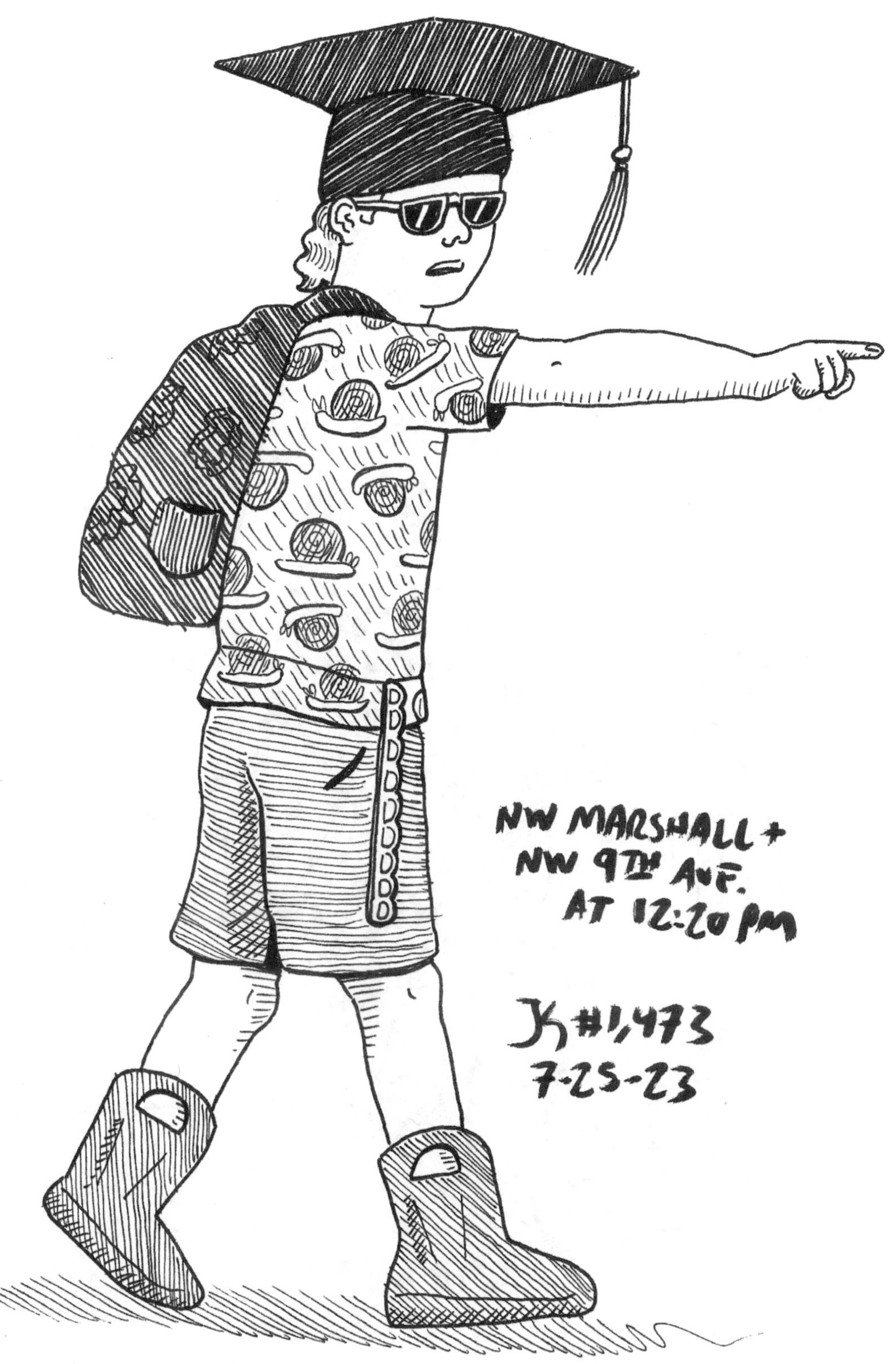

NW MARSHALL +
NW 9TH AVE.
AT 12:20 PM

JK #1,473
7-25-23

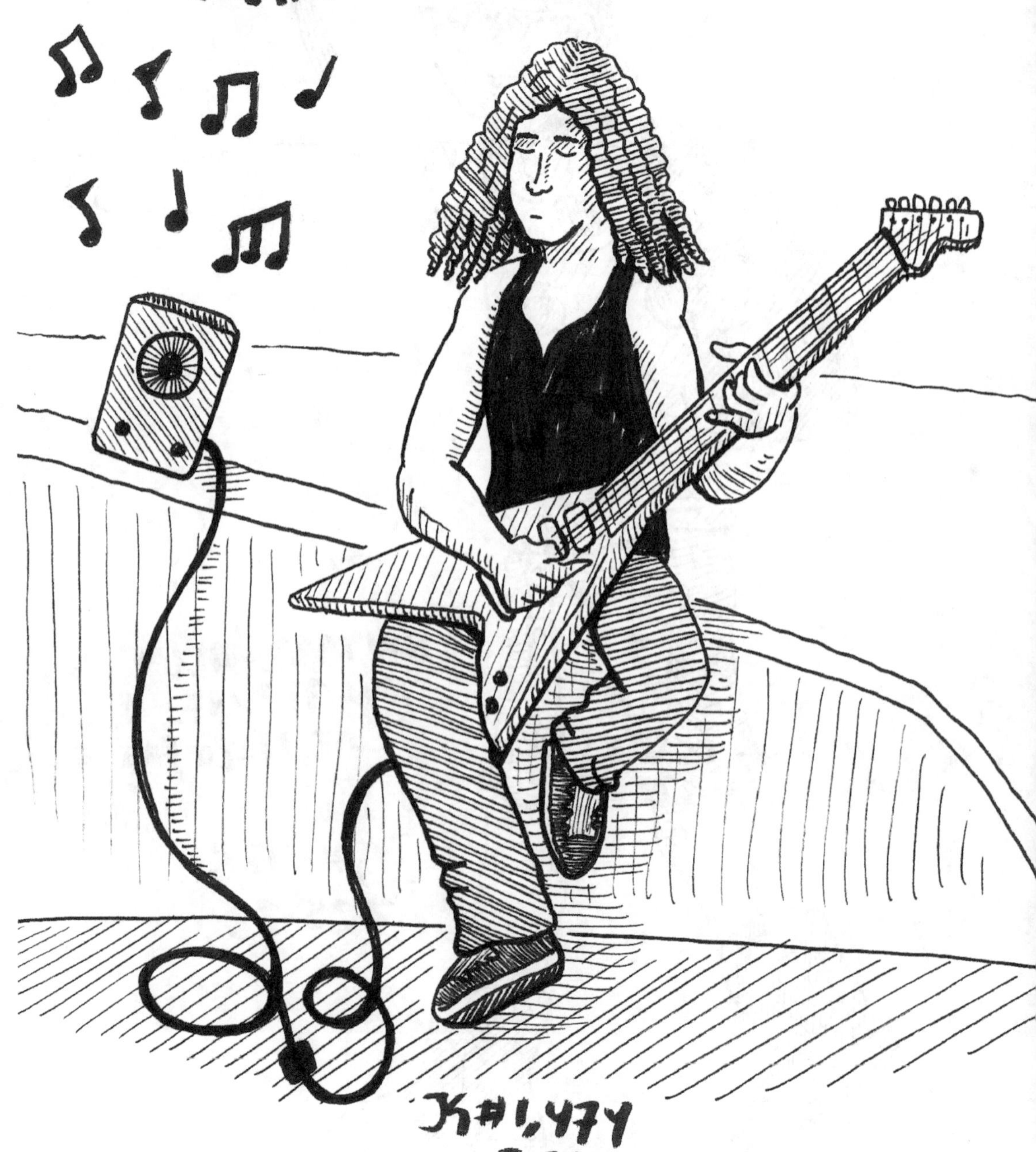

N. COOK ST. +
I-405 KERBY EXIT
6:18 PM
JK #1,474
7-28-23

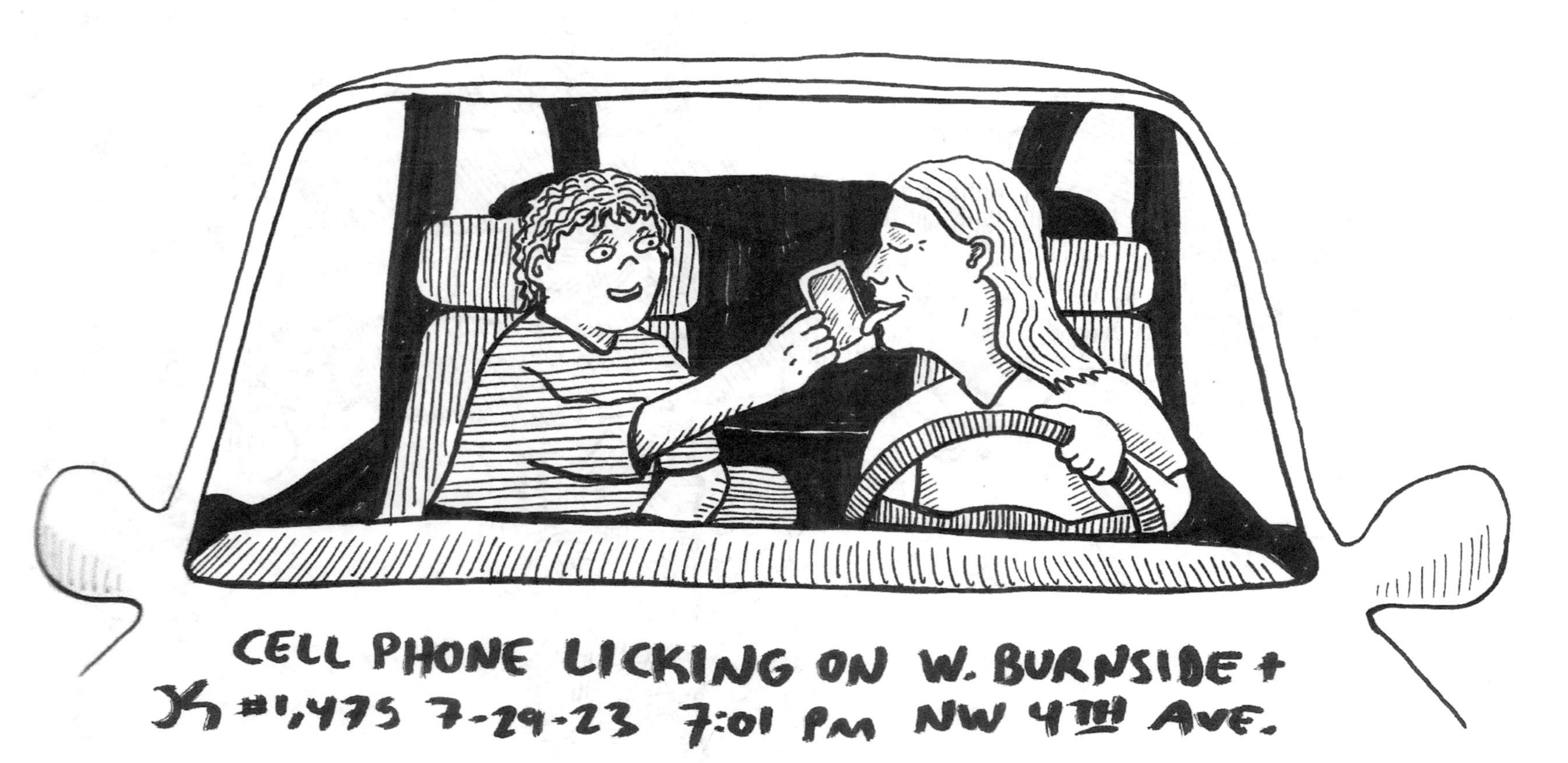

CELL PHONE LICKING ON W. BURNSIDE +
JK #1,475 7-29-23 7:01 PM NW 4TH AVE.

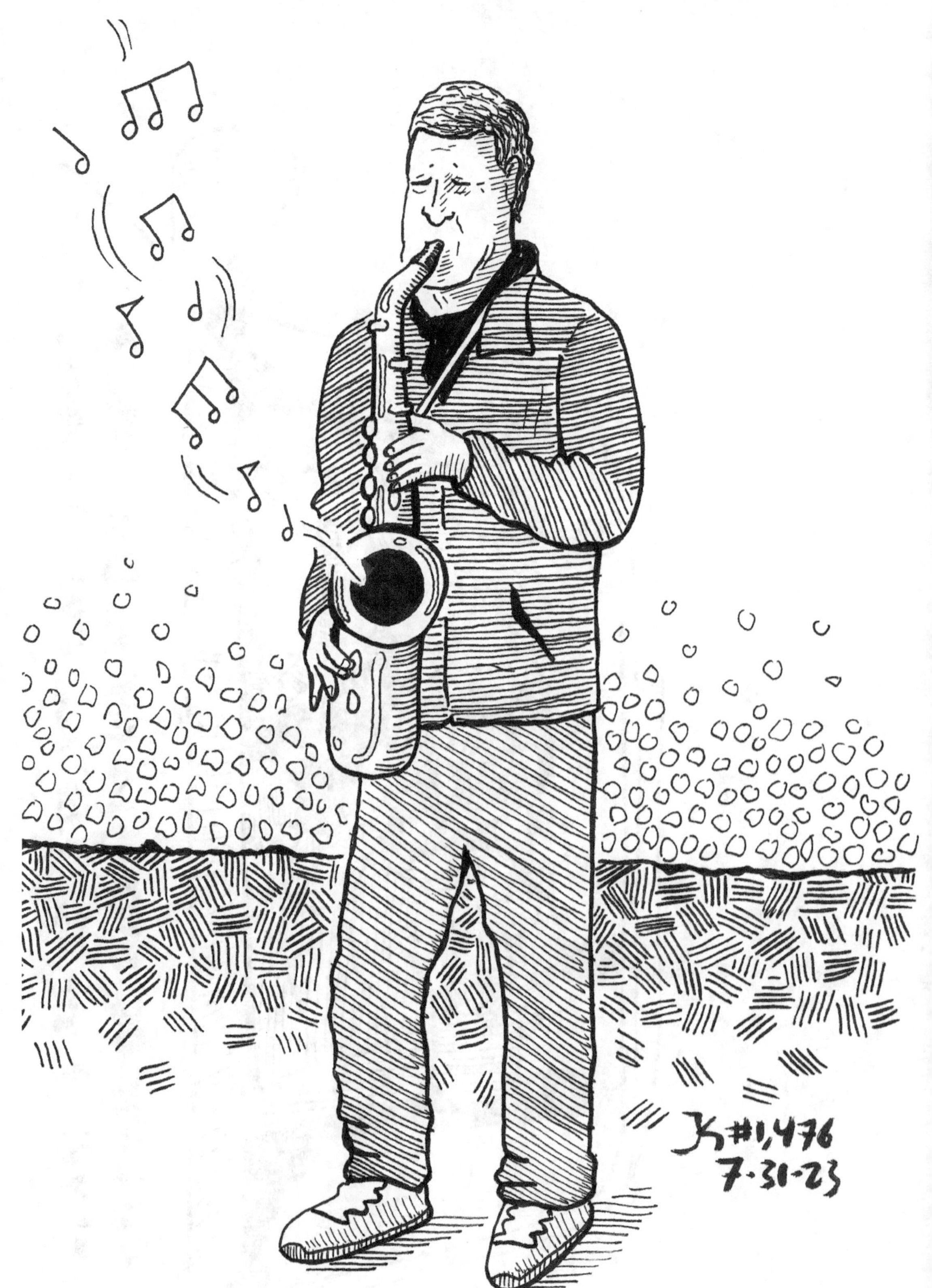

NW YEON + HWY. 30 AT 9:46 AM
ON A LONELY STRETCH OF HWY. 30 AMONGST
THE GRIT OF INDUSTRIAL BUILDINGS,
A LONE MUSICIAN PLAYED ON.

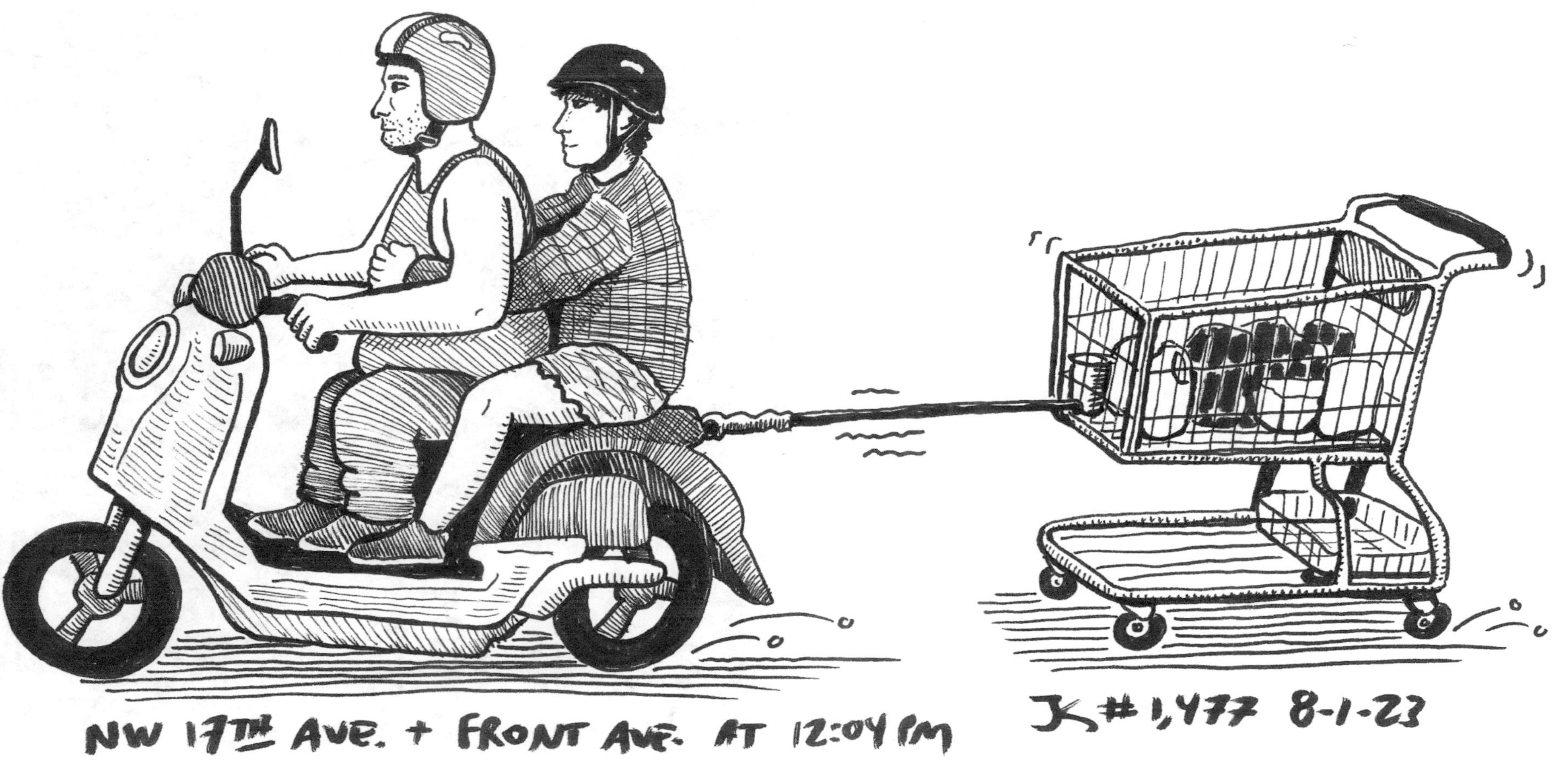

NW 17TH AVE. + FRONT AVE. AT 12:04 PM
JK #1,477 8-1-23

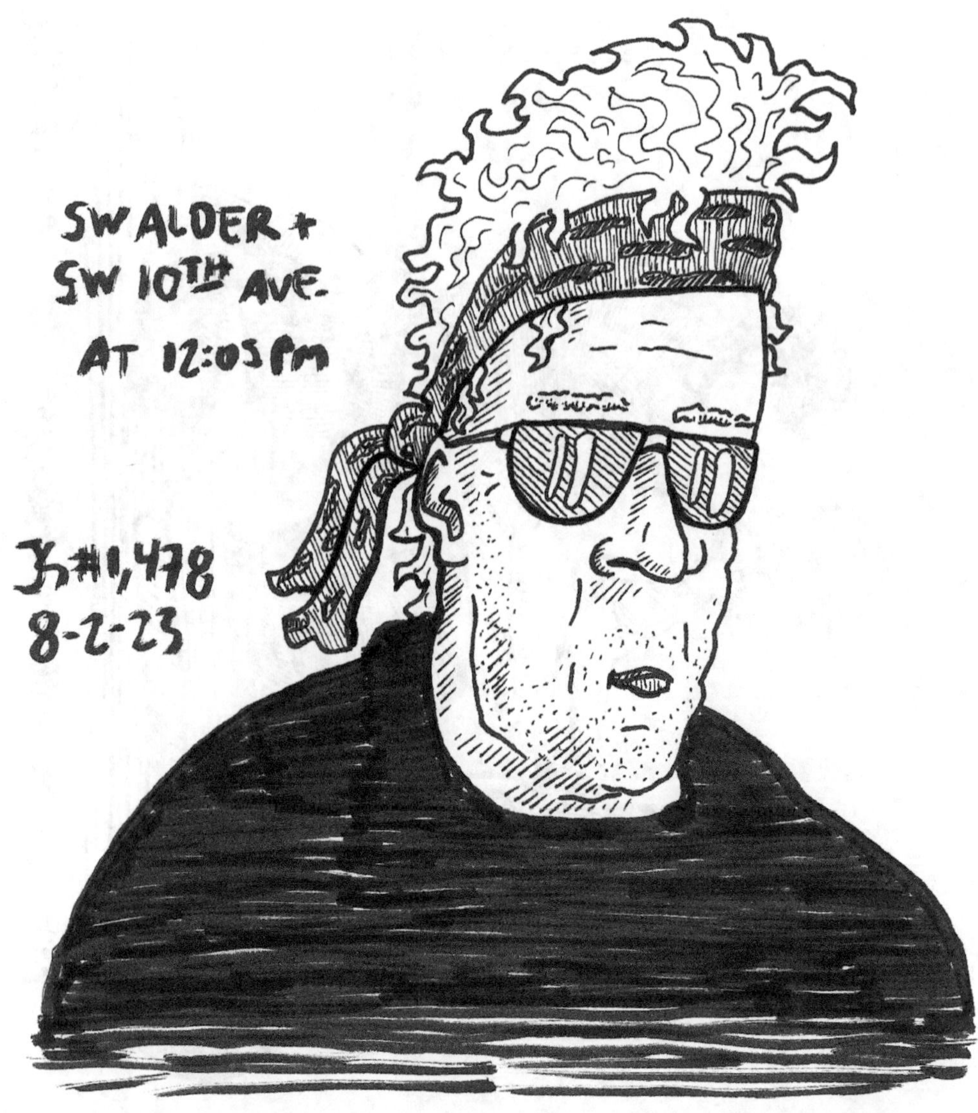
SW ALDER +
SW 10TH AVE.
AT 12:05 PM

#1,478
8-2-23

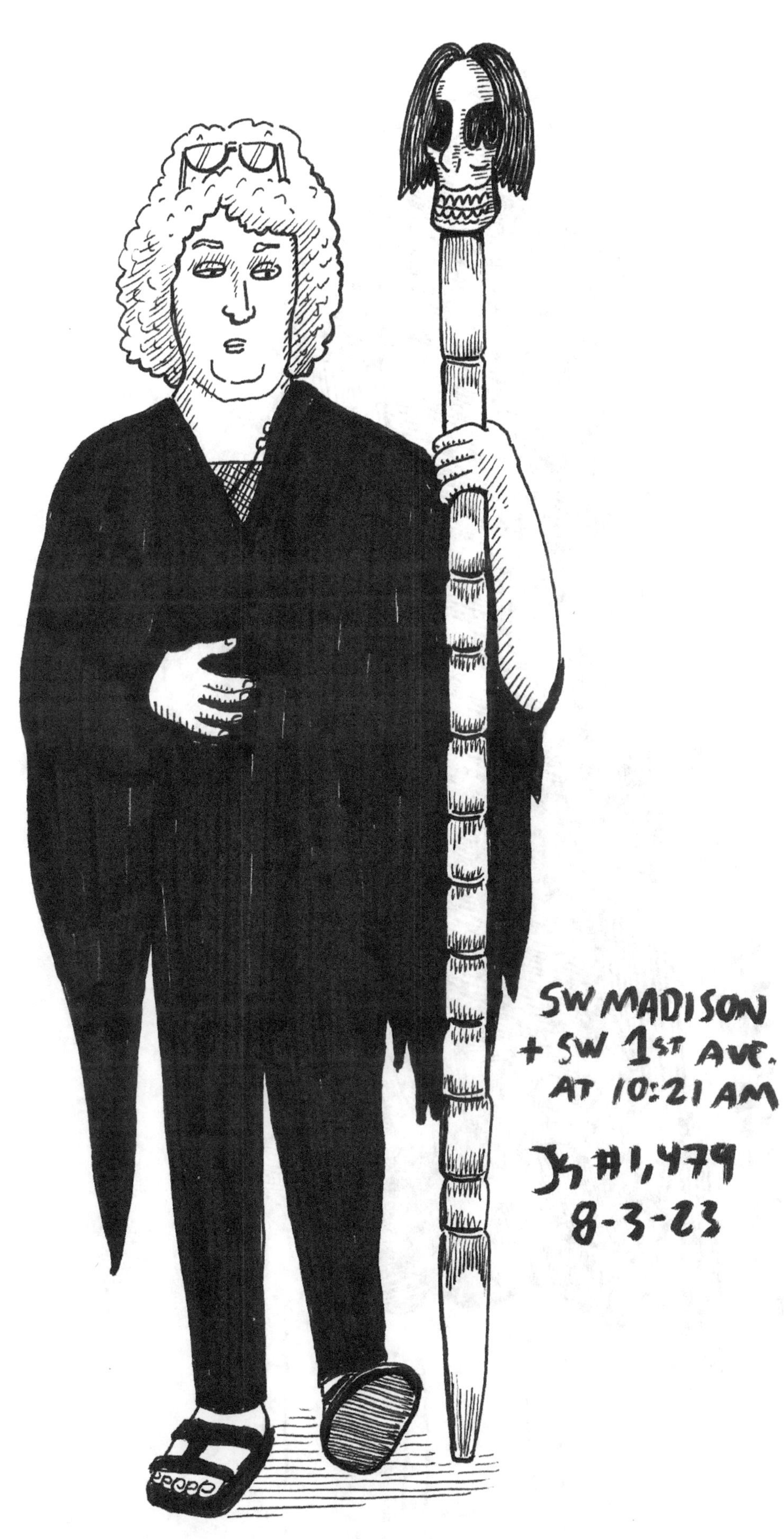

SW MADISON
+ SW 1ST AVE.
AT 10:21 AM

J #1,479
8-3-23

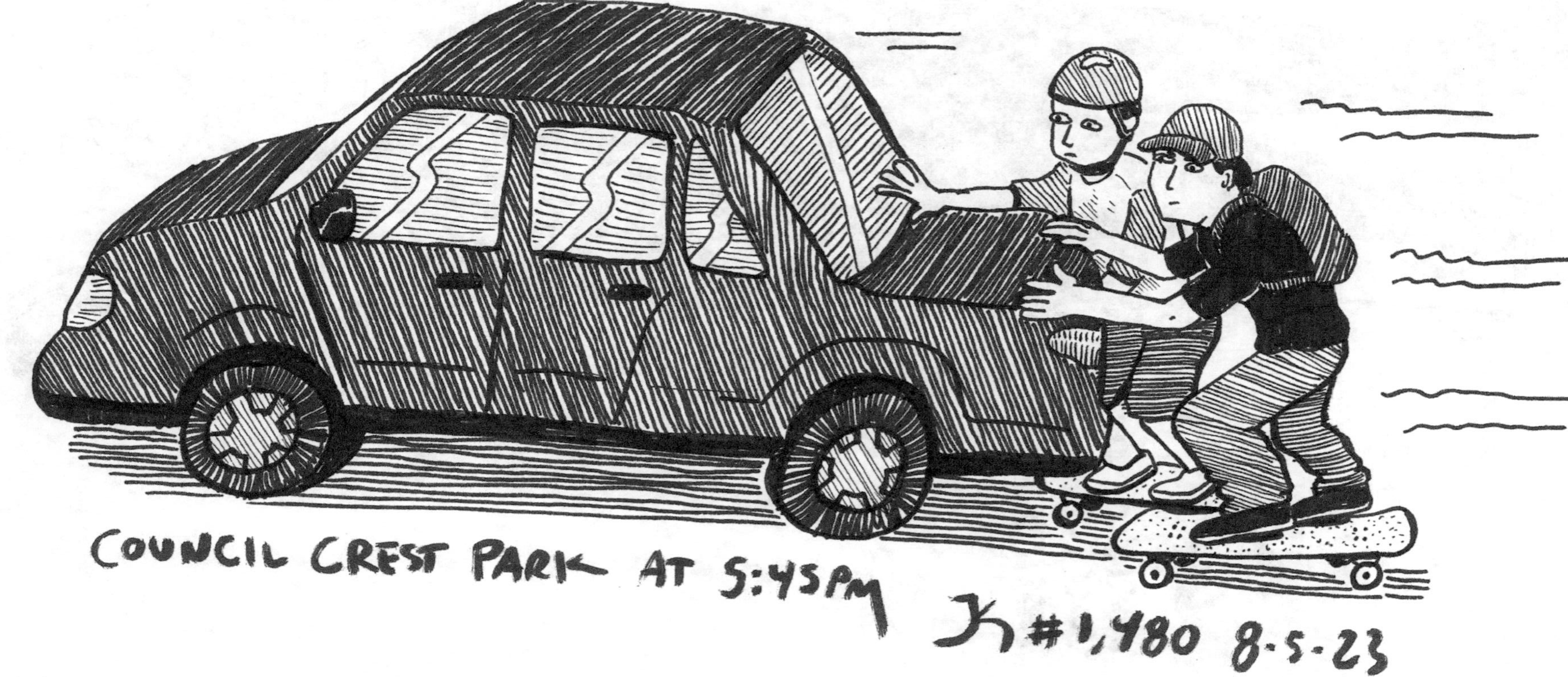

COUNCIL CREST PARK AT 5:45PM
#1,480 8-5-23

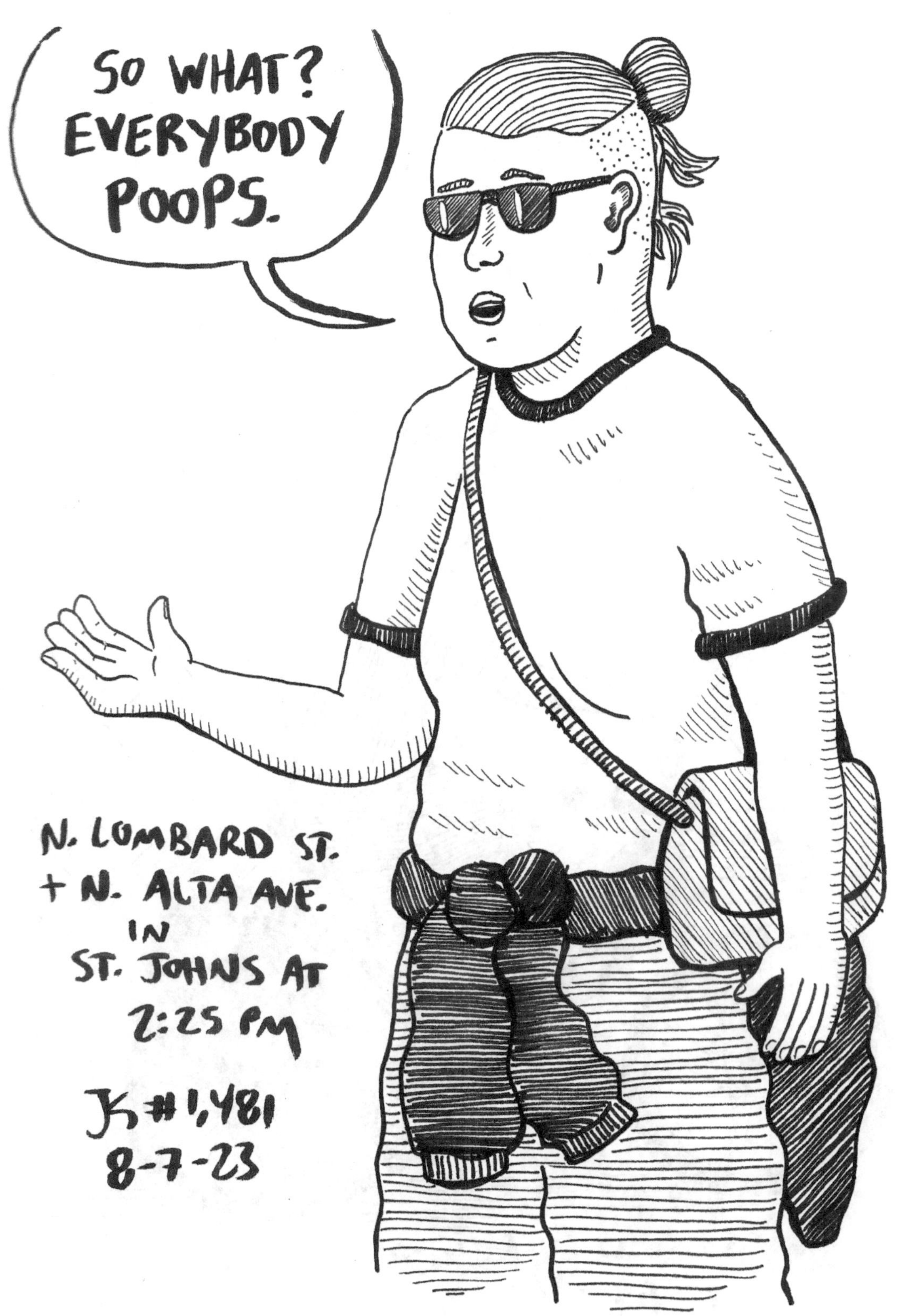

SO WHAT? EVERYBODY POOPS.
N. LOMBARD ST. + N. ALTA AVE. IN ST. JOHNS AT 2:25 PM
JS #1,481
8-7-23

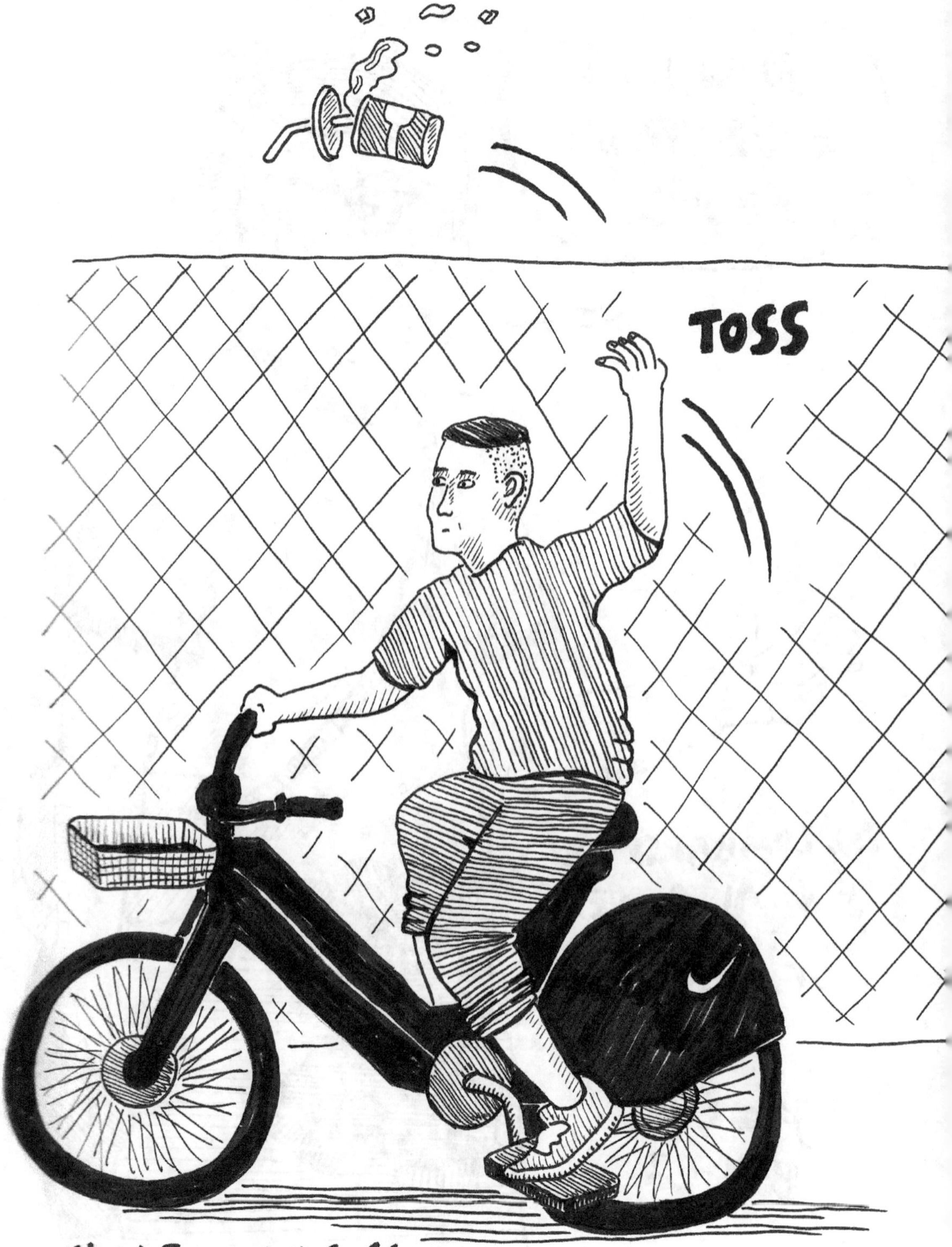

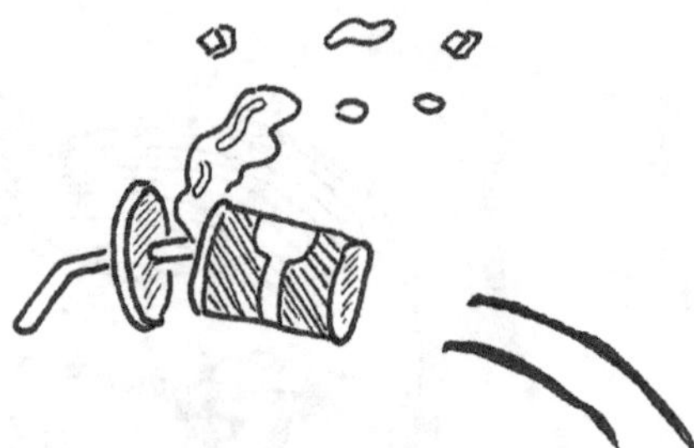

HWY. 30 + NW SUFFOLK ST.
AT 4:41 PM
JK #1,482 8-10-23

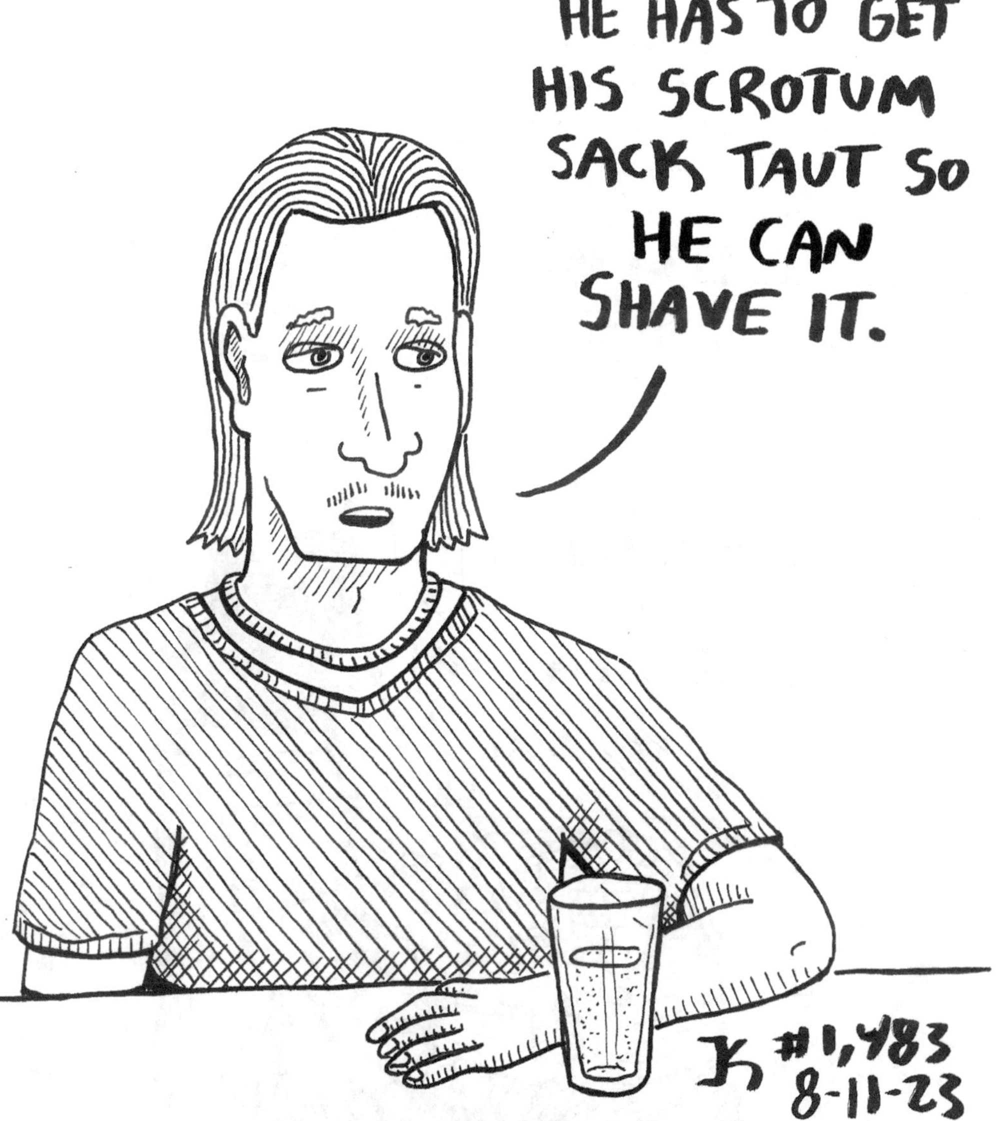
HE HAS TO GET
HIS SCROTUM
SACK TAUT SO
HE CAN
SHAVE IT.

#1,483
8-11-23

HUNGRY TIGER
ON SE 12TH & ASH AT 7:19 PM

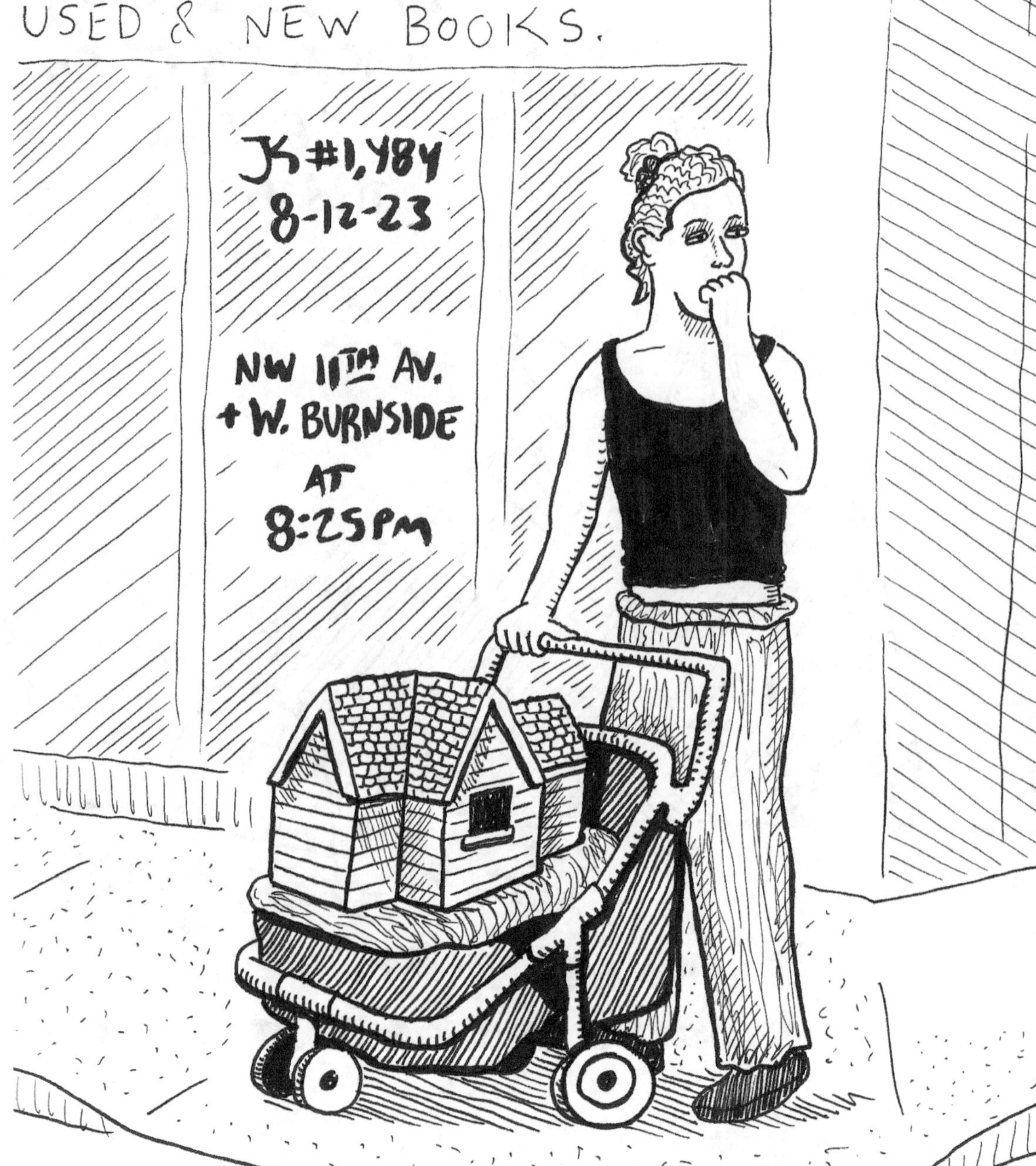
POWELL'S
BOOKS
USED & NEW BOOKS.
JK #1,484
8-12-23
NW 11TH AV.
+ W. BURNSIDE
AT
8:25PM

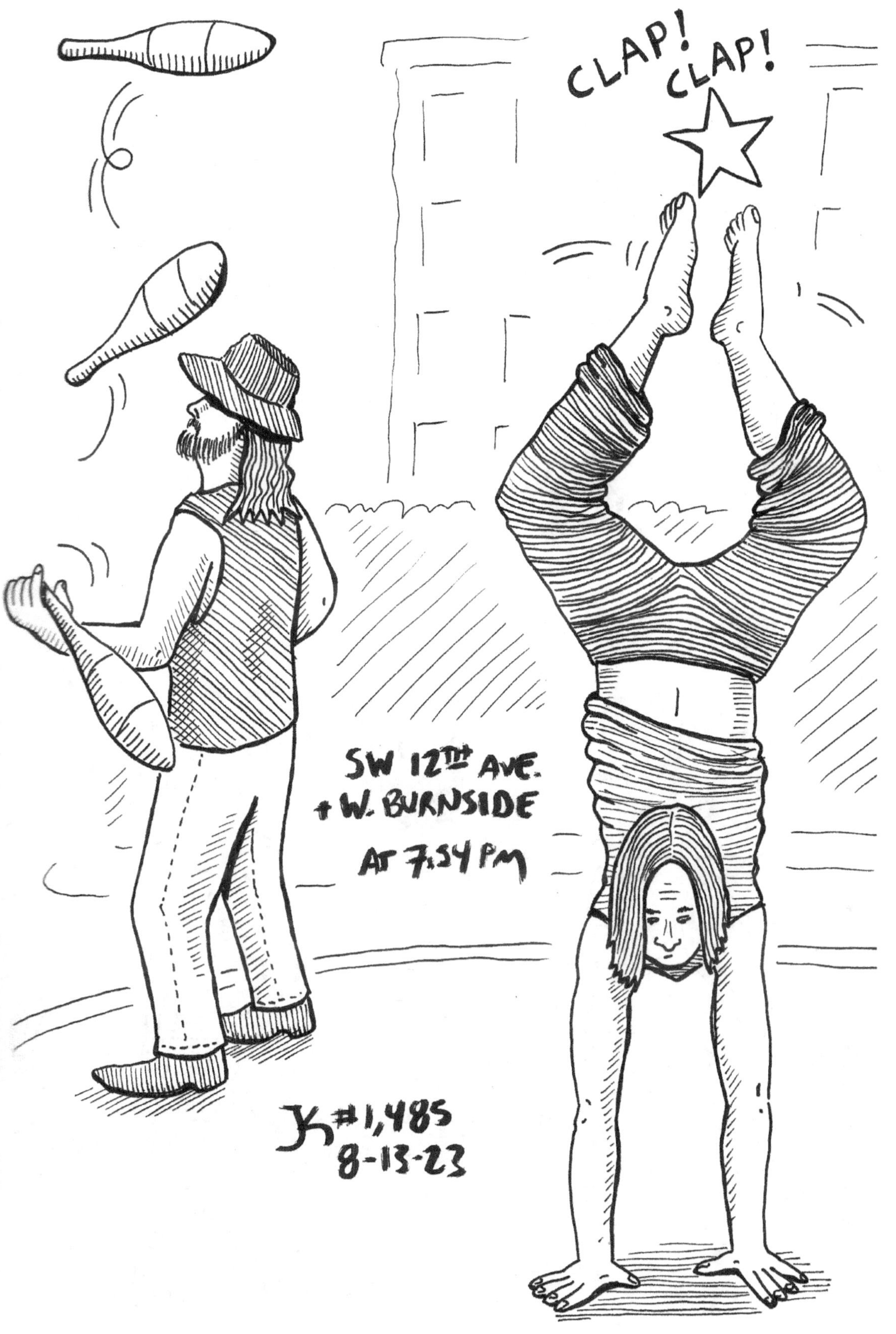

CLAP!
CLAP!
SW 12TH AVE.
+ W. BURNSIDE
AT 7:54 PM
#1,485
8-13-23

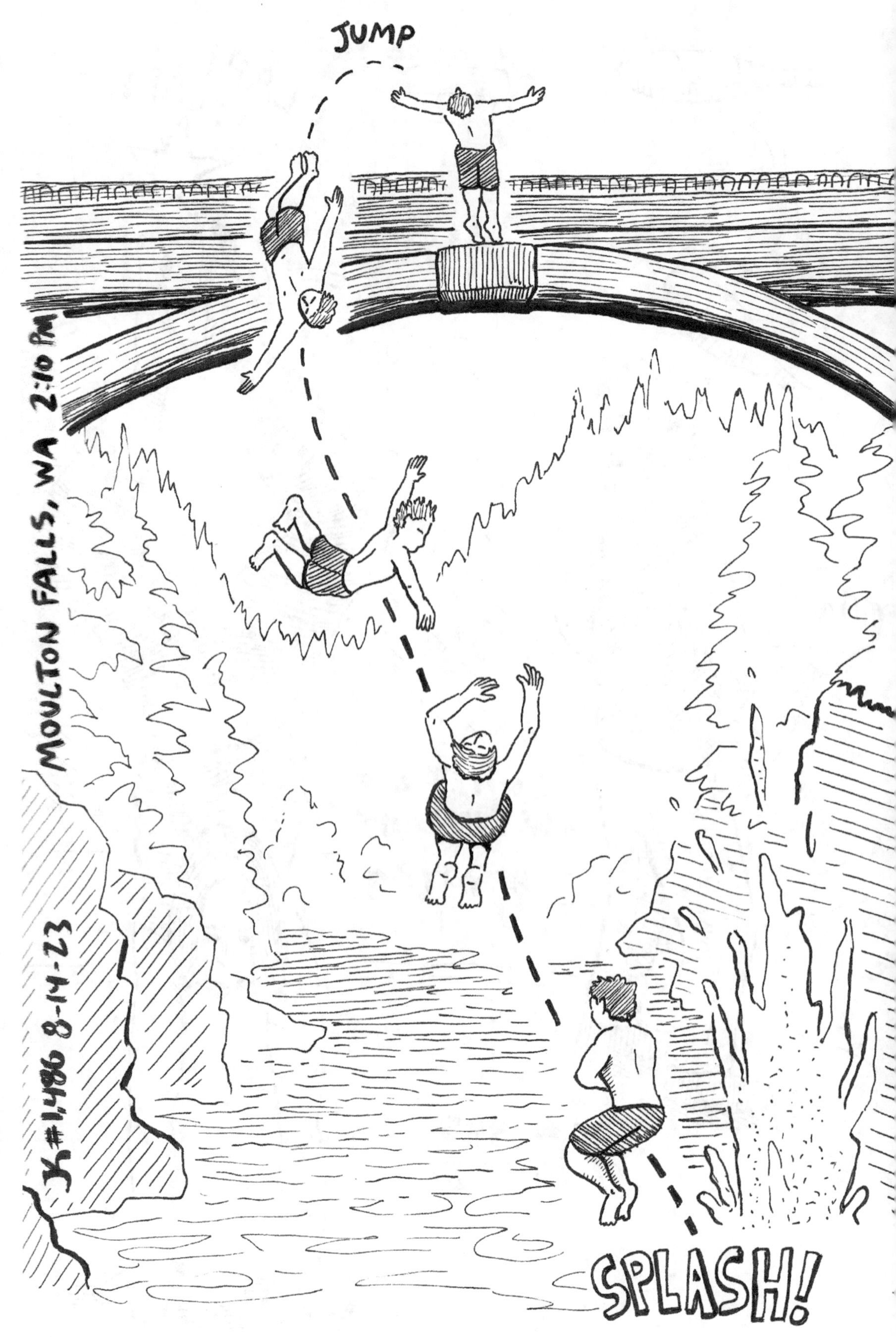
JUMP
MOULTON FALLS, WA   2:10 PM
JX #1,486 8-14-23
SPLASH!

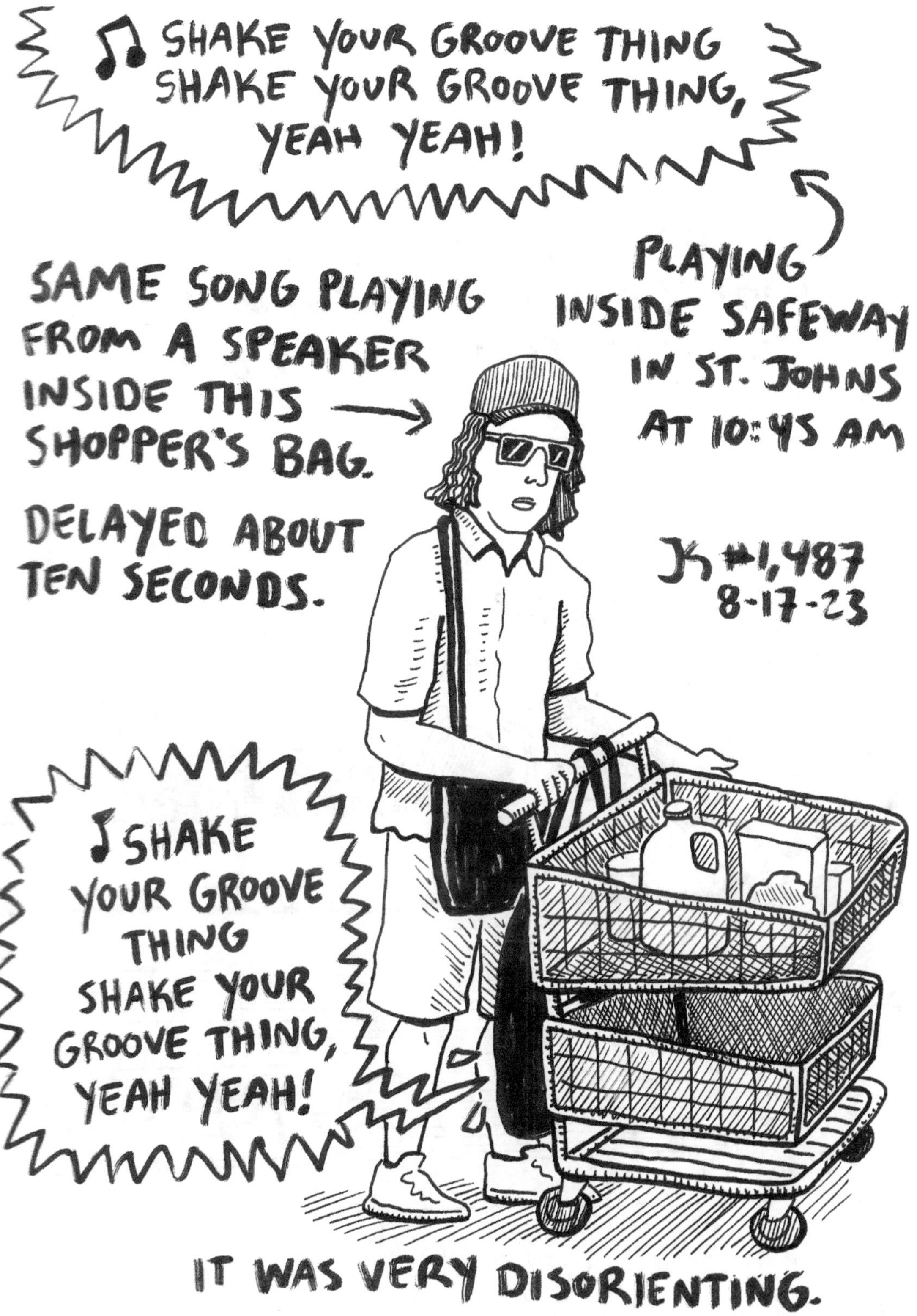

♫ SHAKE YOUR GROOVE THING SHAKE YOUR GROOVE THING, YEAH YEAH!
SAME SONG PLAYING FROM A SPEAKER INSIDE THIS SHOPPER'S BAG.
DELAYED ABOUT TEN SECONDS.
PLAYING INSIDE SAFEWAY IN ST. JOHNS AT 10:45 AM
JJ #1,487
8-17-23
♪ SHAKE YOUR GROOVE THING SHAKE YOUR GROOVE THING, YEAH YEAH!
IT WAS VERY DISORIENTING.

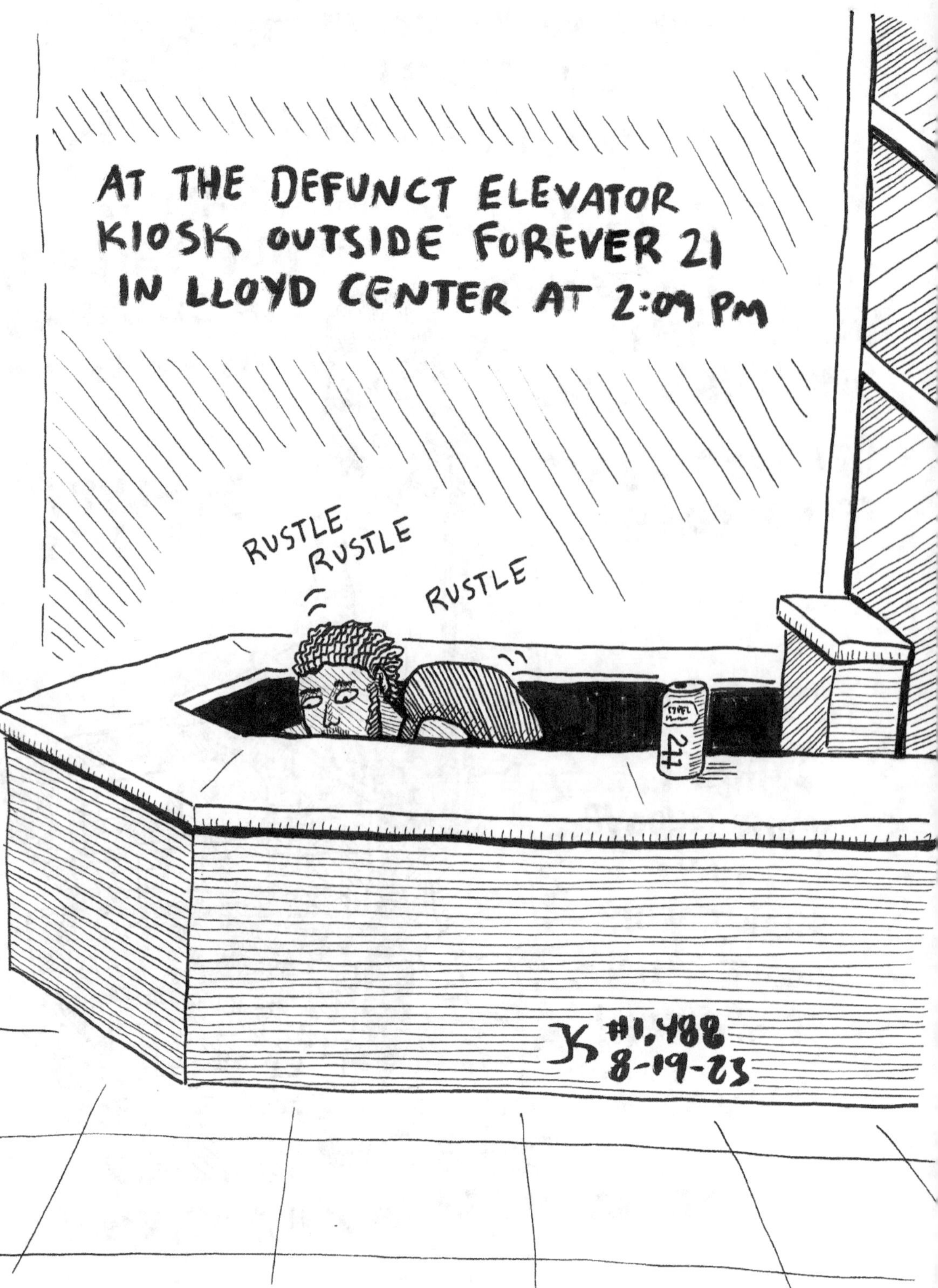

AT THE DEFUNCT ELEVATOR KIOSK OUTSIDE FOREVER 21 IN LLOYD CENTER AT 2:09 PM
RUSTLE RUSTLE
RUSTLE
211
JS #1,488
8-19-23

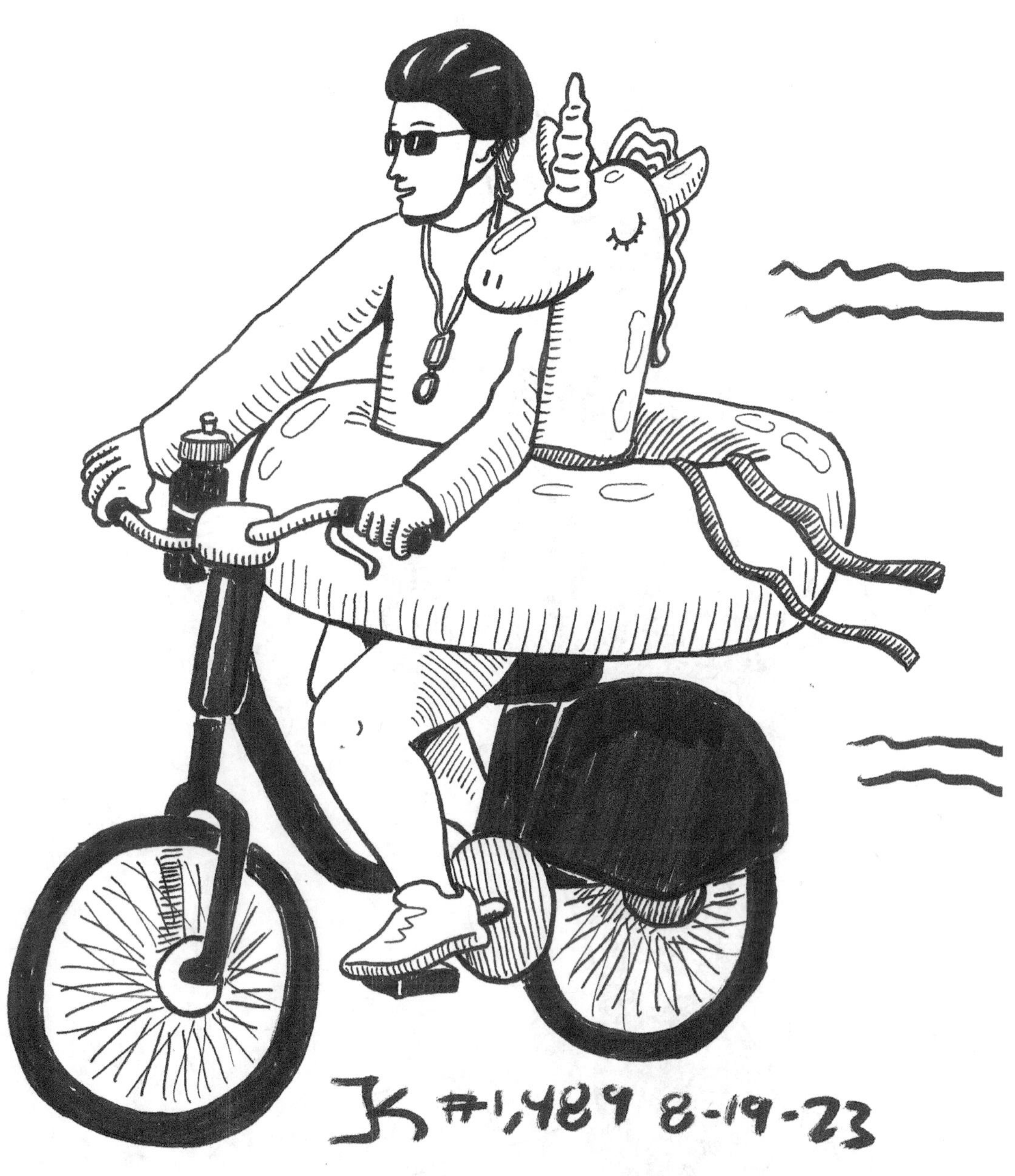

JK #1,484 8-19-23
N. WILLIAMS +
FREMONT AT 5:07 PM

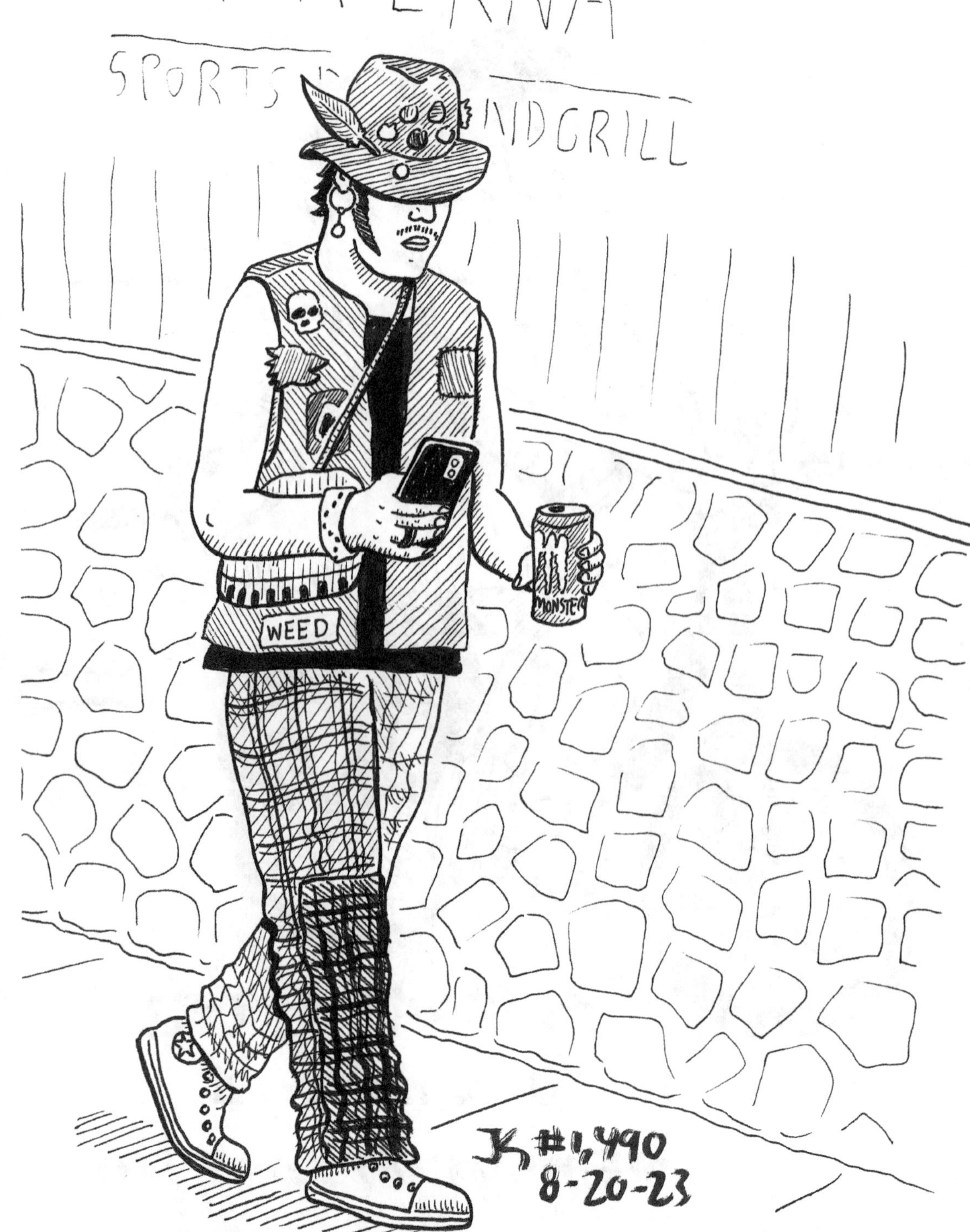

W. BURNSIDE + NW 18ᵀᴴ AVE. AT 2:59 PM

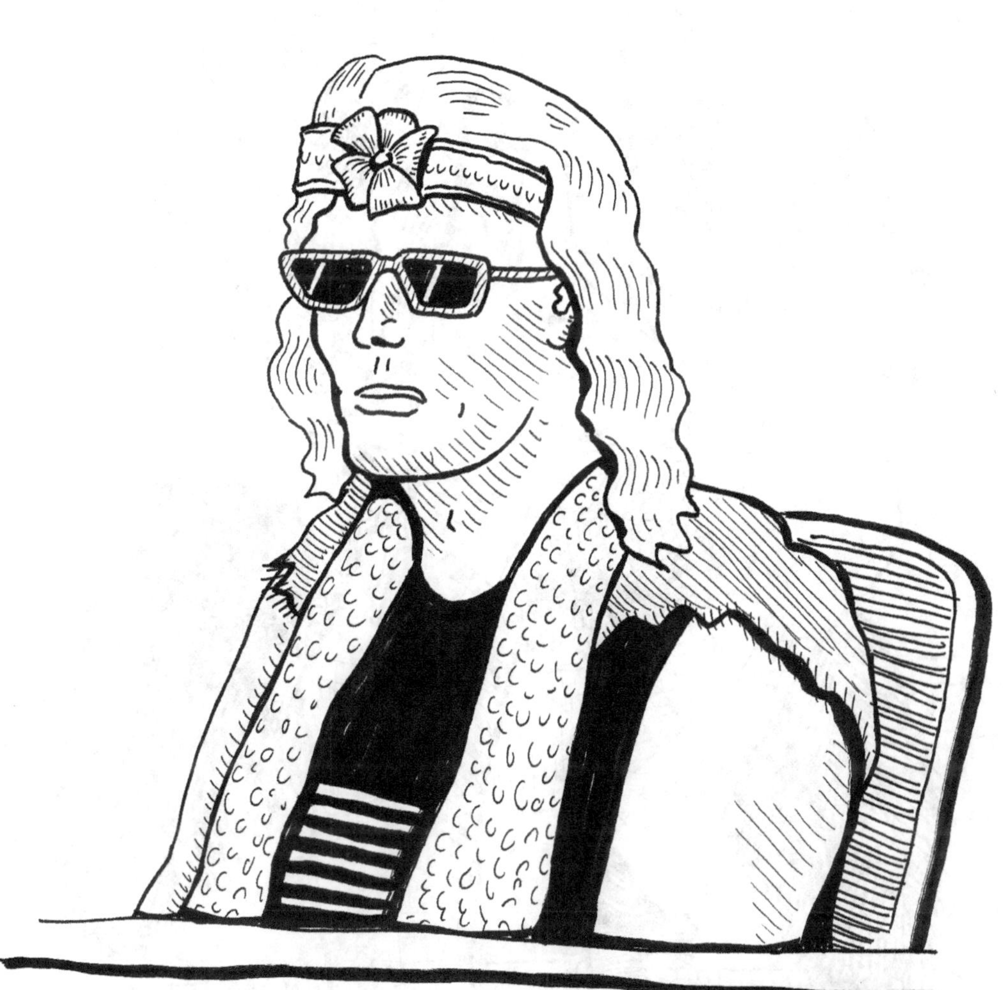

- PINK HEADBAND
- PINK SHADES
- PINK SCARF
- PINK LINES
  ON SHIRT

STREETCAR ON
NW COUCH +
NW 10TH AT
7:40 PM

JK #1,491
8-22-23

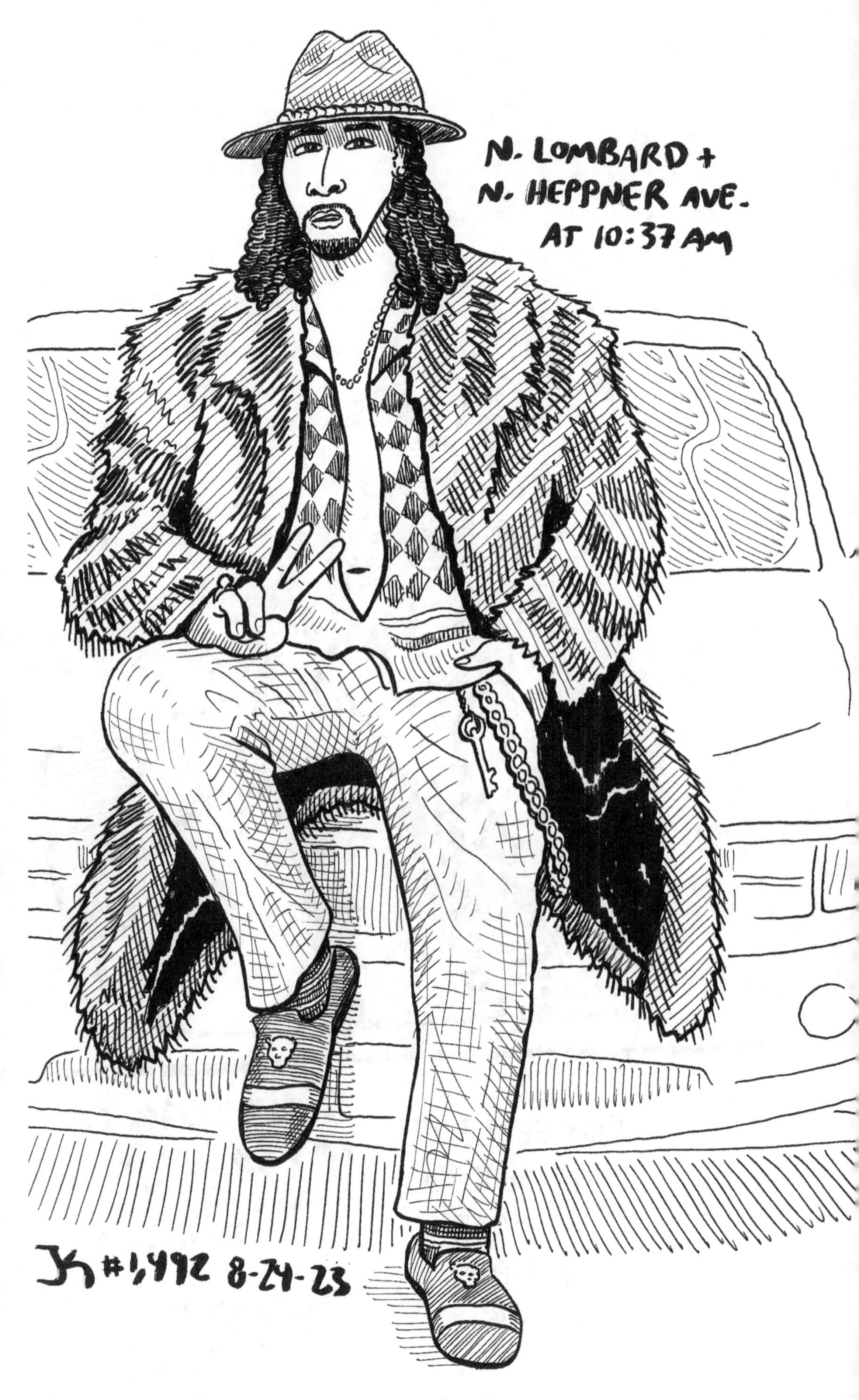

N. LOMBARD +
N. HEPPNER AVE.
AT 10:37 AM
JK #1,492 8-24-23

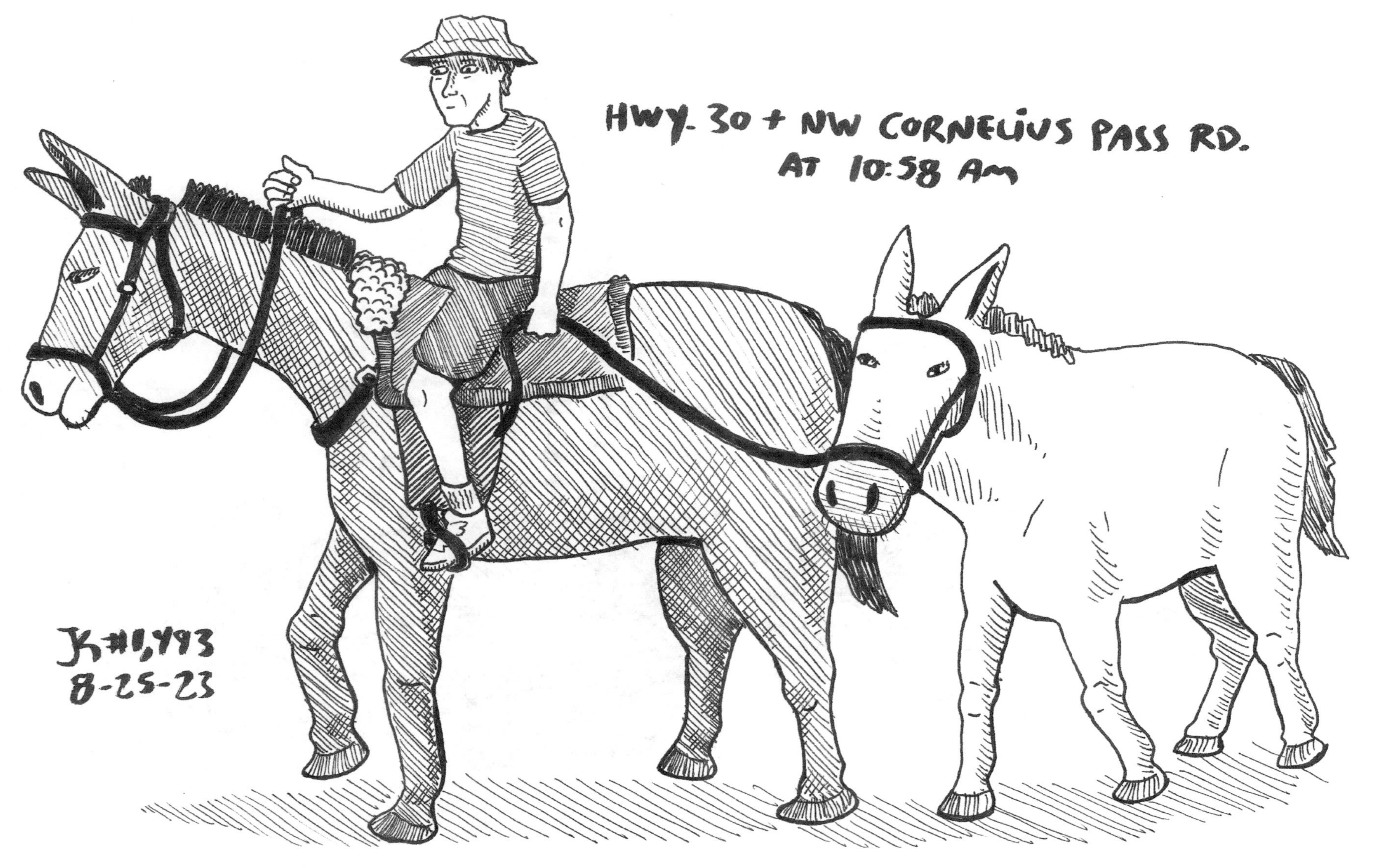

HWY. 30 + NW CORNELIUS PASS RD.
AT 10:58 Am
K#1,443
8-25-23

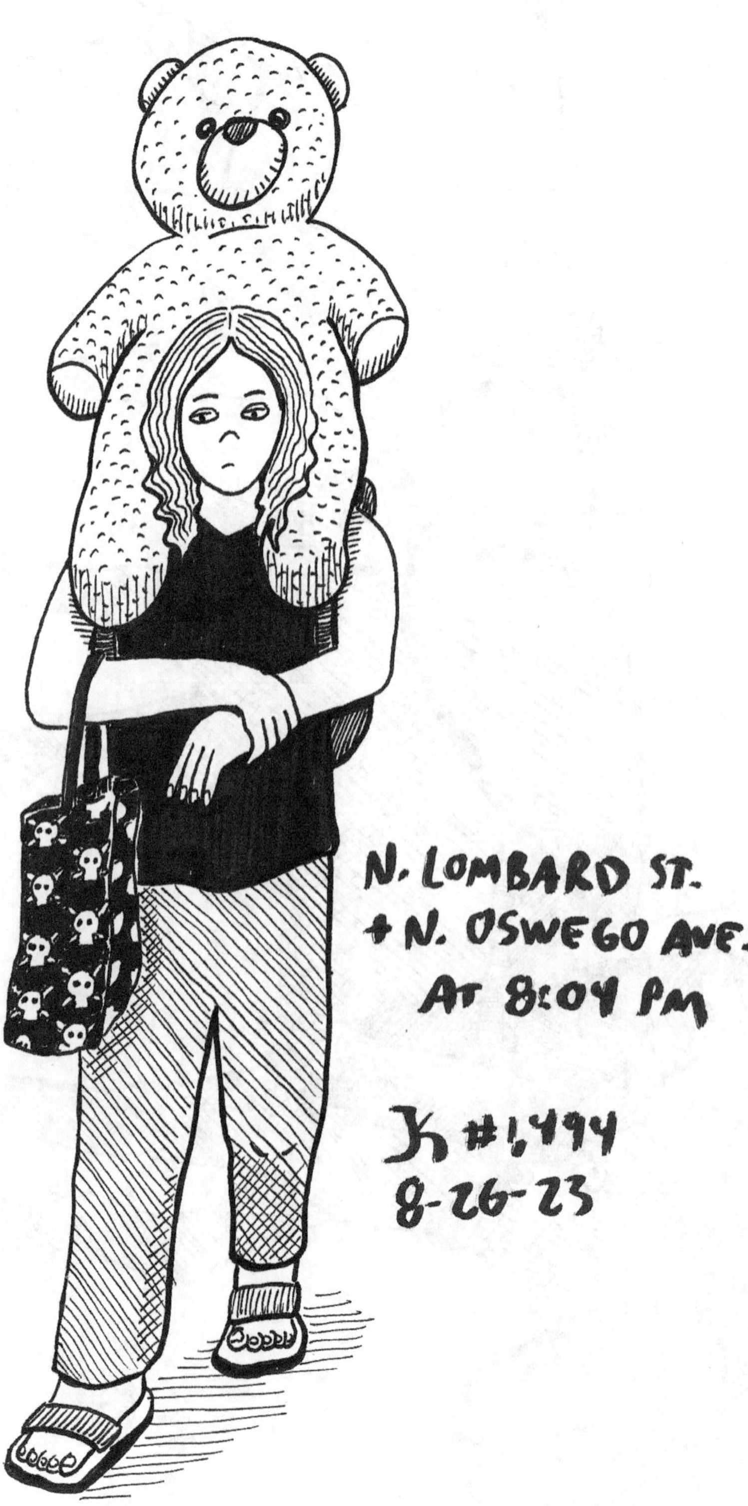

N. LOMBARD ST.
+ N. OSWEGO AVE.
AT 8:04 PM

#1,494
8-26-23

DRESSED IN BLACK W/ A TIE DYE TEE
AT T-MOBILE PARK IN
SEATTLE. VS. ROYALS.
SECTION 329
AT 1:51 PM
RECYCLE PLASTIC BOTTLES HERE
SEATTLE
MARINERS
JK #1,495
8-28-23

PARKING GARAGE AT
T-MOBILE PARK IN SEATTLE
AT 4:30 PM 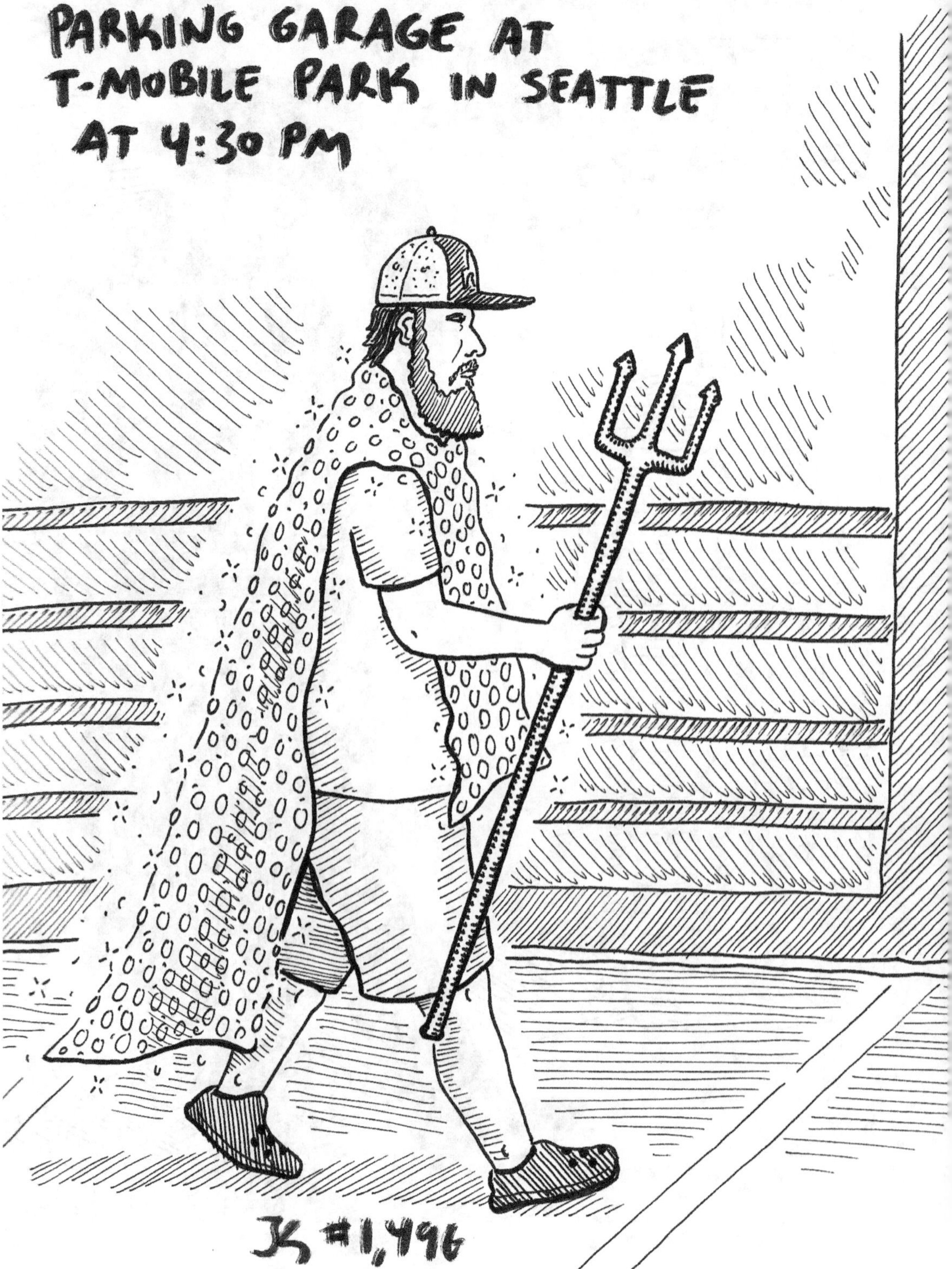
JK #1,496
8-28-23

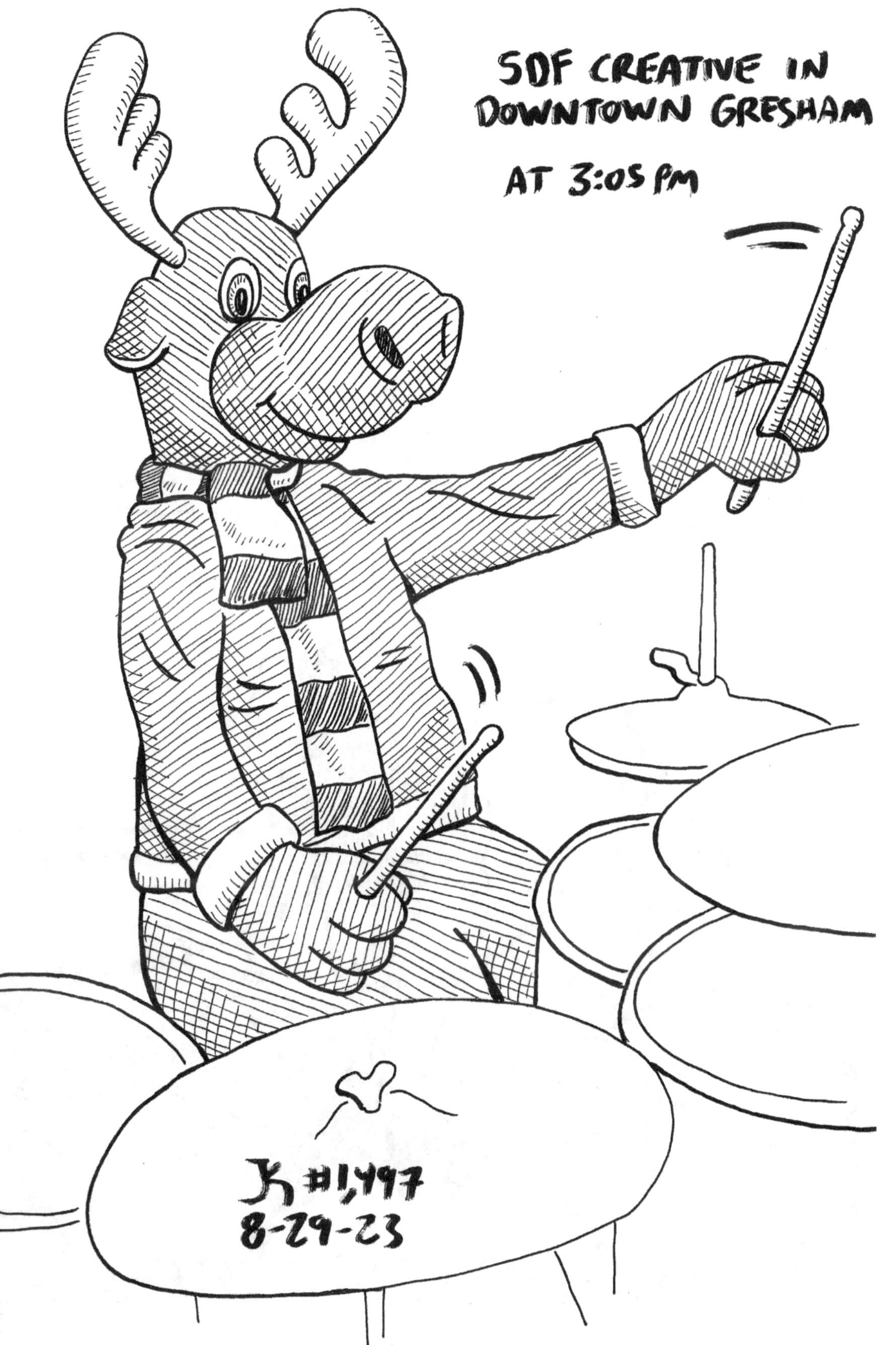

SDF CREATIVE IN
DOWNTOWN GRESHAM
AT 3:05 PM
#1,497
8-29-23

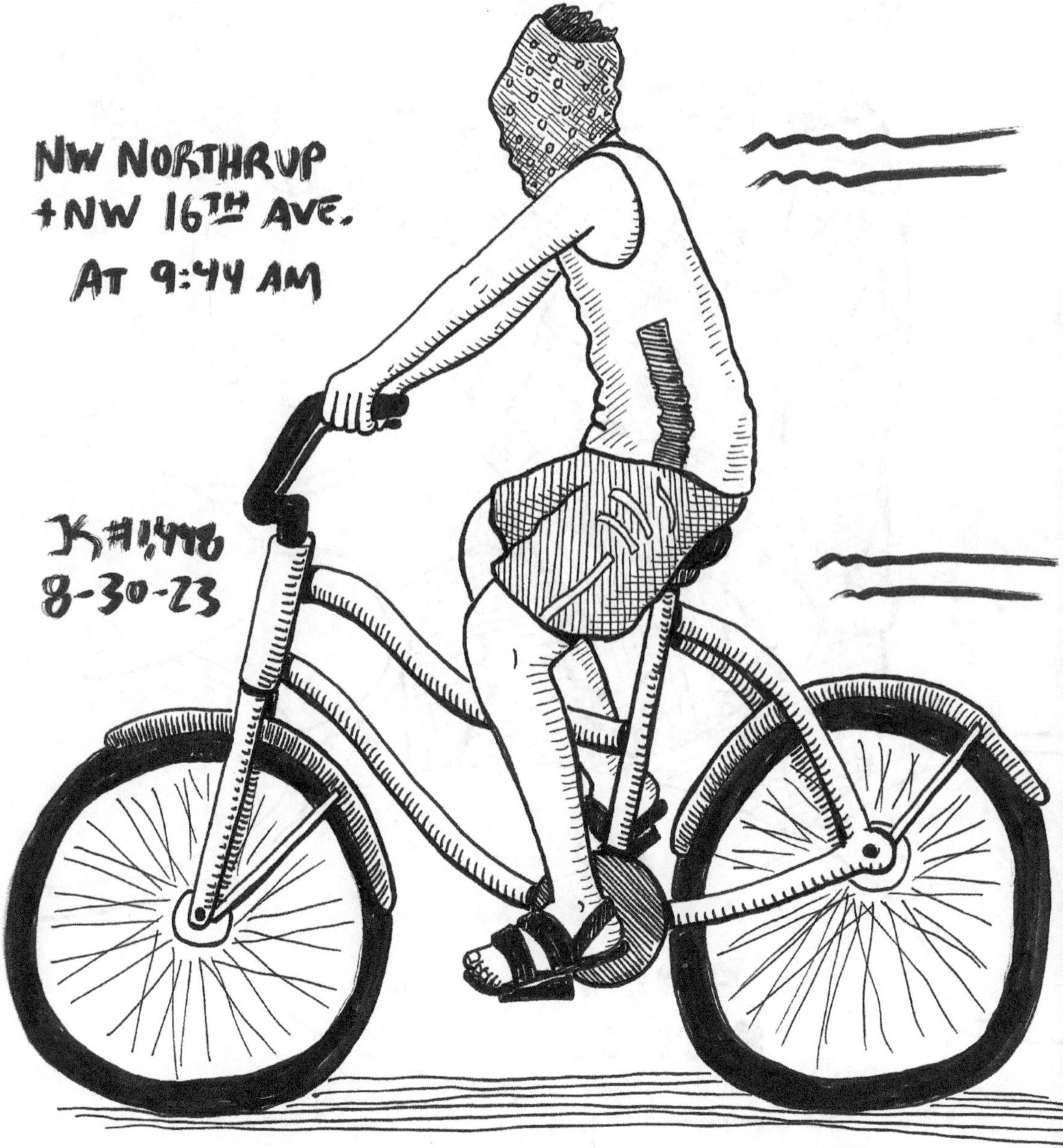

NW NORTHRUP
+ NW 16TH AVE.
AT 9:44 AM

JK #1,496
8-30-23

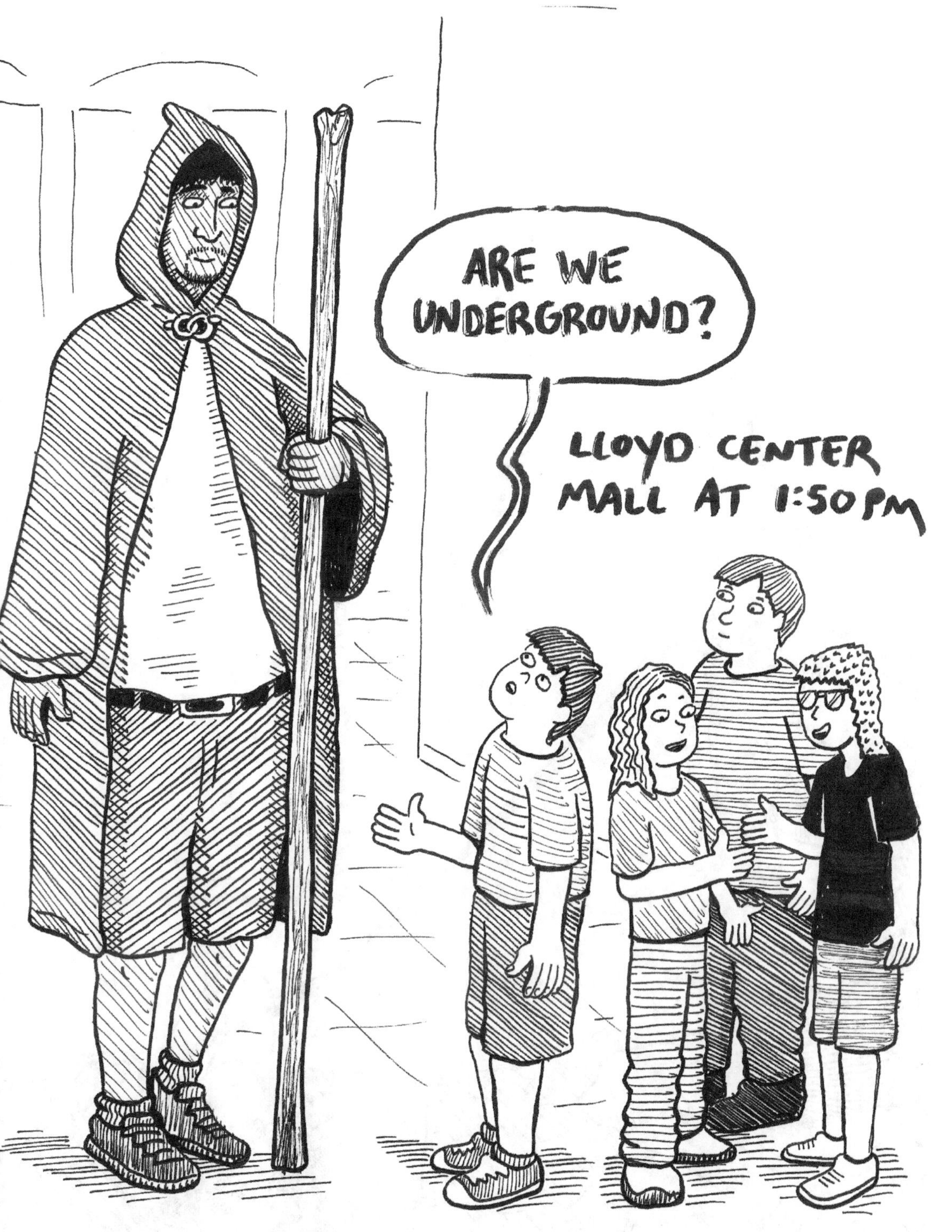

ARE WE UNDERGROUND?
LLOYD CENTER MALL AT 1:50 PM
JS #1,499 8-31-23

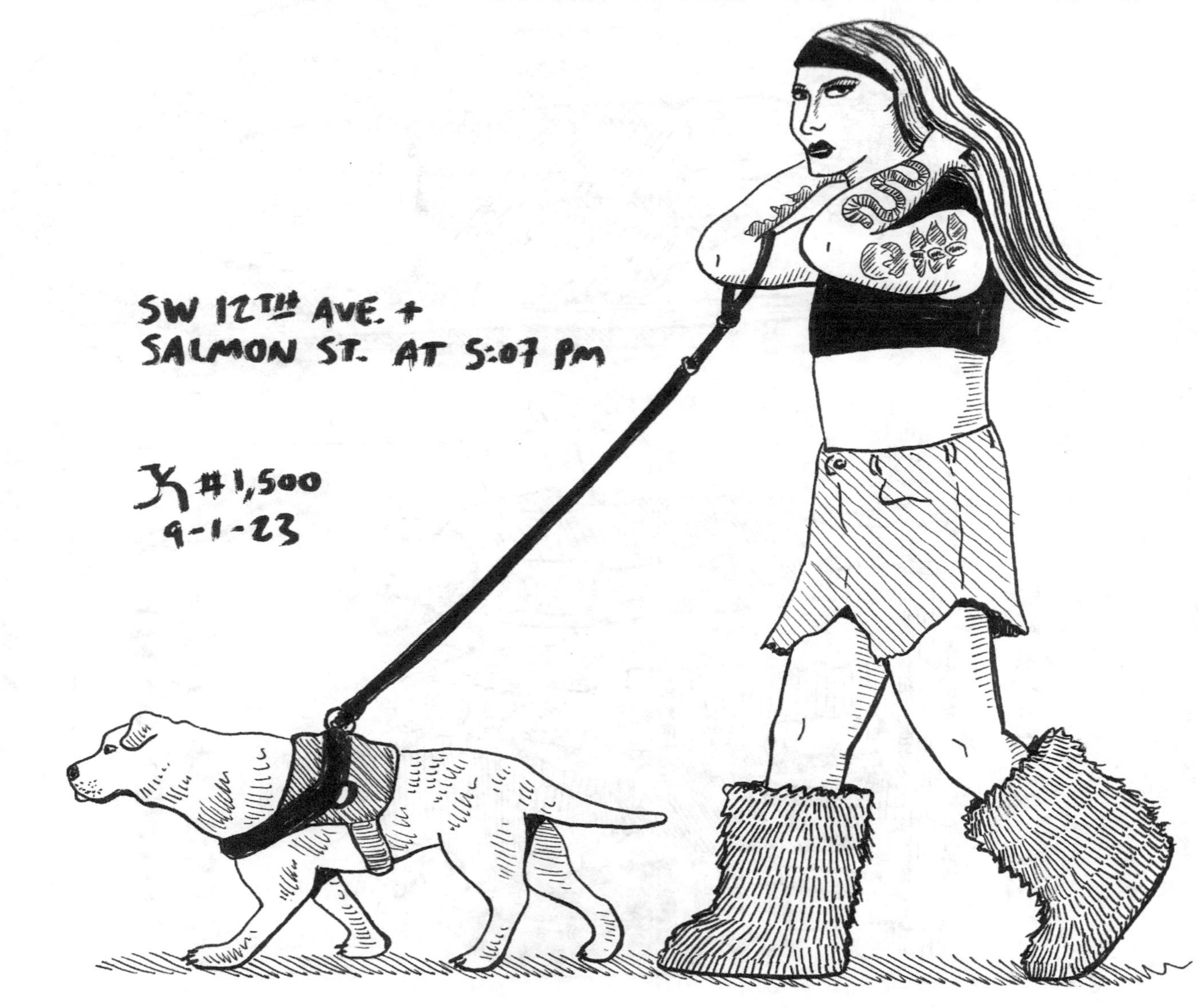

SW 12TH AVE. +
SALMON ST. AT 5:07 PM
#1,500
9-1-23

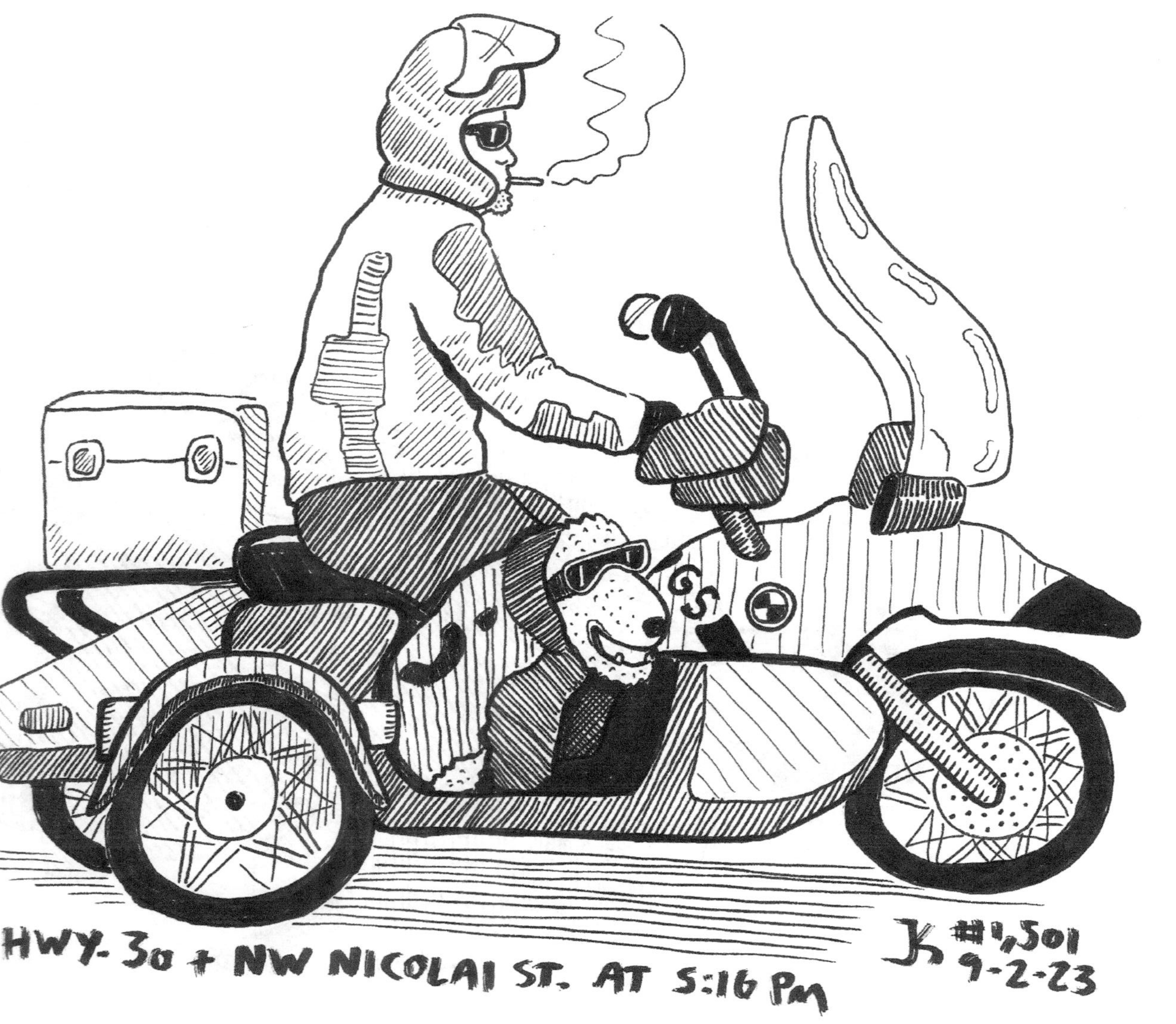
GS
HWY. 30 + NW NICOLAI ST. AT 5:16 Pm
K #1,501
9-2-23

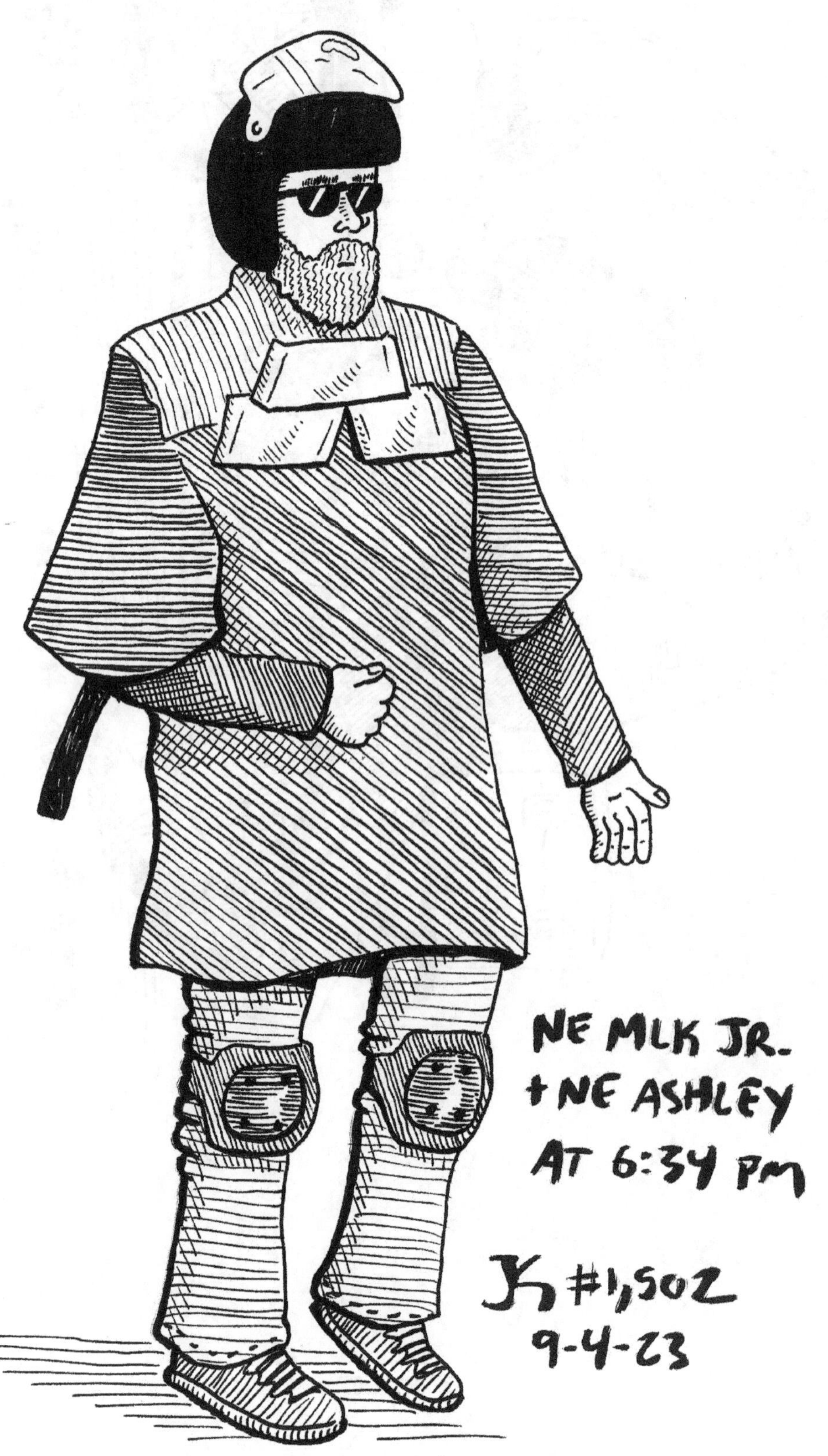

NE MLK JR.
+ NE ASHLEY
AT 6:34 PM

#1,502
9-4-23

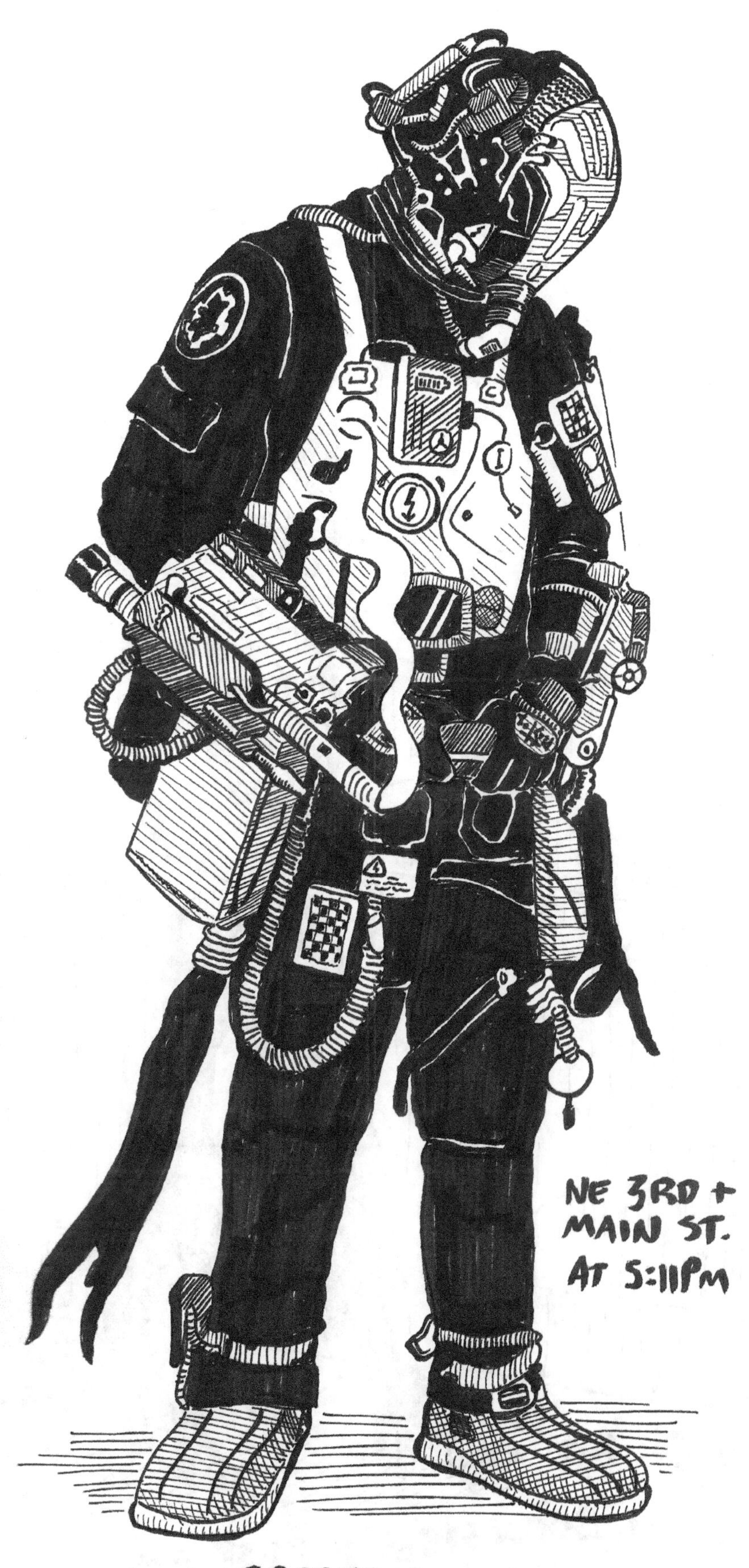

NE 3RD +
MAIN ST.
AT 5:11PM

GRESHAM, OR
JS #1,503 9-5-23

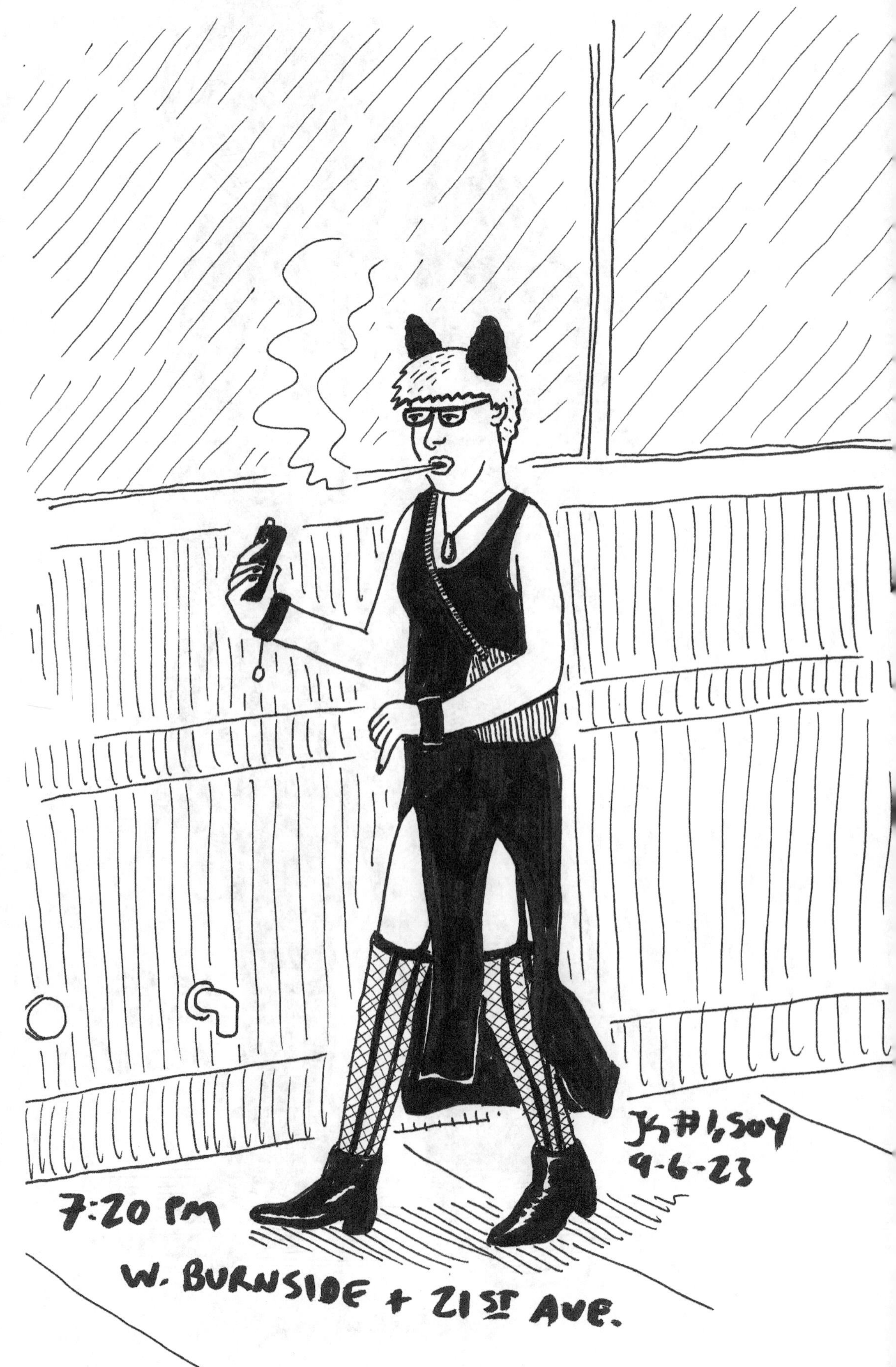

Js#1,504
9-6-23
7:20 PM
W. BURNSIDE + 21ST AVE.

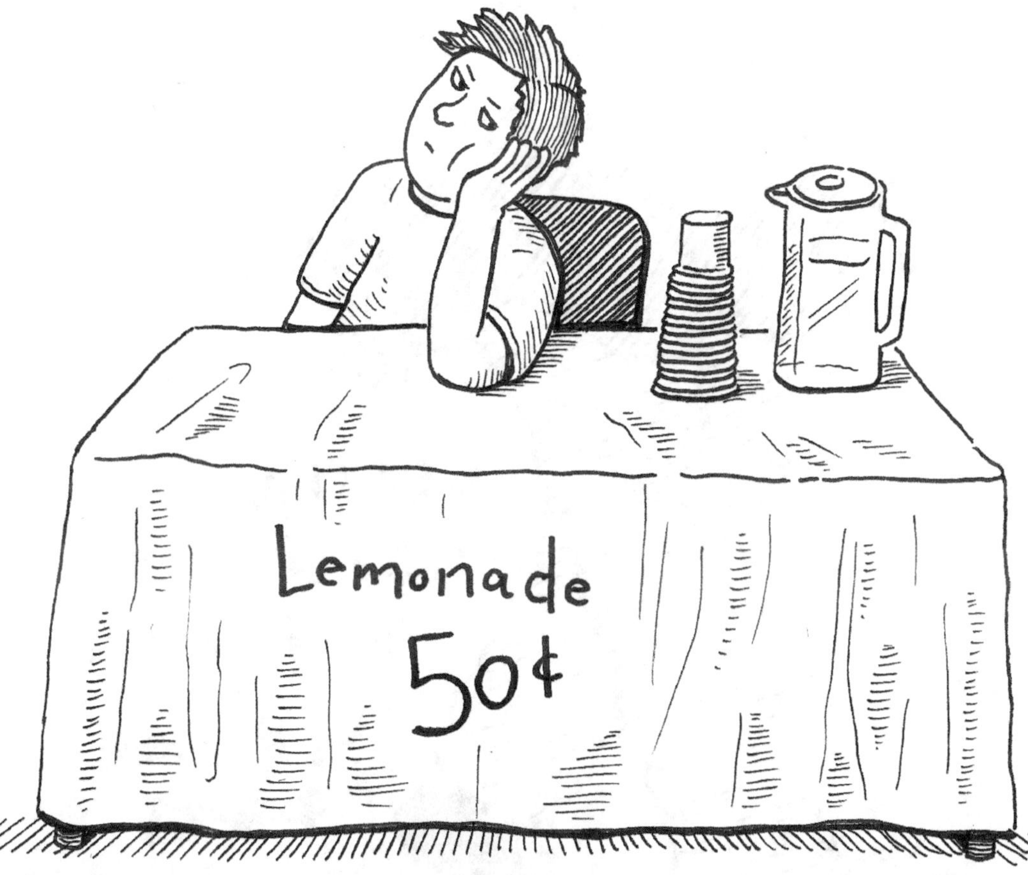

N. 10TH AVE. + N. CLARK ST.
IN CORNELIUS, OR AT 4:05 PM

#1,505
9-7-23

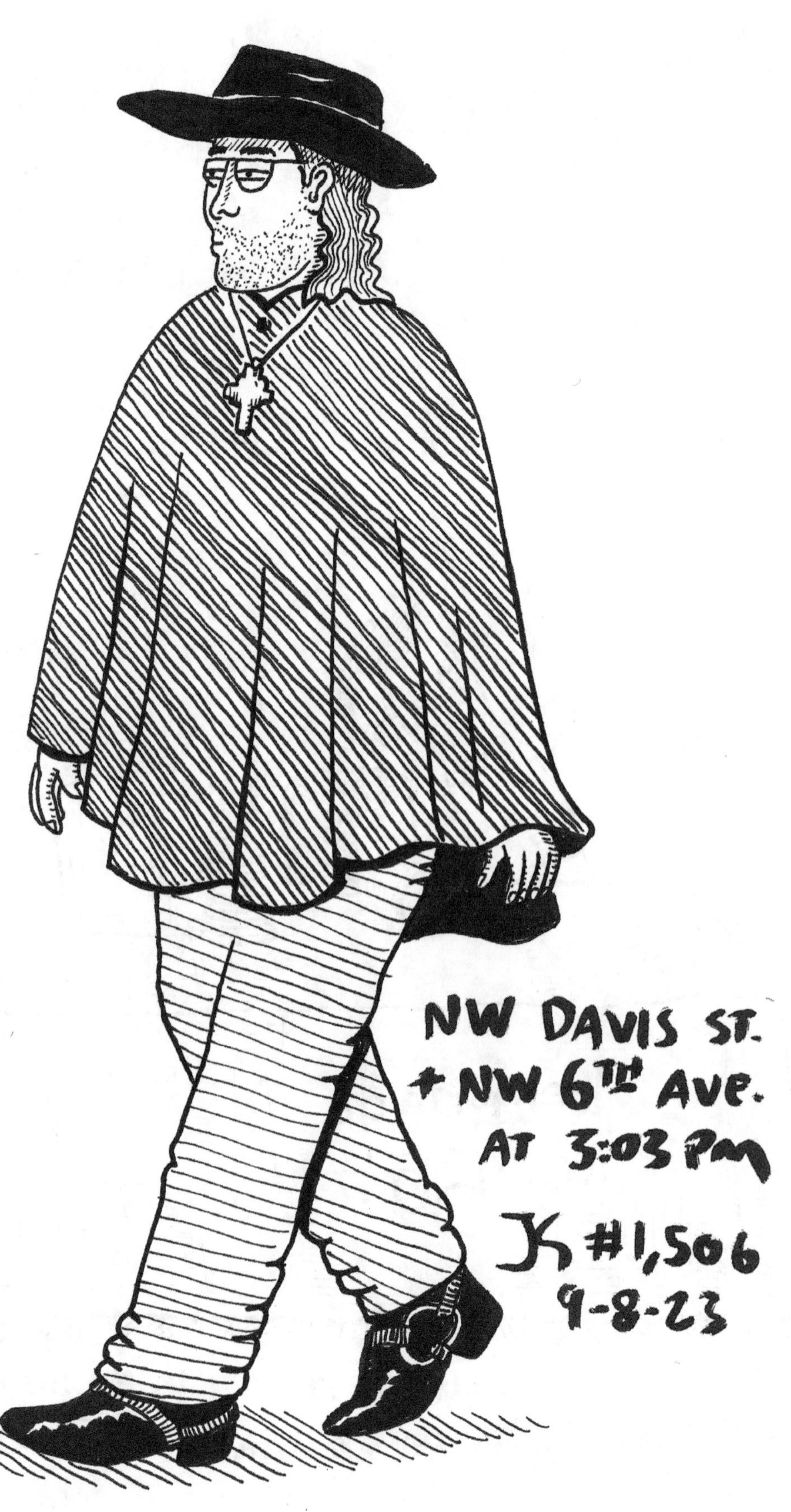

NW DAVIS ST.
+ NW 6TH AVE.
AT 3:03 PM
JK #1,506
9-8-23

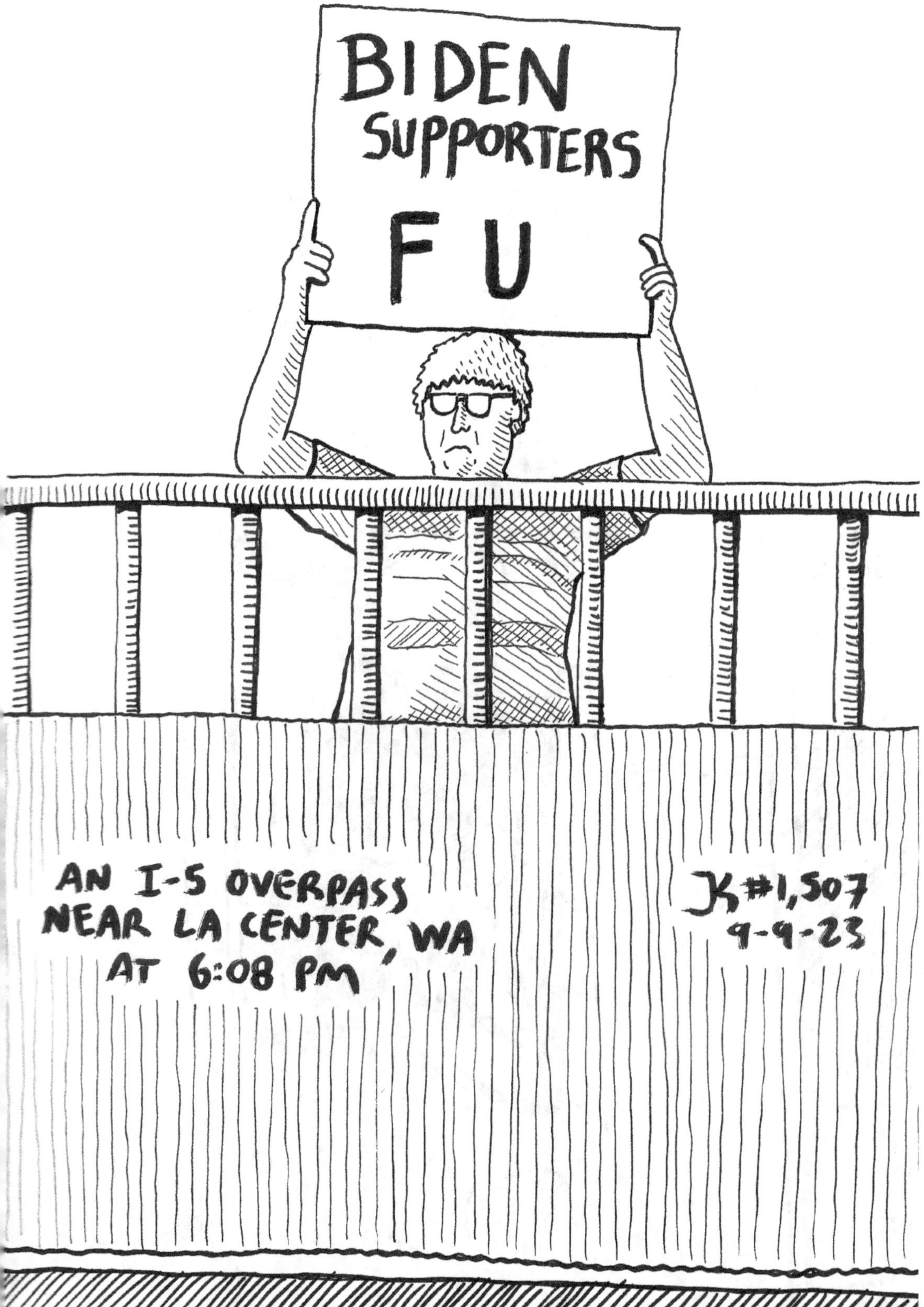

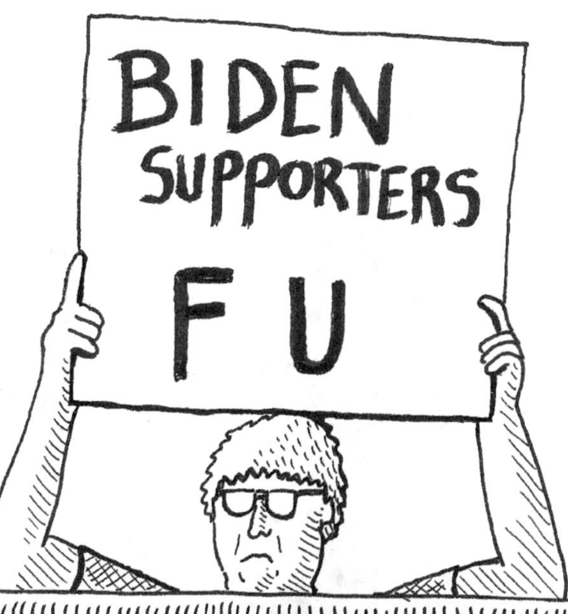

AN I-5 OVERPASS
NEAR LA CENTER, WA
AT 6:08 PM

JK #1,507
9-9-23

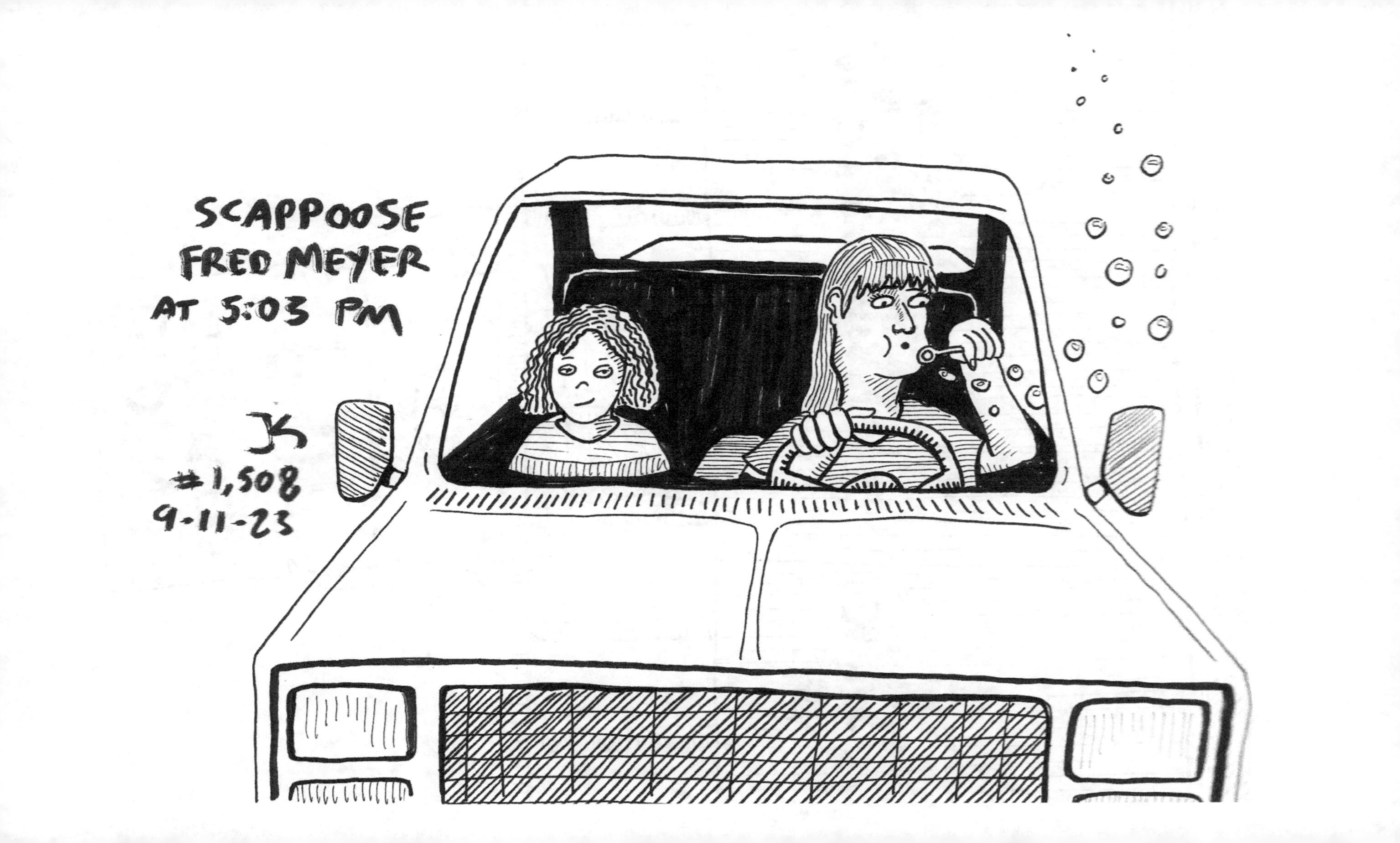

SCAPPOOSE
FRED MEYER
AT 5:03 PM
JS
#1,508
9-11-23

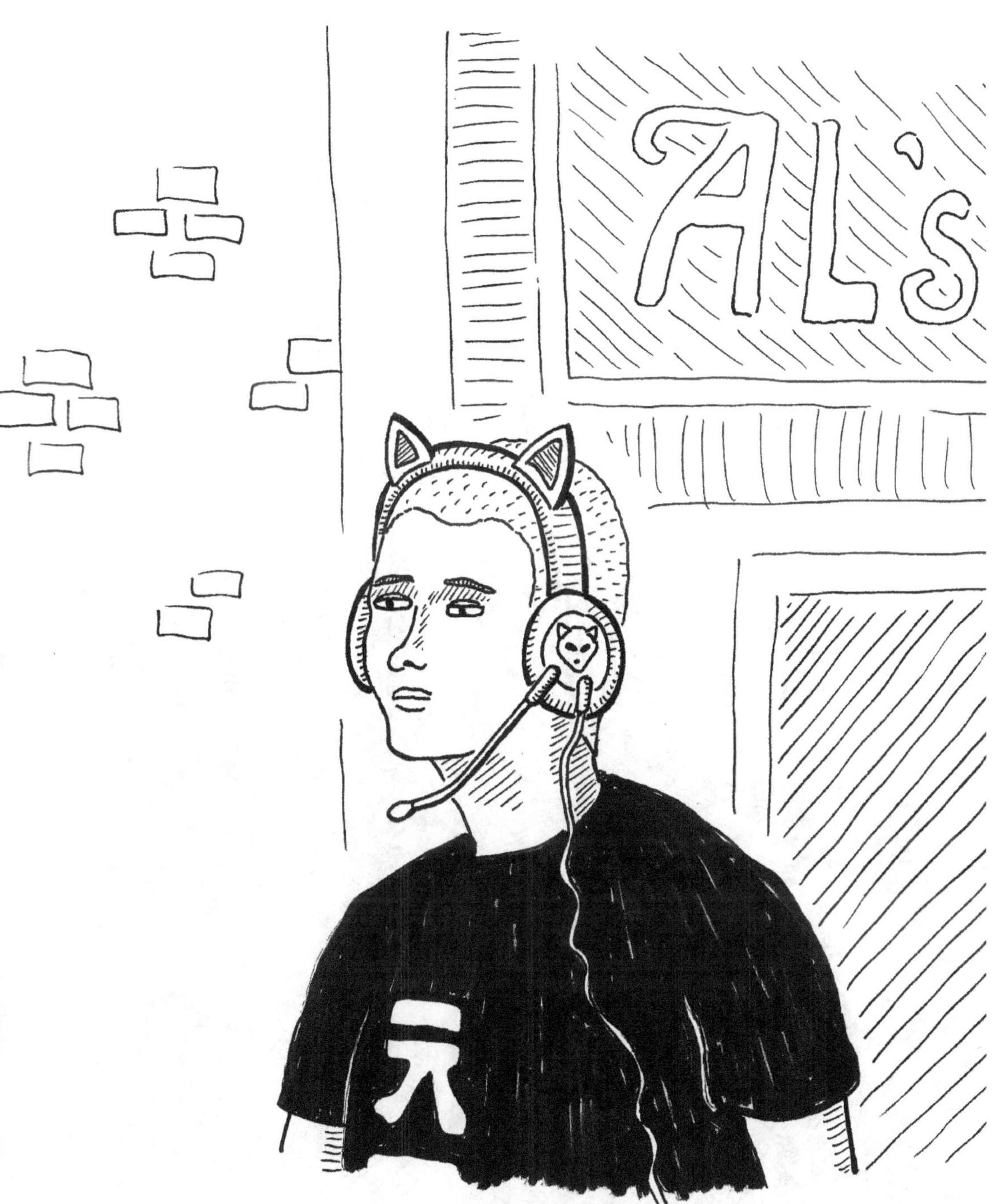
AL'S
W. BURNSIDE +
SW 13TH AVE.
AT 3:28 PM
K #1,509
9-13-23

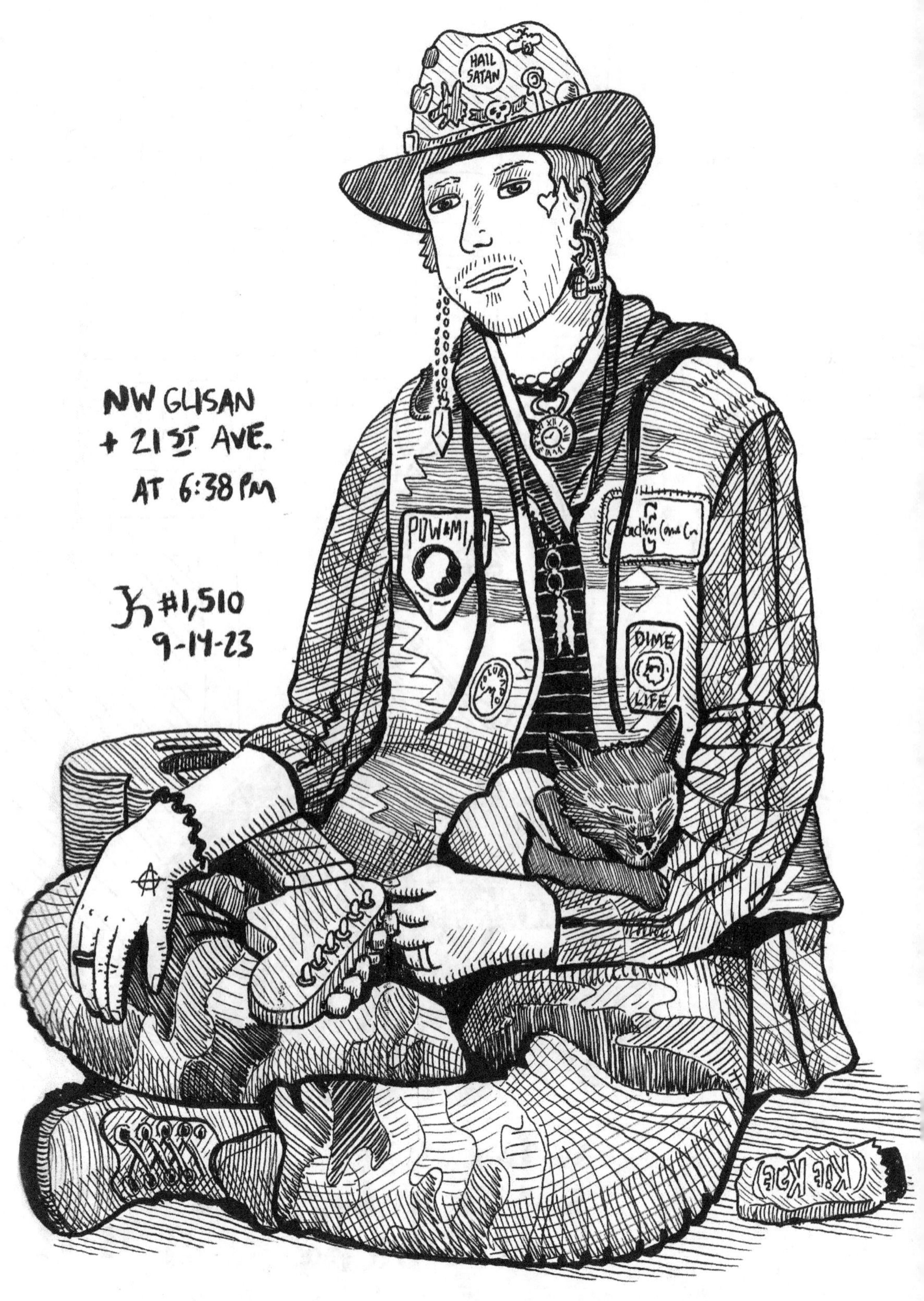

NW GLISAN
+ 21 ST AVE.
AT 6:38 PM

#1,510
9-14-23

HAIL
SATAN

POW*MIA

Dime
Life

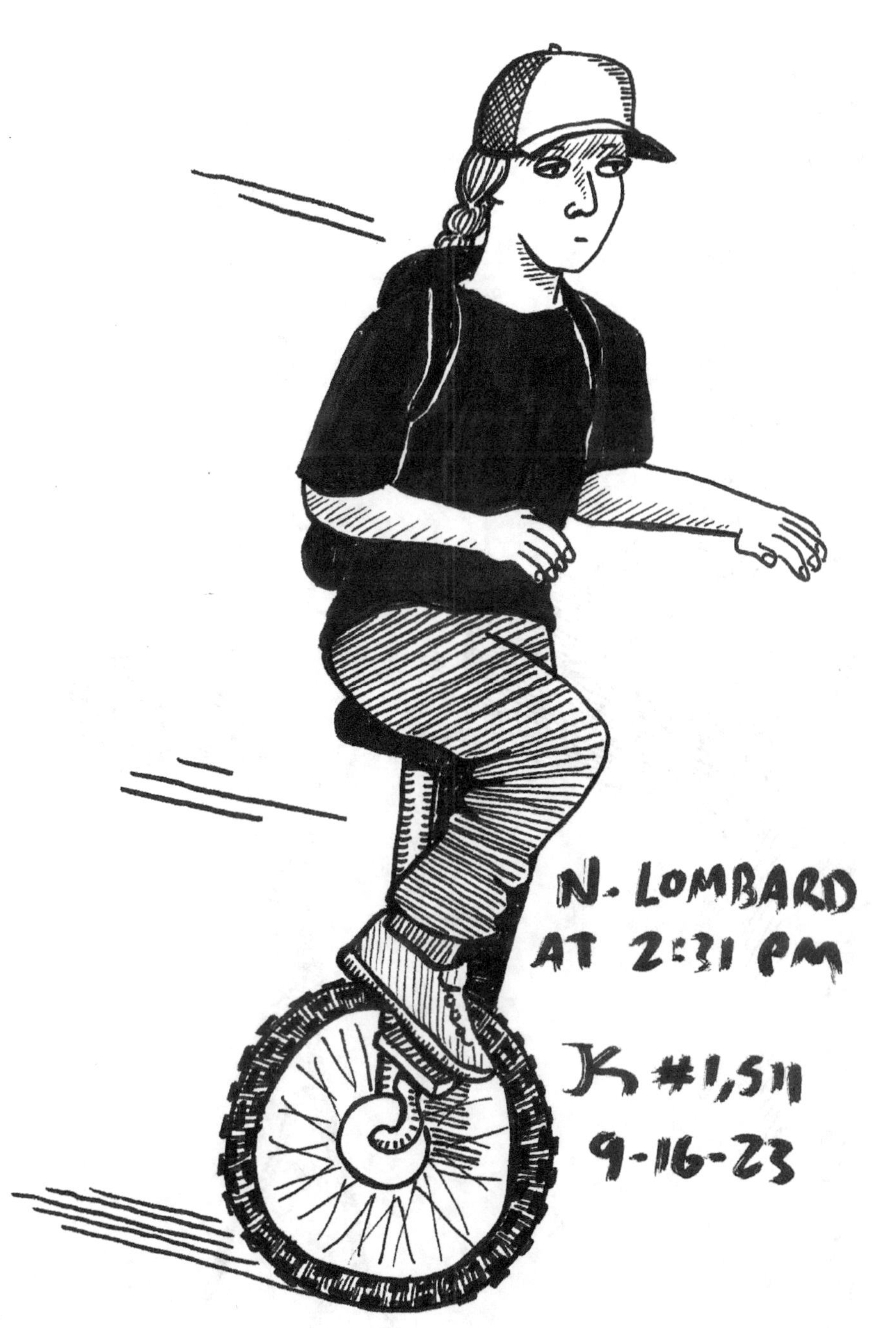

N. LOMBARD
AT 2:31 PM
K #1,511
9-16-23

N. IVANHOE ST. +
N. RICHMOND AVE.   AT 4:51 PM   K # 1,512 9-19-23

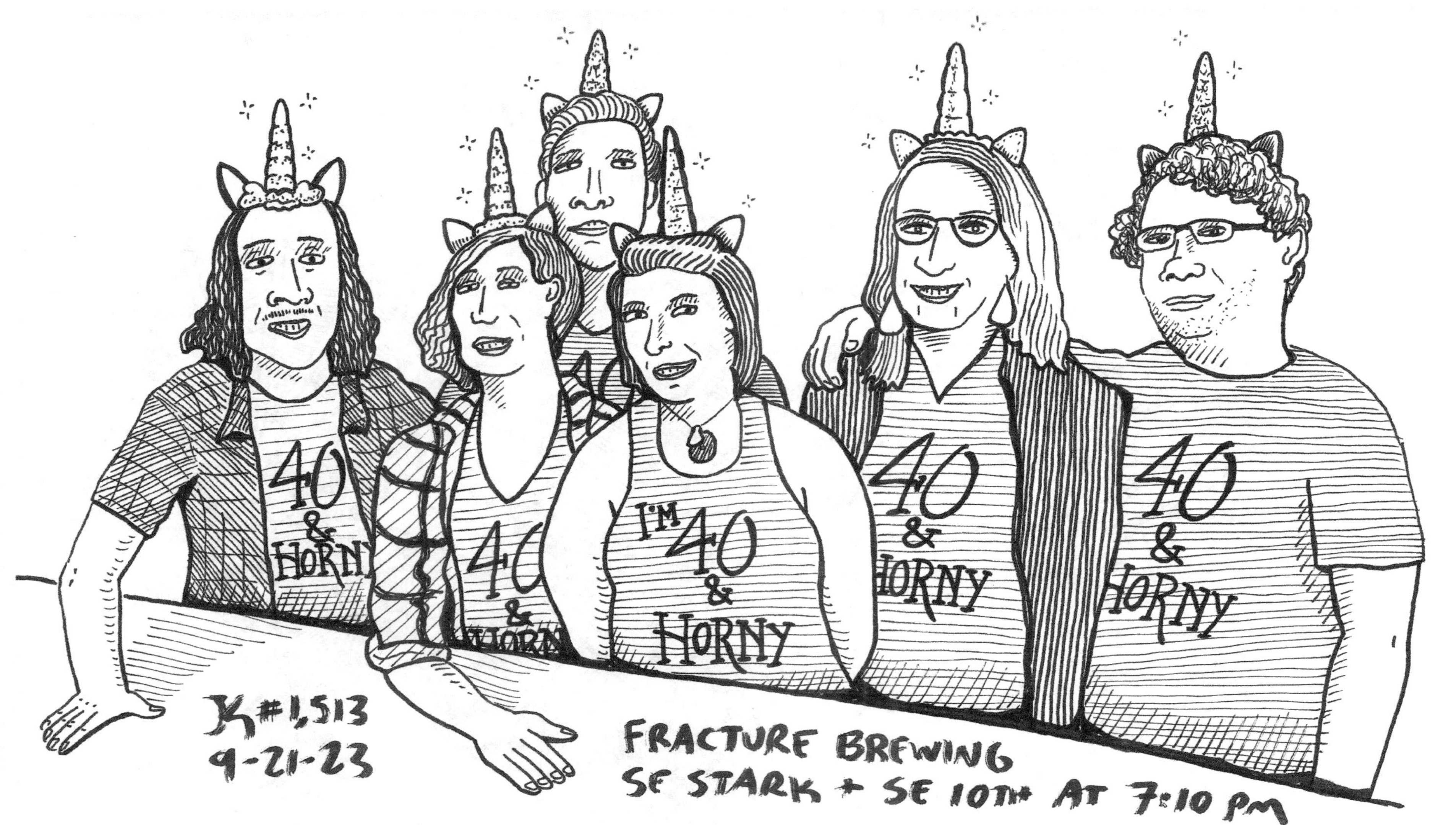
40 & HORNY
40 & HORNY
I'M 40 & HORNY
40 & HORNY
40 & HORNY
JK #1,513
9-21-23
FRACTURE BREWING
SE STARK + SE 10TH AT 7:10 PM

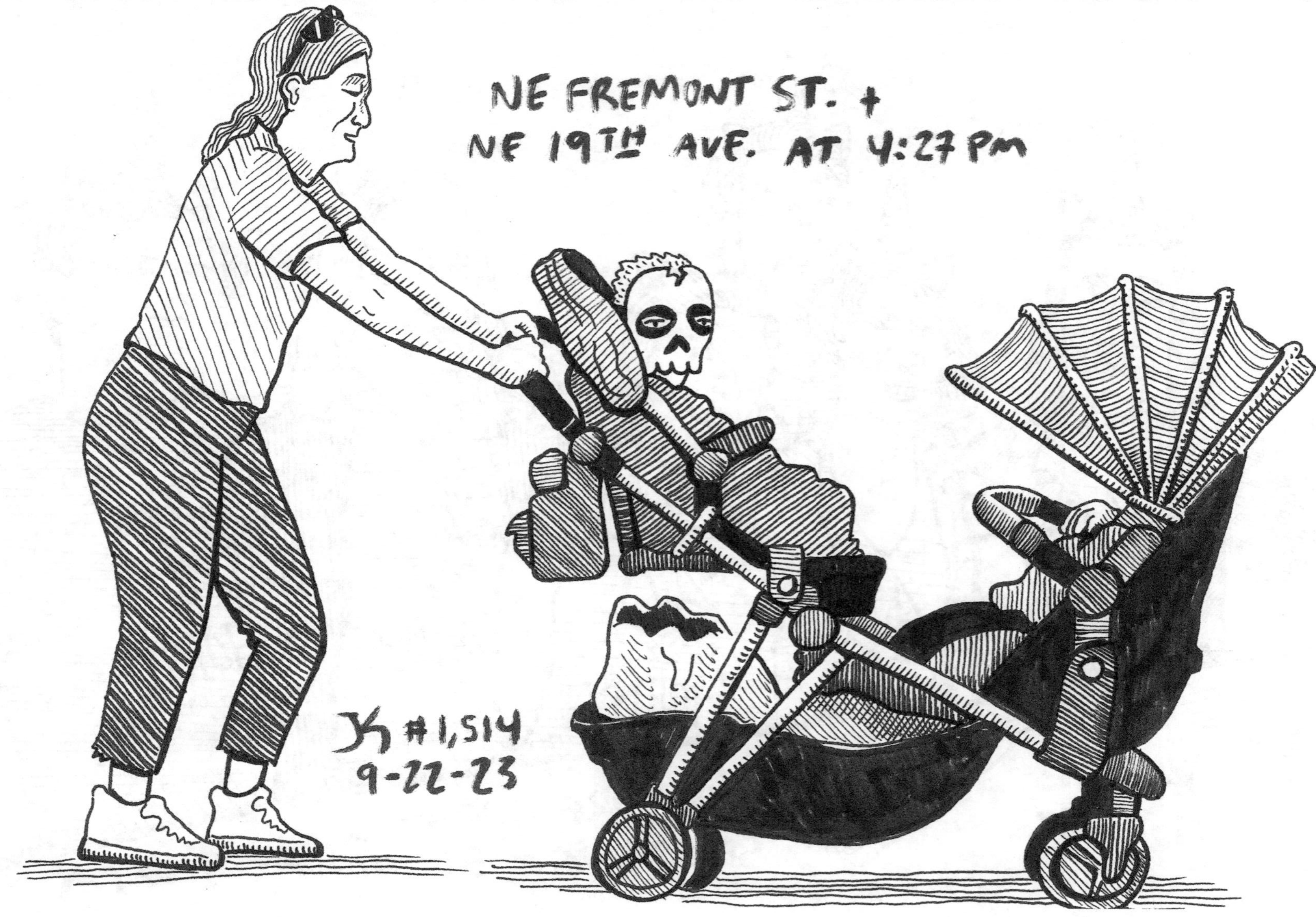

NE FREMONT ST. +
NE 19TH AVE. AT 4:27 PM
JK #1,514
9-22-23

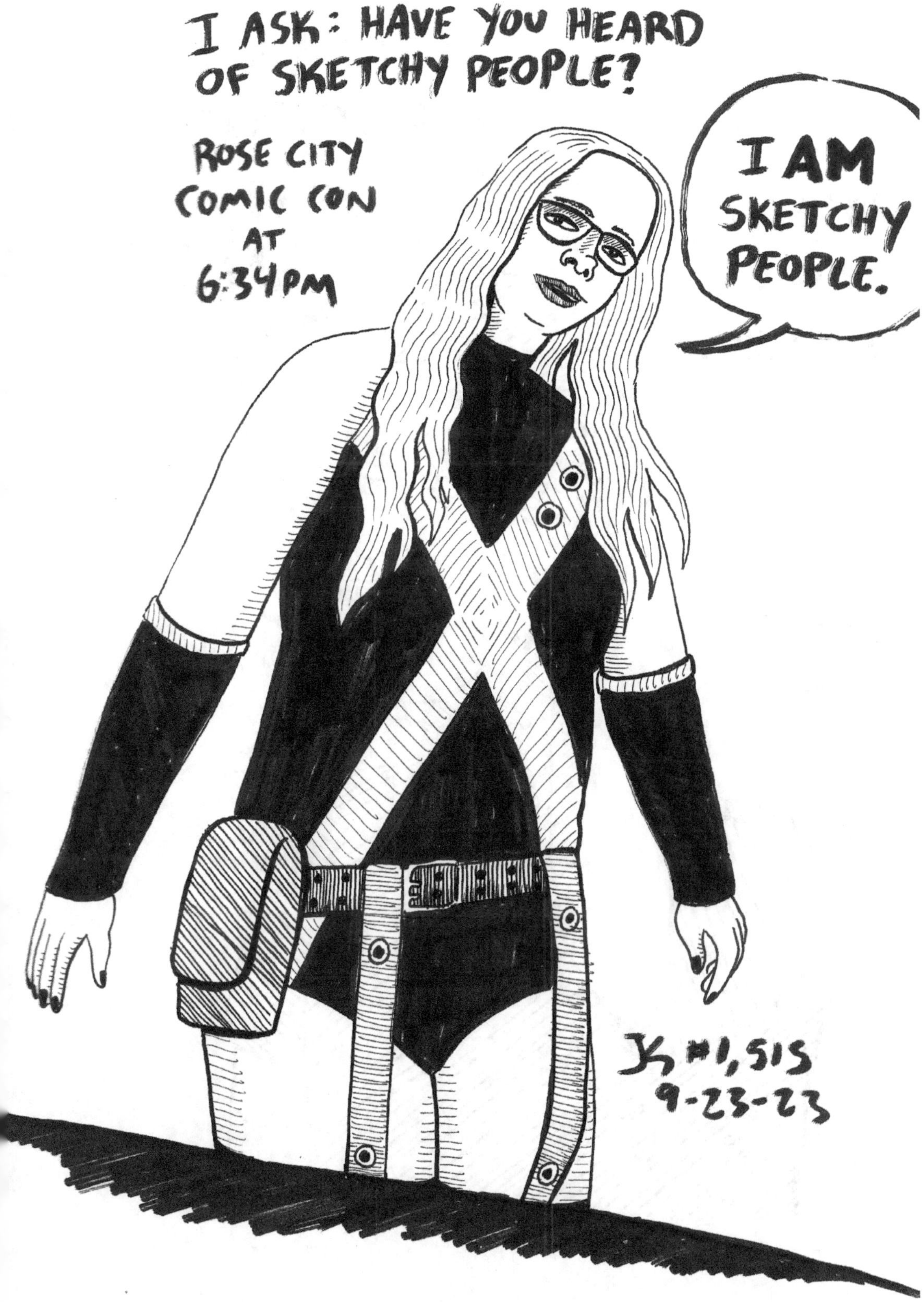

I ASK: HAVE YOU HEARD OF SKETCHY PEOPLE?
ROSE CITY COMIC CON AT 6:34 PM
I AM SKETCHY PEOPLE.

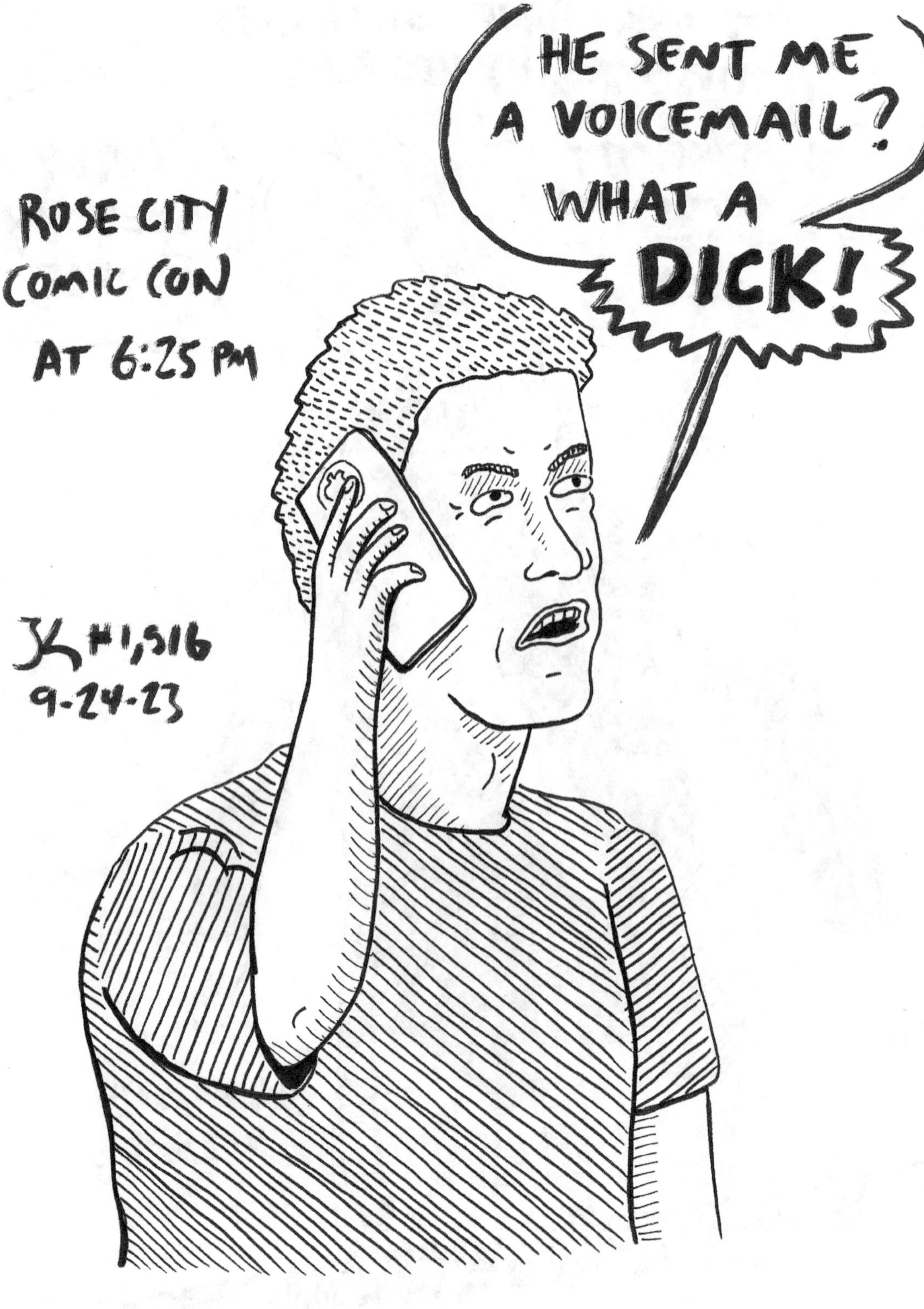

HE SENT ME A VOICEMAIL? WHAT A DICK!
ROSE CITY COMIC CON AT 6:25 PM
#1,516
9-24-23

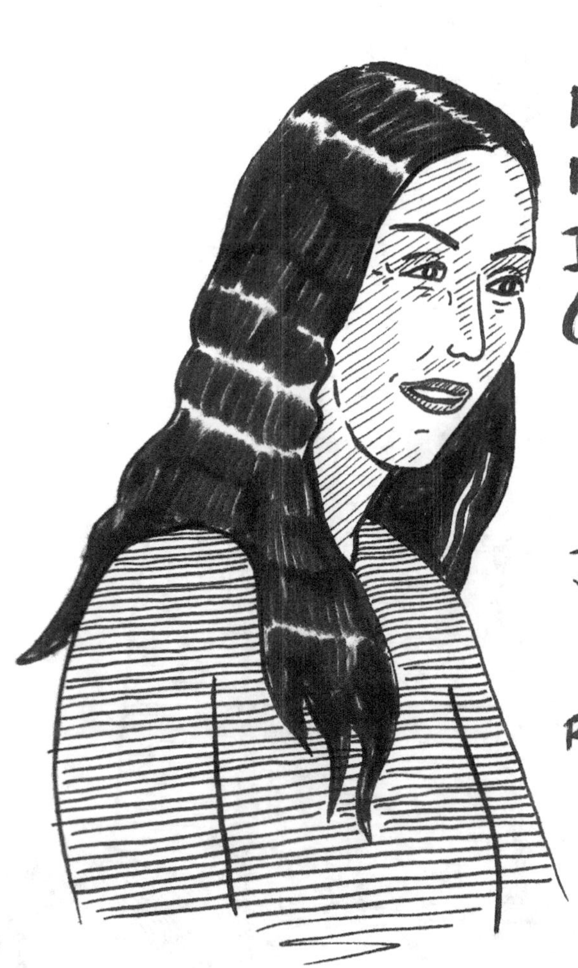

I ASKED
RALPH MACCHIO IF
IT WAS OKAY THAT
I ACCIDENTALLY
GROPED HIM.

HE SAID IT WAS.

THAT GOT MY
JOLLIES OFF FOR
THE DAY.

ROSE CITY COMIC CON
AT 12:01 PM
JK #1,517 9-24-23

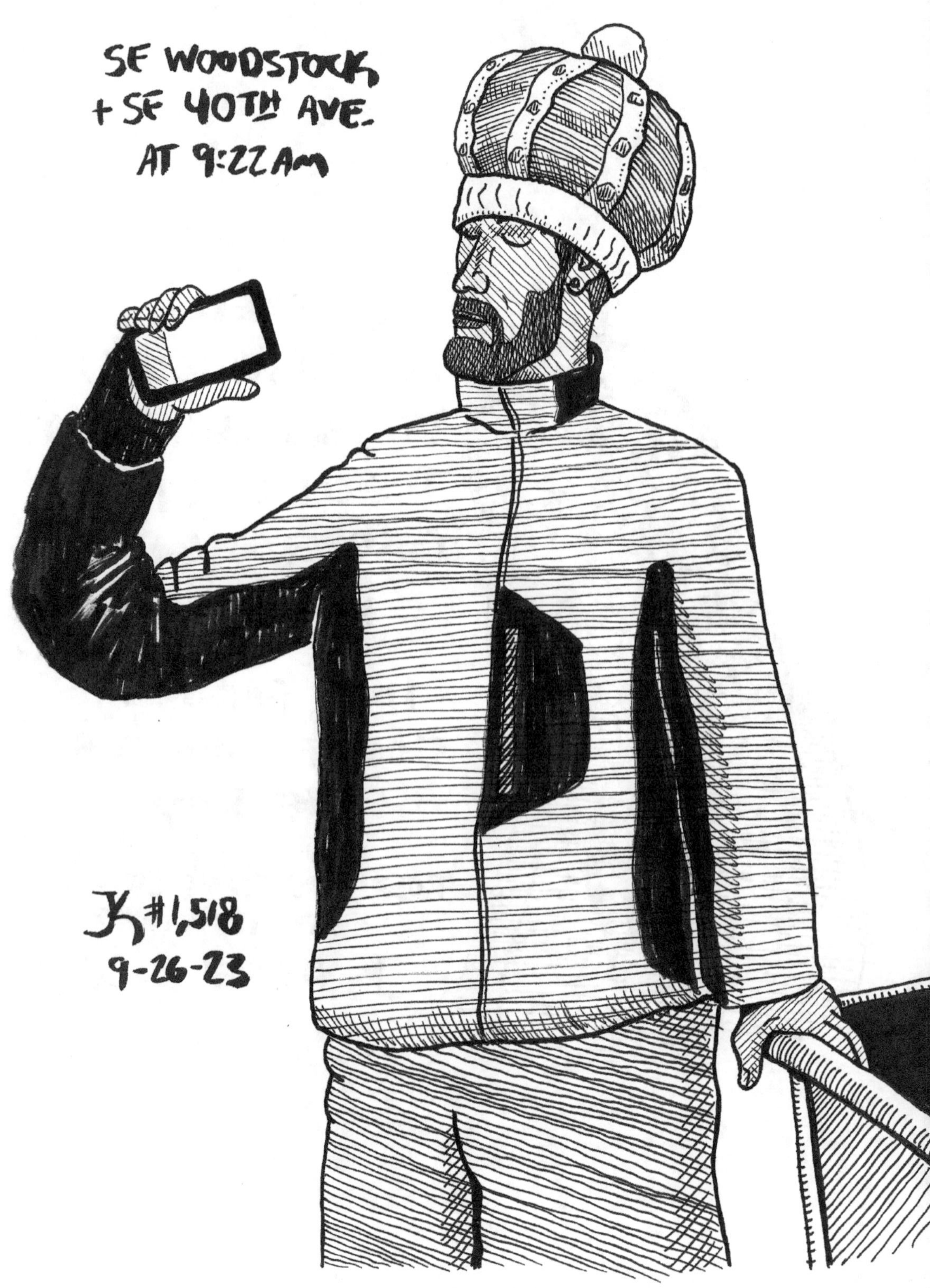

SE WOODSTOCK
+ SE 40TH AVE.
AT 9:22AM
JK #1,518
9-26-23

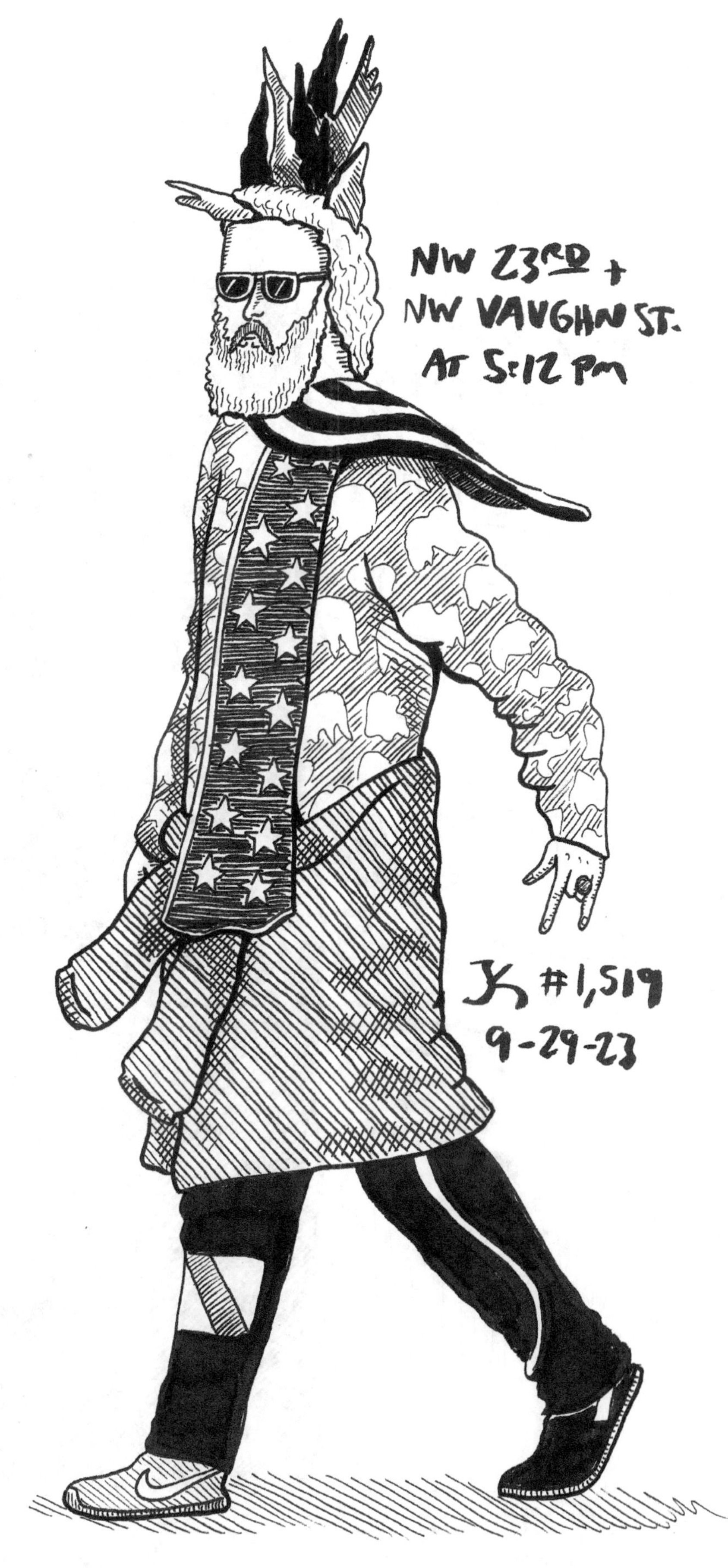
NW 23RD +
NW VAUGHN ST.
AT 5:12 PM
#1,519
9-29-23

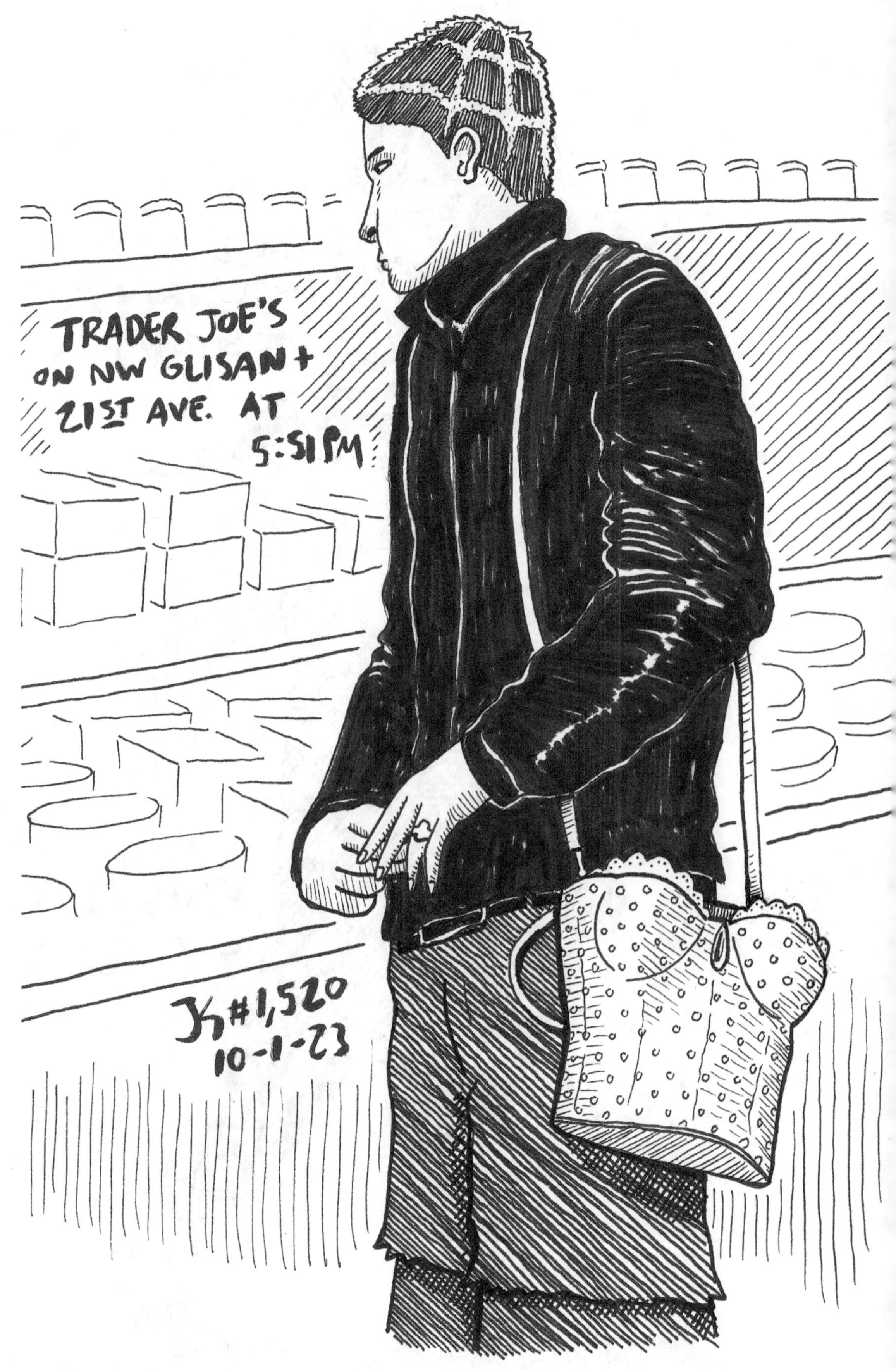

TRADER JOE'S
ON NW GLISAN +
21ST AVE. AT
5:51 PM
#1,520
10-1-23

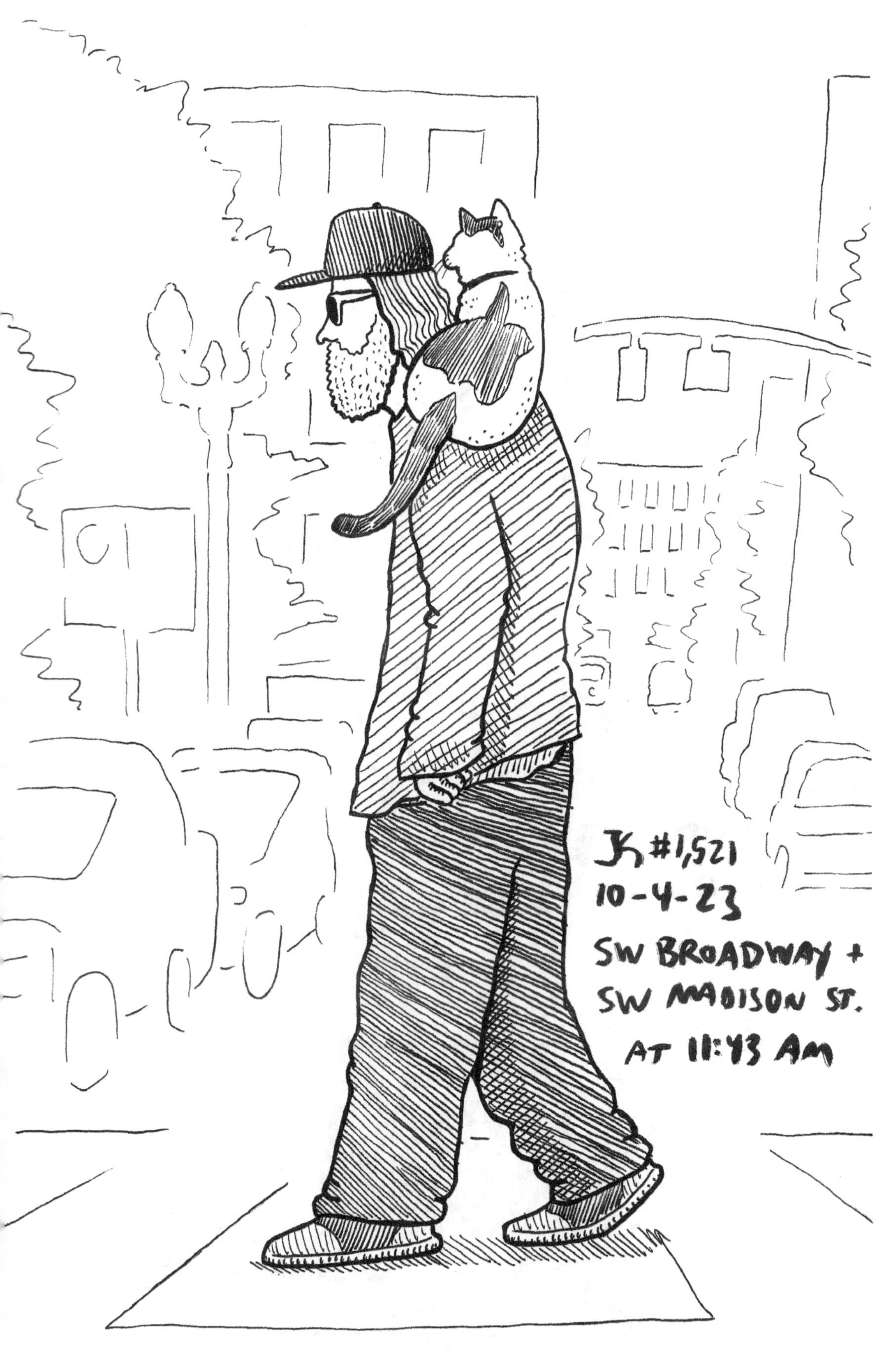
JK #1,521
10-4-23
SW BROADWAY +
SW MADISON ST.
AT 11:43 AM

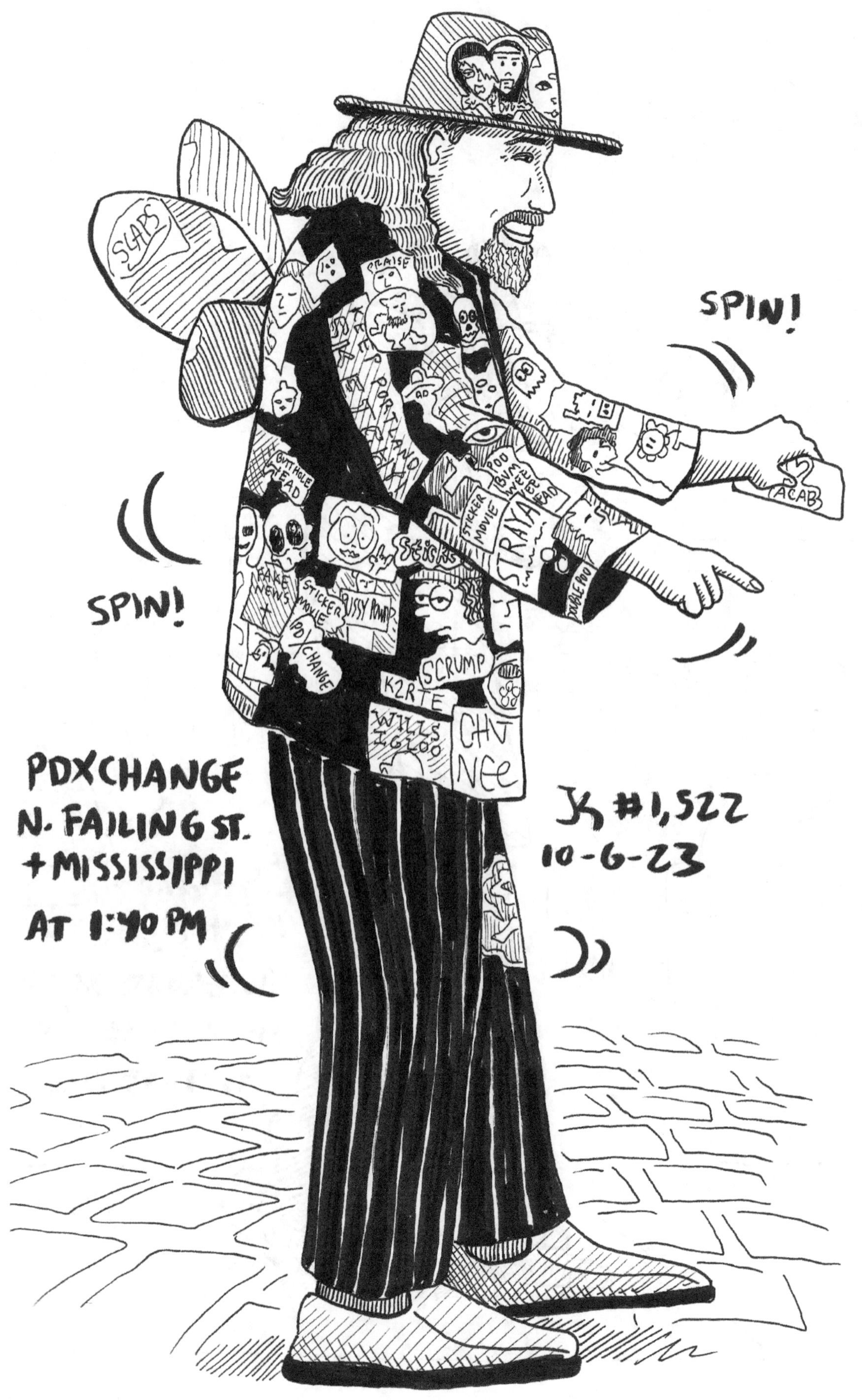

SPIN!
SPIN!
SLAPS
PORTLAND
BUTT HOLE HEAD
PRAISE
STICKS
FAKE NEWS
STICKER MOVIE
PDX CHANGE
PUSSY POWER
STICKER MOVIE
STRAYA
SCRUMP
K2RTE
WILLS IGLOO
CHVNGE
ACAB
PDX CHANGE
N. FAILING ST.
+ MISSISSIPPI
AT 1:40 PM
JK #1,522
10-6-23

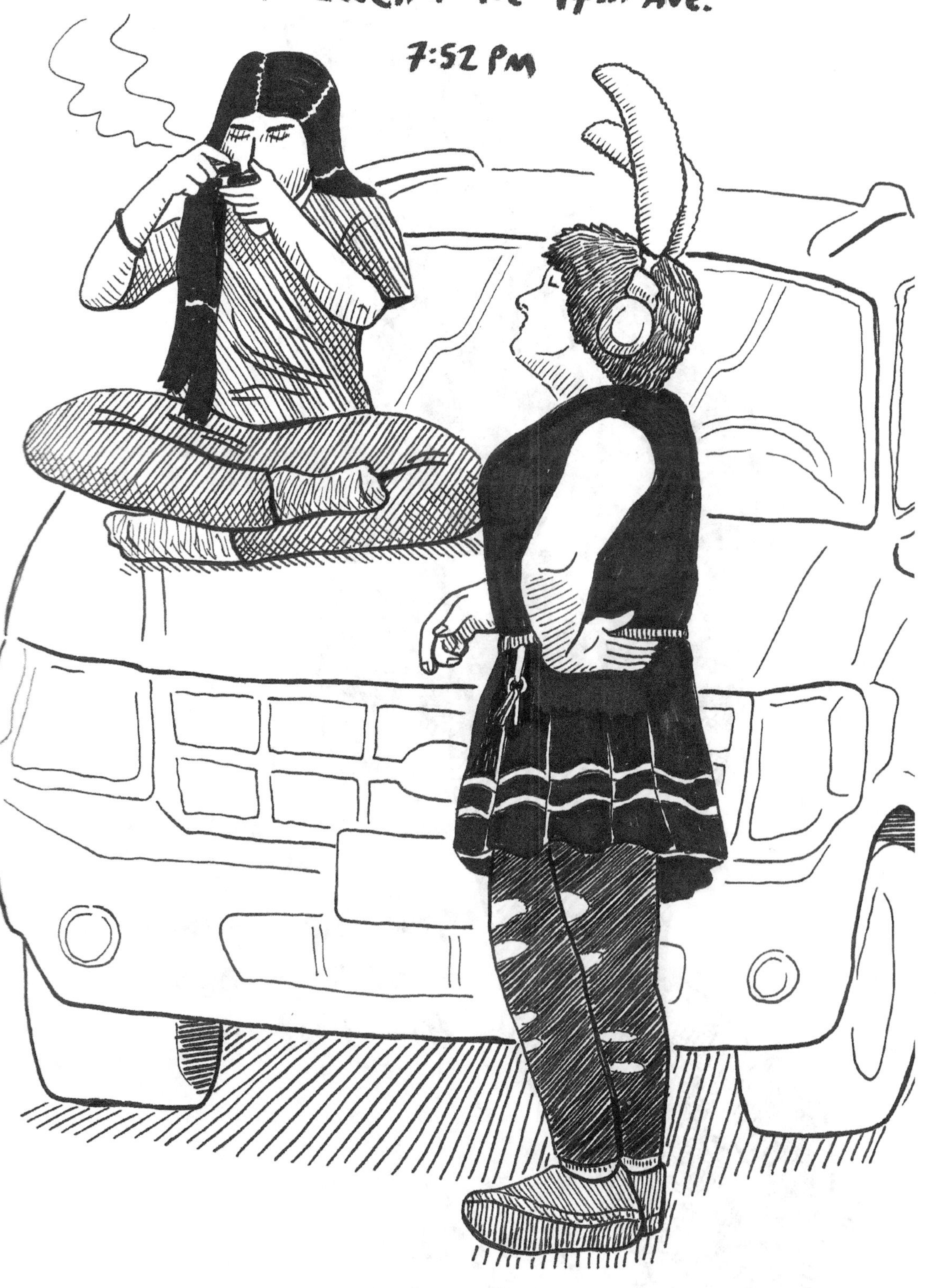

NE BEECH + NE 47TH AVE.
7:52 PM
JS #1,523 10-7-23

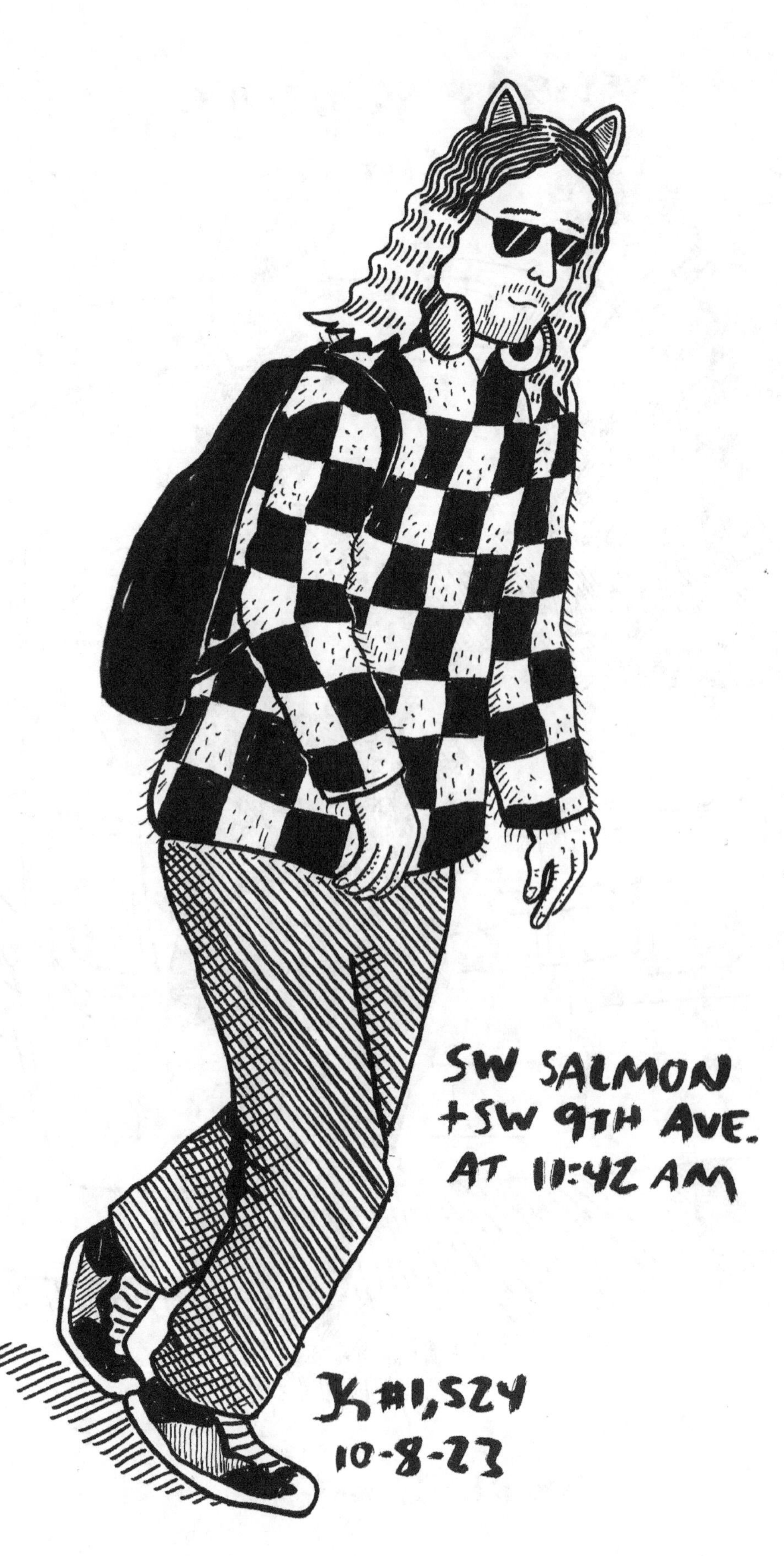

SW SALMON
+SW 9TH AVE.
AT 11:42 AM
K#1,524
10-8-23

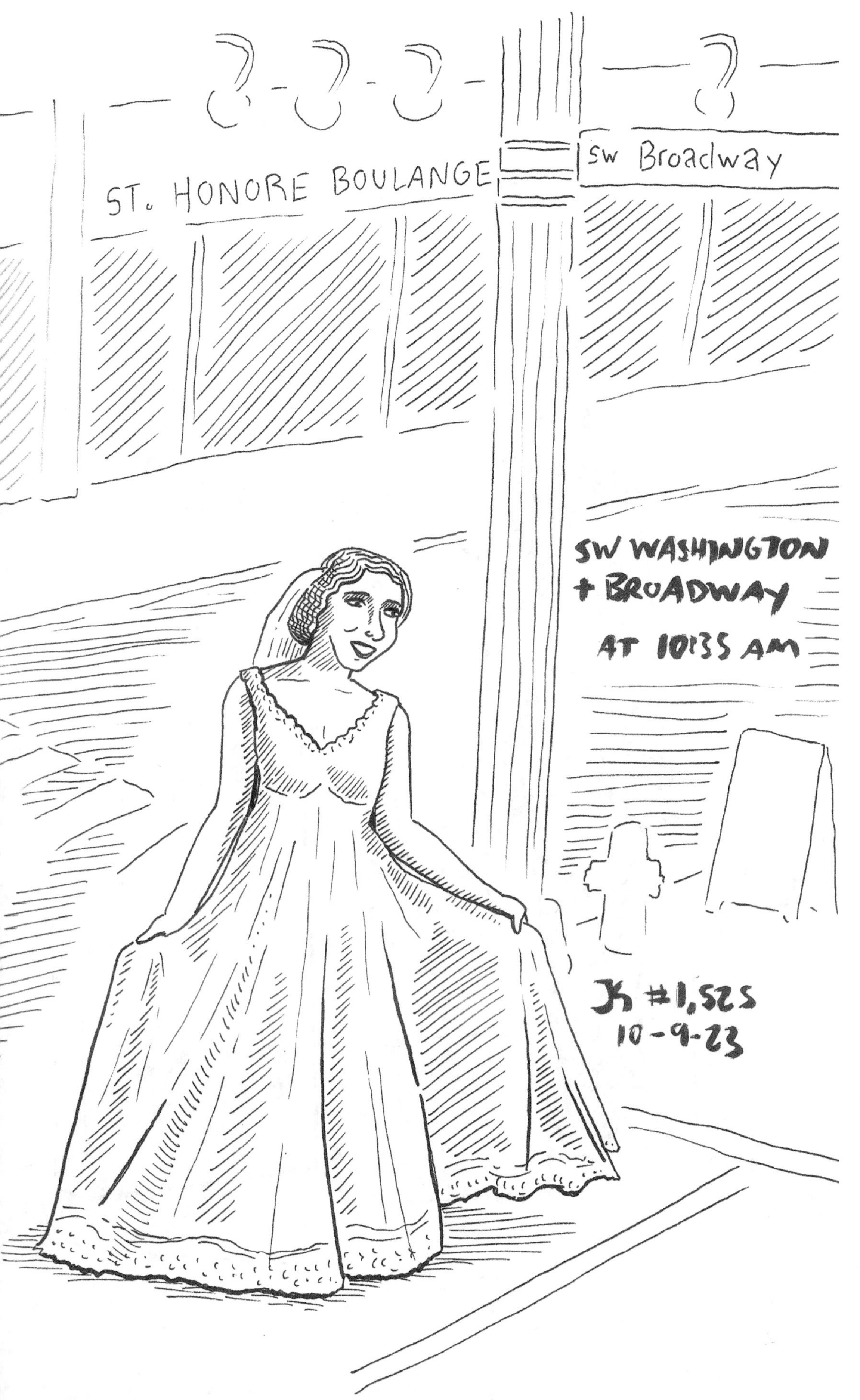

ST. HONORE BOULANGE
sw Broadway
SW WASHINGTON
+ BROADWAY
AT 10:35 AM
JK #1,525
10-9-23

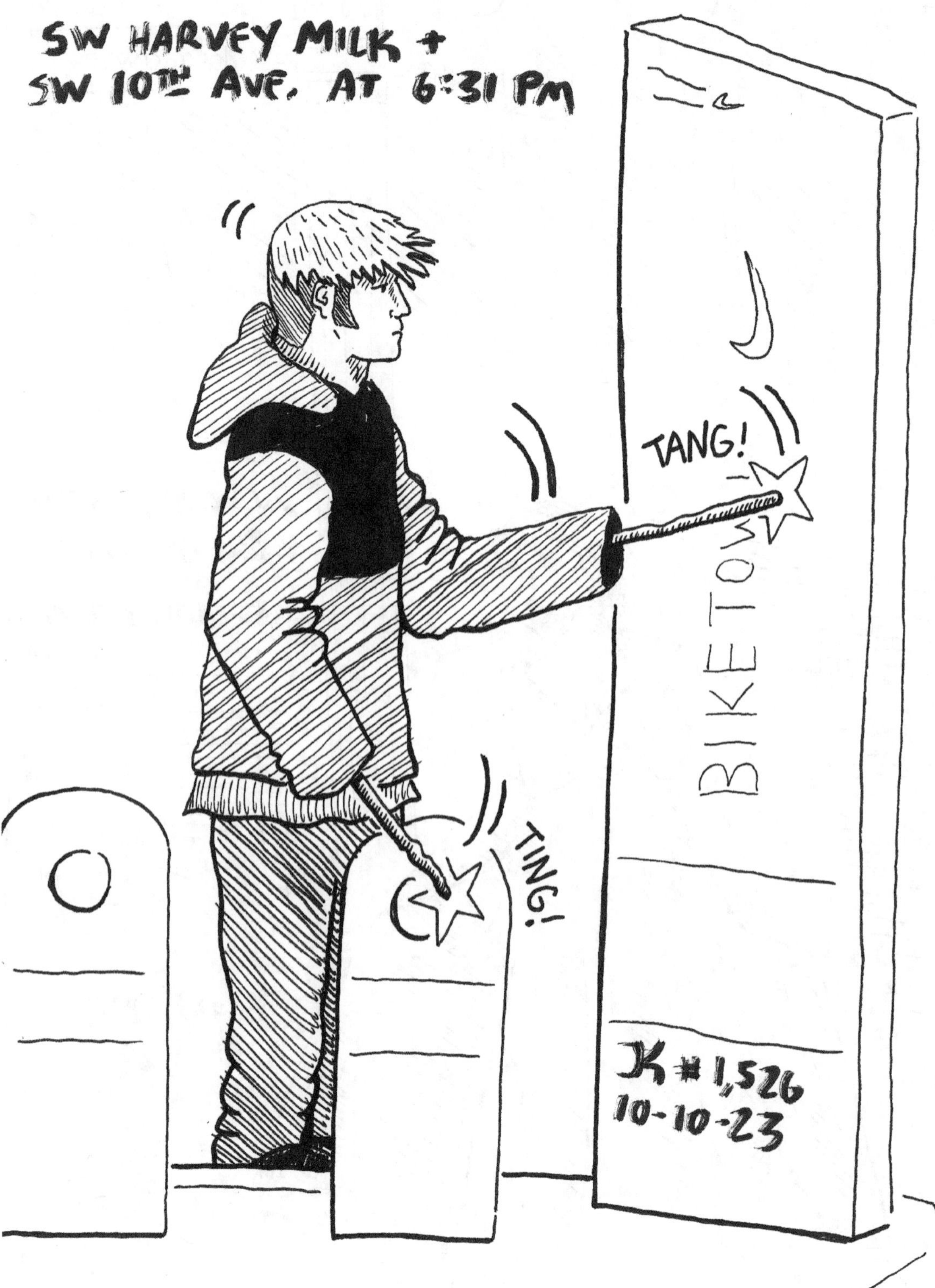

SW HARVEY MILK +
SW 10TH AVE. AT 6:31 PM
TANG!
TING!
BIKETOWN
K # 1,526
10-10-23

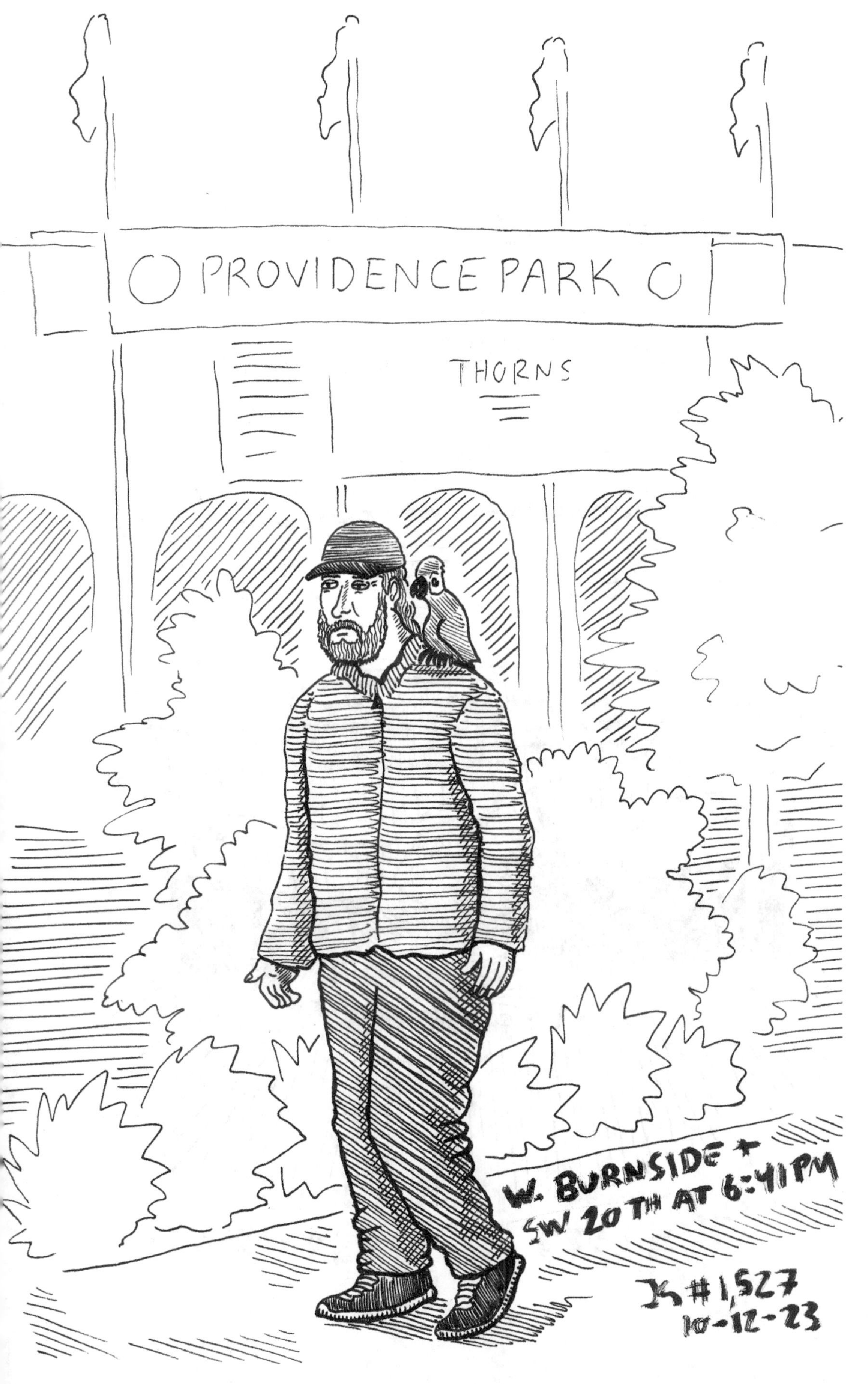

PROVIDENCE PARK
THORNS
W. BURNSIDE +
SW 20TH AT 6:41 PM
#1,527
10-12-23

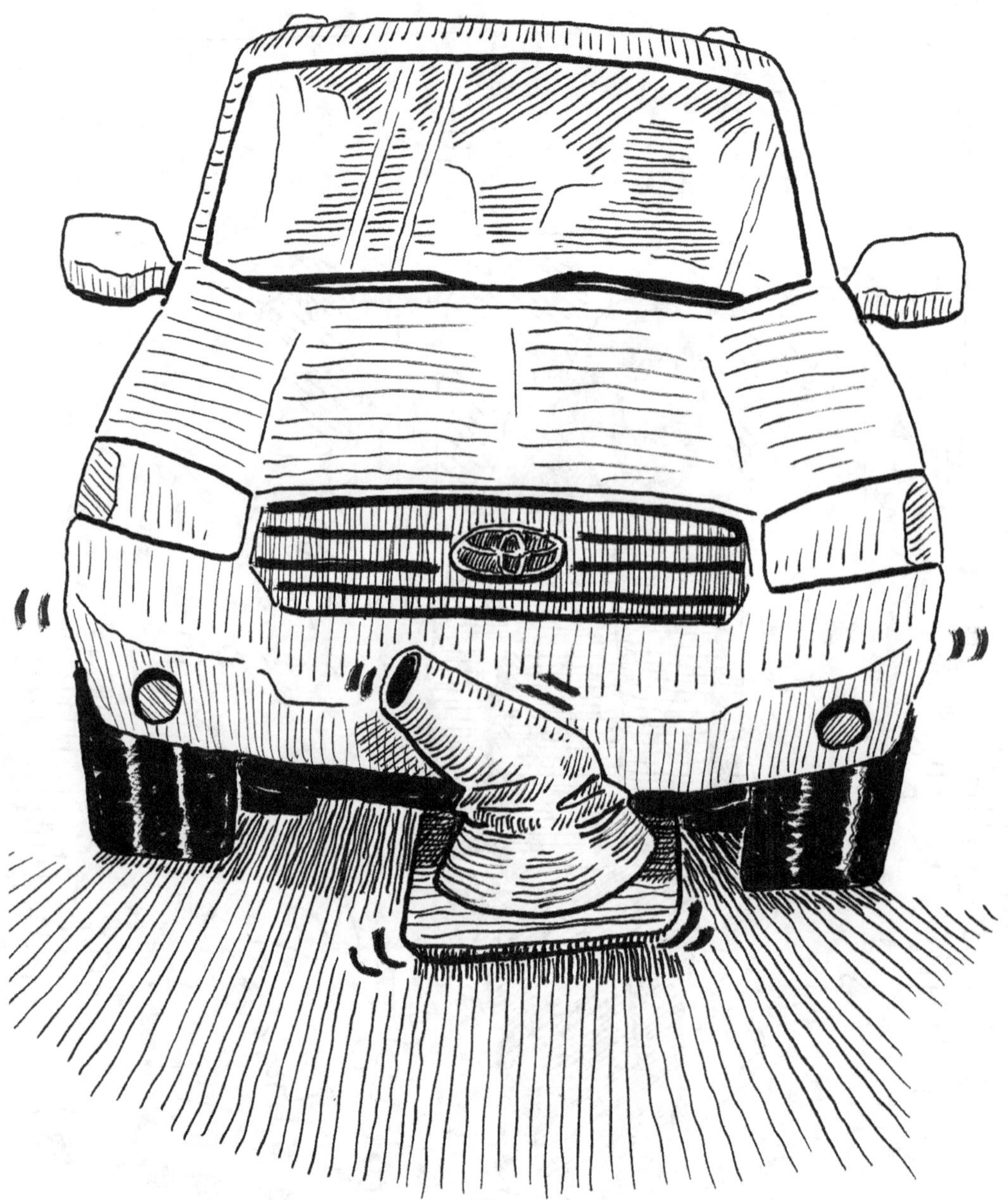

SW SALMON ST. +
SW 12TH AT 8:33AM
1,528
10-13-23

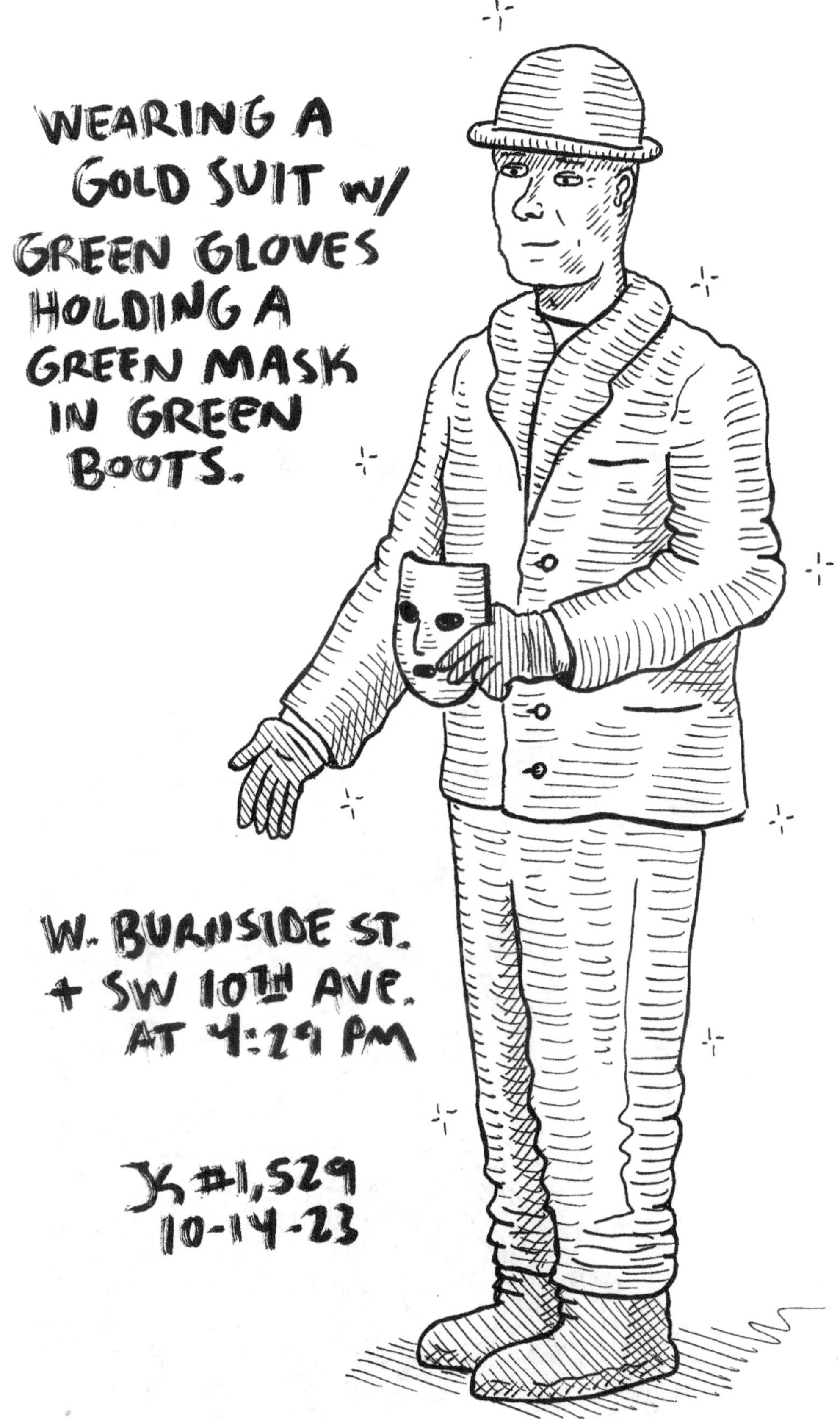
WEARING A
GOLD SUIT w/
GREEN GLOVES
HOLDING A
GREEN MASK
IN GREEN
BOOTS.

W. BURNSIDE ST.
+ SW 10TH AVE.
AT 4:29 PM

JS #1,529
10-14-23

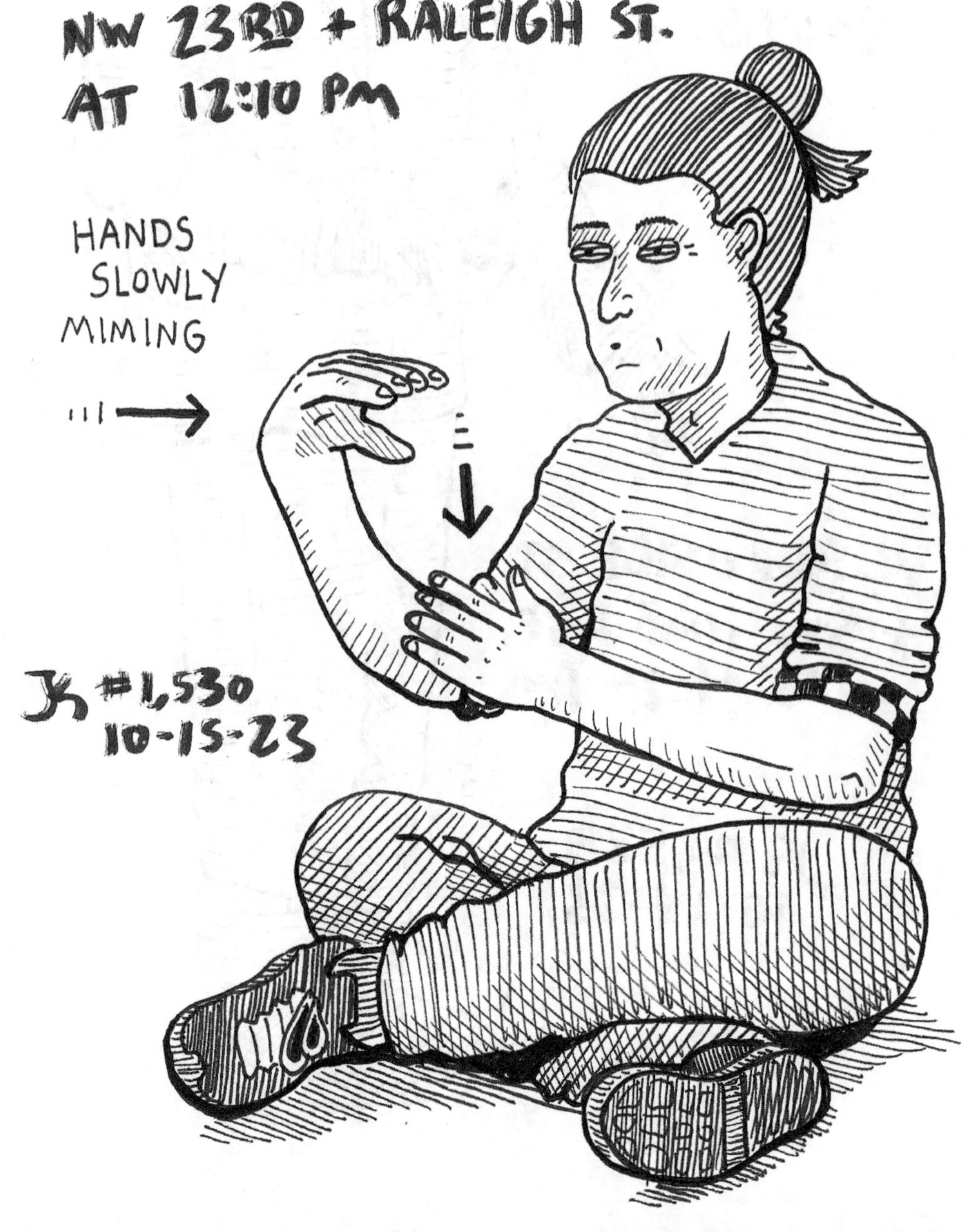

NW 23RD + RALEIGH ST.
AT 12:10 PM

HANDS
SLOWLY
MIMING

JK #1,530
10-15-23

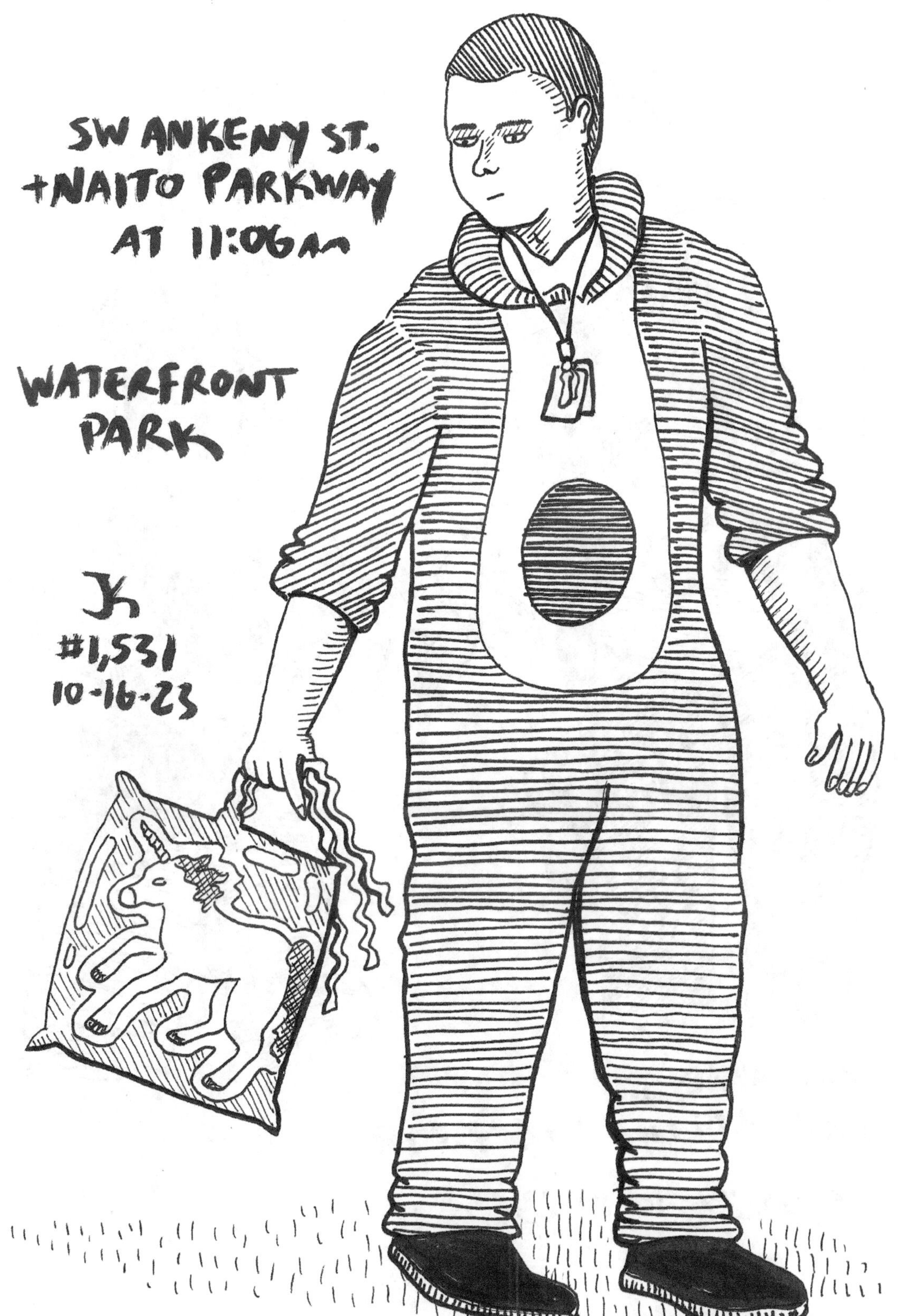

SW ANKENY ST.
+ NAITO PARKWAY
AT 11:06AM

WATERFRONT
PARK

#1,531
10-16-23

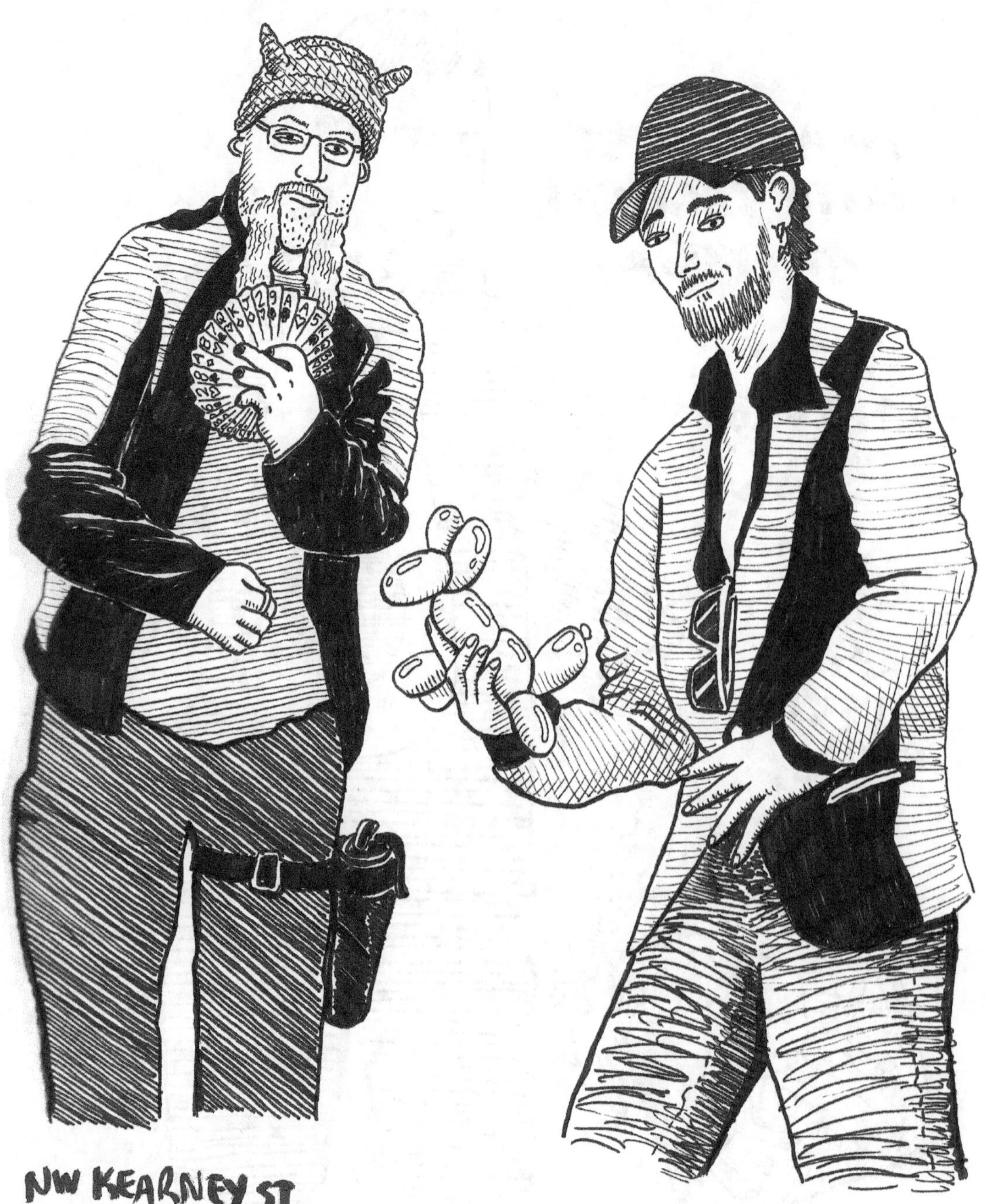

NW KEARNEY ST.
† NW 13TH AVE. AT 5:45 PM
JS #1,532 10-19-23

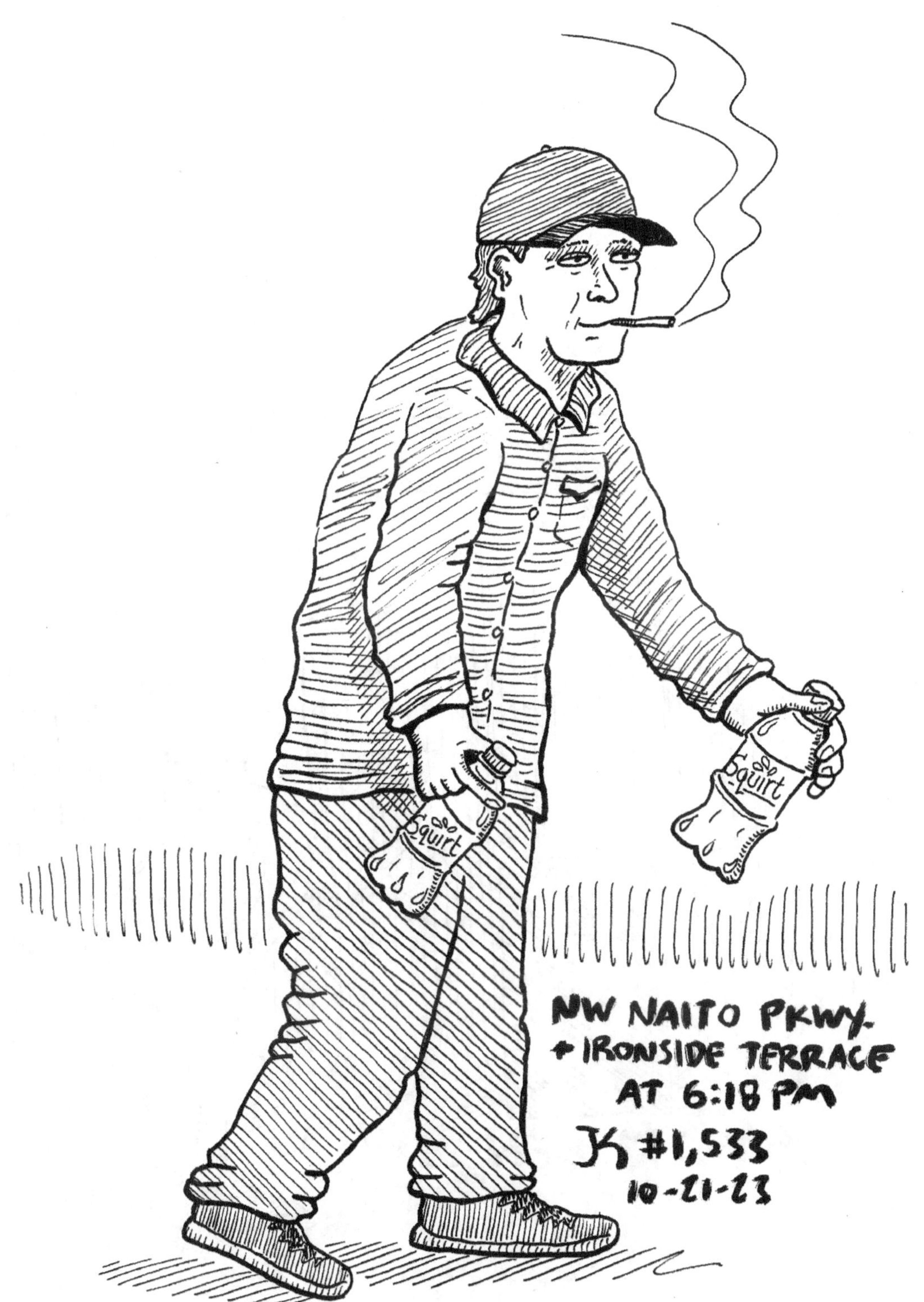

squirt
squirt
NW NAITO PKWY.
+ IRONSIDE TERRACE
AT 6:18 PM
JK #1,533
10-21-23

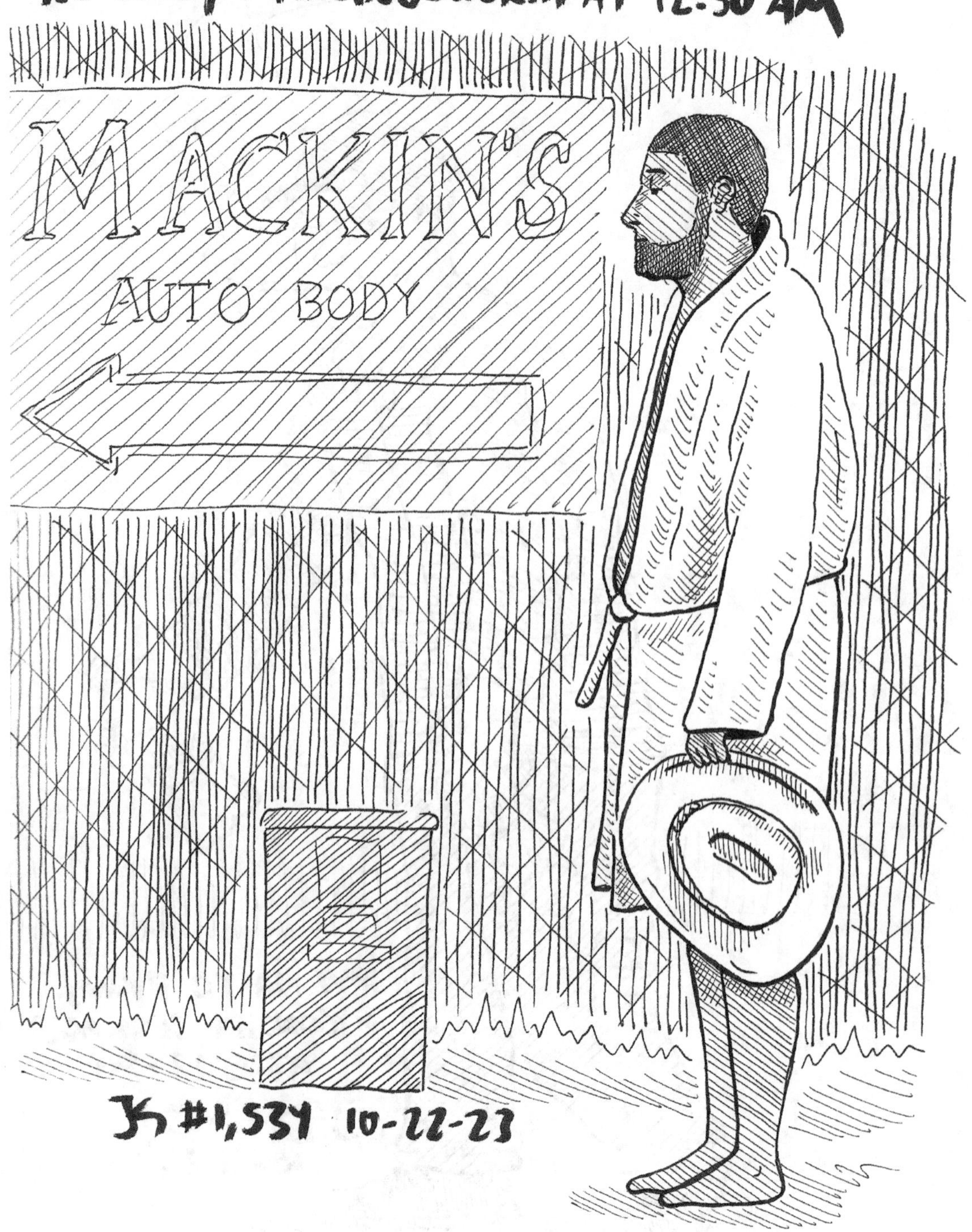

NE CULLY + KILLINGSWORTH AT 12:50 AM
MACKIN'S
AUTO BODY
JS #1,534 10-22-23

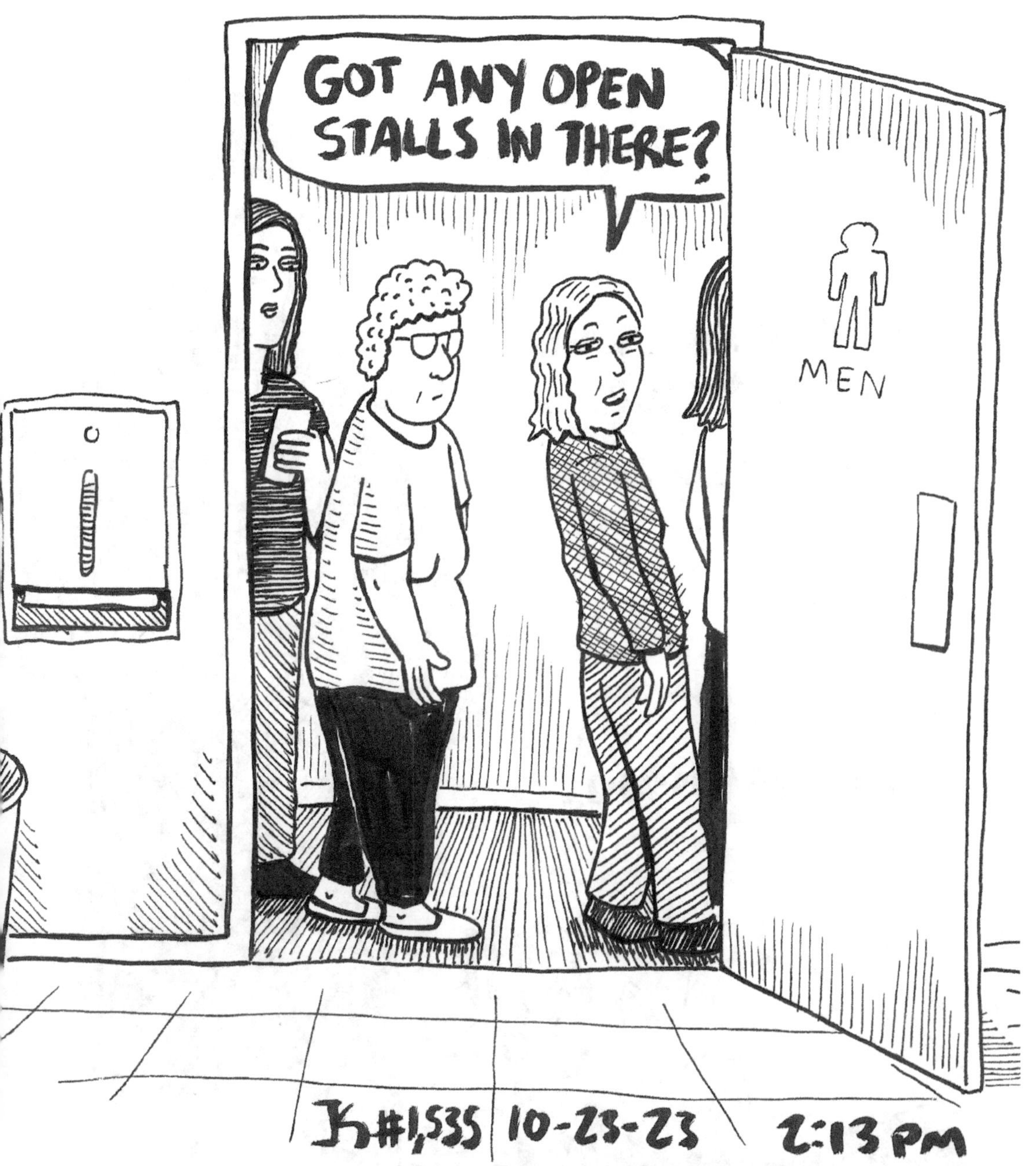

K #1,535 | 10-23-23 | 2:13 PM
BRIX TAVERN IN TUALATIN,
LAKE AT THE COMMONS

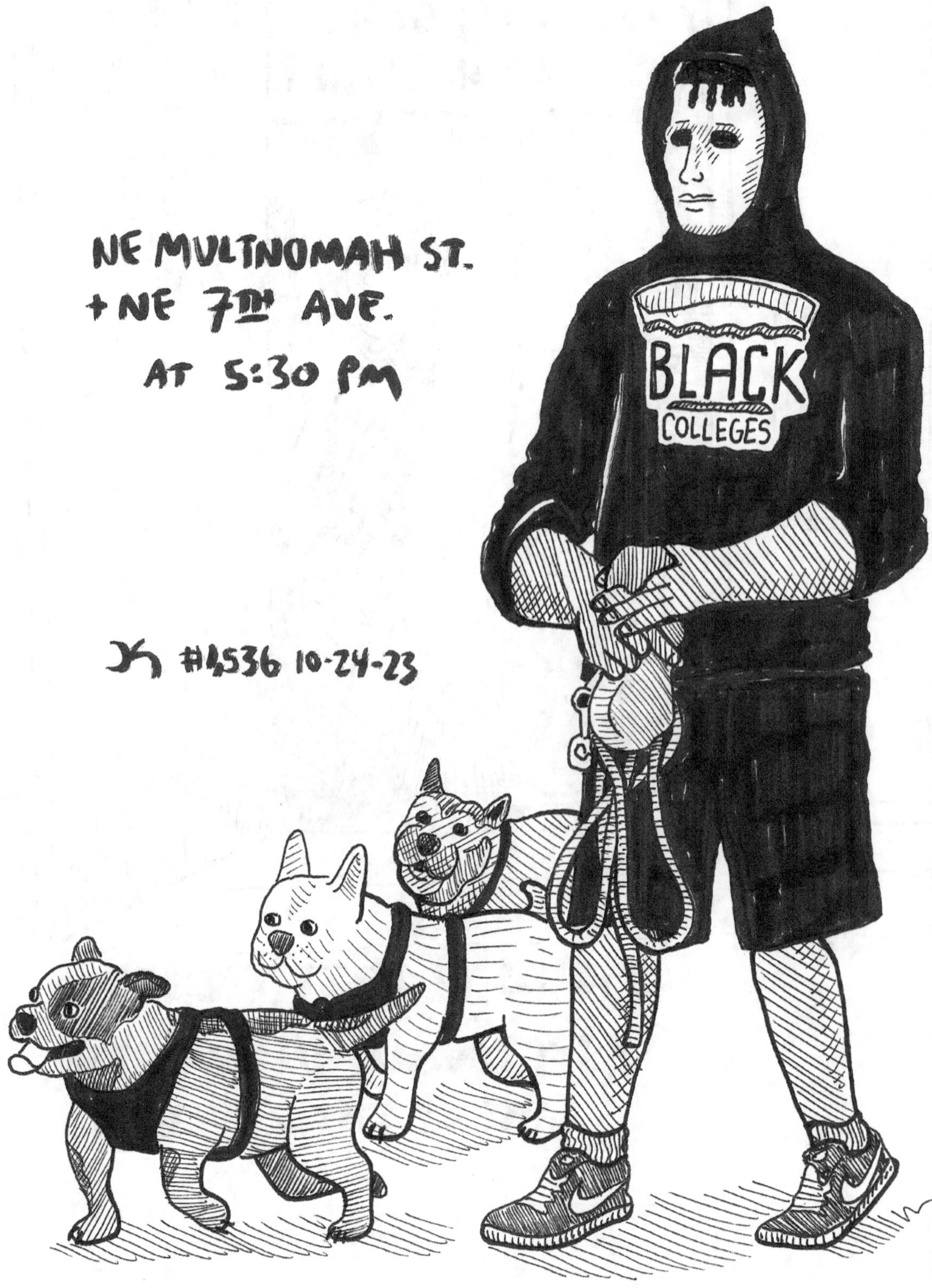

NE MULTNOMAH ST.
+ NE 7TH AVE.
AT 5:30 PM
#4536 10-24-23
BLACK
COLLEGES

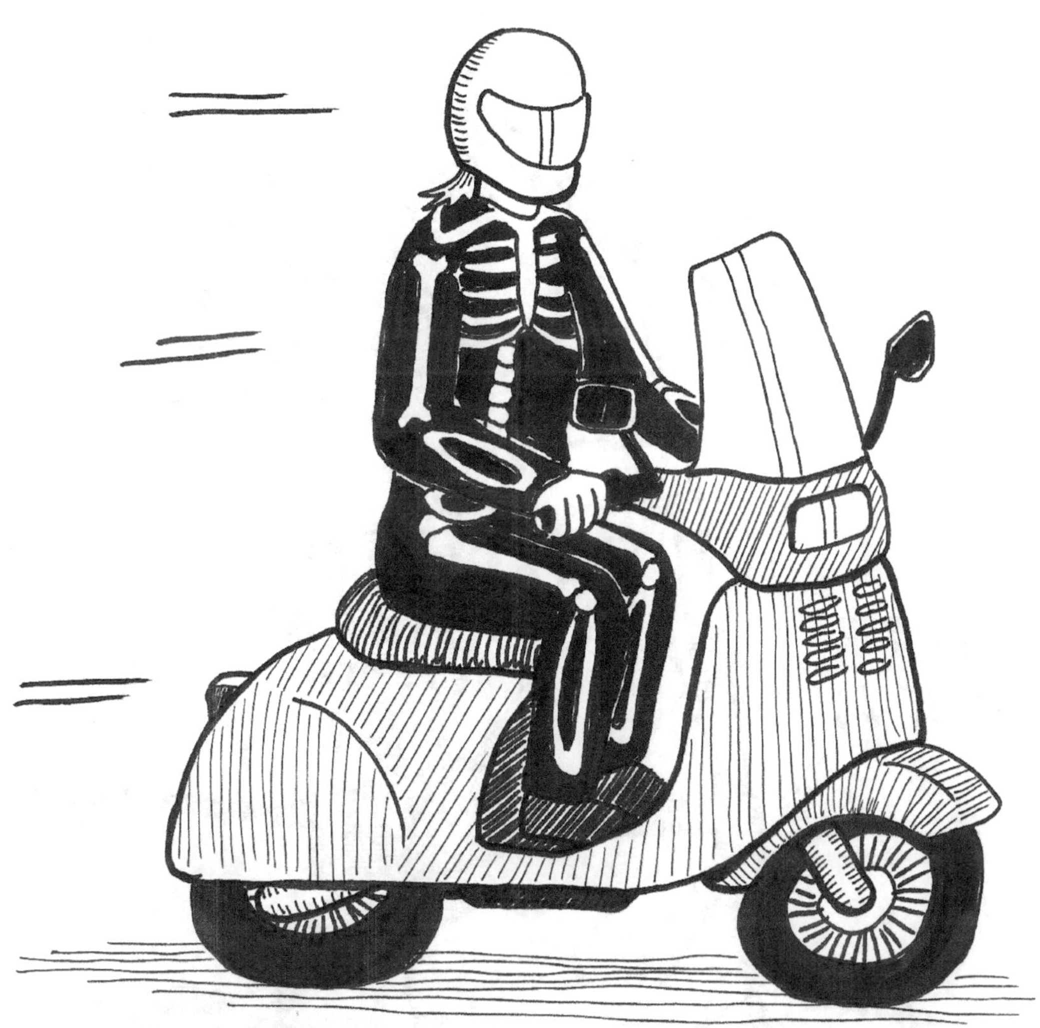

JS #1,537 10-25-23   7:15 PM
SE GLADSTONE + SE 29TH AVE.

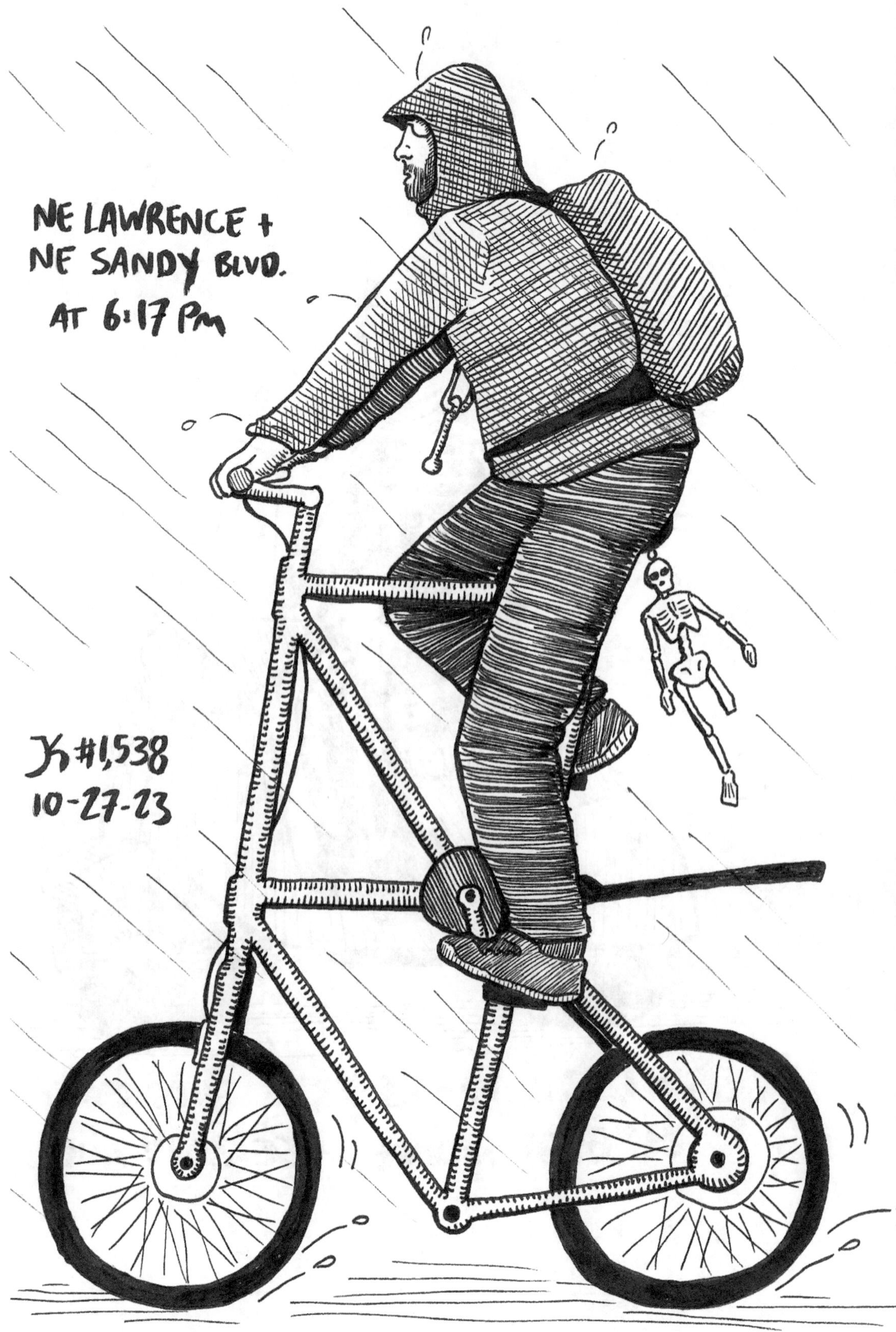

NE LAWRENCE +
NE SANDY BLVD.
AT 6:17 PM
#1,538
10-27-23

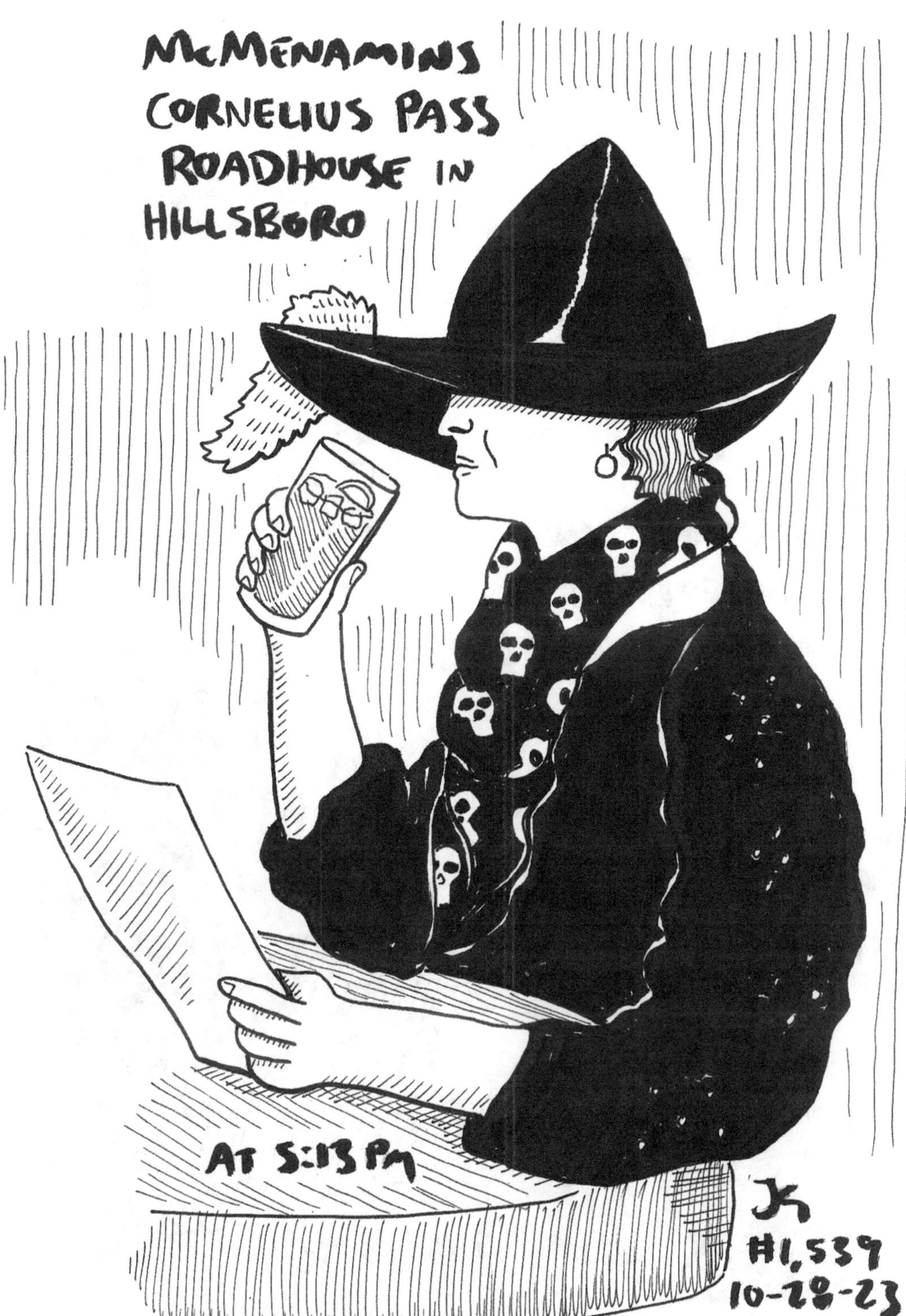

McMenamins
Cornelius Pass
Roadhouse in
Hillsboro
at 5:13 pm
JK
#1,539
10-28-23

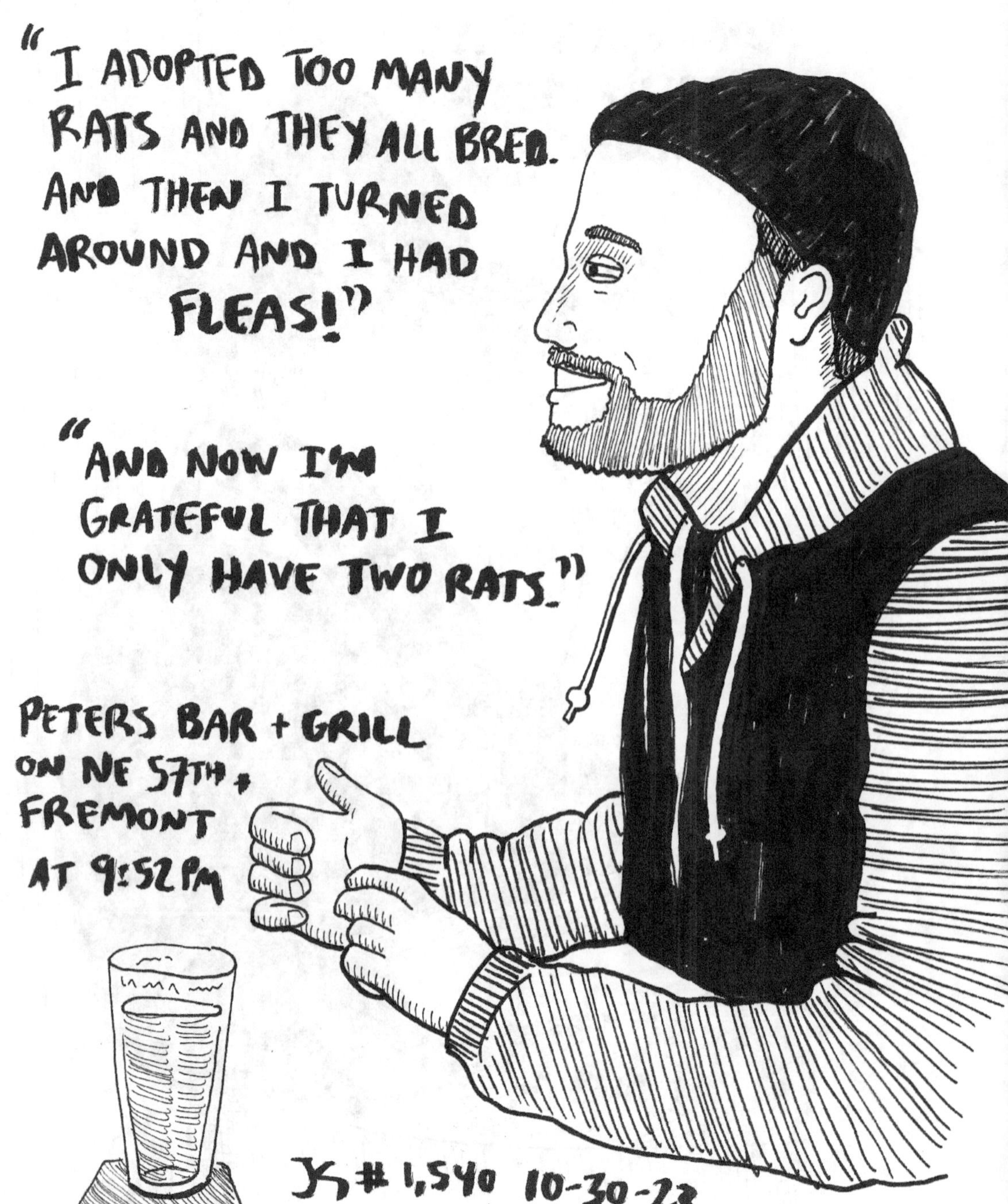

"I ADOPTED TOO MANY RATS AND THEY ALL BRED. AND THEN I TURNED AROUND AND I HAD FLEAS!"

"AND NOW I'M GRATEFUL THAT I ONLY HAVE TWO RATS."

PETERS BAR + GRILL ON NE 57TH & FREMONT AT 9:52 PM

JS #1,540 10-30-23

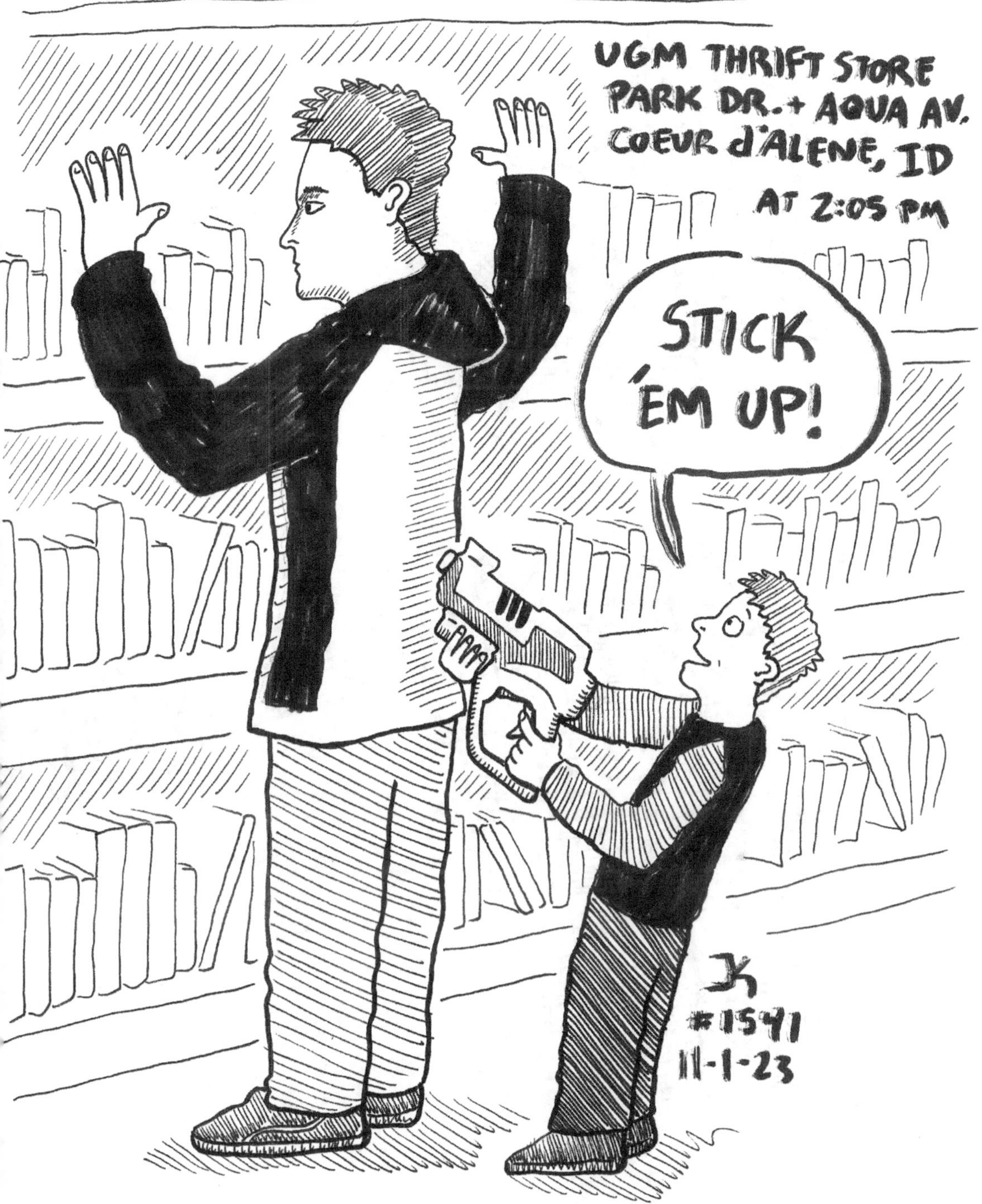

BOOKS
$2
$3
$5
UGM THRIFT STORE
PARK DR. + AQUA AV.
COEUR d'ALENE, ID
AT 2:05 PM
STICK 'EM UP!
#1541
11-1-23

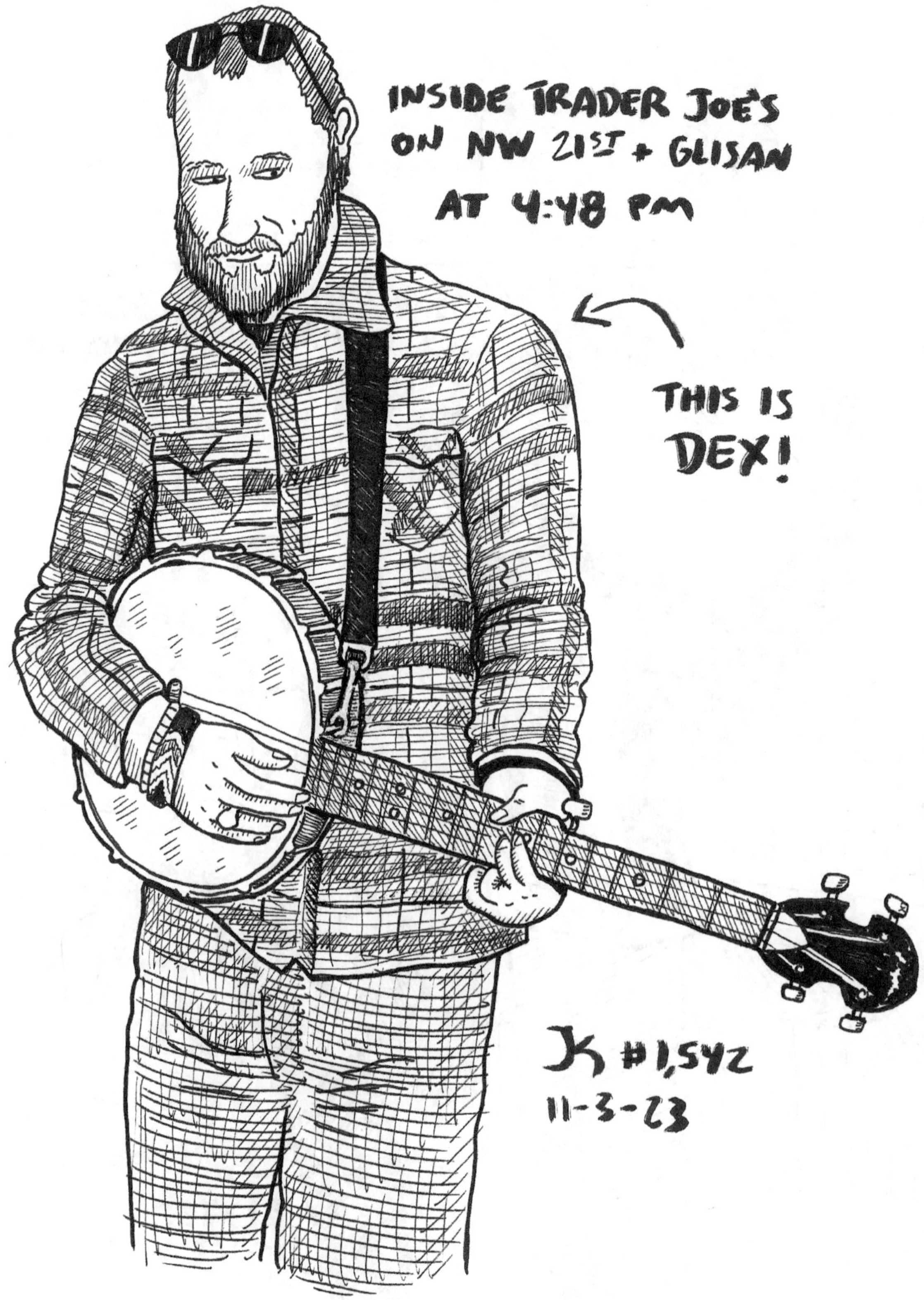

INSIDE TRADER JOE'S ON NW 21ST + GLISAN AT 4:48 PM
THIS IS DEX!
#1,542
11-3-23

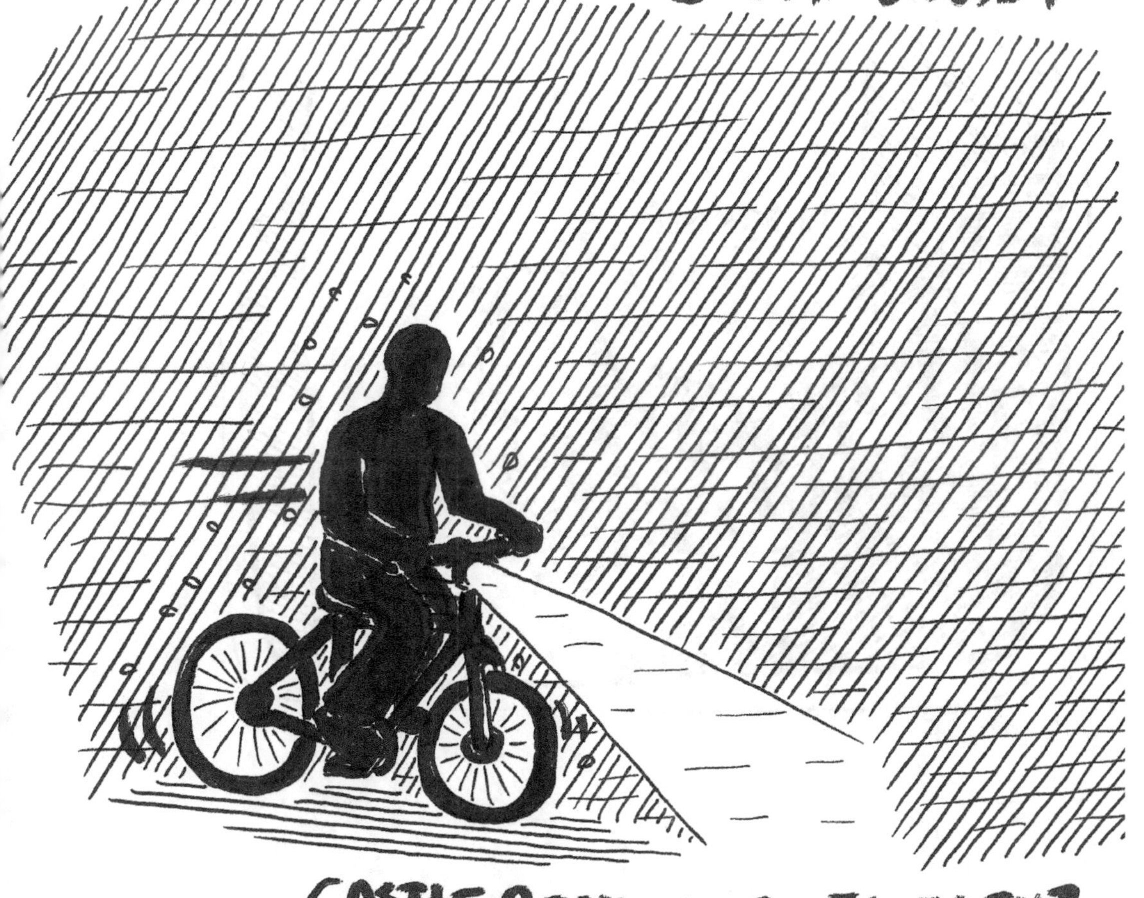

PITCH DARK IN
SIDEWAYS RAIN
RIDING AGAINST
THE TRAFFIC ALONG
I-5 AT 6:58 AM
CASTLE ROCK, WA   #1,543
11-4-23

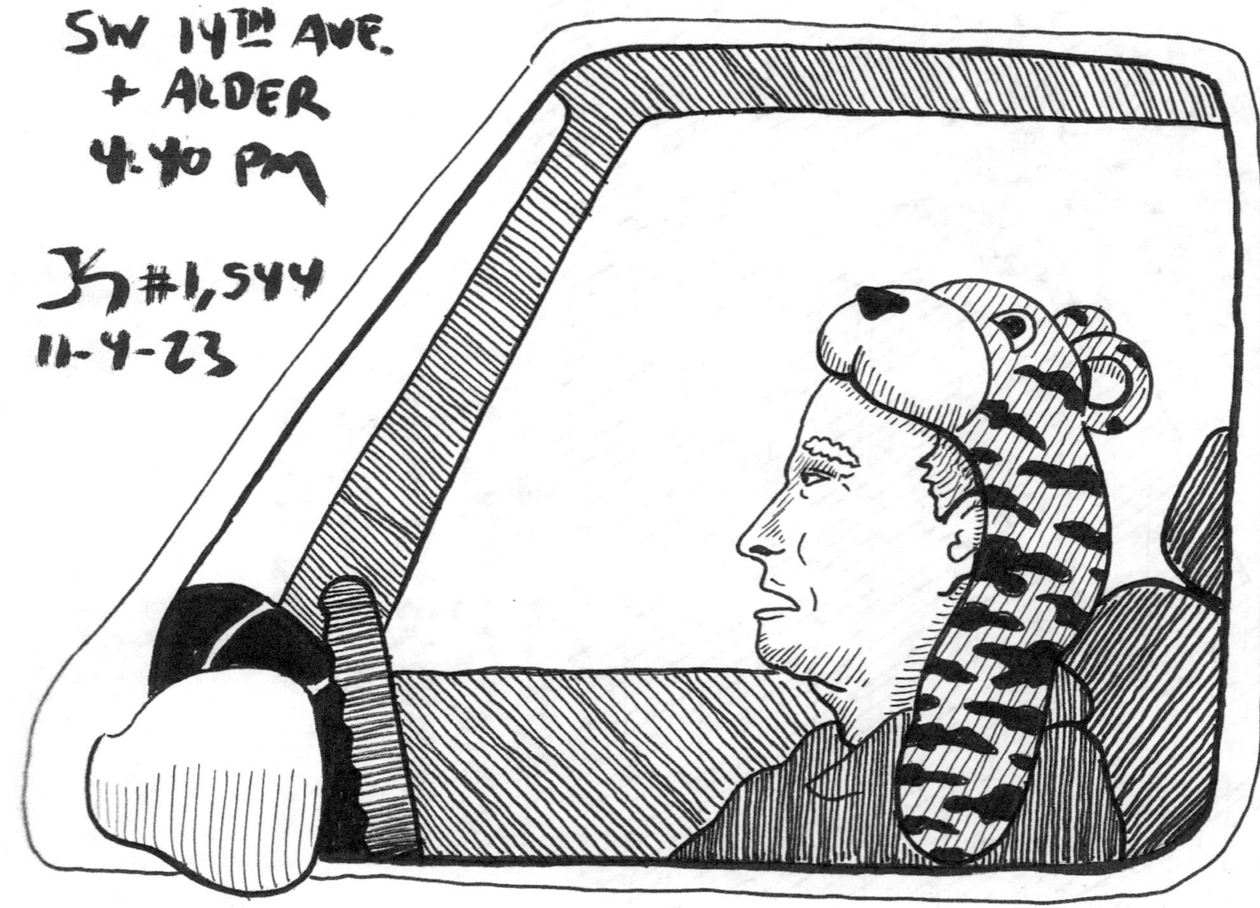

SW 14TH AVE.
+ ALDER
4:40 PM
#1,544
11-4-23

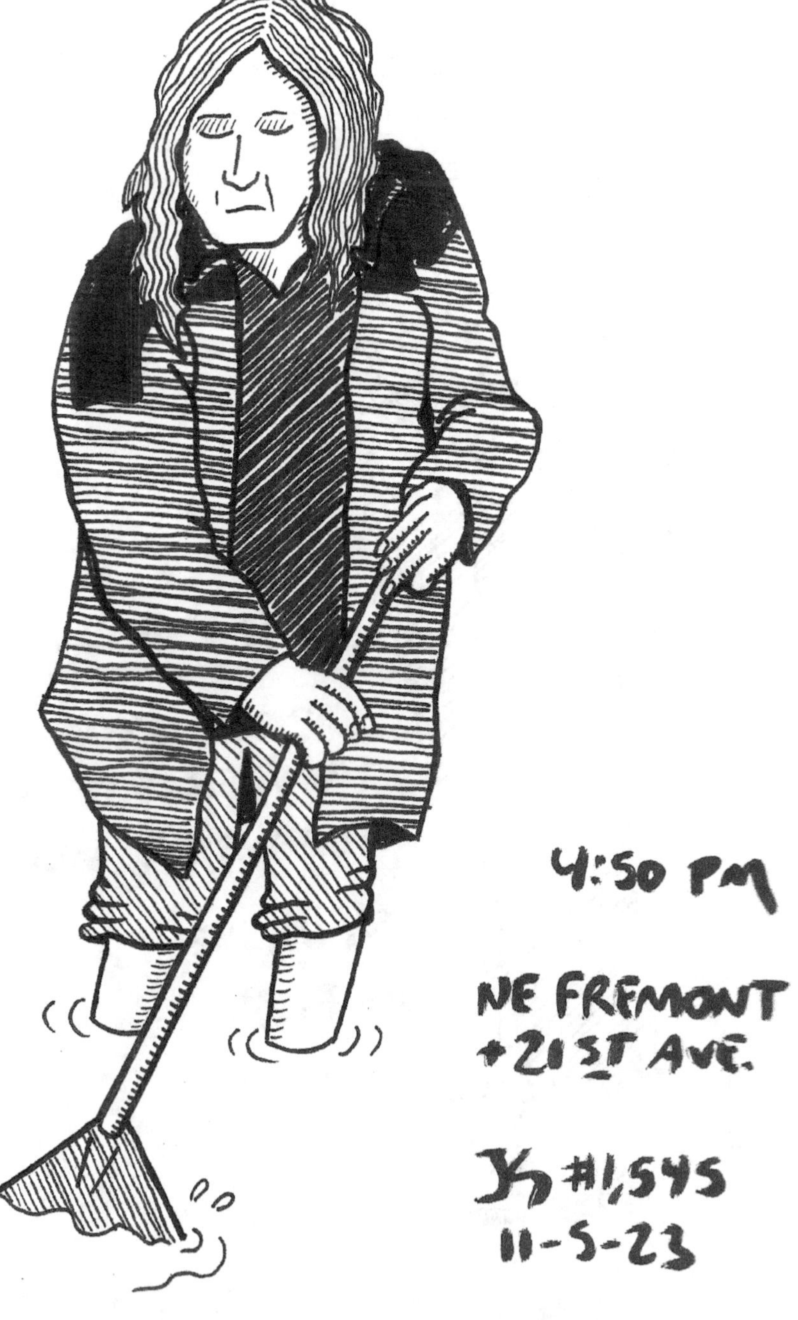
4:50 PM
NE FREMONT
+ 21 ST AVE.
#1,545
11-5-23

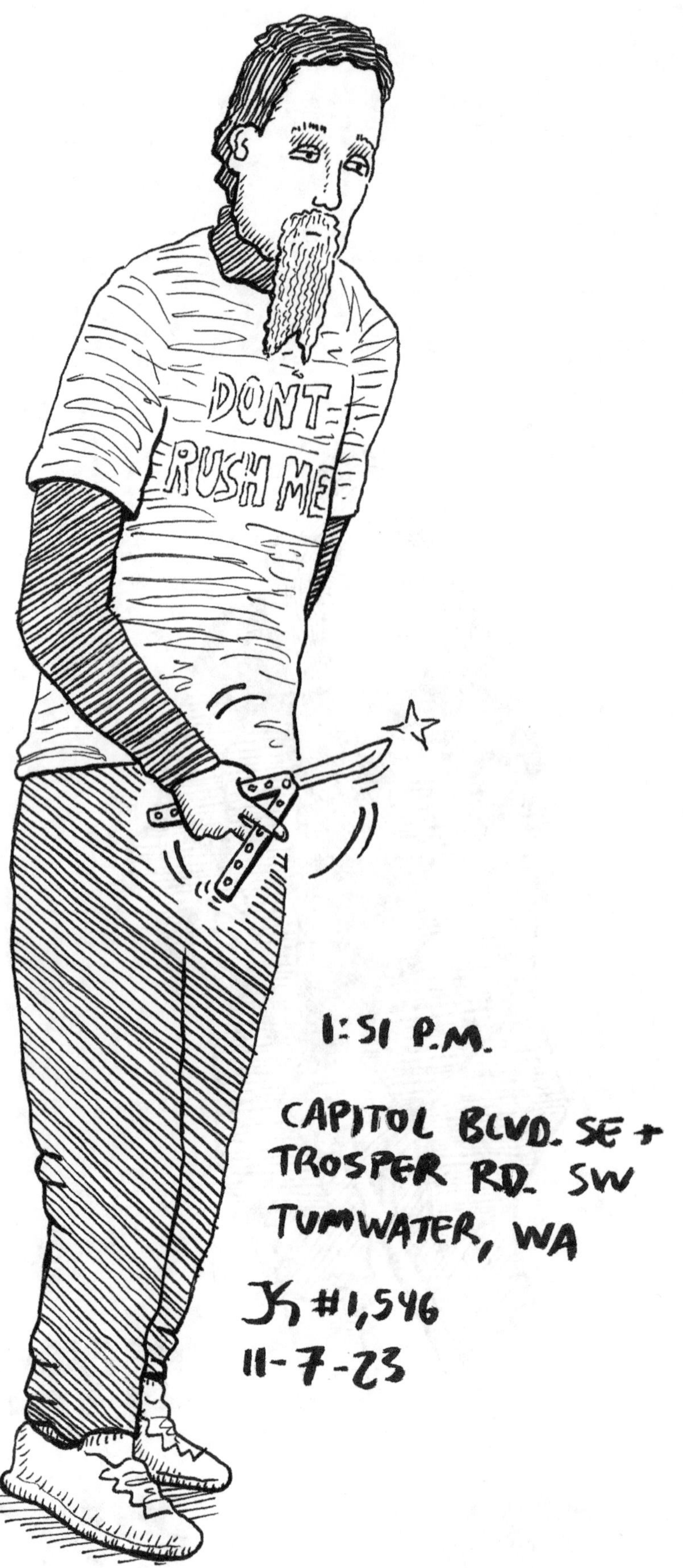

DON'T
RUSH ME
1:51 P.M.
CAPITOL BLVD. SE +
TROSPER RD. SW
TUMWATER, WA
JS #1,546
11-7-23

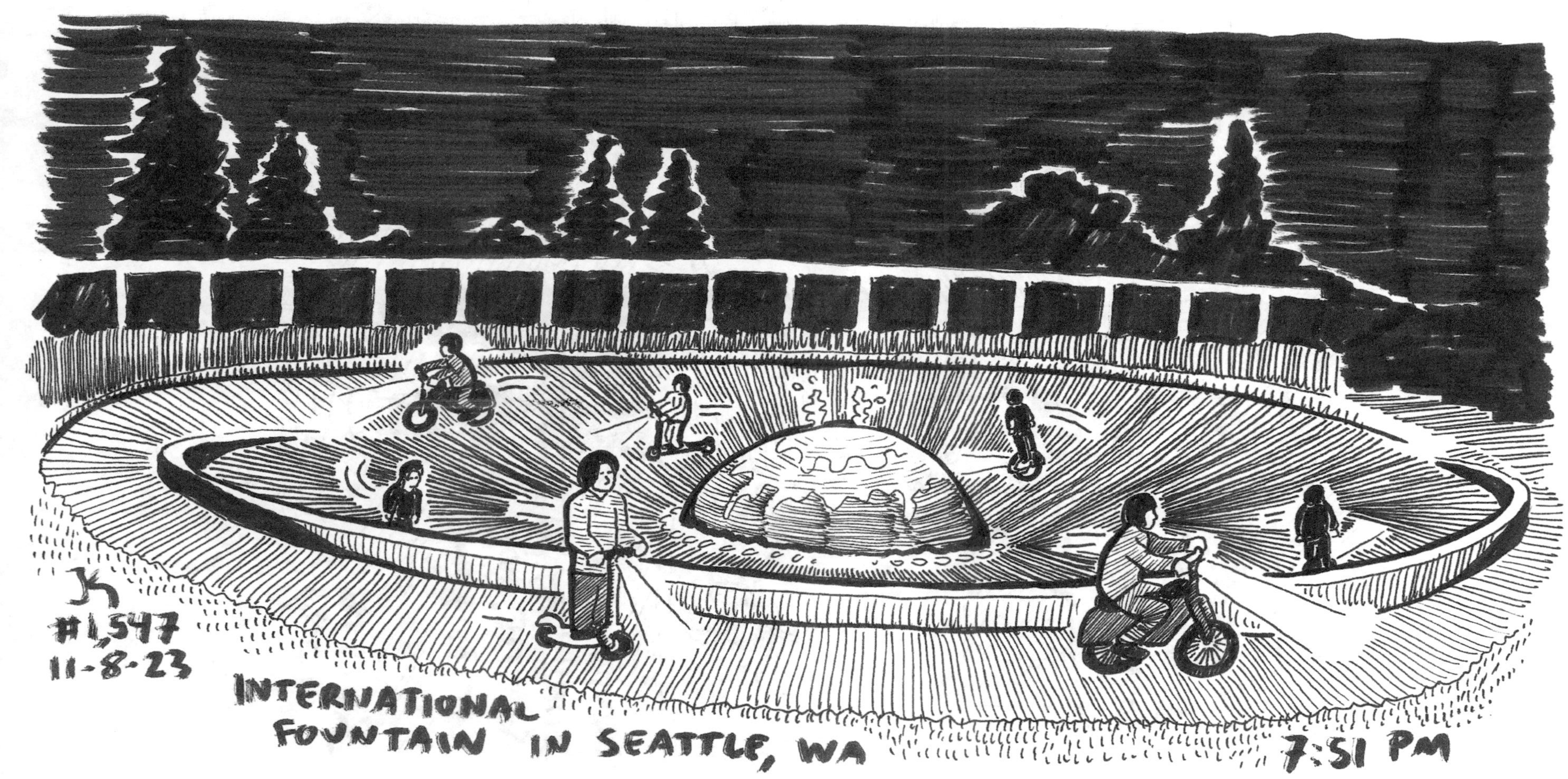

#1,547
11-8-23
INTERNATIONAL FOUNTAIN IN SEATTLE, WA
7:51 PM

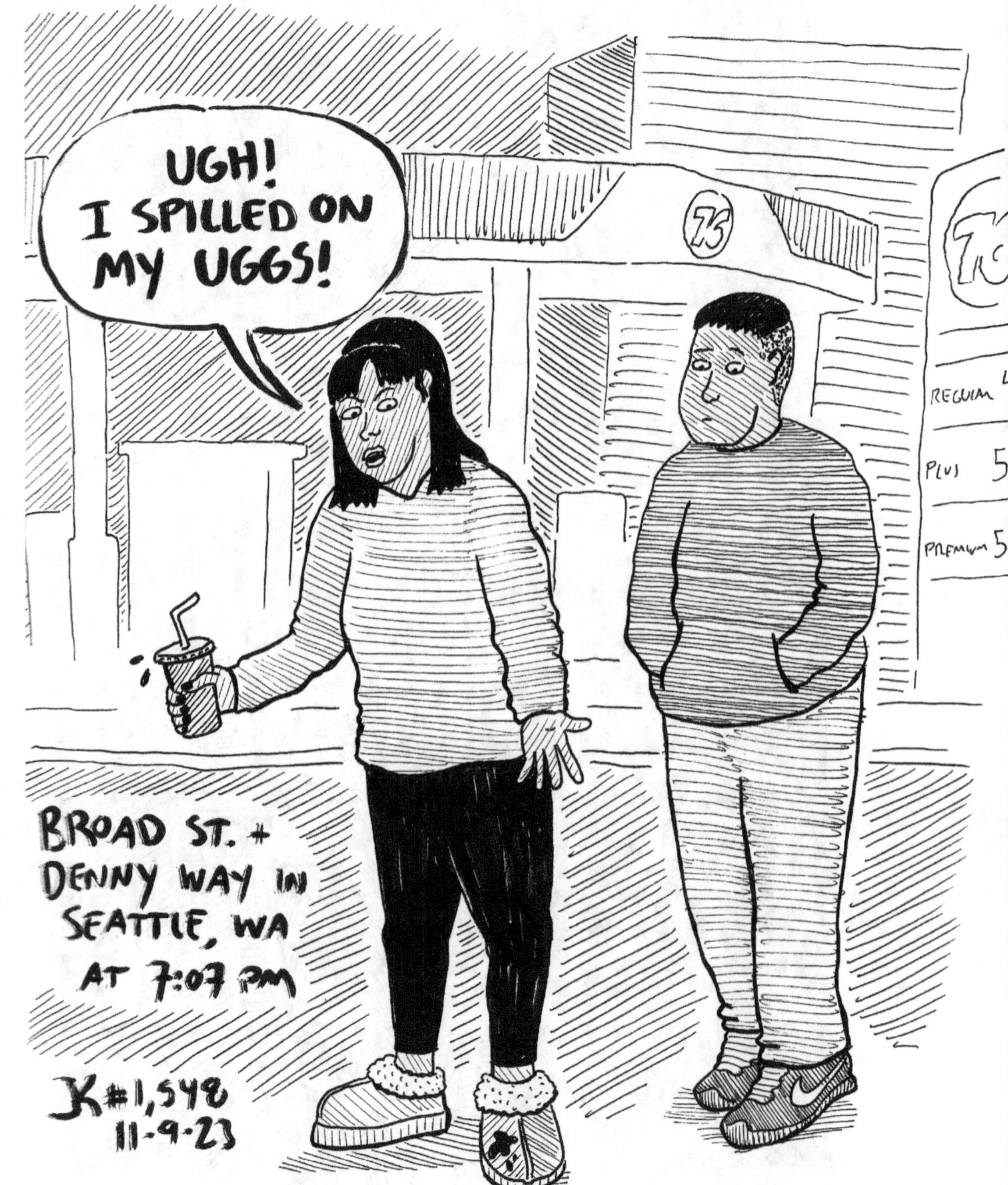

UGH! I SPILLED ON MY UGGS!
76
76
REGULAR
PLUS 5.
PREMIUM 5.
BROAD ST. + DENNY WAY IN SEATTLE, WA AT 7:07 PM
JK #1,548
11-9-23

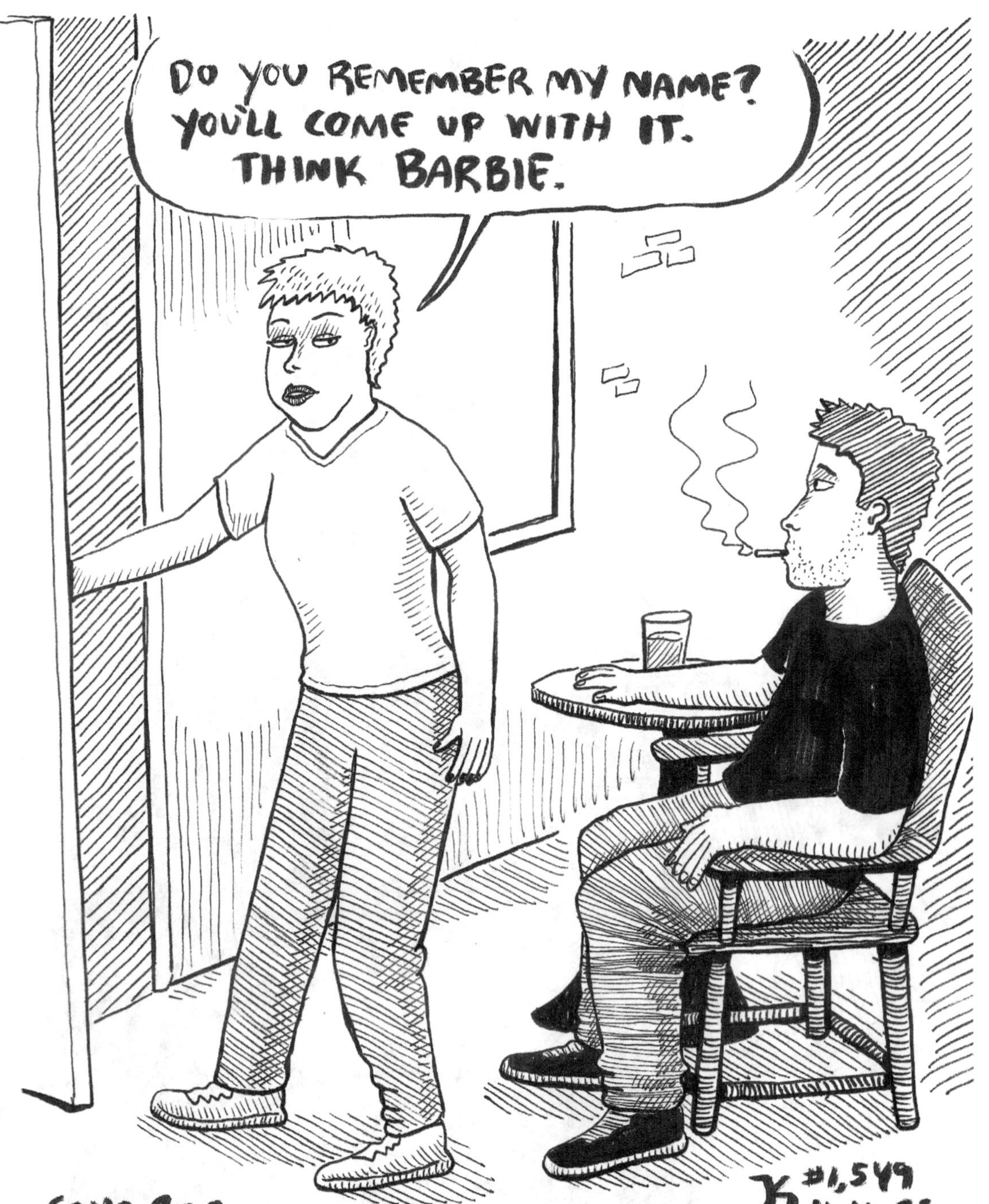

SOHO BAR ON 3RD AVE. N. + ROY ST. IN SEATTLE, WA AT 8:05 PM

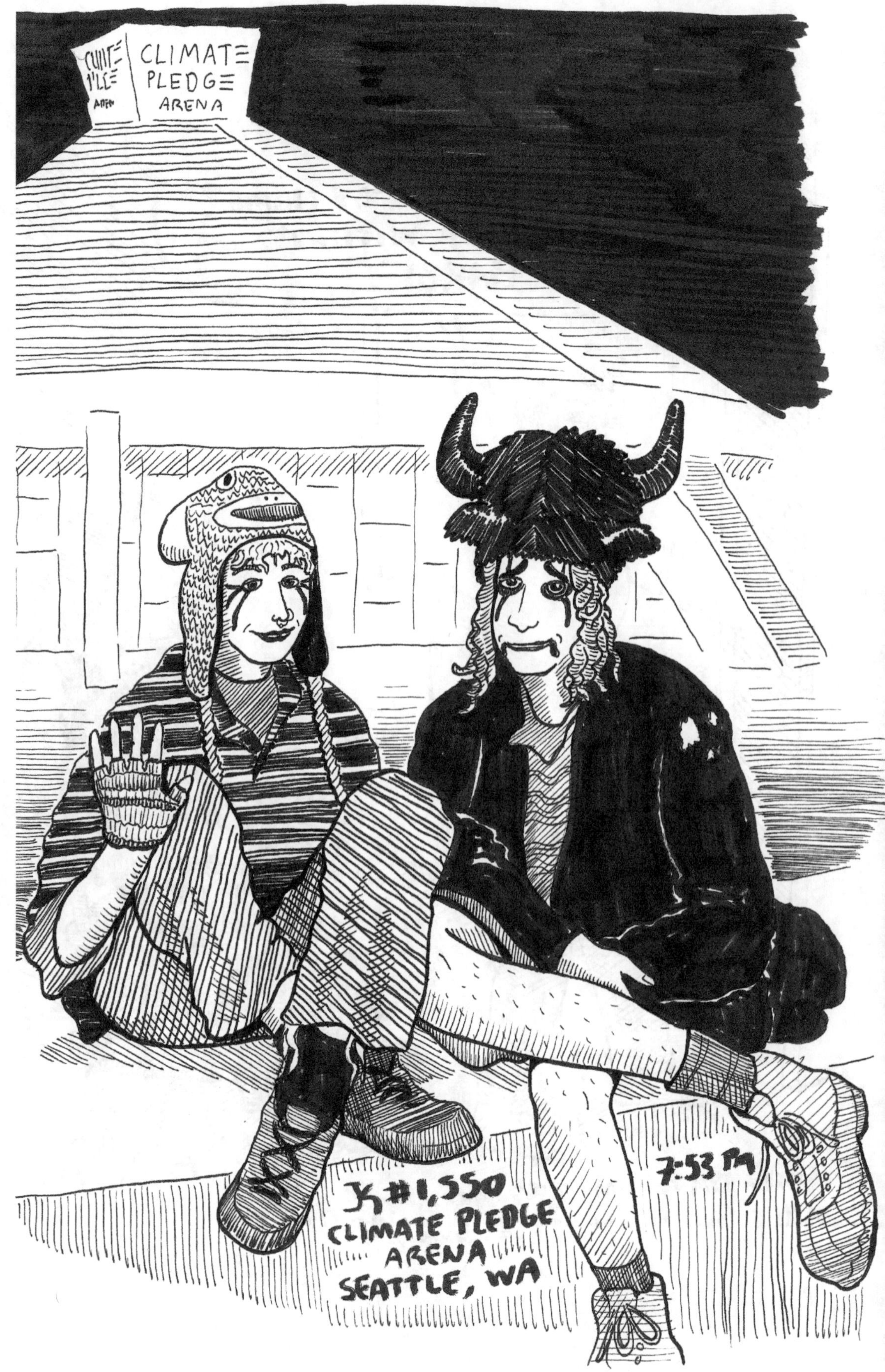

CLIMATE
PLEDGE
ARENA
K #1,550
CLIMATE PLEDGE
ARENA
SEATTLE, WA
7:53 PM

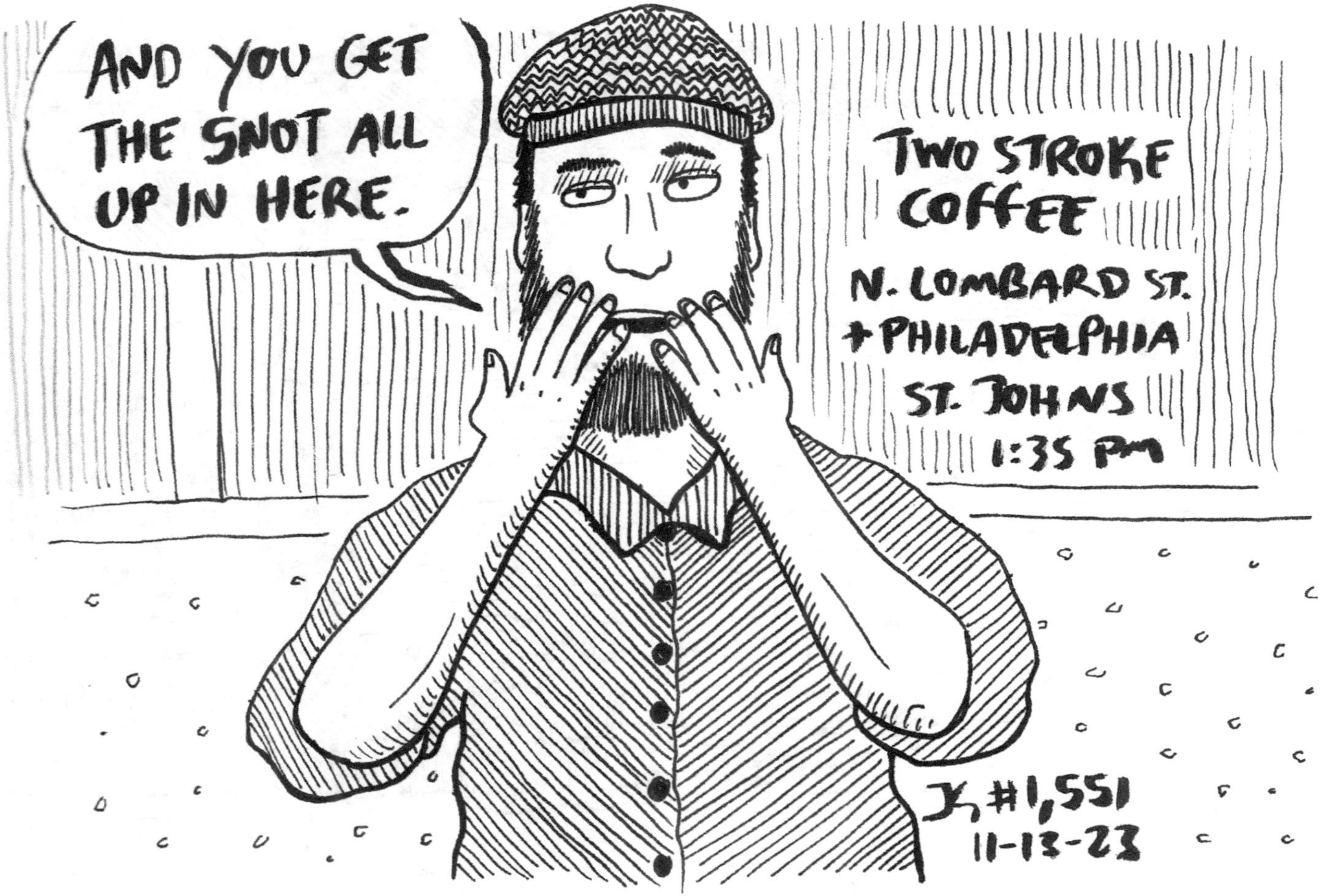

AND YOU GET THE SNOT ALL UP IN HERE.
TWO STROKE COFFEE
N. LOMBARD ST.
+ PHILADELPHIA
ST. JOHNS
1:35 PM
JS #1,551
11-13-23

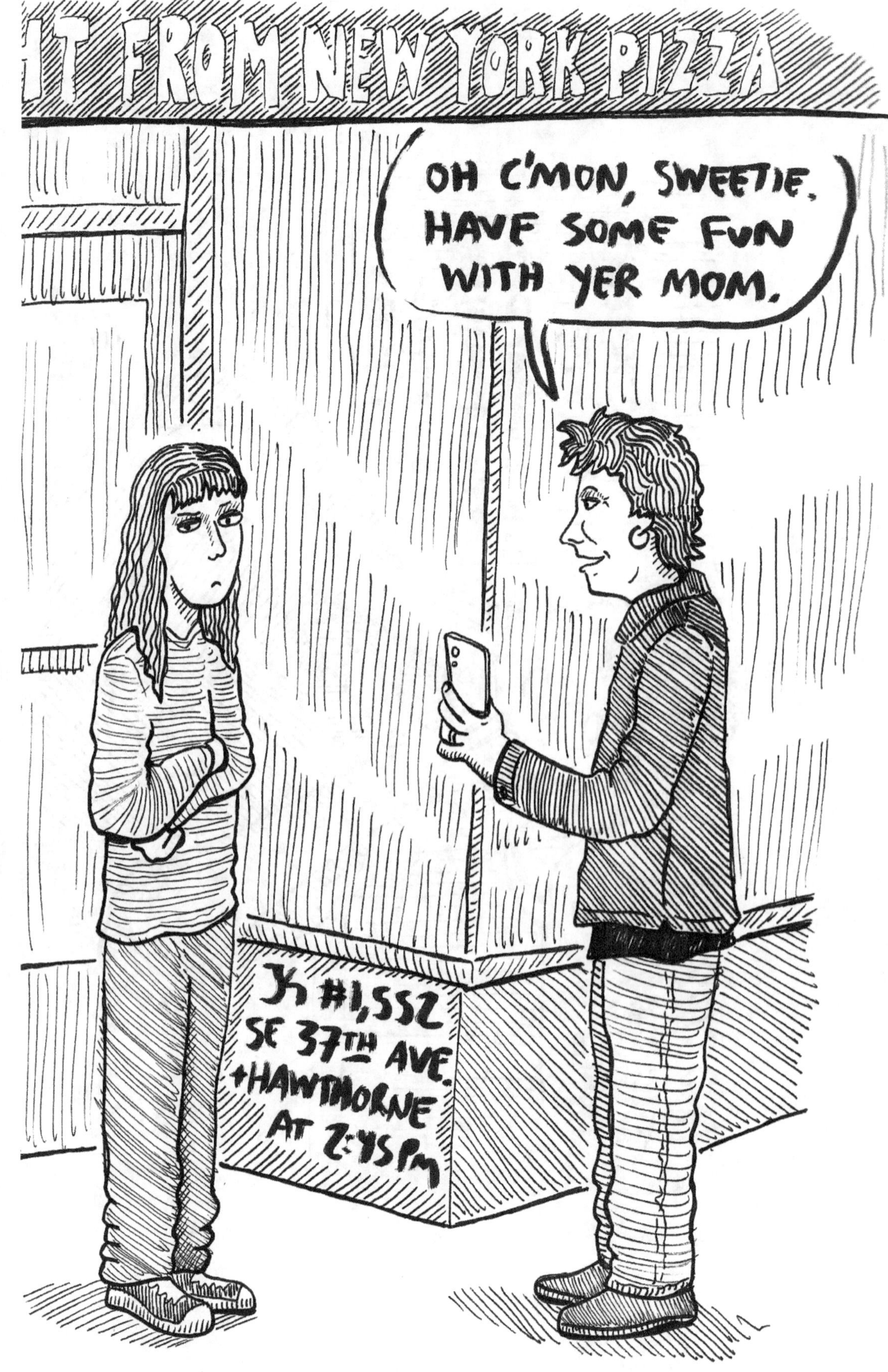

IT FROM NEW YORK PIZZA
OH C'MON, SWEETIE.
HAVE SOME FUN
WITH YER MOM.
#1,552
SE 37TH AVE.
+HAWTHORNE
AT 2:45 PM

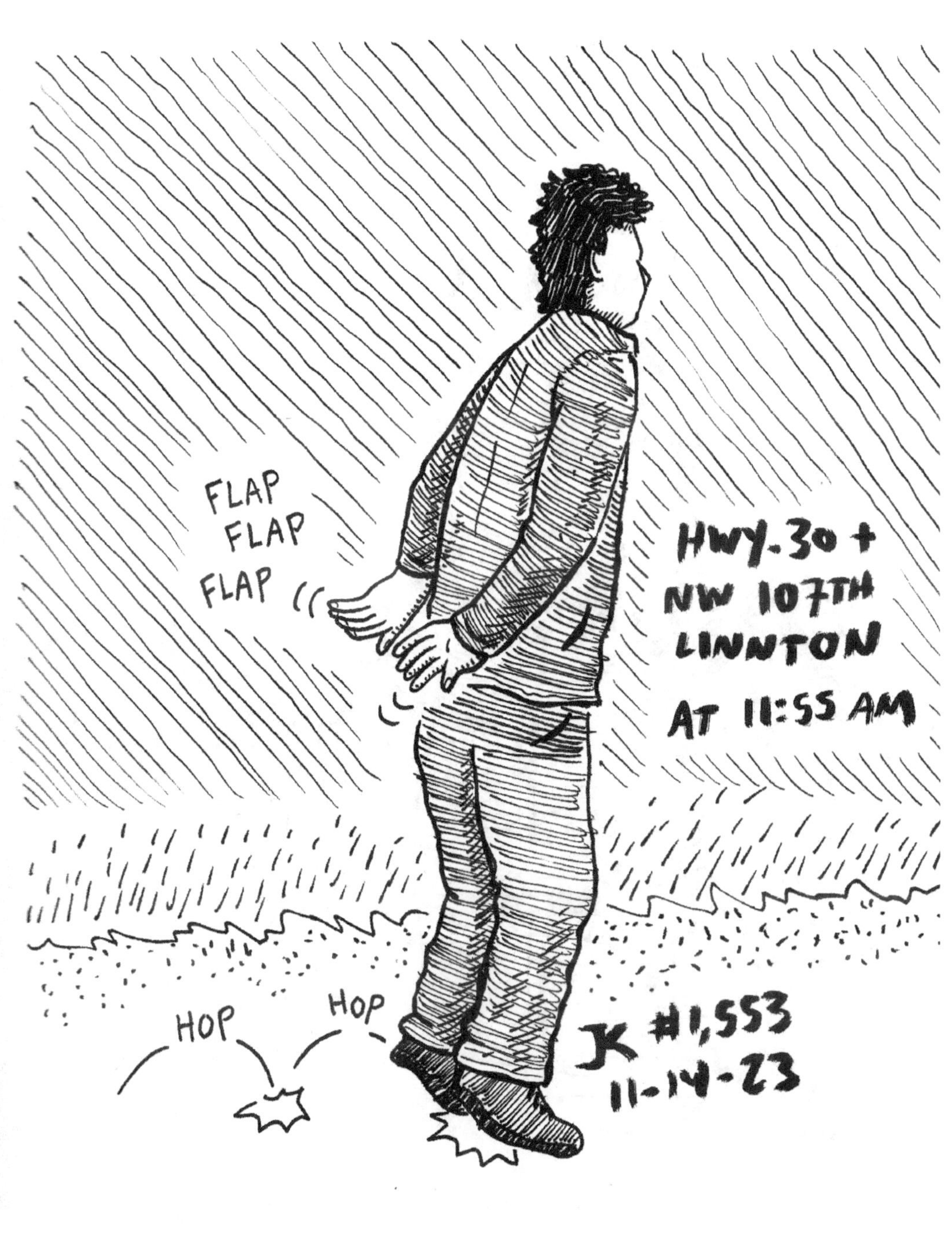

FLAP
FLAP
FLAP
HWY. 30 +
NW 107TH
LINNTON
AT 11:55 AM
HOP
HOP
JK #1,553
11-14-23

N. ROSA PARKS WAY + N. MOORE AVE.
AT 12:24 PM

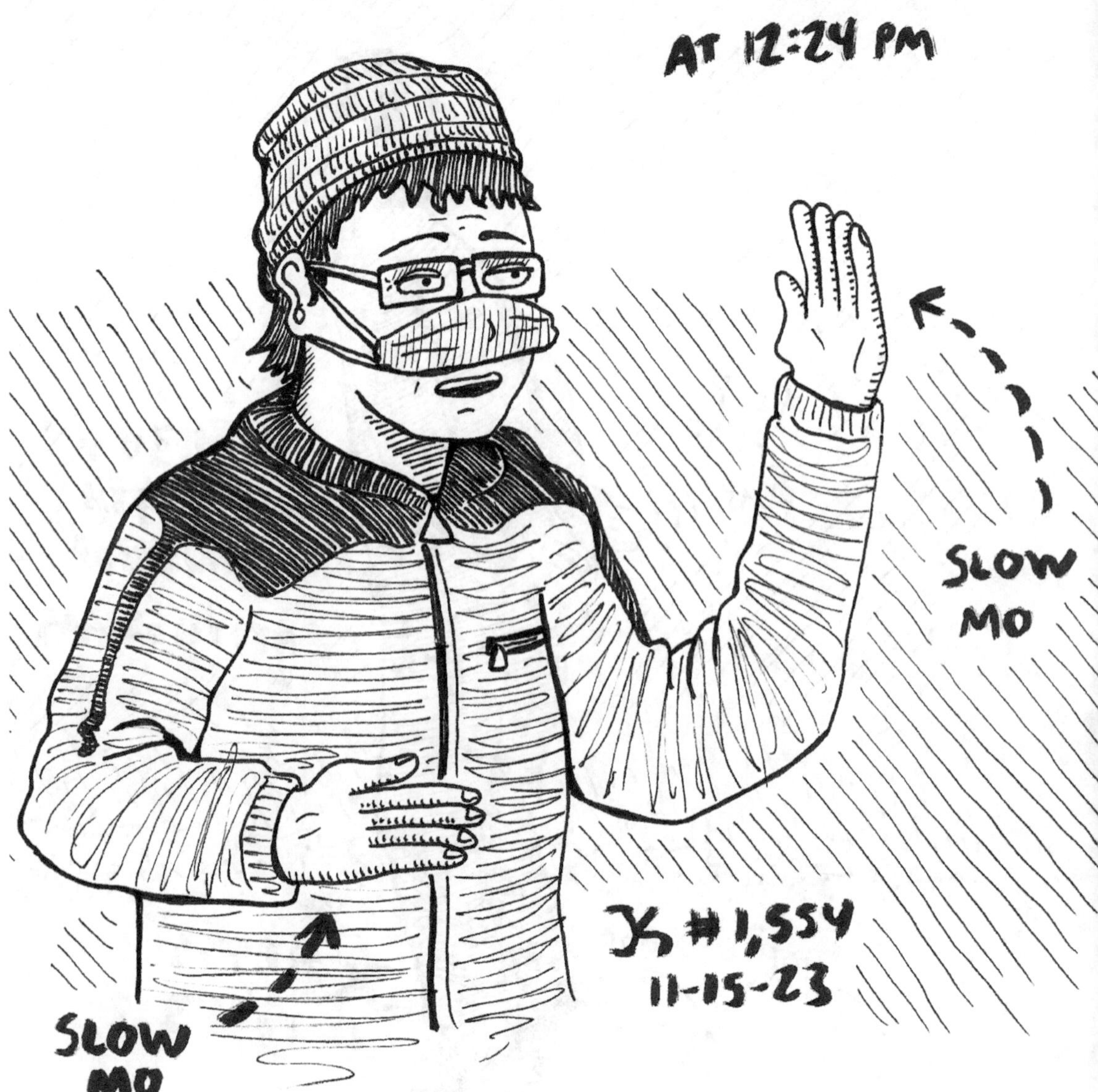

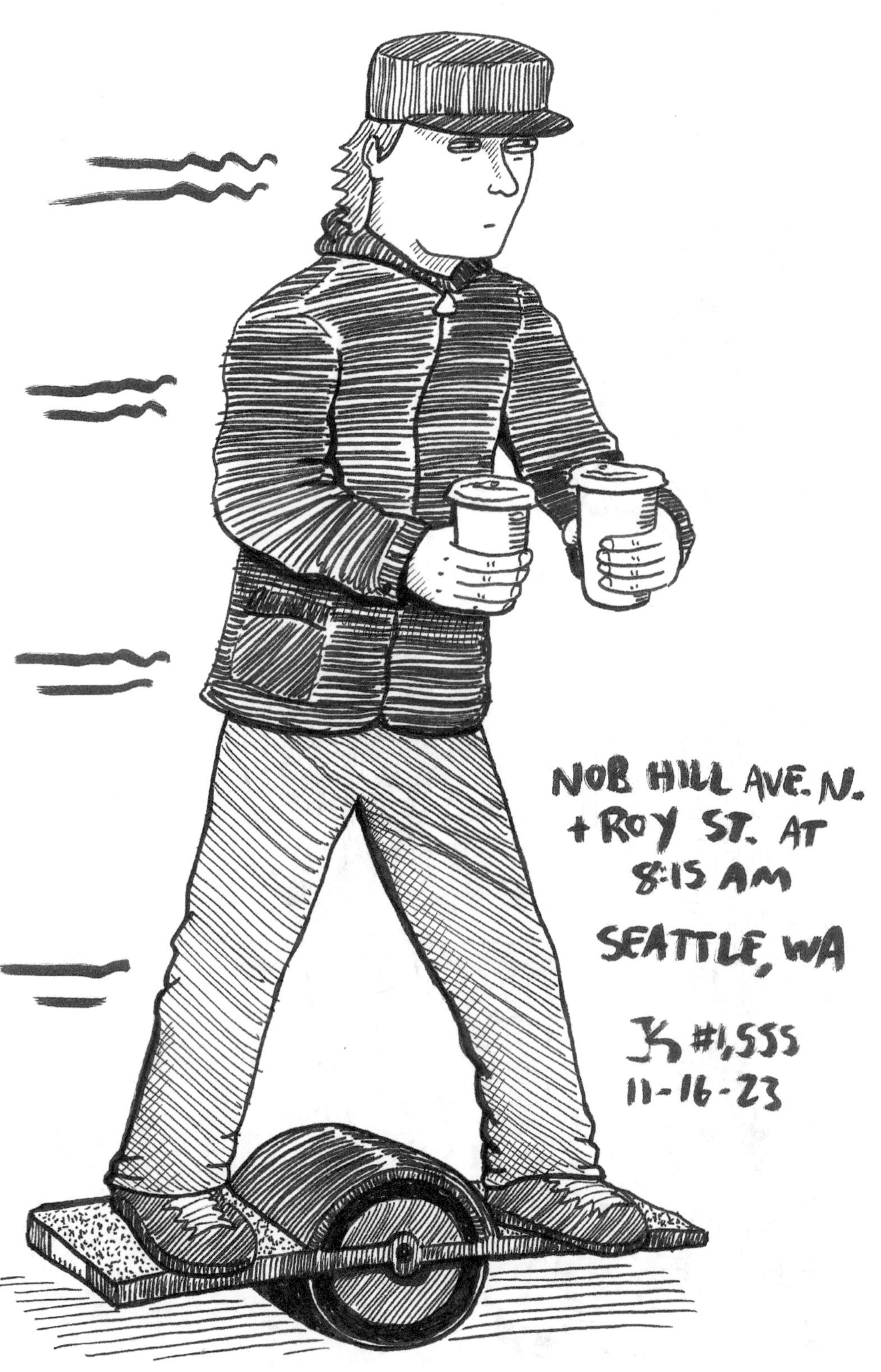

NOB HILL AVE. N.
+ ROY ST. AT
8:15 AM
SEATTLE, WA
#1,555
11-16-23

bluevelo
N. Rosa Parks Way + Greeley Ave.
At 6:13 PM
#1,556 11-17-23

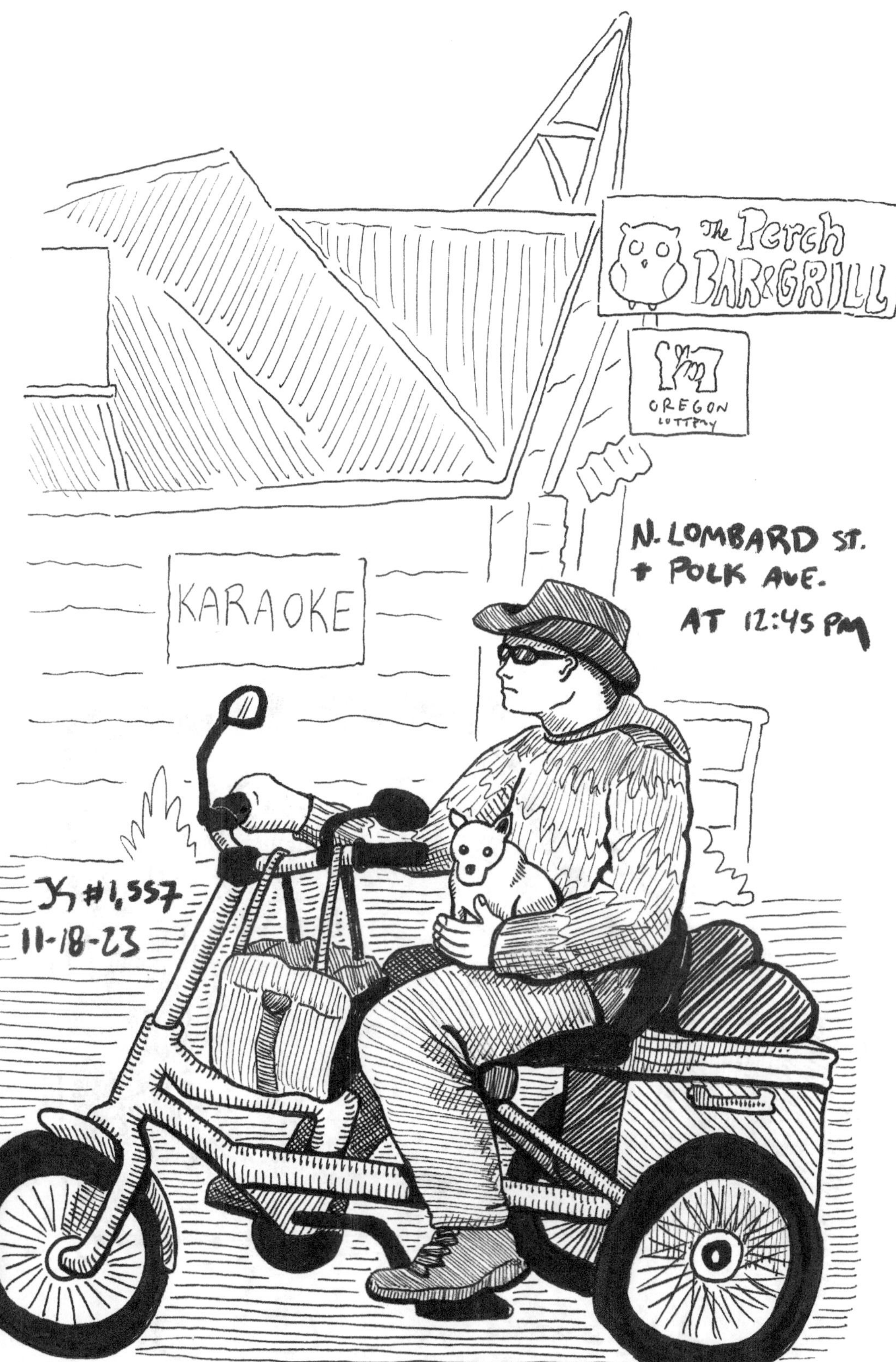

The Perch
BAR&GRILL
OREGON
LOTTERY
KARAOKE
N. LOMBARD ST.
+ POLK AVE.
AT 12:45 PM
JK #1,557
11-18-23

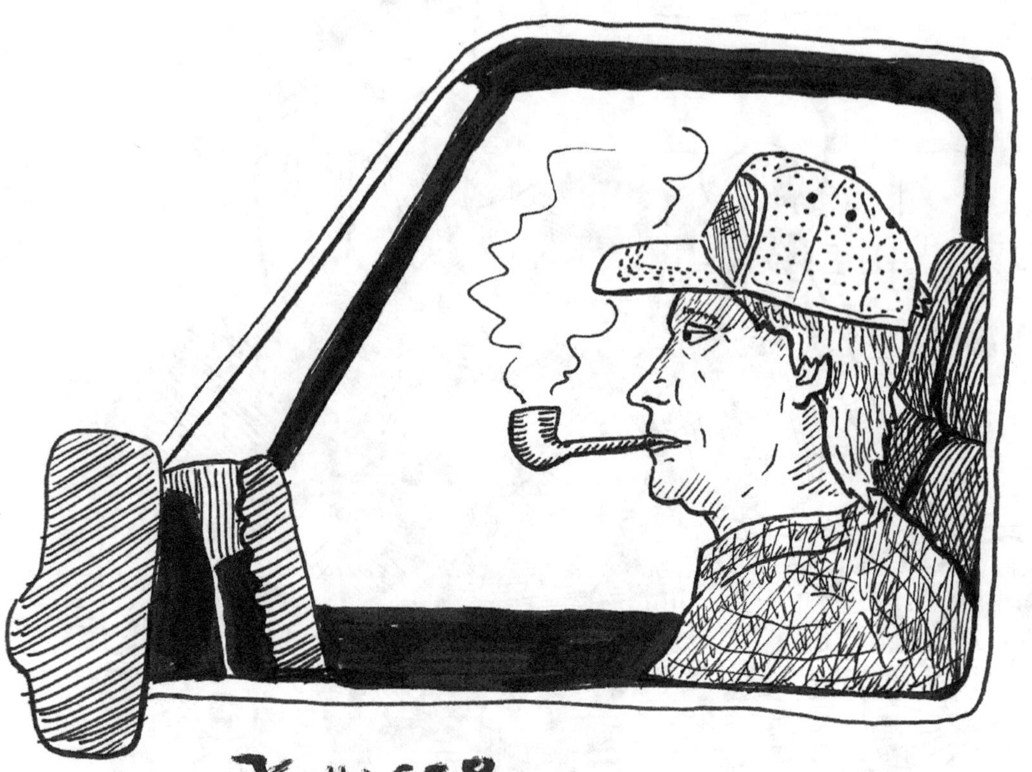
FRED MEYER IN SCAPPOOSE, OR
AT 1:41 PM
JK #1,558
11-19-23
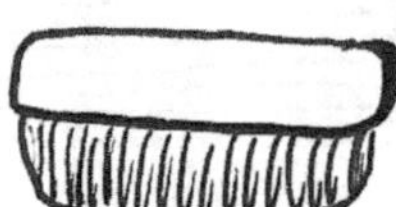

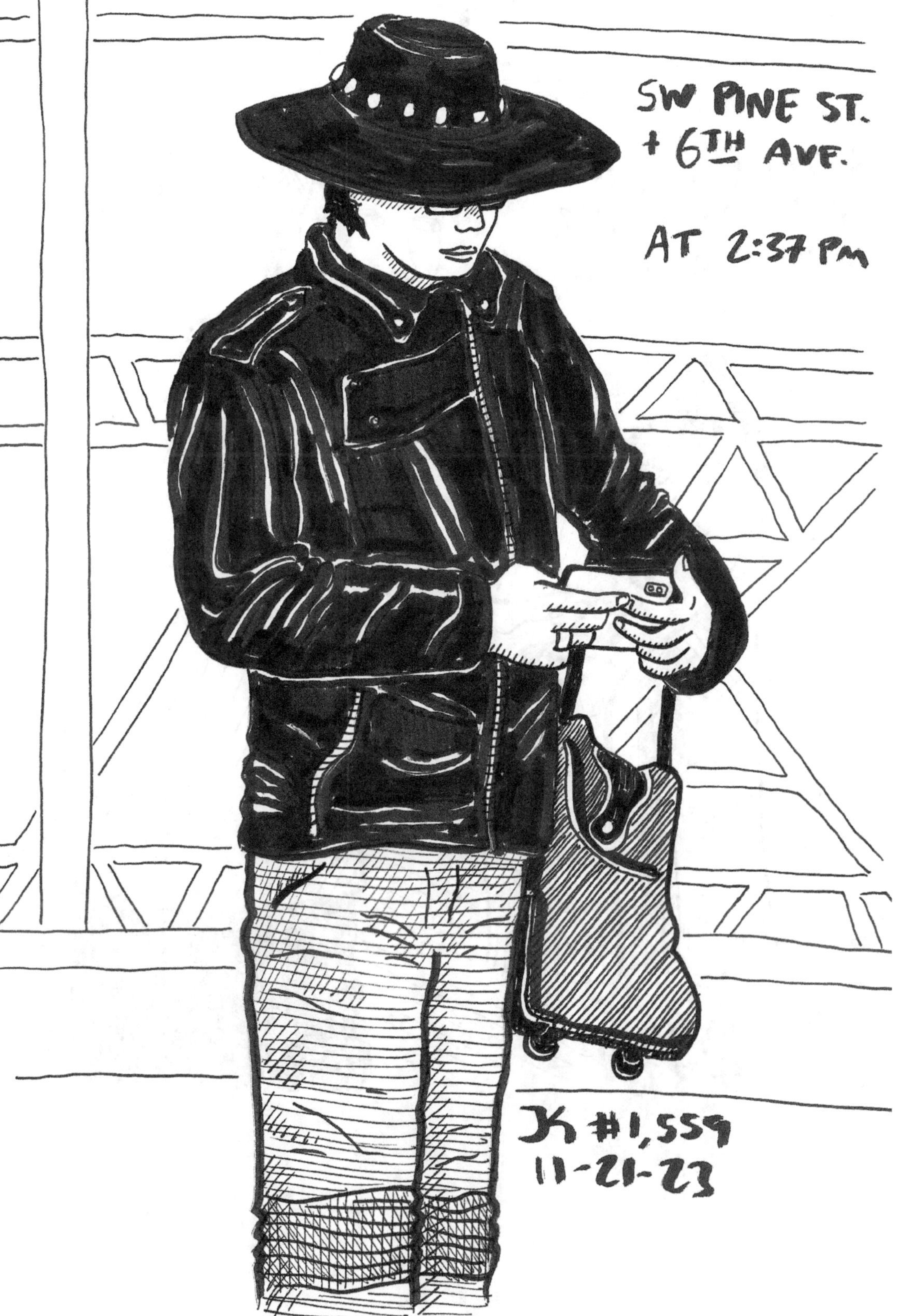

SW PINE ST.
+ 6TH AVE.

AT 2:37 PM

JK #1,559
11-21-23

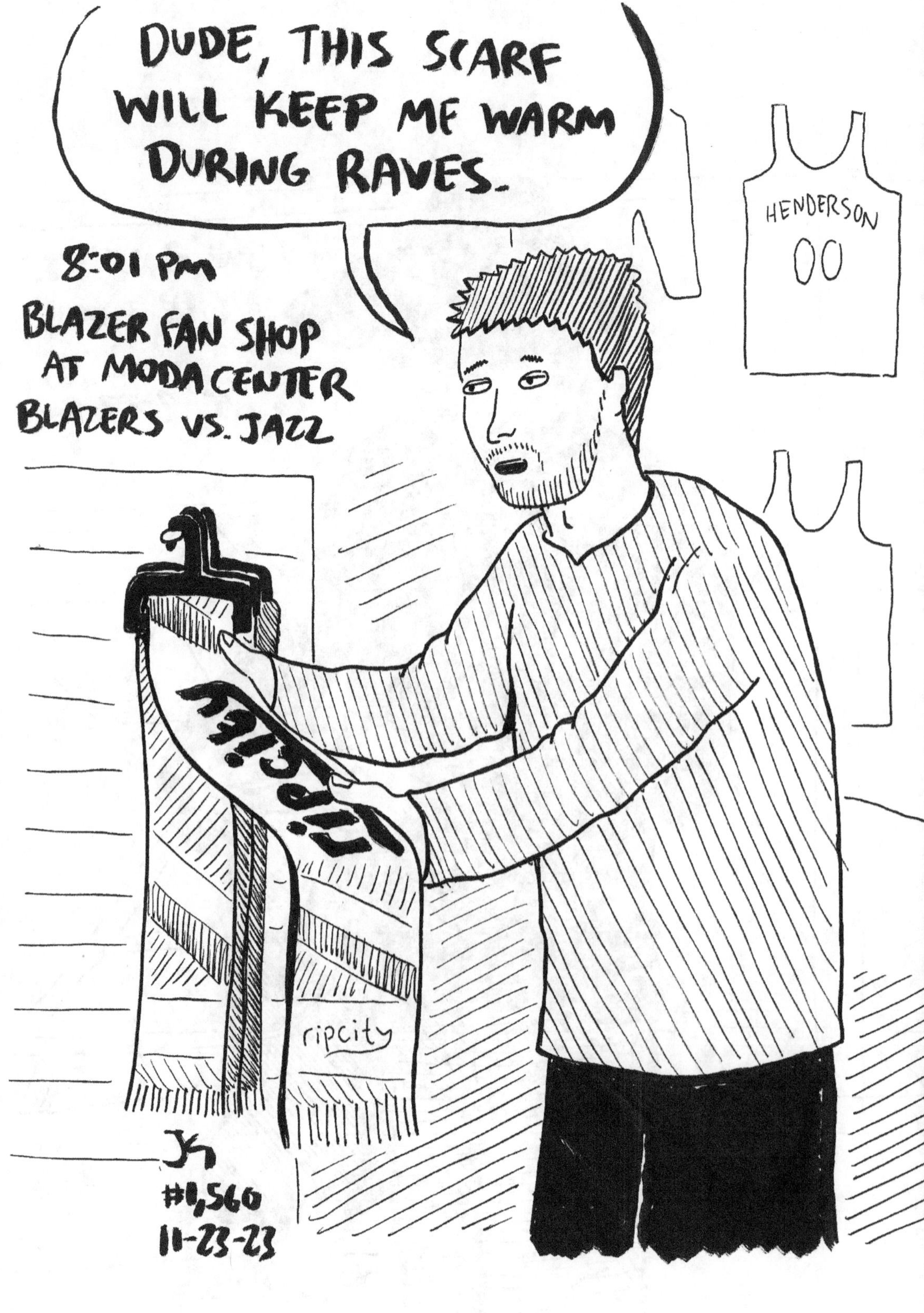
DUDE, THIS SCARF WILL KEEP ME WARM DURING RAVES.
8:01 PM
BLAZER FAN SHOP AT MODA CENTER
BLAZERS VS. JAZZ
HENDERSON 00
ripcity
#1,560
11-23-23

BLAZER FAN SHOP AT MODA CENTER
BLAZERS VS. JAZZ
#1,561
11-25-23
7:58 PM
UTAH JAZZ
BASKETBALL

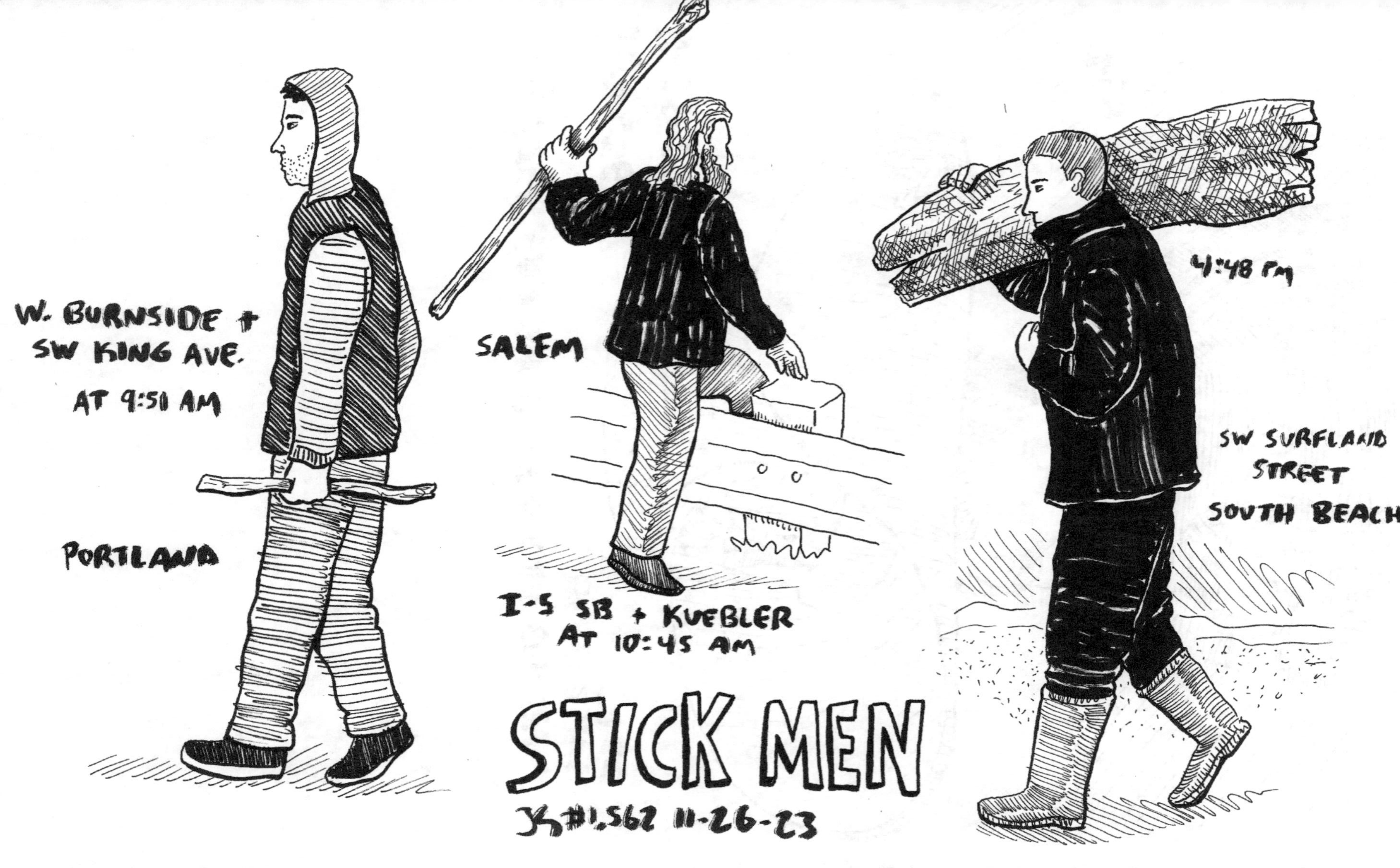

W. BURNSIDE +
SW KING AVE.
AT 9:51 AM
PORTLAND
SALEM
I-5 SB + KUEBLER
AT 10:45 AM
4:48 PM
SW SURFLAND
STREET
SOUTH BEACH
STICK MEN
JS #1,562 11-26-23

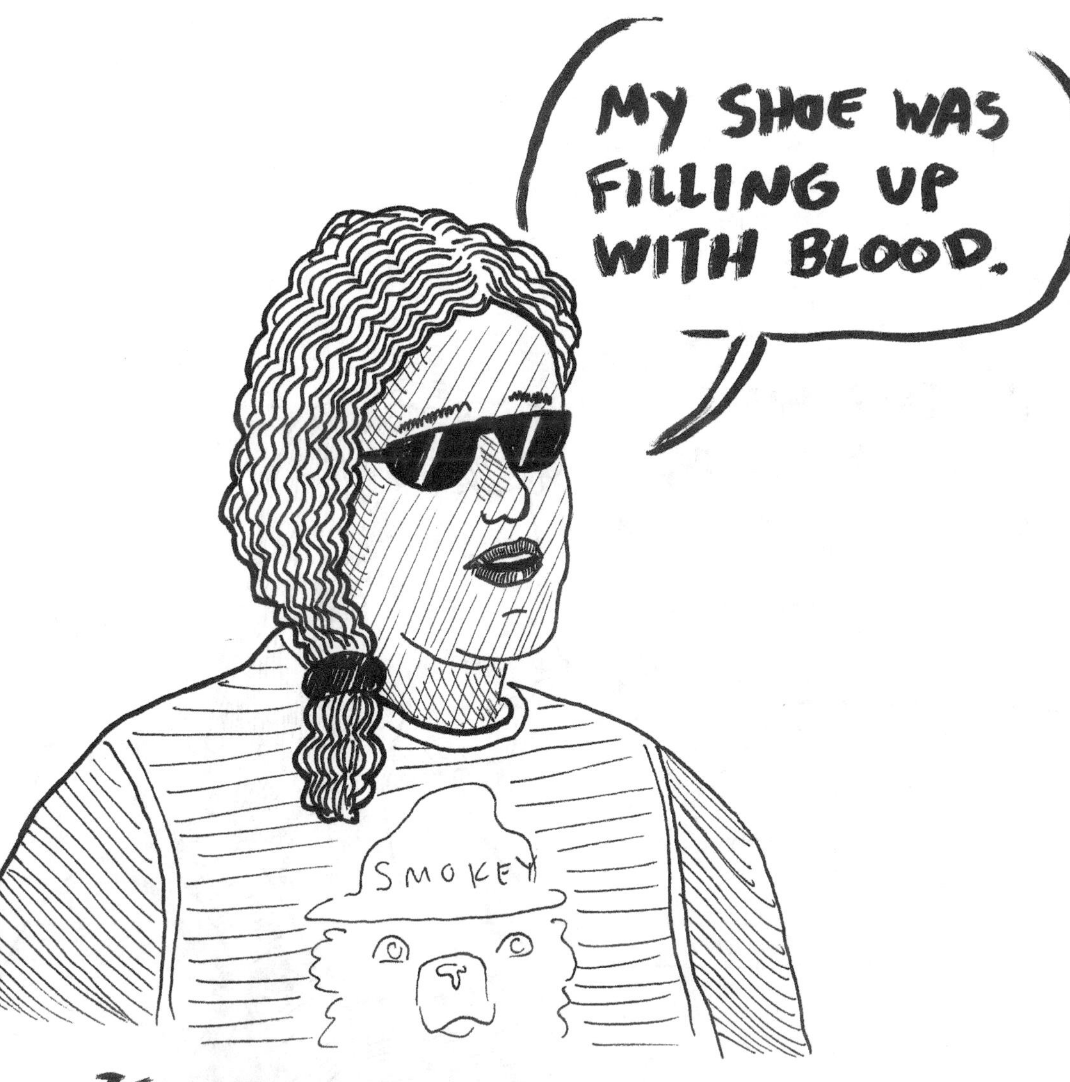

JS #1,563 11-26-23
BAYFRONT IN NEWPORT, OR
AT 2:11 PM

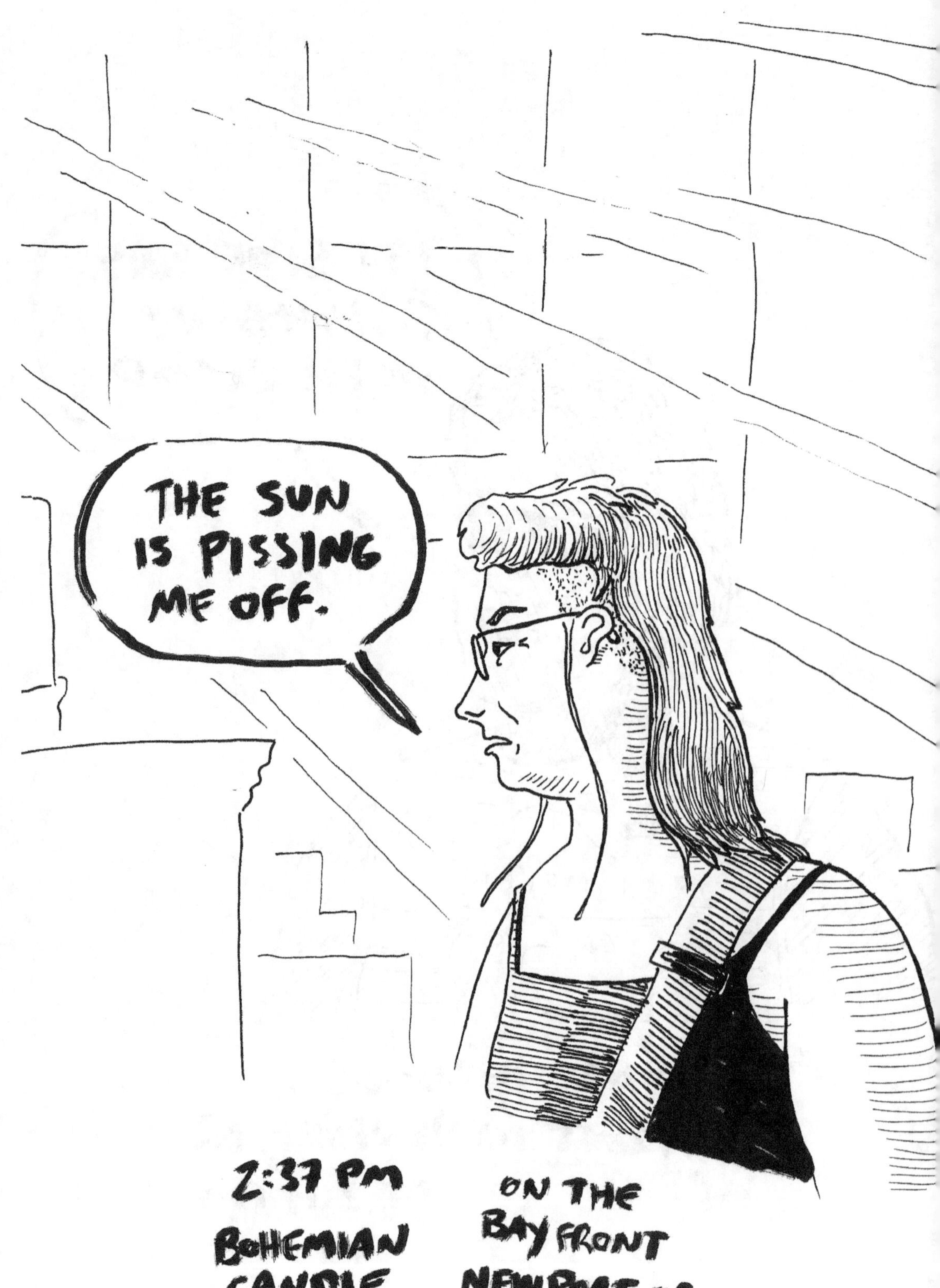

THE SUN IS PISSING ME OFF.
2:37 PM
BOHEMIAN CANDLE
ON THE BAY FRONT
NEWPORT, OR
#1,564 11-26-23

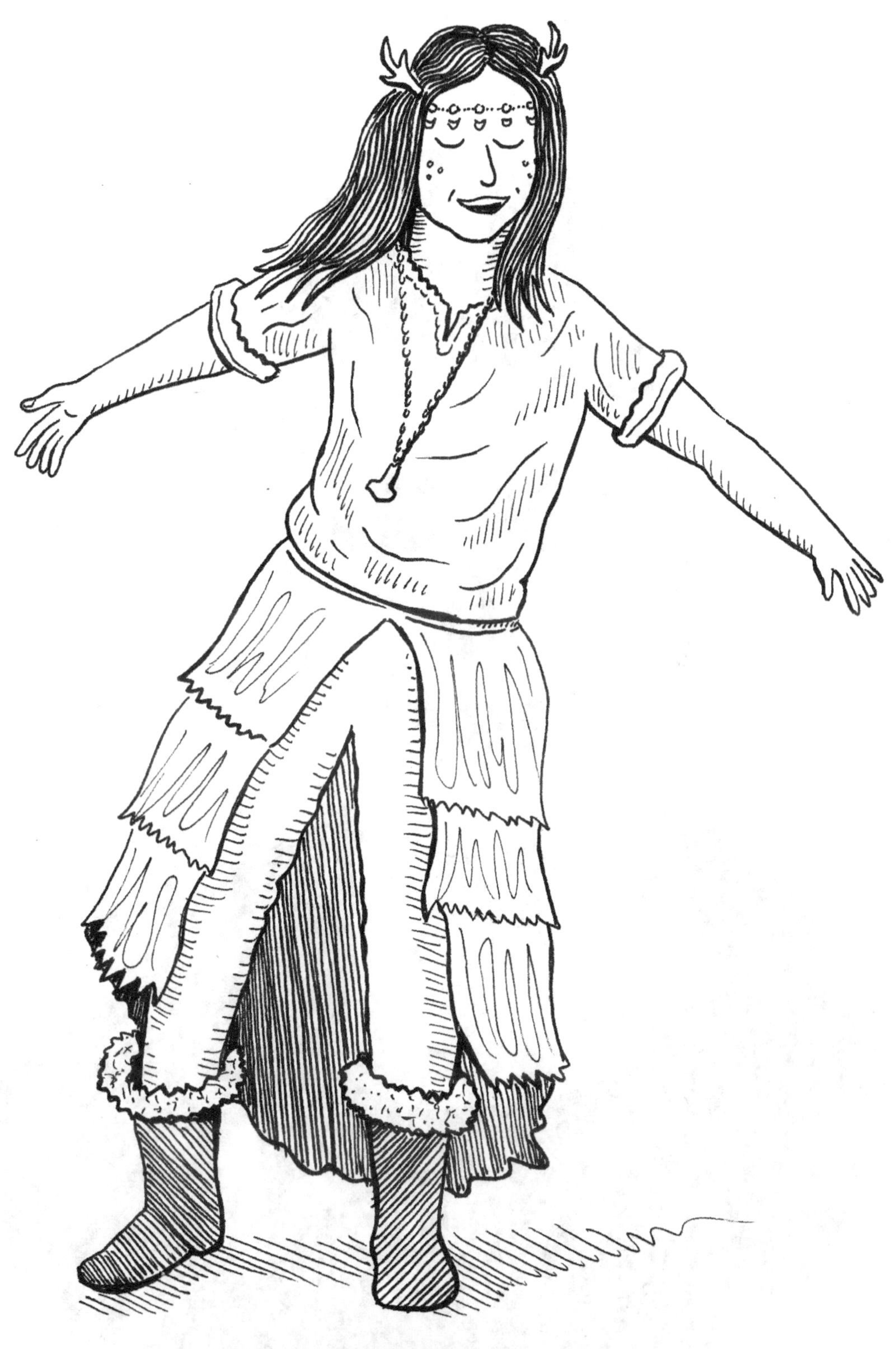

SW WASHINGTON
+ SW 2ND ST.
CORVALLIS, OR
1:51 PM
JK #1,365
11-27-23

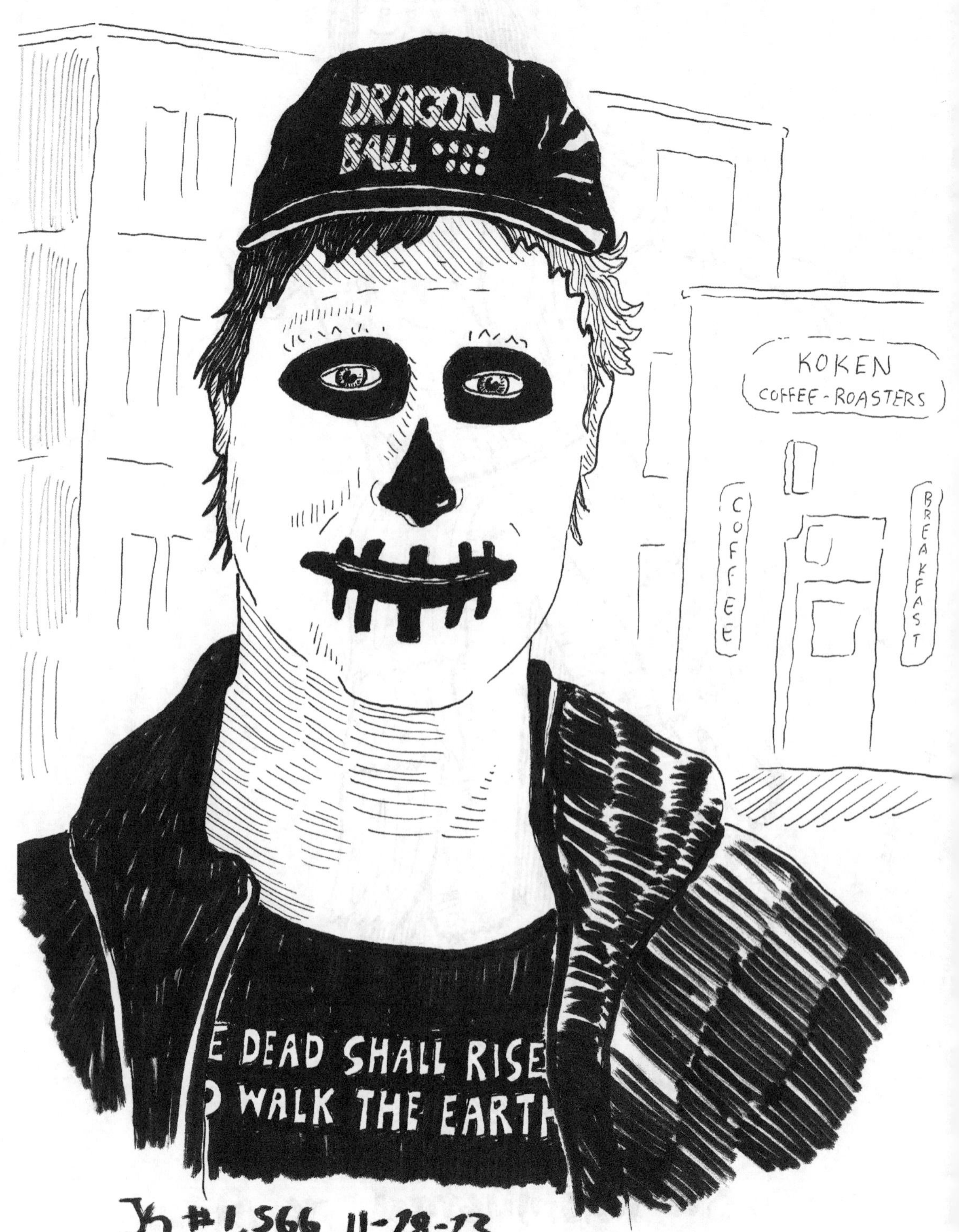

Jh #1,566 11-28-23
NE MLK JR BLVD. + NE DEKUM ST. AT 1:53 PM

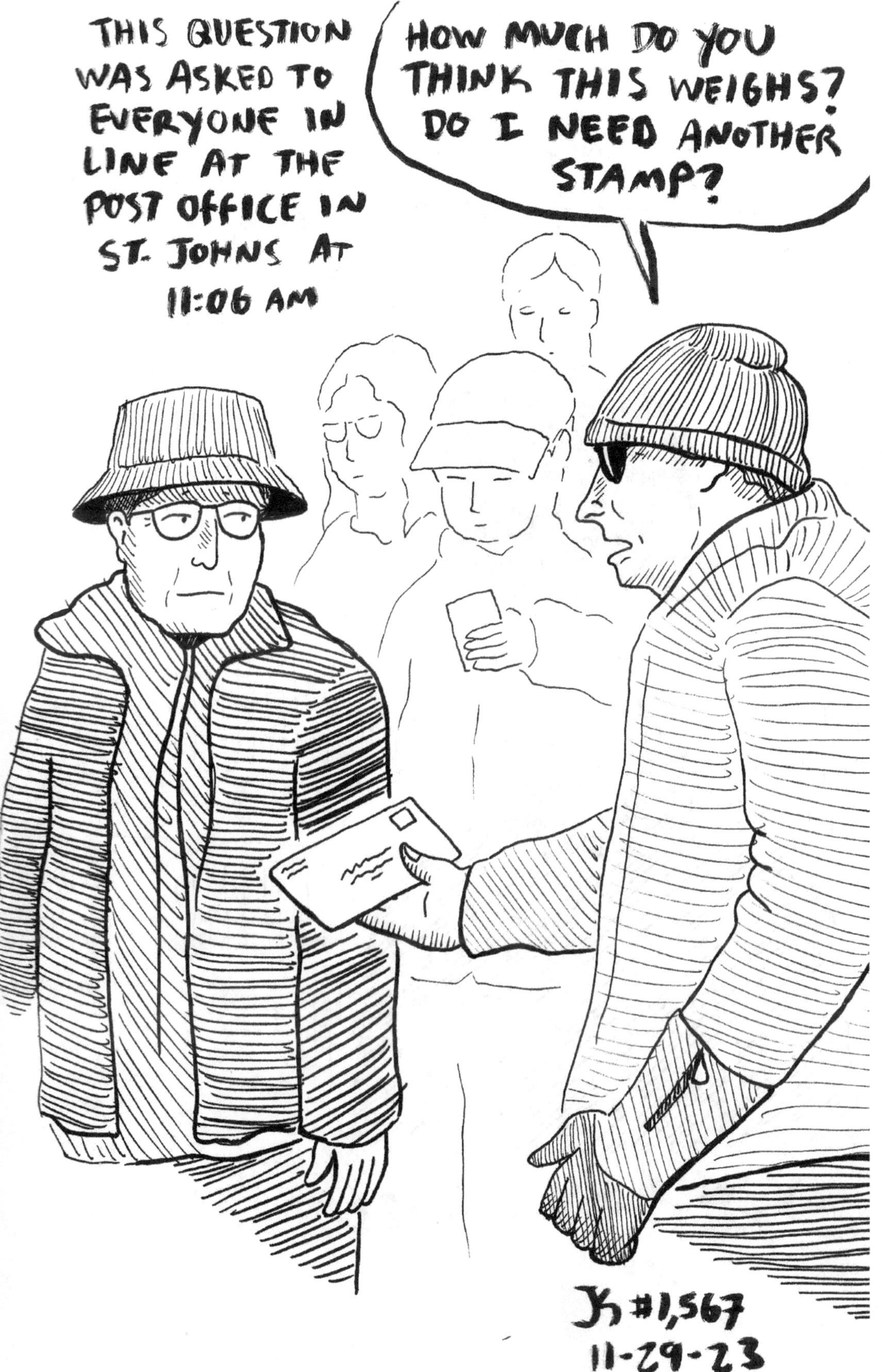

THIS QUESTION WAS ASKED TO EVERYONE IN LINE AT THE POST OFFICE IN ST. JOHNS AT 11:06 AM
HOW MUCH DO YOU THINK THIS WEIGHS? DO I NEED ANOTHER STAMP?
JS #1,567
11-29-23

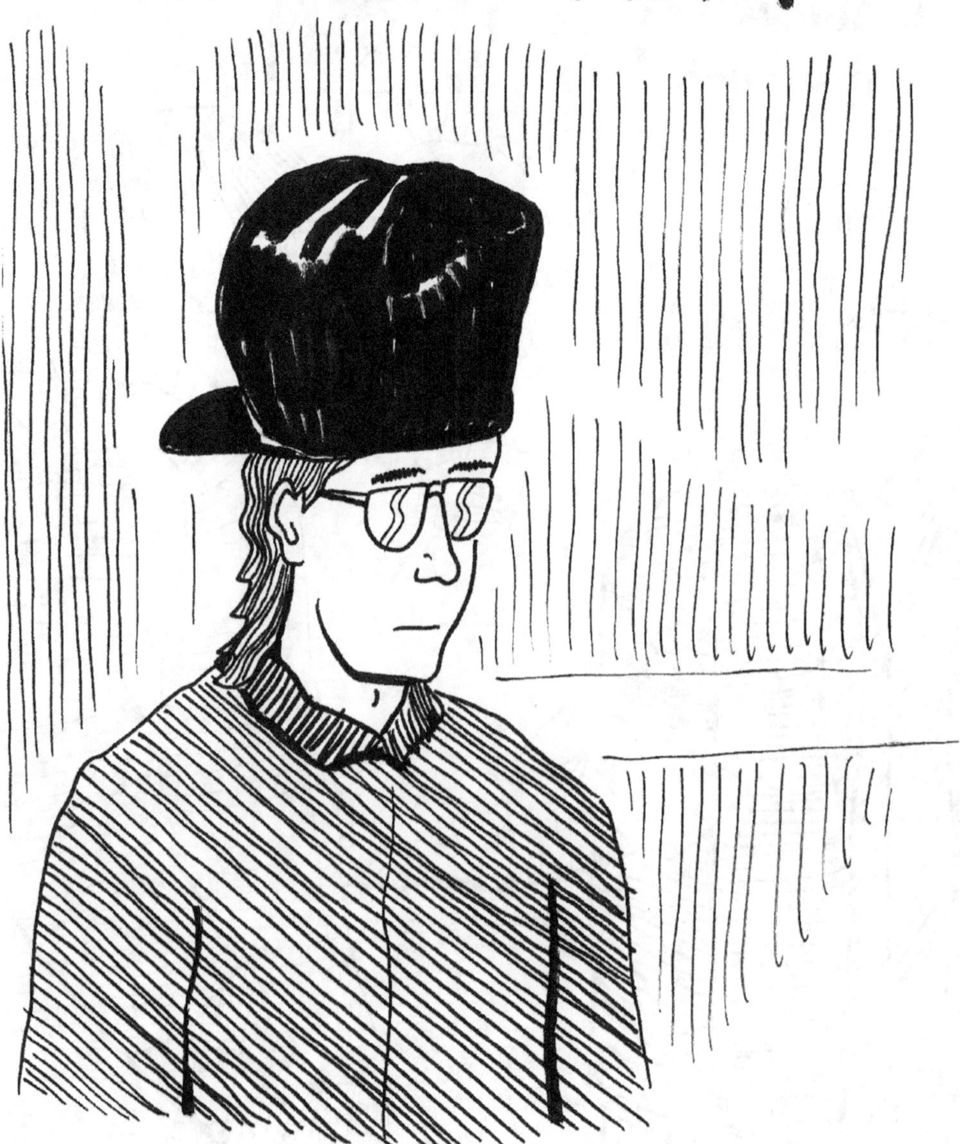

SE 28TH AVE. +
E. BURNSIDE AT 9:45 PM
1,568 12-6-23

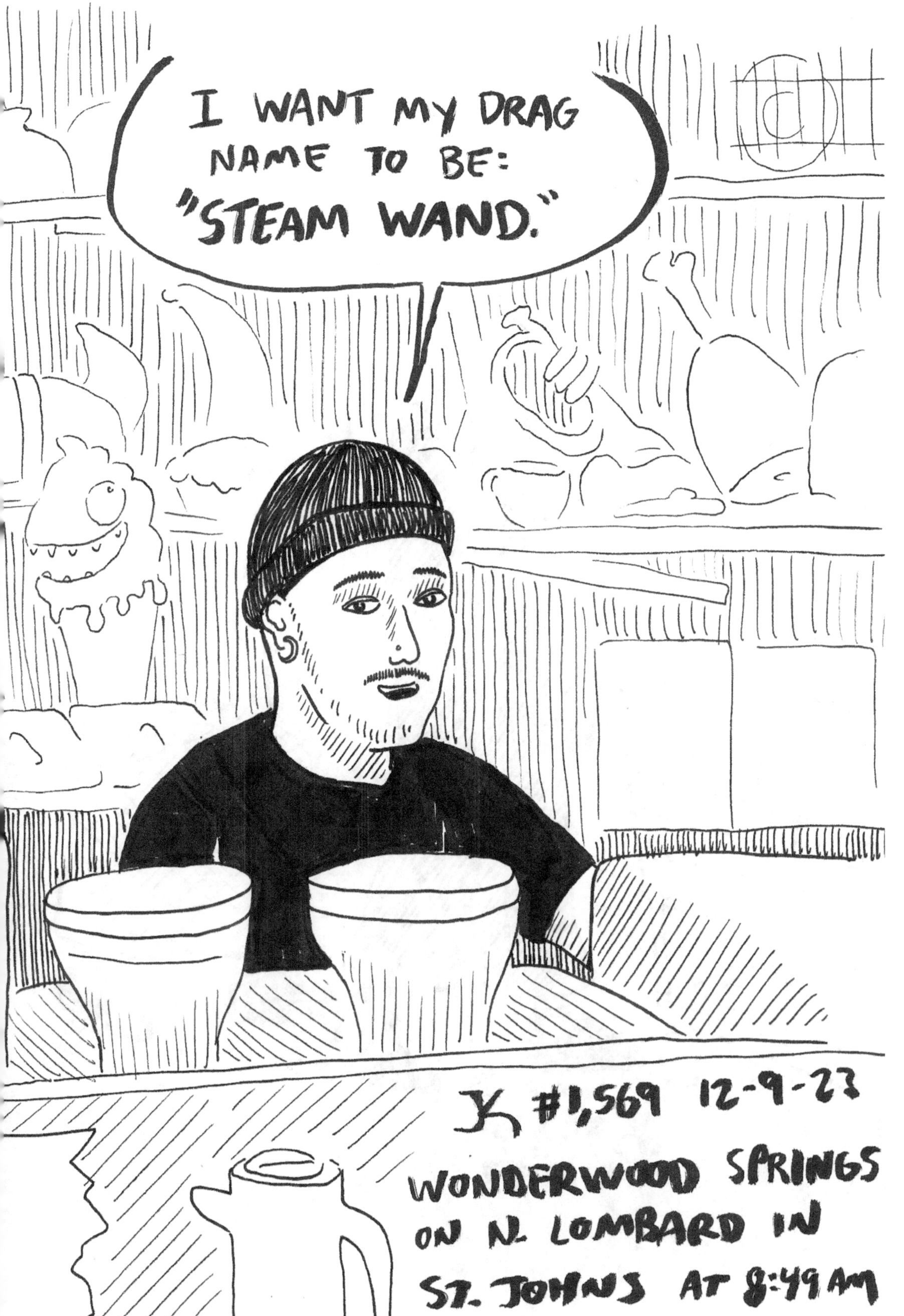

I WANT MY DRAG NAME TO BE: "STEAM WAND."
#1,569 12-9-23
WONDERWOOD SPRINGS ON N. LOMBARD IN ST. JOHNS AT 8:49 AM

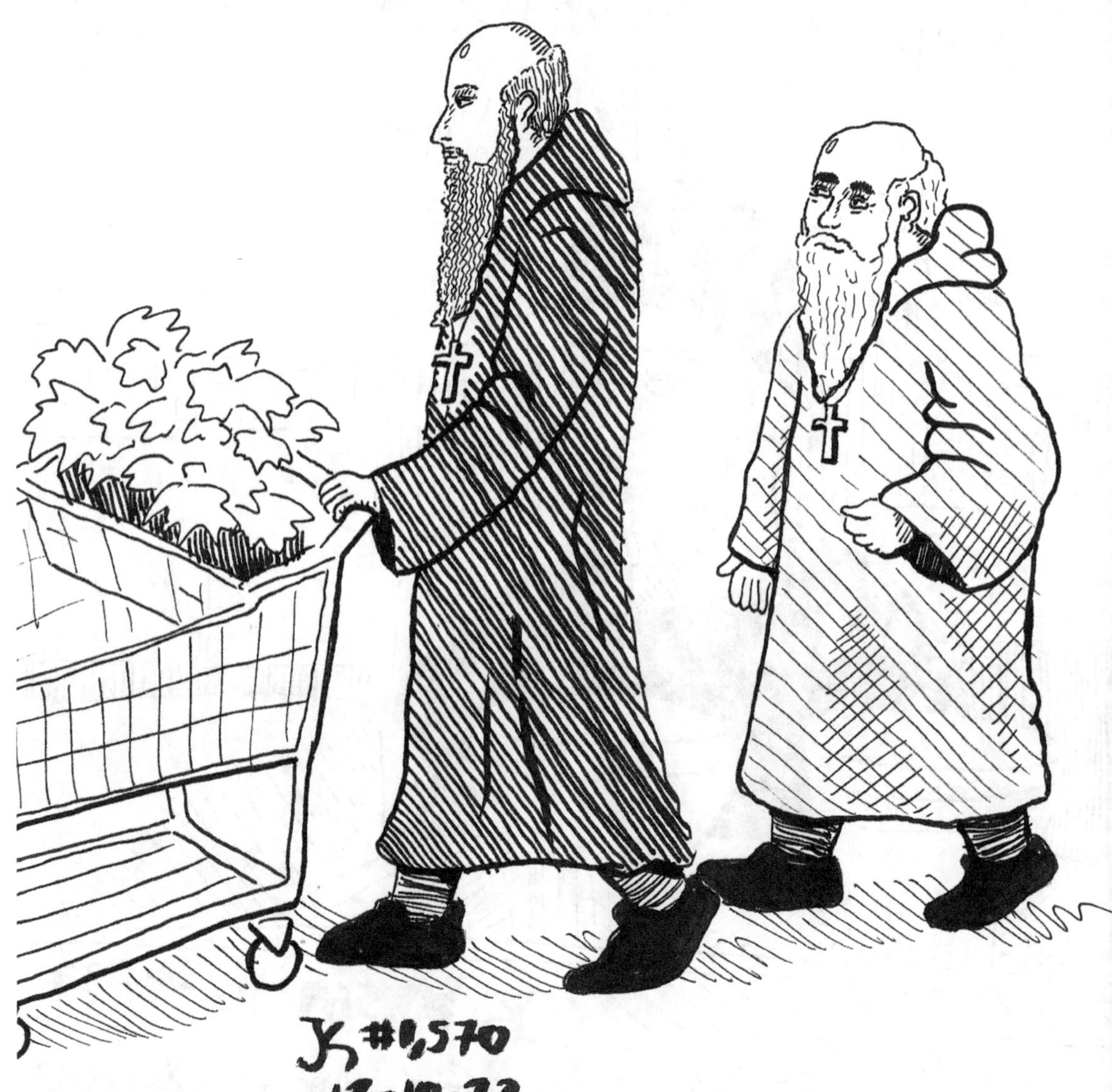

SCAPPOOSE FRED MEYER
AT 1:10 PM
JS #6,570
12-10-23

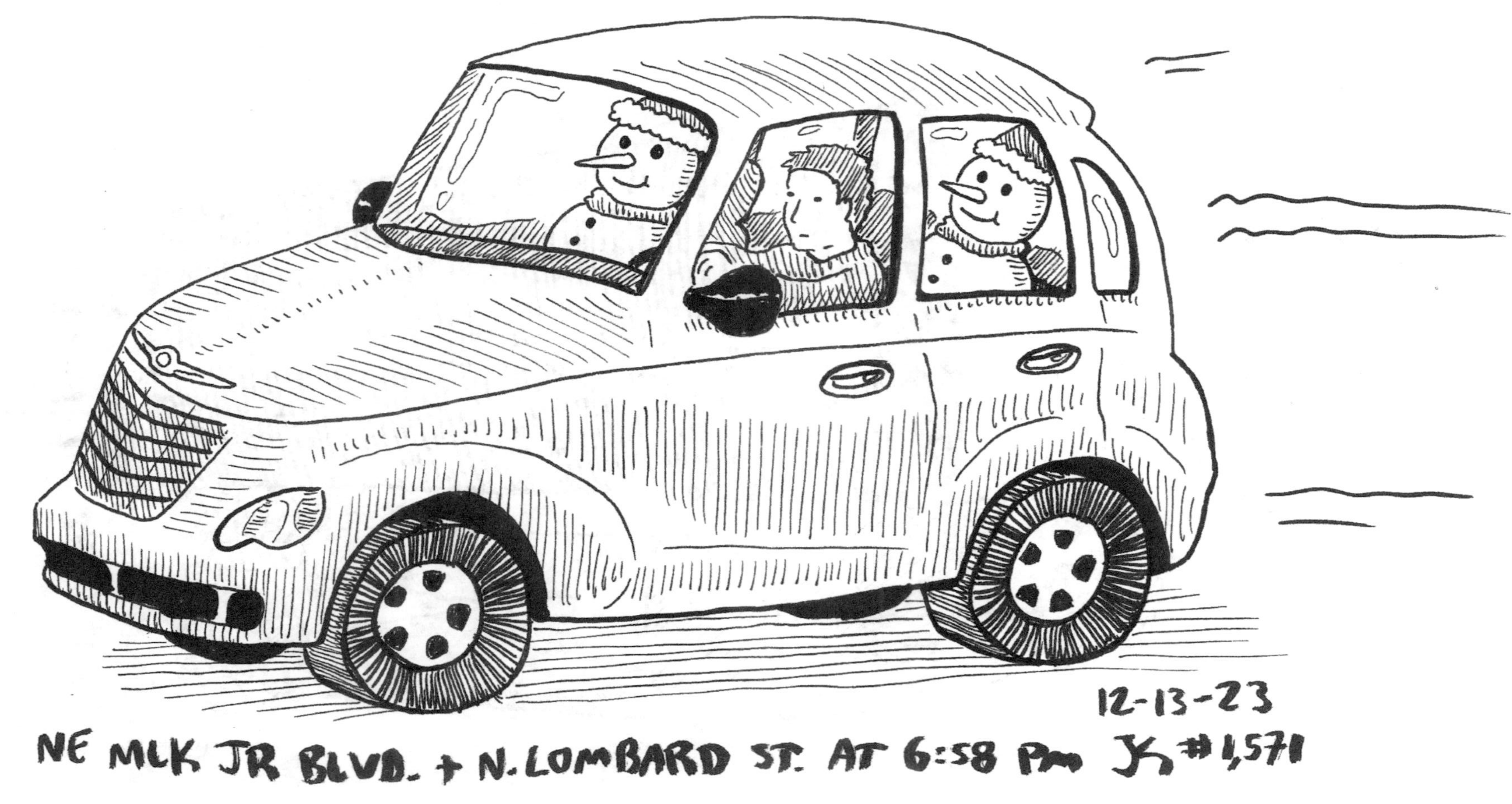

12-13-23

NE MLK JR BLVD. + N. LOMBARD ST. AT 6:58 PM JS #1,571

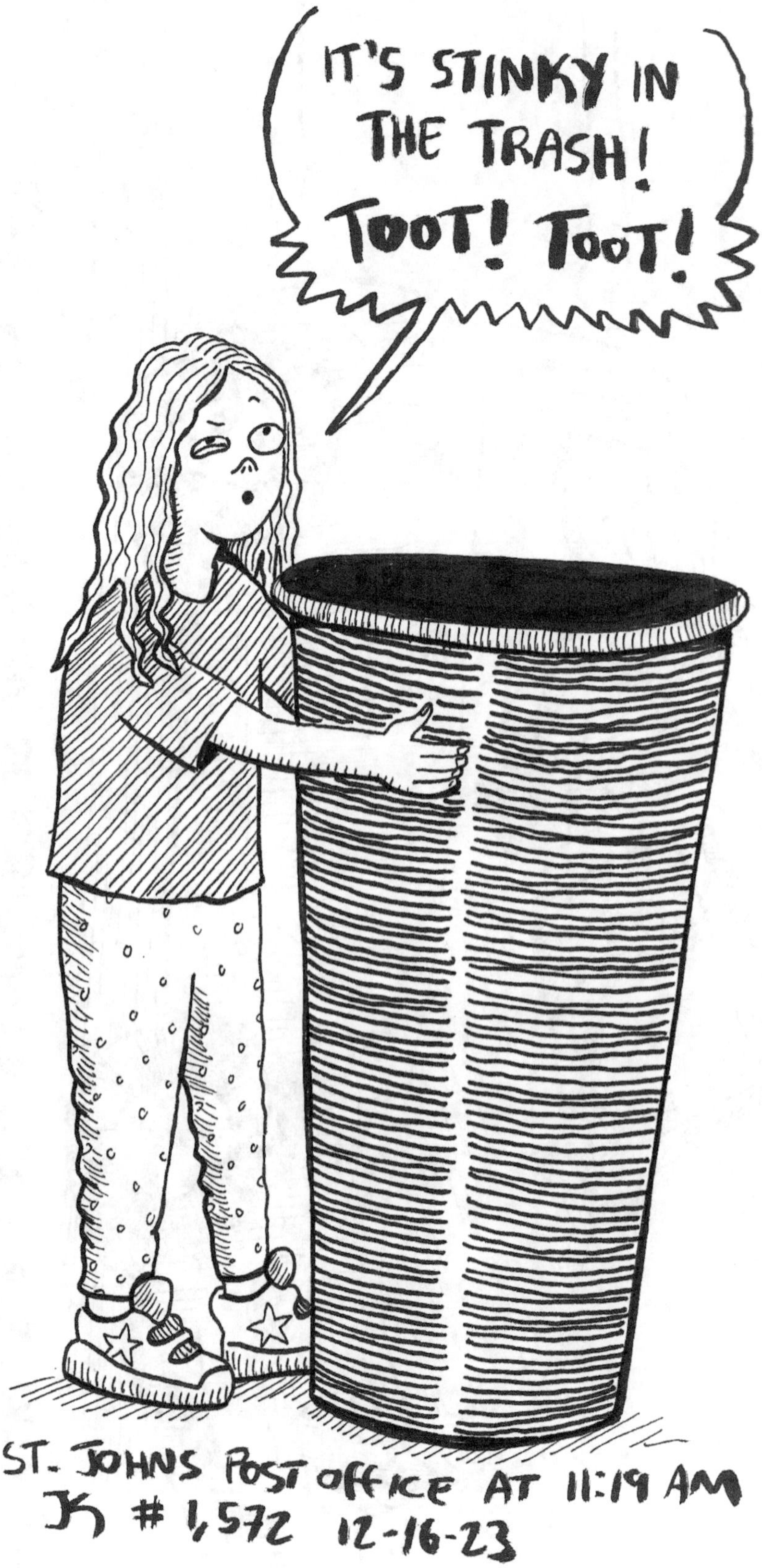

IT'S STINKY IN THE TRASH! TOOT! TOOT!
ST. JOHNS POST OFFICE AT 11:19 AM
JK #1,572 12-16-23

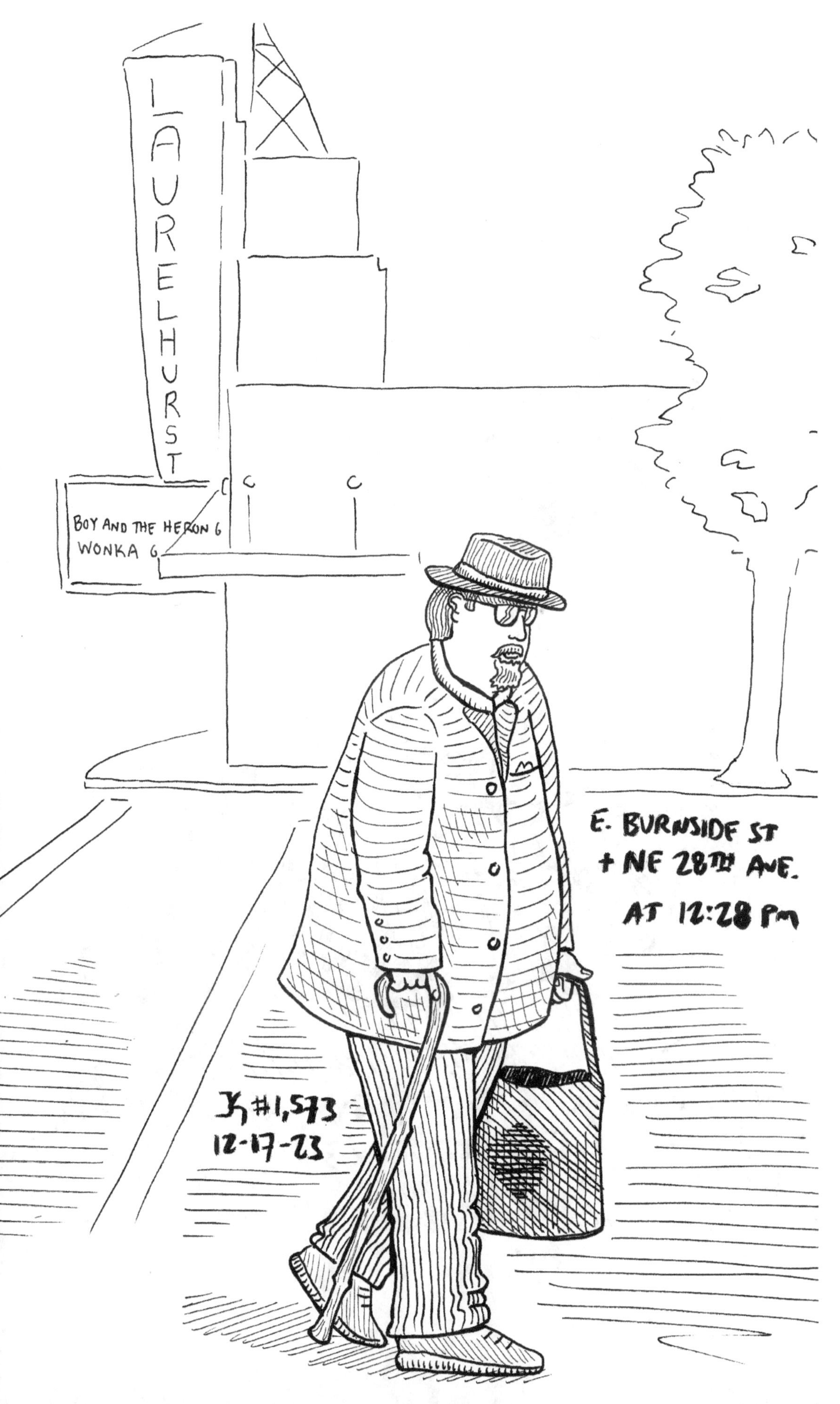

LAURELHURST
BOY AND THE HERON G
WONKA G
E. BURNSIDE ST
+ NE 28TH AVE.
AT 12:28 PM
#1,573
12-17-23

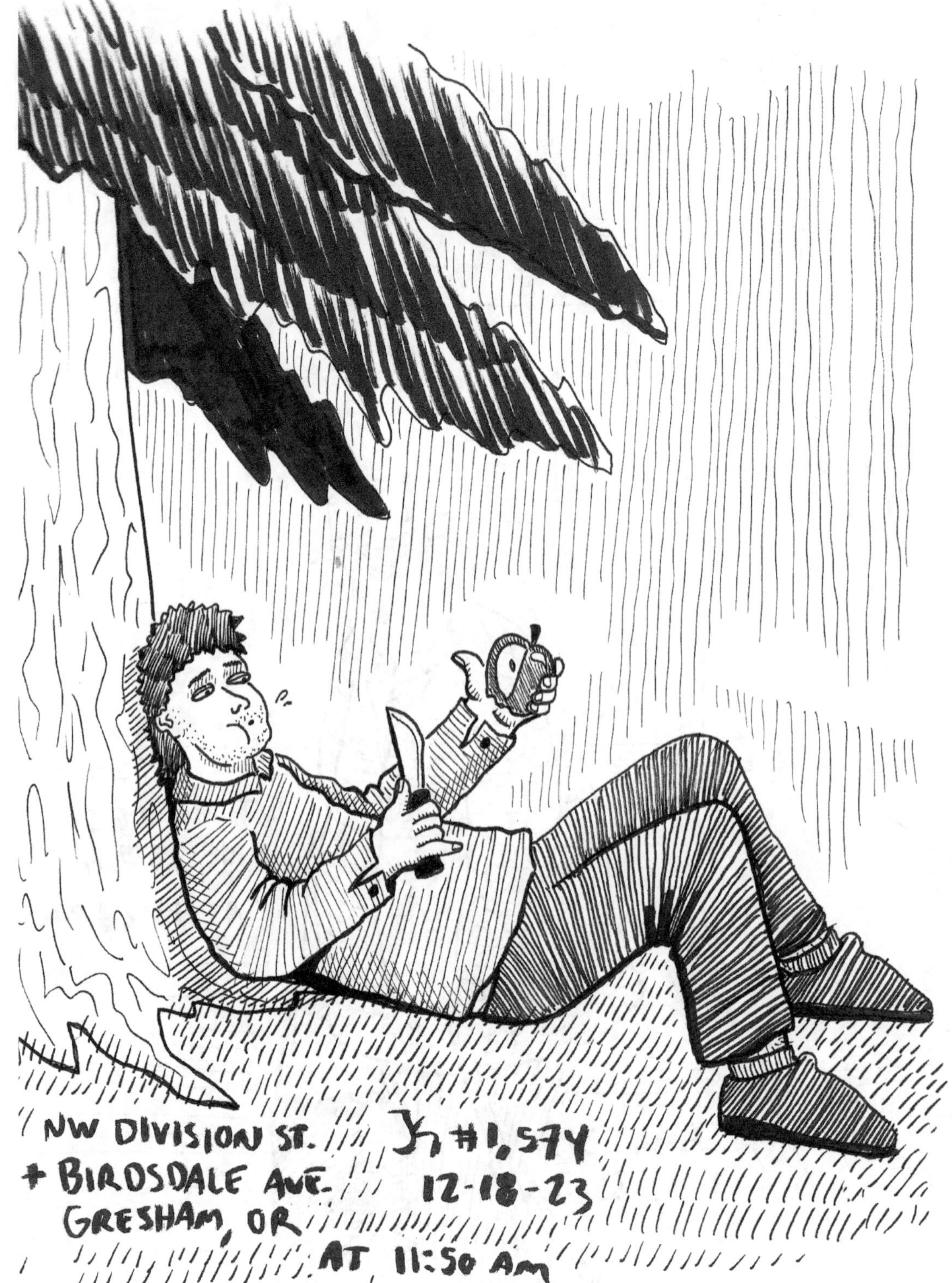

NW DIVISION ST.
+ BIRDSDALE AVE.
GRESHAM, OR
#1,574
12-18-23
AT 11:50 AM

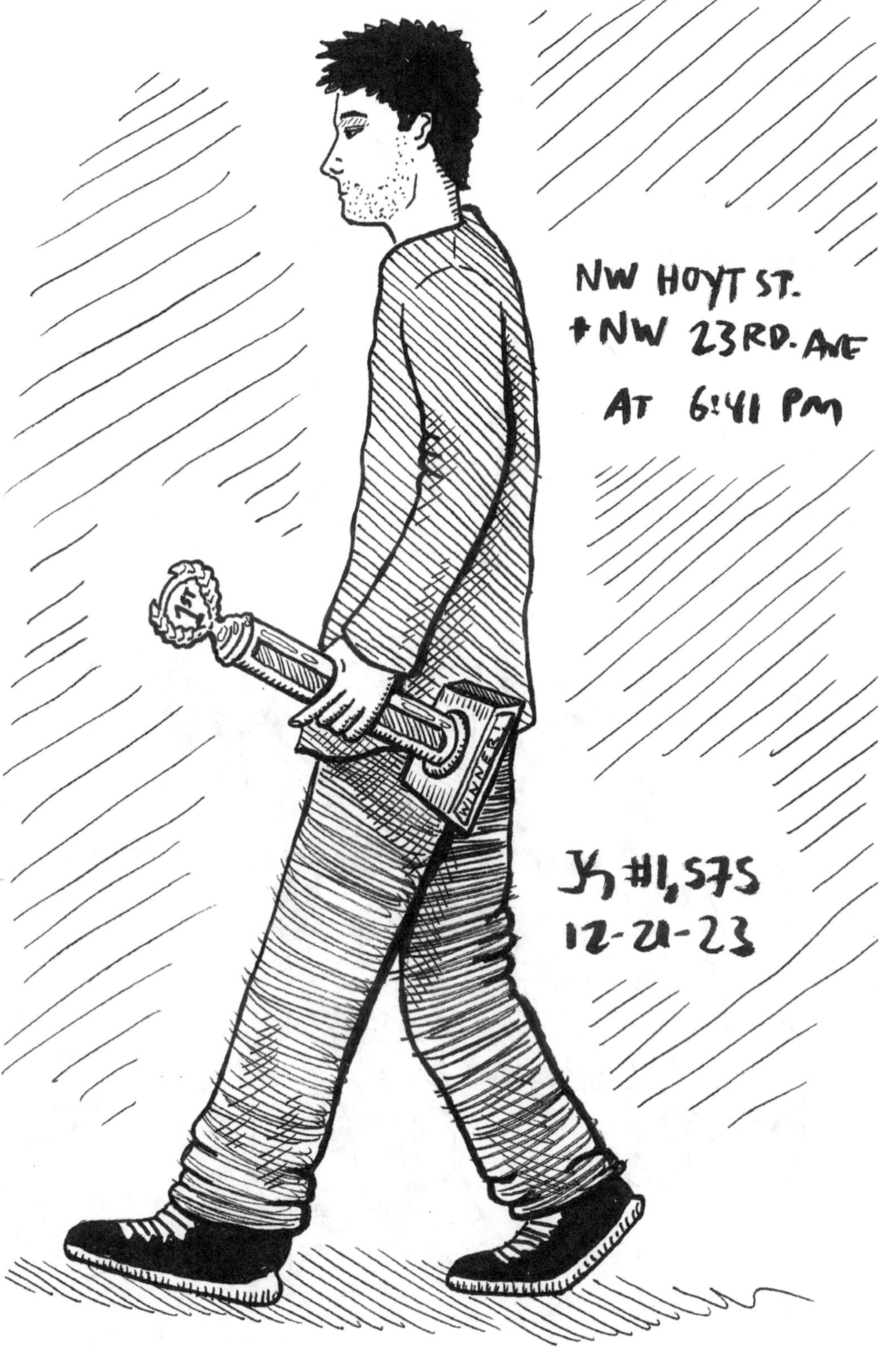
NW HOYT ST.
+ NW 23RD. AVE
AT 6:41 PM
#1,575
12-21-23

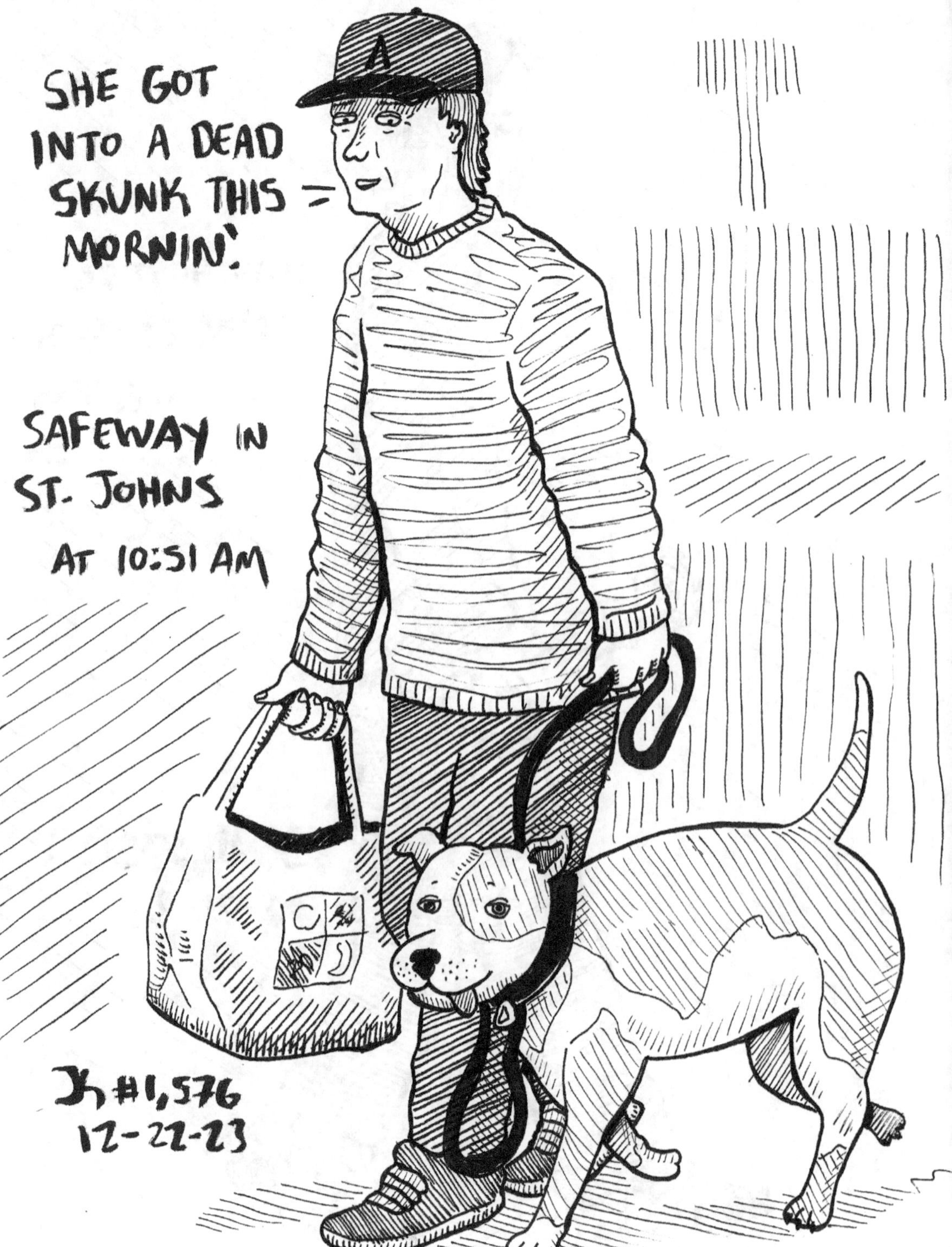

SHE GOT INTO A DEAD SKUNK THIS MORNIN'.
SAFEWAY IN ST. JOHNS
AT 10:51 AM
#1,576
12-22-23

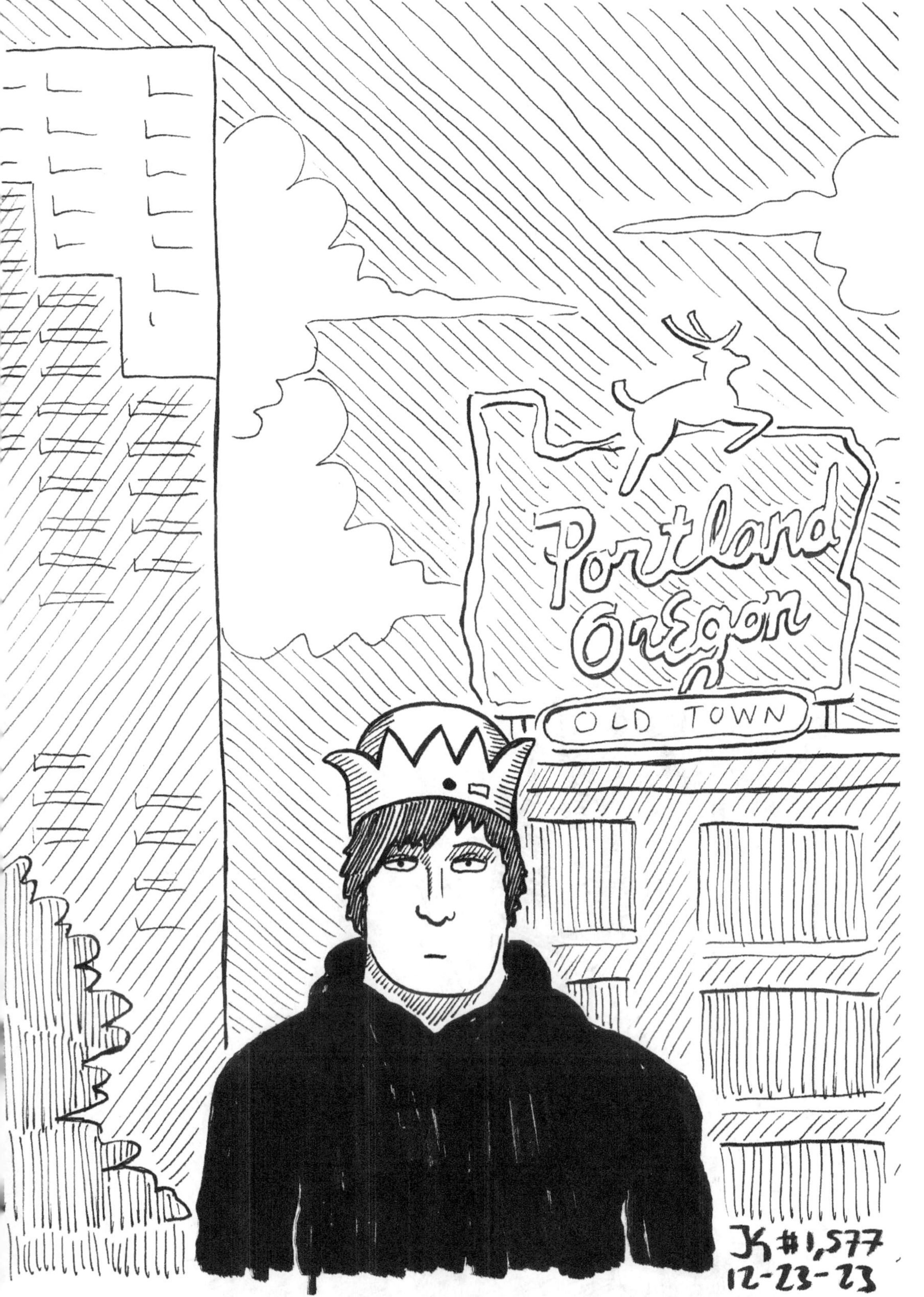

W. BURNSIDE BRIDGE AT 1:54 PM

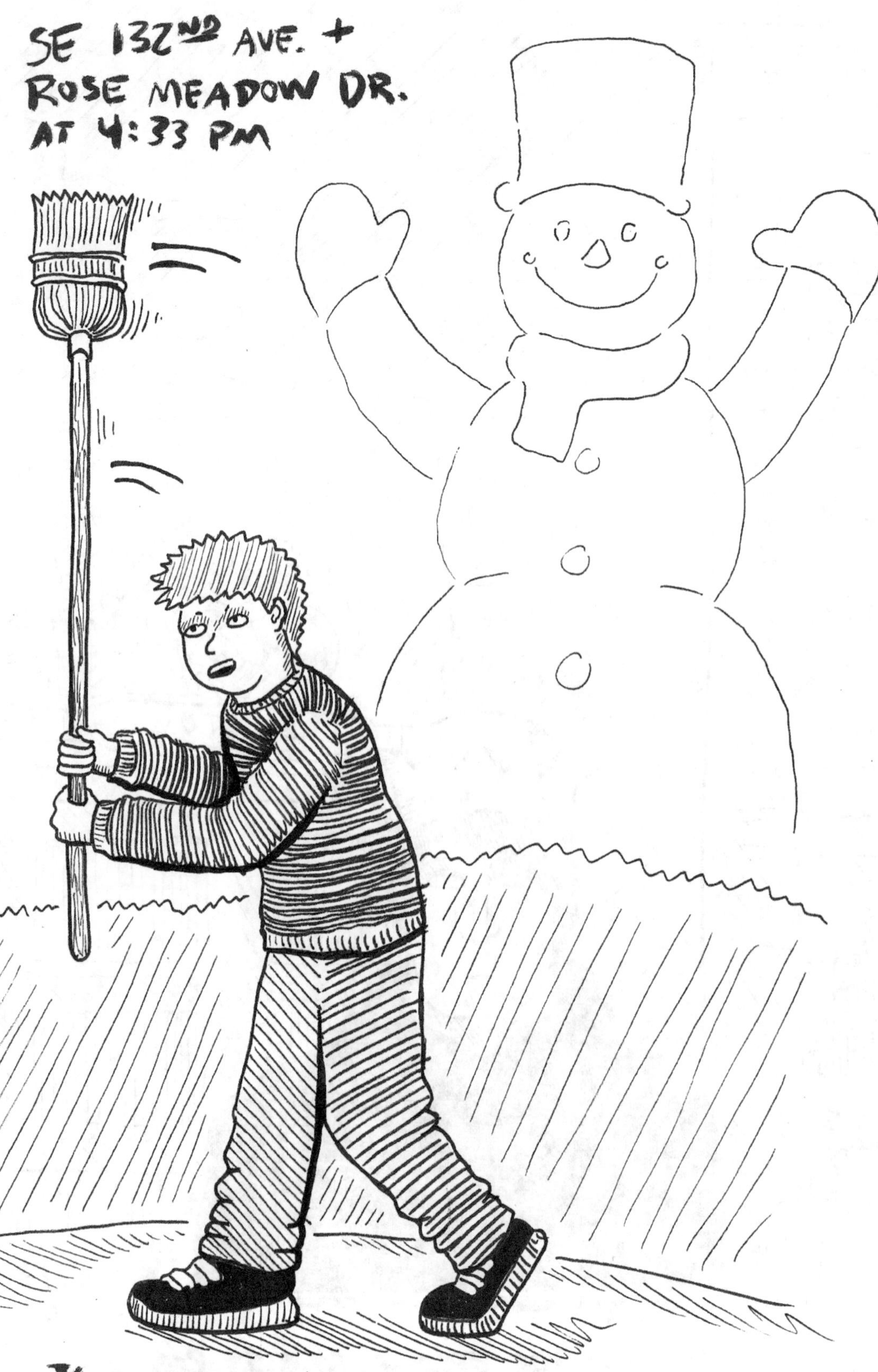

SE 132ND AVE. +
ROSE MEADOW DR.
AT 4:33 PM
JK #1578 12-27-23

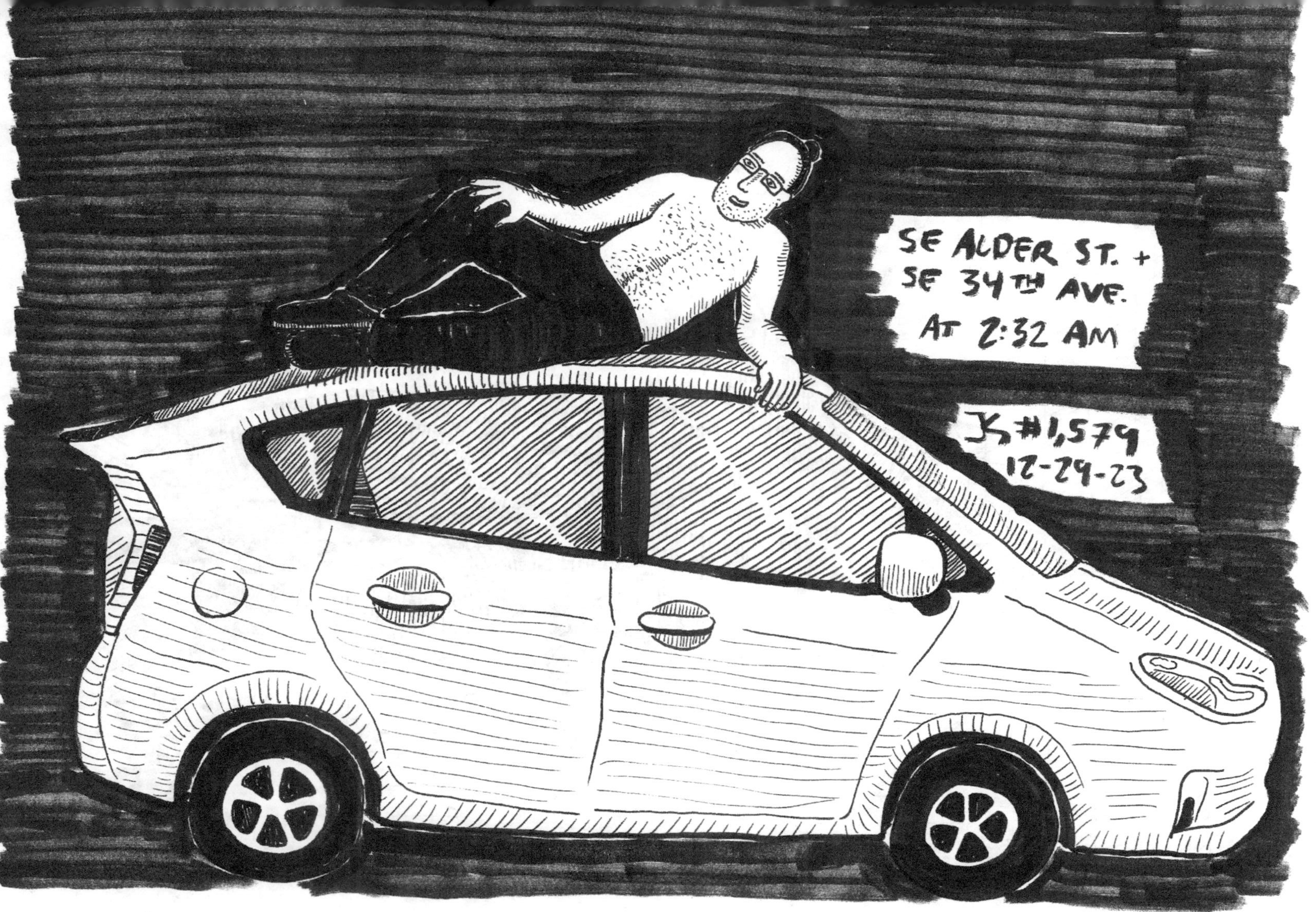

SE ALDER ST. +
SE 34TH AVE.
AT 2:32 AM
JS #1,579
12-29-23

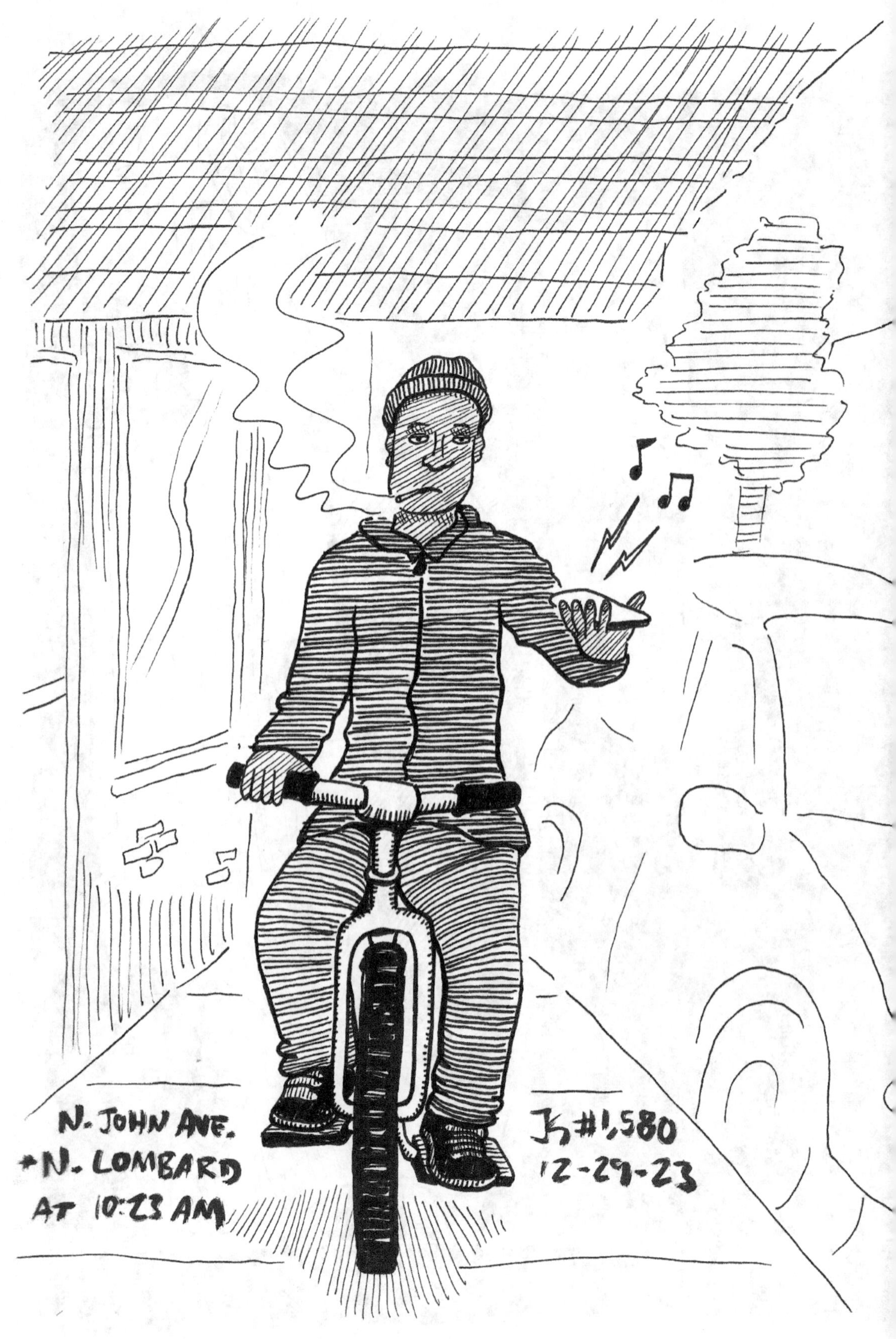
N. JOHN AVE.
+ N. LOMBARD
AT 10:23 AM
JG #1,580
12-29-23

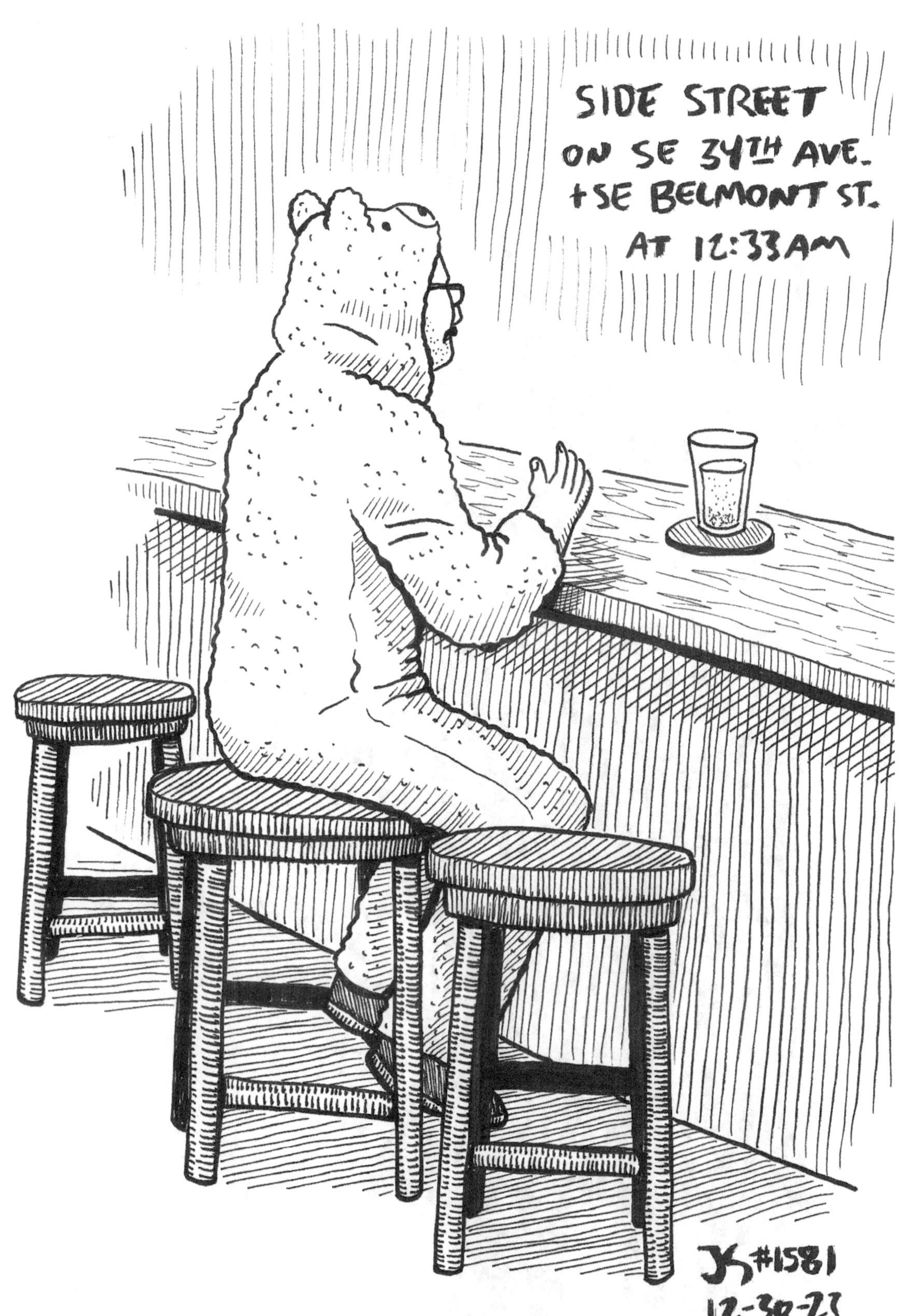

SIDE STREET
ON SE 34TH AVE.
+ SE BELMONT ST.
AT 12:33 AM
JKS #1581
12-30-23

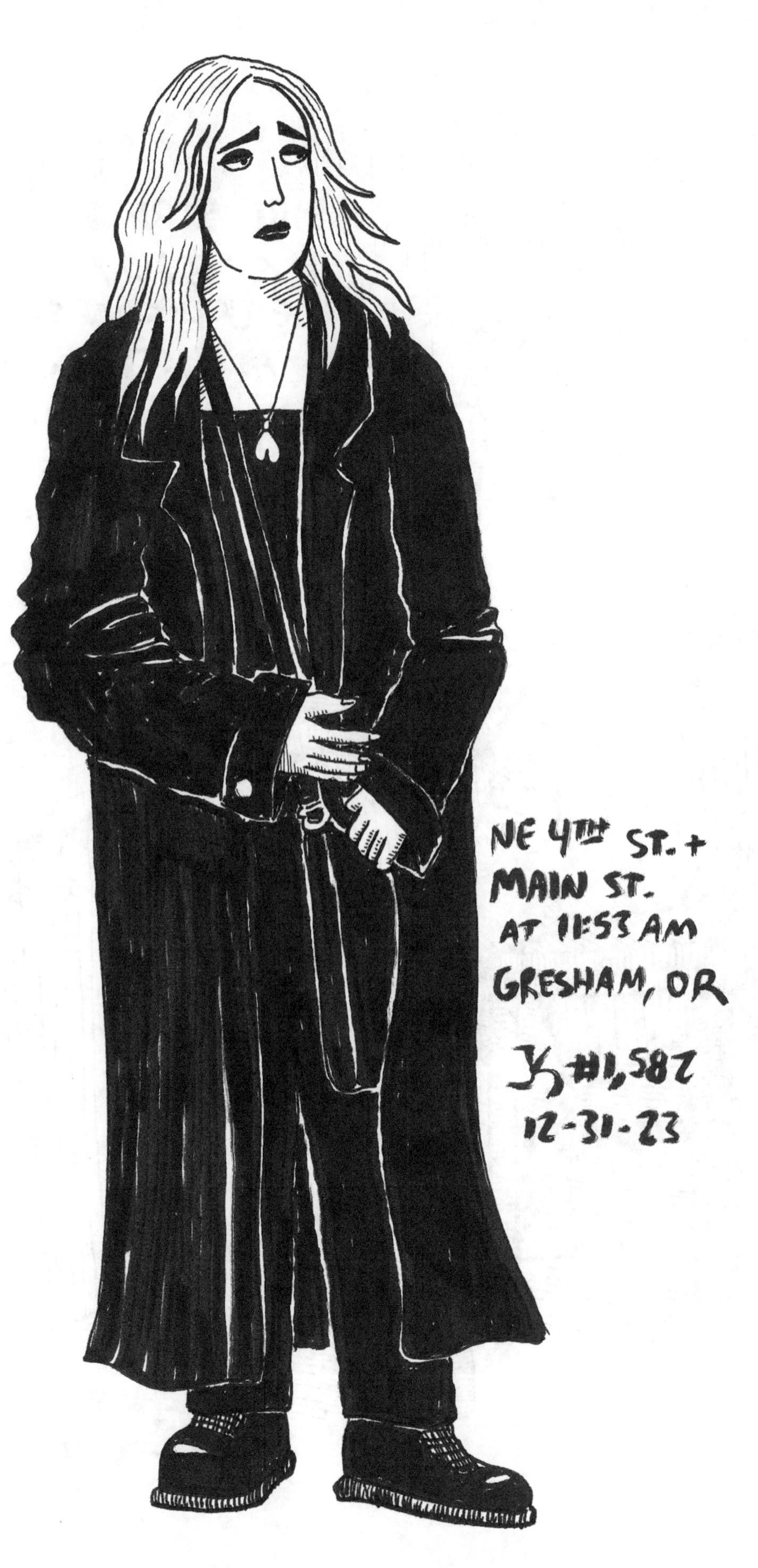

NE 4TH ST. +
MAIN ST.
AT 11:53 AM
GRESHAM, OR
#1,582
12-31-23

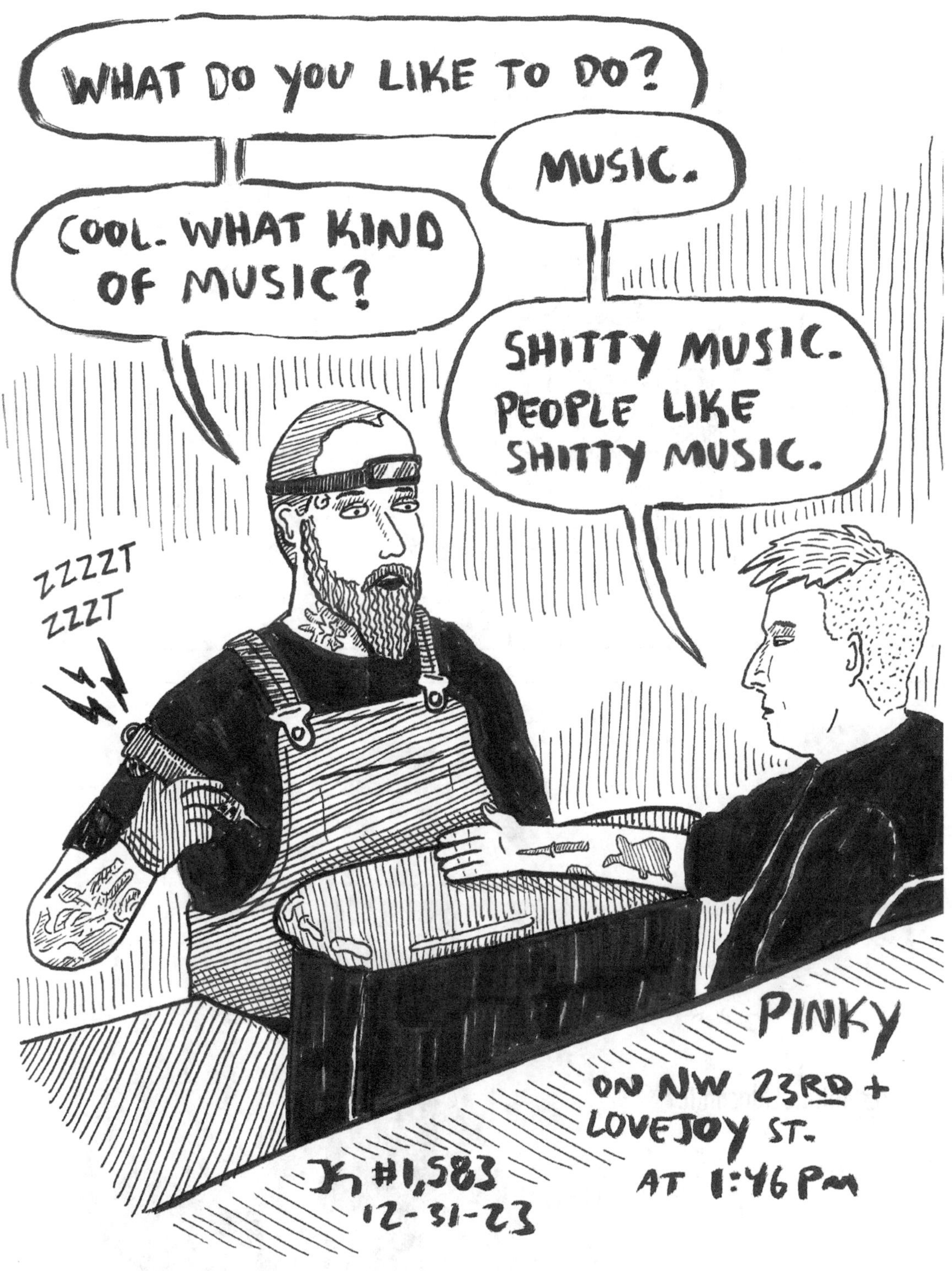

WHAT DO YOU LIKE TO DO?
MUSIC.
COOL. WHAT KIND OF MUSIC?
SHITTY MUSIC. PEOPLE LIKE SHITTY MUSIC.
ZZZZT
ZZZT
PINKY
ON NW 23RD + LOVEJOY ST.
AT 1:46 PM
JK #1,583
12-31-23

Other comics by Jack

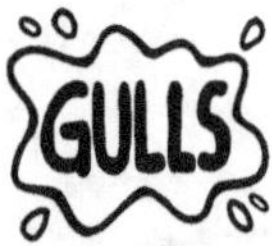

@ gullscomicstrip

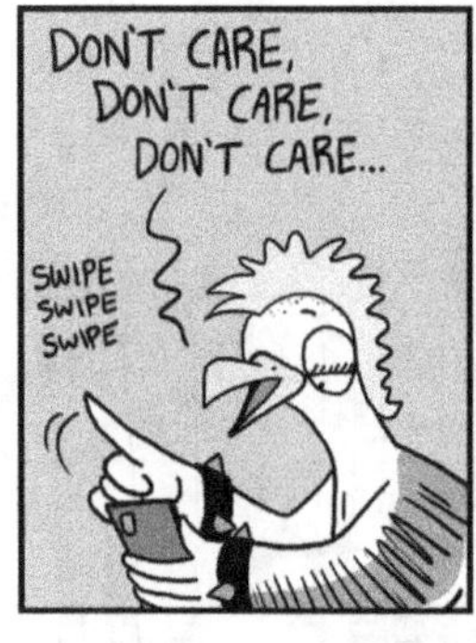

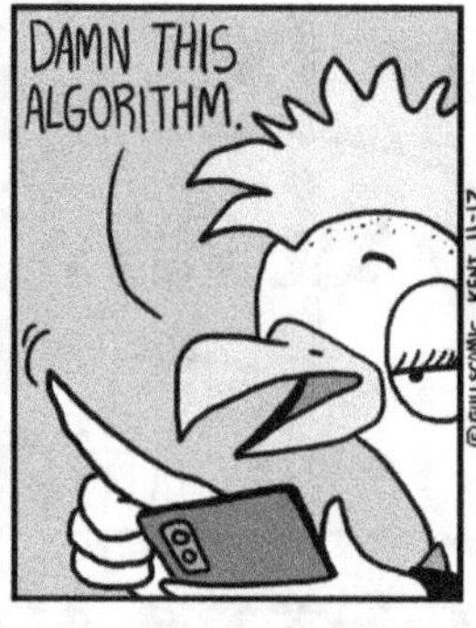

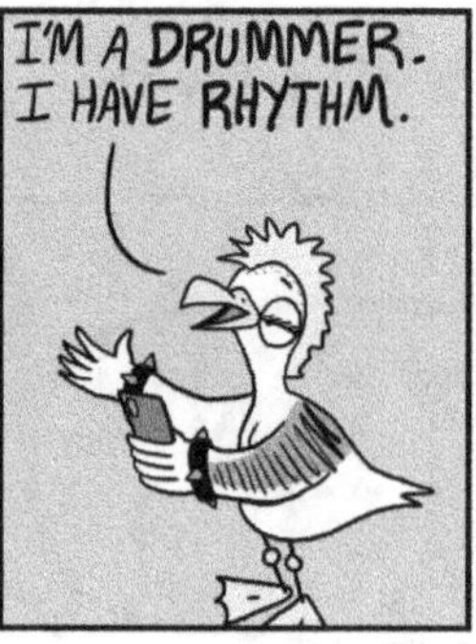

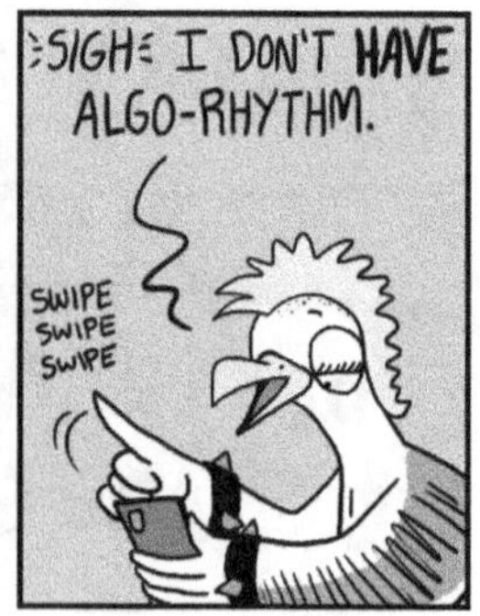

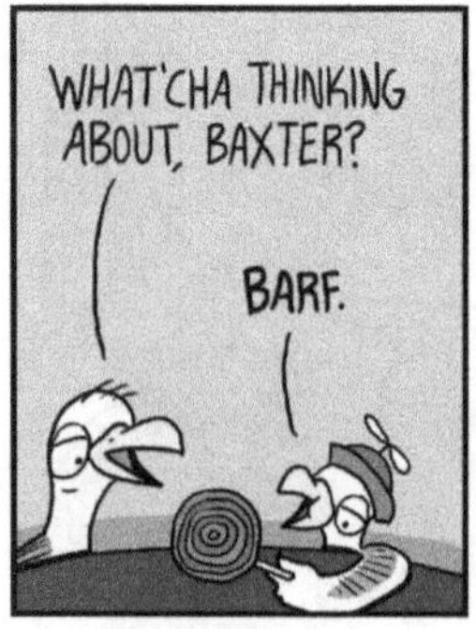

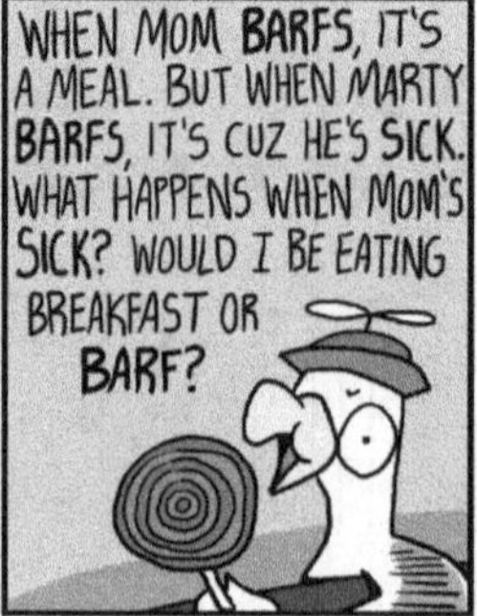

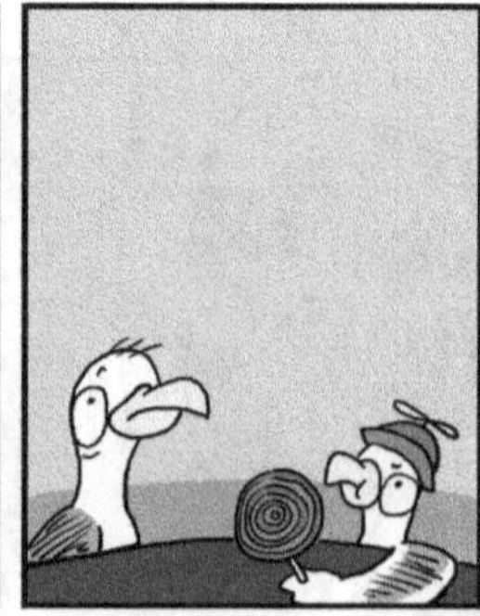

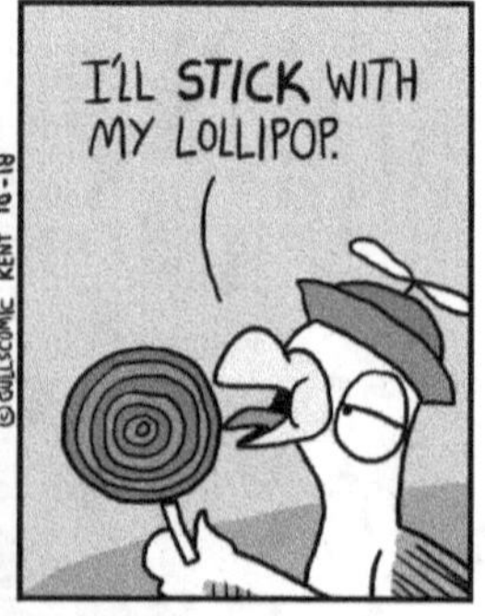

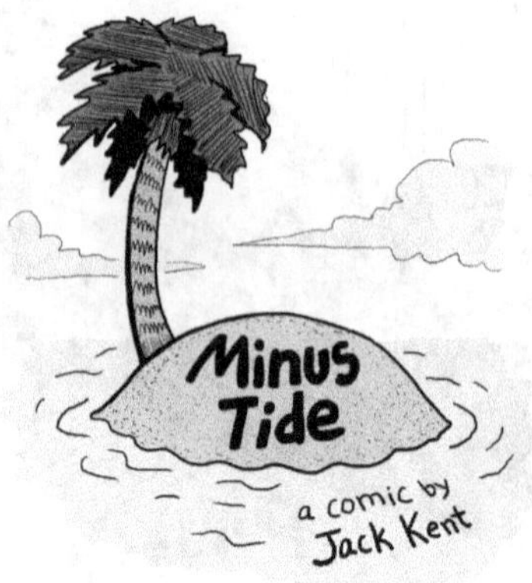

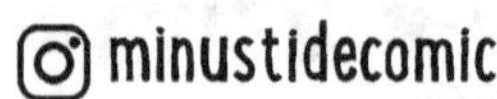

@ minustidecomic

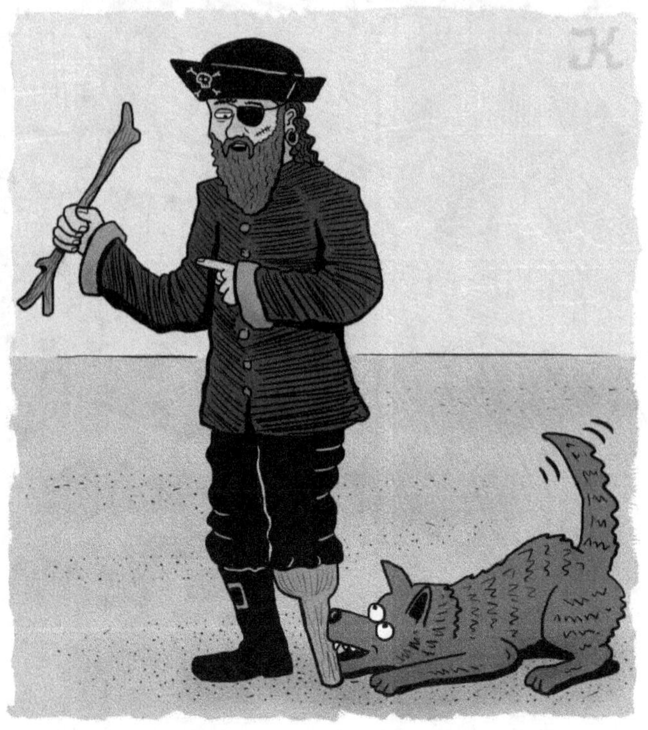

For all of Jack's cartooning projects visit:

kentcomics.com

Make sure your library is extra sketchy with these titles.

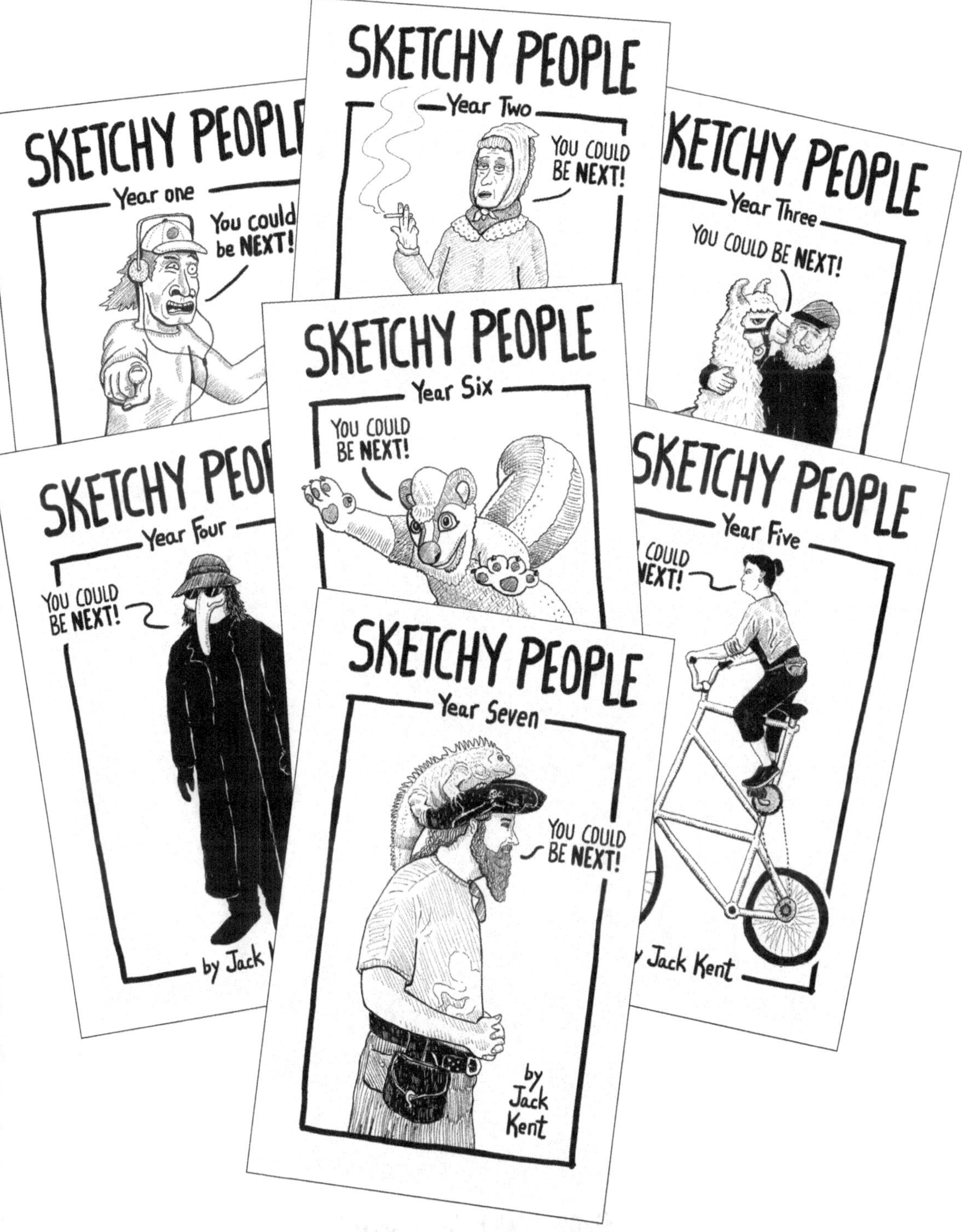